S. P. CERASANO is the Edgar W. B. Fairchild Professor of Literature at Colgate University. She has published numerous books, as well as articles in *Shakespeare Quarterly, Shakespeare Survey, Shakespeare Studies,* and other academic journals. She is the editor of *Medieval and Renaissance Drama in England* and has served as a consultant to members of the Archaeology Division of the Museum of London concerning the excavation of the Rose Playhouse site.

A NORTON CRITICAL EDITION

William Shakespeare
JULIUS CAESAR

AN AUTHORITATIVE TEXT
CONTEXTS AND SOURCES
CRITICISM
PERFORMANCE HISTORY

Edited by

S. P. CERASANO
COLGATE UNIVERSITY

W · W · NORTON & COMPANY · *New York* · *London*

W. W. Norton & Company has been independent since its founding in 1923, when William Warder Norton and Mary D. Herter Norton first published lectures delivered at the People's Institute, the adult education division of New York City's Cooper Union. The firm soon expanded its program beyond the Institute, publishing books by celebrated academics from America and abroad. By midcentury, the two major pillars of Norton's publishing program—trade books and college texts—were firmly established. In the 1950s, the Norton family transferred control of the company to its employees, and today—with a staff of four hundred and a comparable number of trade, college, and professional titles published each year—W. W. Norton & Company stands as the largest and oldest publishing house owned wholly by its employees.

Manufacturing by Maple Press
Composition by Westchester
Production manager: Sean Mintus

Library of Congress Cataloging-in-Publication Data

Shakespeare, William, 1564–1616.
   Julius Caesar : an authoritative text, sources and contexts, criticism,
performance history / William Shakespeare ; edited by S. P. Cerasano.
      p. cm. — (A Norton critical edition)
   Includes bibliographical references.
   ISBN 978-0-393-93263-8 (pbk.)
   1. Shakespeare, William, 1564–1616. Julius Caesar.
2. Caesar, Julius—Assassination—Drama.   3. Conspiracies—
Drama.   4. Assassins—Drama.   5. Rome—Drama.   I. Cerasano,
S. P.   II. Title.
   PR2808.A2C45 2012
   822.3'3—dc23

                                                              2012010728

W. W. Norton & Company, Inc., 500 Fifth Avenue, New York, NY 10110
wwnorton.com

W. W. Norton & Company Ltd. 15 Carlisle Street, London W1D 3BS

2   3   4   5   6   7   8   9   0

Contents

Illustrations

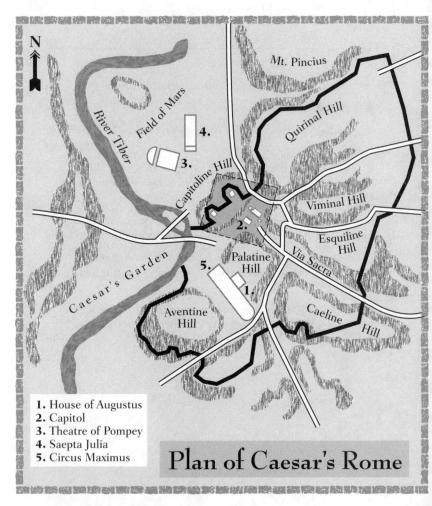

N

River Tiber

Field of Mars

Mt. Pincius

Quirinal Hill

4.

3.

Capitoline Hill

Viminal Hill

2.

Caesar's Garden

5.

Palatine Hill

Via Sacra

Esquiline Hill

1.

Aventine Hill

Caeline Hill

1. House of Augustus
2. Capitol
3. Theatre of Pompey
4. Saepta Julia
5. Circus Maximus

Plan of Caesar's Rome

The maps are reproduced by permission of Deborah Whitman.
Whitman Studios, Norwich, NY.

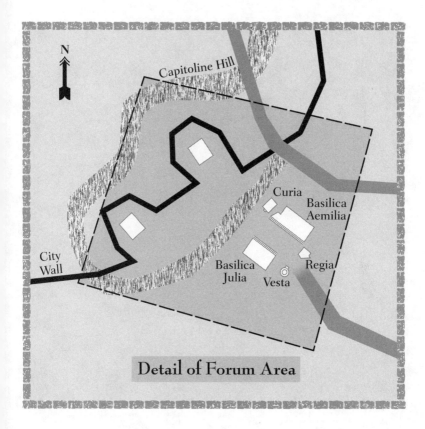

Detail of Forum Area

Introduction

Sources, Images of Caesar, and Romanization

> They on thother side that had conspired his death, compassed
> him in on everie side with their swordes drawen in their handes,
> that Caesar turned him[self] no where, but he was stricken at by
> some, and still had naked swords in his face, and was hacked and
> mangeled among them, as a wilde beaste taken of hunters. For it
> was agreed among them, that every man should geve him a
> wound, bicause all their partes should be in this murther: and
> then Brutus him selfe gave him one wounde about his privities.
> Men reporte also, that Caesar did still defende him selfe against
> the rest, running everie waye with his bodie: but when he sawe
> Brutus with his sworde drawen in his hande, then he pulled his
> gowne over his heade, and made no more resistaunce, and was
> driven either casually, or purposedly, by the counsell of the con-
> spirators, against the base whereupon Pompeys image stoode,
> which ranne all of a goare blood, till he was slaine.
>
> Plutarch, *The Life of Julius Caesar*[1]

Shakespeare's Julius Caesar is murdered only seventy-five lines into
3.1, at the center of the play, in an action marked by the simple stage
direction "They stab Caesar." In truth we know little about how the
actual killing would have taken place on stage in 1600 when, according to the German traveler Thomas Platter, the play was performed
at the newly opened Globe Playhouse; however, Shakespeare's
sources report elements of the assassination, together with the circumstances leading up to it, that are much more richly envisioned
than Shakespeare's text might initially convey.

In 1579, the publication of Plutarch's *Parallel Lives of the Greeks
and Romans*, translated from the French into English by Thomas
North, made a significant account of Caesar available to those who
couldn't read the Greek original. Previous to this, readers depended
upon Latin narratives—a variety of classical, medieval, and
sixteenth-century sources—and particularly Suetonius's life of Caesar in *The Twelve Caesars*, for sketches of the legendary conqueror.
However, while the basic details in Suetonius's account of Caesar's

---

1. Geoffrey Bullough, ed., *Narrative and Dramatic Sources of Shakespeare* (London: Routledge and Kegan Paul, 1957–77), 9 vols., 5: 86.

death are repeated by Plutarch (and others), Plutarch's lives are fuller and more detailed, and essentially more three-dimensional than Suetonius's. Additionally, Plutarch provided lives of not only Caesar, but also Brutus, Antony, and Cicero that, together, contributed different elements to Shakespeare's play. Of these, the lives of Caesar and Brutus supplied much of the background for *Julius Caesar*, although ample evidence from many of Shakespeare's plays suggests that he read more widely in Plutarch's collection than we might initially suspect.[2] Moreover, as I shall mention later, other sources contributed heavily to Shakespeare's reading, not only in terms of providing historical information, but also in shaping his sense of historical motivation and the role of providence in human history.

By selecting Julius Caesar as the subject of his tragedy Shakespeare chose a character whose mythic life was well known, a larger-than-life presence who could easily take over the Globe stage. Generations of English school boys had translated Caesar's *Gallic Wars*, as well as Cicero's orations addressing Cataline's thwarted conspiracy and other aspects of contemporary politics during the period when Caesar ruled the Roman Republic. There were, as well, references to Caesar and his time in the writings of many classical authors whose works were standard reading for sixteenth-century students.

Aside from Alexander the Great, no figure arguably had a greater effect on the history of the classical world than Julius Caesar.[3] An iconic figure, as well known for his statesmanship as for his military genius, Caesar provided Shakespeare with a complex presence that was resonant with ambiguity. His death, carefully portrayed by Plutarch, marked the crucial turning point in Roman history when the well-respected Republic—lauded for its representative government—gave way to a series of tyrants during the Empire that followed. Ancient historians generally construed the reign of Caesar as a period of relative stability amid a stream of civil war and unrest; for the early modern audience Caesar metaphorically embodied all that was "civilized" in Roman culture. Consequently, his death was interpreted as an event that unleashed chaos, war, and ultimately tragedy. Yet Caesar's reign and his assassination were controversial. While some ancient authors acclaimed Caesar and condemned the civil wars, Plutarch's extended portrait presented Shakespeare with both positive and negative attributes, allowing the playwright to explore the possibility that Caesar possessed the kinds of ambitious tendencies that would have favored his elevation to the status of a

2. E. A. J. Honigmann, "Shakespeare's Plutarch," *Shakespeare Quarterly* 10.1 (1959): 31–32.
3. For further commentary in light of plays by Shakespeare's contemporaries see Lisa Hopkins, *The Cultural Uses of the Caesars on the English Renaissance Stage* (Aldershot, Hampshire: Ashgate, 2008).

king. To this was added the particular interpretations of medieval commentators, chief among whom was Augustine, who, in his writings on history, saw Caesar as embodying the sin of pride, a characterization that found a place in other dramatic treatments during Shakespeare's time. Slanting the portrait of Caesar in the direction of providential history only made his assassination more predictable.[4] And also the actions of Brutus and the conspirators were thereby somewhat vindicated. Instead of bloodthirsty savages they became, in Augustine's view, the agents for divine change within the annals of history ordained by God.

Lastly, an important aspect of Julius Caesar's profile, one seldom observed by commentators, was his "personal divinity," an element attributed to Caesar by his contemporaries, for he had held the prestigious position of "pontifex maximus" (the High Priest of the College of Pontiffs) for over twenty years at the time of his death. As chief pontifex Caesar enjoyed sacred authority and carried out priestly responsibilities, such as the consecration of temples, sacrificial rites, and other rituals. The pontifex also administered *jus divinum*, or divine law; and he lived in an official residence close to the house of the Vestal Virgins and the Via Sacra in the Forum Romanum. Within Shakespeare's play this aspect of Caesar's historical portrait emerges in his willingness to believe Decius's interpretation of his dream:

> This dream is all amiss interpreted.
> It was a vision, far and fortunate.
> Your statue spouting blood in many pipes
> In which so many smiling Romans bathed
> Signifies that from you great Rome shall suck
> Reviving blood, and that great men shall press
> For tinctures, stains, relics . . . (2.2.83–89)

And it is his divine status, Caesar thinks, that will protect him when he goes to the Senate. He is, of course, wrong; but following his death Caesar was deified.[5]

In addition to the threats of civil war in the air during the 1590s in England, there is reason to think that Shakespeare's audience might have felt that Caesar's life was entwined with London and Londoners in a physical, geographical sense. Not only were Shakespeare and his contemporaries familiar with stories of Julius Caesar

4. J. Leeds Barroll, "Shakespeare and Roman History," *MLR* 53 (1958): 327–43.
5. There are many excellent biographies of Gaius Julius Caesar, including the well-known study by Christian Meier, *Caesar*, trans. David McLintock (New York: Basic Books/ HarperCollins, 1995) and Adrian Goldsworthy's more recent *Caesar: Life of a Colossus* (New Haven: Yale University Press, 2006). Another worthy source, one that traces the ways in which Caesar has become a mythological figure, is Maria Wyke, *Caesar: A Life in Western Culture* (Chicago: The University of Chicago Press, 2008).

that formed part of their own early history, they also witnessed Roman roads, walls, and other structures, or remains of those structures all around them, particularly in London. The *Survey of London*, written by the Tudor chronicler John Stow, published first in 1603, provides a representative record. Here, in narrating the foundation of what was eventually to become England, Stow discusses the Roman invasion, the seizure of the realm of "Brytaine" in order to pay a yearly tribute to Rome, and Caesar's eventual founding of "Troynovant" (the "new Troy," later Londinium, i.e., London).[6] As part of his description of the antiquities found in Spittlefield, not far from the site of the Theater, the original playhouse used by Shakespeare and his fellow actors, Stow describes a Roman burial ground, "full of Ashes, and burnt bones of men, to wit, of the Romanes that inhabited here."[7] Moreover, Stow reiterates the legend that Caesar was the first builder of structures integral to the Tower of London, as well as other structures, still evident as ruins in the Tudor era.[8] Not only did Roman civilization seem "alive" in these ways, but Shakespeare's contemporaries attributed to Caesar the invention of the Julian calendar.

In addition to all this, when Shakespeare chose Julius Caesar as a subject for tragedy he recognized an opportunity for capitalizing on a type of play that was fashionable. The craze for Roman plays was already established when Shakespeare first came to London, and it remained strong throughout his lifetime. As Clifford Ronan points out, forty-three extant Roman plays were written and performed between 1585 and 1635, most of which were "serious works." "Indeed," he writes, "it is astonishing to calculate the sheer number and prestige of the authors who provided sixteenth- and seventeenth-century France and England with Ancient Roman characters and dramatic settings." Concurrently, the Roman plays of the period gained popularity because they were embedded in a popular dramatic tradition—that of revenge tragedy—which overlapped with the long-standing genre of Senecan tragedy.[9] Here, it is important to bear in mind that Shakespeare decided to write *Julius Caesar* within a vital, ongoing dramatic tradition. As Ronan concludes, Roman plays were far from being museum pieces; they offered a place to interface with larger philosophical and intellectual trends of the time: "To write a Roman history play must have been a central humanist endeavor: a re-presenting of the genre in which Rome itself

---

6. John Stow, *A Survey of London* (Oxford: Clarendon Press, 1908), 2 vols., 1:2–3.
7. Stow, *A Survey of London*, 1: 168.
8. Stow, *A Survey of London*, 1: 44, 136.
9. Clifford Ronan, *"Antike Roman": Power, Symbology and The Roman Play in Early Modern England, 1585–1635* (Athens, Ga., and London: The University of Georgia Press, 1995): 1, 2.

re-presents its history." Furthermore, Ronan comments that writing such dramas meant "confront[ing] the basic Renaissance issues of continuity, discontinuity, and mutability."[1]

For generations, readers and audiences have been asking, "How 'Roman' are Shakespeare's Roman plays?" Not surprisingly, perhaps, here much of the discussion centers on characterization, setting, issues relating to Latin rhetoric, and Shakespeare's anachronisms.[2] In 1957, T. J. B. Spencer noted that Shakespeare has been frequently complimented for his portrait of the ancient Romans, as well as for his characterization of the Roman world and of its people at key historical moments. During the Restoration and eighteenth century John Dryden, Alexander Pope, and many other writers speculated on the "genuineness" of Shakespeare's Romans.[3] What Spencer notes of special significance, however, is that "the Romans in the imagination of the sixteenth century were Suetonian and Tacitan rather than Plutarchan." There was more interest in the Roman Empire than in the Republic. That Suetonius generated greater enthusiasm was attributable to the gossipy nature of his narrative, while the Empire, with its extravaganza of bloodshed and power presented itself as the natural stuff from which to make tragedies.[4] Consequently, Shakespeare was unusual in terms of his fascination with Plutarch's *Lives*. More of his spectators would actually have been interested in Plutarch's *Moralia* than the *Lives*, primarily because then, as in later centuries, the issues raised by the history of Caesar and his times created a natural bridge to questions of political morality and statecraft.[5]

Helping to redefine our questions regarding historical authenticity, John W. Velz in 1978 underscored M. W. MacCallum's conclusion, articulated early in the twentieth century, that "there was a good deal of . . . correspondence between Elizabethan life and Roman life" in Shakespeare's time.[6] And it was, in many ways, the "style" or "Romanitas" depicted by Shakespeare that defined Rome and its inhabitants. Thus, for Shakespeare, the sense of "Rome" changed from one Roman setting to another. For Velz, the Rome of

1. Ronan, 7. For further discussion of contemporary versions of *Julius Caesar* see Harry Morgan Ayres, "Shakespeare's *Julius Caesar* in Light of Some Other Versions," *PMLA* 25.2 (1910): 183–227.
2. Ronan takes up the issue of anachronism in a fascinating way, arguing that it was intentional. See Chapter 1 *passim*.
3. See the excerpts from Spencer's essay in this volume, taken from "Shakespeare and the Elizabethan Romans," *Shakespeare Survey* 10 (1957): 27–38. The reference here is from pp. 27–28 in the original. Unless otherwise noted, page citations in the Introduction refer to the original, not to excerpts in this volume.
4. Spencer, 31.
5. Spencer, 33, 37.
6. MacCallum, quoted in John W. Velz, "The Ancient World in Shakespeare: Authenticity or Anachronism? A Retrospect," *Shakespeare Survey* 31 (1978): 1–12.

Julius Caesar differs from that of *Titus Andronicus, Antony and Cleopatra*, and *Coriolanus*. "Yet in all four plays," he writes, "style is prominent—and 'Roman,' or so Shakespeare would have thought." Further, he notes, other "Roman" elements (apart from the rhetorical modes that Shakespeare creates for various characters in the play) include a Stoic temperament, a strain of antifeminism, and the political institutions that history has associated with Roman culture. And these are literally part of Rome as *urbs*, i.e., that city, ringed with a wall "outside of which the dark forces of barbarism lurk."[7]

According to Velz, it is the specific places mentioned in the play—the Forum, the Senate House, Pompey's Theatre, Brutus's and Caesar's houses, the Via Sacra of Caesar's great processions, the marketplace where the ruler's body is taken after the assassination—that create Shakespeare's Rome.[8] At the beginning of the play the runners are set to run the Lupercalian race that would have started on the outskirts of the city, at the cave of Romulus and Remus, and eventually the runners would have come down to the city's center (see the plan of Caesar's Rome). Consequently, the Forum Romanorum, simply known as "The Forum" in its time, takes on a special meaning. In 46 BCE, at the time of his great triumph, Caesar entertained the whole Roman people at a single banquet, for which 22,000 dining tables were set out in the Forum. Several equestrian statues (of Pompey and Caesar) stood in the vicinity of the official speaker's platform. Caesar displayed his authority publicly by constructing a new, larger senate house on the Forum (the Curia Julia), and Antony "gave the oration at the funeral pyre of Caesar, which stood in an open space on the east side of the Forum."[9] When we think about the geography of Shakespeare's play, it is necessary to realize that a large portion of the action occurs in a very small part of the city, much of it adjacent to, near, or in the area demarcated as the Forum (see detail of Forum area). As a result, the frenzy of Caesar's death and the chaos of its aftermath feel contained, geographically and physically; the violence builds to a fever pitch, not only because of the mob's gathering anger, but because the events transpire in a relatively restricted area. The death of Cinna the Poet takes place not far from the murder of Caesar. In Shakespeare's play the domiciles of Caesar, Brutus, and Antony don't appear to be very far apart.

However, in writing *Julius Caesar*, Shakespeare was not attempting to create an historically accurate model of Republican Rome, but rather to construct a place that would have seemed "Roman-

---

7. Velz, "The Ancient World in Shakespeare," 10–11.
8. Velz, 11.
9. Albert J. Ammerman, "The Forum in Rome" in *The Oxford Encyclopedia of Ancient Greece and Rome,* ed. Michael Gagarin and Elaine Fantham (Oxford: Oxford University Press, 2010), 7 vols., 3: 212–22. This reference is from p. 215.

ized," showcasing characters who would have been thought by his audience to have been historically plausible. In this undertaking, Plutarch was a valuable source, as Robert Miola explains, because, in his choice of material and dialogue-like moments, Shakespeare understands what makes good drama. He "brings to life the ancients in all their noisy, grand, greedy, pompous, brave, and passionate glory. . . . Conflicted individuals, with mixed motivations hidden under deceptive appearances, create history."[1] As Gary Miles points out, "Shakespeare's emphasis upon the private, interior dilemmas of his characters may be understood as an enrichment of the material that he found in his ancient sources." This is not to argue that Romans were conceived of as two-dimensional persons, Miles explains, but that their interior thoughts were judged, by historians such as Plutarch, to be less important than the "terms on which Roman aristocrats acted out their lives," terms dictated largely by public power and authority, wealth, and public distinction.[2]

Although a thorough examination of Shakespeare's sources is impossible in this introduction, some overview is instructive because, in adapting his sources, Shakespeare was retelling history in light of his own interests.[3] In the course of this process Shakespeare absorbed Plutarch's narratives in various ways. As in the writing of other history plays Shakespeare freely reorganized chronology, cutting down the number of events recorded by Plutarch and reducing the amount of time in which these occur. For instance, the Feast of the Lupercal was actually celebrated in February, but it occurs in *Julius Caesar* nearer to the Ides of March. Similarly, Octavius arrives in Rome shortly after the assassination of Caesar, but, historically, the event didn't occur for some time thereafter. Symbolically, the rearrangement of time compresses events and generates tension; by such rearrangement the audience gets the sense that once Caesar is murdered, events build quickly toward the tragic ending. And also, the specific marking of time within the play reinforces the perception that time runs out quickly for the conspirators.

In narrating his story of Caesar's murder and the fall of the Republic Shakespeare also added details of his own, some not mentioned by Plutarch. For instance, Shakespeare's Caesar is deaf in one ear, which makes him vulnerable to flattery, but "deaf to reason" and warnings such as that offered by the soothsayer. Likewise, many

---

1. Robert S. Miola, *Shakespeare's Reading* (Oxford: Oxford University Press, 2000), 99.
2. For a more historically based reading of "authenticity" see Gary B. Miles, "How Roman Are Shakespeare's 'Romans'?", *Shakespeare Quarterly* 40 (1989): 257–83.
3. In addition to the sources listed in the notes to this section, see Kenneth Muir, *The Sources of Shakespeare's Plays* (New Haven: Yale University Press, 1978); Vivian Thomas, *Shakespeare's Roman Worlds* (London and New York: Routledge, 1989); and the introduction to Geoffrey Bullough's volume of sources on the play, plus other citations in the general bibliography.

Stage set used at Her Majesty's Theatre, January 29, 1898. Reproduced by permission of the Folger Shakespeare Library (Washington, DC).

editors and literary critics have noted that Shakepseare expands upon the number and kind of dark portents presented before the murder. While Plutarch mentions fire in the sky, spirits, the slave's burning hand, and the sacrificed beast that lacks a heart, the playwright adds thunder and lightning, a lioness whelping in the street, blood raining on the Capitol, and other signs of doom.[4]

Because Shakespeare was a careful reader, North's translation also proved enormously influential in terms of rhetoric. Shakespeare borrowed particular phrases and words from the English translation, which he recycled freely, "finding poetry in North's prose." A term such as "constancy," at the center of sixteenth-century political theory—predominantly through the ongoing conversation surrounding Justus Lipsius's *De Constantia Sapientis* (*On the Constancy of the Wise Man*)—becomes a defining concept in the characterizations of all of the major characters in the play.[5] Moreover, the quality of constancy was central in the imagining of a culture which widely accepted the tenets of Stoic philosophy.

---

4. Here, see Miola, *Shakespeare's Reading*, 103.
5. See Miola, *Shakespeare's Reading*, 100–101, and Adriana McCrae, *Constant Minds* (Toronto: University of Toronto Press, 1997).

with one Roman life—so that readers are encouraged to evaluate each subject in light of historical currents that are larger than any one subject alone. Most significantly, Plutarch's structure prompts readers to consider not only the oft-discussed ambiguity of each character, but also the subtle human possibilities of the men who shaped some of the most turbulent and exciting history of Roman civilization.

In *Julius Caesar* Shakespeare implies that the most influential figures of the ancient world were capable of causing incredible misery, not as a result of their grandeur but through common human flaws and failings. In other words he fashioned them to human scale rather than presenting them as monsters. Caesar needn't have been a tyrant in order to provoke chaos; Brutus and Cassius needn't have been forces of insidious evil. Rather, they could emerge as misdirected human beings, in the process of their lives discovering a tragic end instead of the road to the perfect republic.[3]

A Brief Critical Overview

The earliest commentators on *Julius Caesar*, writing in the eighteenth century, were united in applauding what one anonymous writer in 1789 called the play's "dramatic excellence and historical truth"; but they were not without censure. Samuel Johnson (1709–1784)—known as much for his personal eccentricity as for his acute insights into literature and human nature—found the tragedy "cold and unaffecting, compared with some other of Shakespeare's plays." The problem, he hypothesized, was that Shakespeare's "adherence to the real story, and to Roman manners, seems to have impeded the natural vigour of his genius." George Steevens (1736–1800), whose edition of Shakespeare's plays appeared in 1773, felt obliged to defend Shakespeare's portrayal of women from critics who characterized them as represented in "a disagreeable light," or even "depraved." Steevens indicted his contemporaries who complained of Shakespeare's "cruelty to the ladies" by explaining that "His women are always as important as the nature of his fable requires them." There are times, he argued, when women "have equally the advantage" to the men in the plays. Speaking more particularly about *Caesar*, Steevens cited the obvious comparison with *Macbeth*, which was

---

3. Other sources for Shakespeare's play, such as Appian's *The Civil Wars*, J. Higgin's *The Mirror for Magistrates*, and Suetonius's *Twelve Caesars*, are included in the Sources section. Many of the authors working on Plutarch and Shakespeare give them at least a brief mention in their surveys. The excerpt from Ernest Schanzer's book, in the readings section, provides a good survey of some of these additional sources, as does the full essay written by T. J. B. Spencer, cited above in note 3, p. xv.

written only a few years after *Caesar*. Each, he writes, provides good proof that "a very excellent play could have been written without the assistance even of a love episode." Nevertheless, Steevens applauded Shakespeare for his portrait of Portia who displays "conjugal tender-ness" in her anxiety for Brutus and the assassination plot which, Steevens asserts, she probably suspects.[4]

The anonymous author alluded to a few sentences earlier demon-strates how quickly the conversation on *Julius Caesar* moved to character-based criticism, a trend that was to continue for well over a century. Moreover, this author emphasized what seemed to be Shakespeare's shortcomings. Cassius, he decided, was deficient because Shakespeare didn't offer a clear sense of his motives in the conspiracy. Neither Antony nor Cicero was portrayed in a manner that was true to history, Antony's rhetoric being influenced by a style of oratory that was "Asiatic, or diffuse and flowery" and Cicero being a prominent figure, rather than a shadowy presence in the back-ground. The critic also found the opening of the play to be too full of "low humour, ill suited to the grandeur of the business which fol-lows, and unlikely to have passed between the Comons and their Tribunes." In other matters as well, incidents and interactions in the play were written off as being out of step with "any authentic record."

By the time William Hazlitt wrote his commentary (1817), criti-cal thinking was fastened on specific characters and comparisons between Shakespeare's play and his sources. By contrast with the writer of the unsigned 1789 essay, Hazlitt declared that "the truth of history in *Julius Caesar* is very ably worked up with dramatic effect. The councils of generals, the doubtful turns of battles, are repre-sented to the life. The death of Brutus is worthy of him." Cassius, when compared with Brutus, is "the better cut for a conspirator," and the quarrel scene between Brutus and Cassius is "managed in a mas-terly way." Moreover, Hazlitt was the first critic to raise the issue of tyranny (which, as we will see later, has become a major issue in discussing the play).[5] Despite his praise, however, Hazlitt was unsat-isfied with the representation of Caesar that fell short of "the portrait given of him in his Commentaries. He makes several vapouring and rather pedantic speeches, and does nothing." "Indeed," the author fulminated, "he has nothing to do."[6]

---

4. Coppélia Kahn traces the women and the purpose of Portia's wound interestingly in her chapter on the play in *Roman Shakespeare: Warriors, wounds, and woman* (London and New York: Routledge, 1997), 77–105. And for another feminist view of the play see also, Mary Hamer, *William Shakespeare: 'Julius Caesar'* (Horndon, UK: Northcote House, 1998). George Steevens's essay can be found on pp. 155–57. The anonymous essay is excerpted on pp. 158–62.

5. For a more modern account see Robert S. Miola, "*Julius Caesar* and the Tyrannicide Debate," *RQ* 38.2 (1985): 271–89.

6. See William Hazlitt's essay in this volume, 162–64.

In the early twentieth century, at a time when literary critics, and particularly those writing on Shakespeare, had gained some autonomy, Harley Granville-Barker contributed his *Prefaces to Shakespeare* to what had then become an ongoing critical conversation. Presenting verbal portraits of individual characters in the play, he proposes that the play centers on Brutus, whose first sentence is "measured, dispassionate, tinged with disdain," all characteristics that stand out in Shakespeare's senator. Like Hazlitt, Granville-Barker emphasized that Cassius is "blest—and curst—with a temperament." The character of Octavius, he wrote, is drawn with a kind of subtleness that shows his astuteness to changing politics. Calphurnia and Portia, are astonishingly lifelike, and Portia he found especially remarkable: "A quiet beauty is the note of Portia." She is "a portrait in miniature," Granville-Barker concluded, with "a dignity of soul and an innate courage that might well leave the cleverest of them humble."

For many decades, *Julius Caesar* has prompted literary critics to continue debating the issues surrounding source study, although other areas of interest have emerged. Irving Ribner's *Patterns in Shakespearian Tragedy* (1960) featured a chapter on "Historical Tragedy" wherein the author countered the trend of separating Shakespeare's history plays from his tragedies, bringing together concerns of dramatic genre with character study. "That the plays are histories conditions the symbolic function of character," Ribner stated. "The hero-king stands always for England, and the principle implicit in his life-journey is one of national destiny. . . . The fate of Brutus or Caesar is secondary to that of Rome, and, as tragic heroes, they also reflect in specific human terms principles of general political conduct."[7] Of course, Caesar is not finally a king, as Ribner points out. Nevertheless, Caesar's ambition to attain kingship has encouraged some commentators to see him as a "would-be tyrant" (Ribner's term), a tendency illustrated in many early modern plays involving Caesar and his Republic. Thus, Shakespeare's contemporaries could be readily interested in debate surrounding Caesar and tyrannicide. Such an issue not only played to contemporary concerns, but initiated some of the critical questions that persist today: How many tragic heroes are in the play? Which characteristics make Brutus, Caesar, or Cassius heroes (or villains)? What can be known about Caesar in the play, and what happens when we begin to investigate the mystery surrounding him? What is the relationship among the terms "king," "monarch," and "tyrant"?

The fragility of the political system, rooted as it is in the personal loyalties (and disloyalties) of the many characters presented in the

---

7. See Irving Ribner's essay, 171–81 in this volume.

play, is at the center of G. Wilson Knight's essay from *The Imperial Theme,* which foregrounds love and honor in the play.[8] In this way, Knight demonstrates, Shakespeare emphasizes the tension between the ties that bind characters to each other and the divisions ultimately created by members of the conspiracy. He explains, "Through making a division between Caesar the man and Caesar the national hero and dictator, Brutus, Cassius, and indeed Caesar himself, all have plunged Rome and themselves into disaster." As a result, Knight suggests, the audience must be ready to see Caesar as Antony sees him—as "both man and demi-god curiously interwoven" and the person who holds Rome together through the sheer force of his identity. Simultaneously, spectators must be ready to sympathize with Brutus, who substitutes his honor for his love of Caesar, allowing his idealism to cloud his judgment. Complicating the audience's response, according to John W. Velz, is our sense that Brutus, Cassius, and Antony unwittingly end by re-enacting an earlier historical moment when Pompey, Marcus Cato, and Lucius Junius Brutus reacted against tyranny. "The republicans see themselves in roles from the heroic past," Velz points out, "while the monarchists look to a prototype who appears onstage and who belongs fully to the Rome of the present."[9]

Confusion, in its many manifestations, whether of a personal, political, or rhetorical nature, seems to be the order of the day in *Julius Caesar.* It is, in part, a search for constancy, set against the conspirators' confusion over Caesar, that leads to the pathetic demise of so many characters. Yet for all of Caesar's claims to be "the northern star," as Jan H. Blits observes, "the northern star, as Caesar seems to forget, is visible only at night. It may indeed display an unrivaled 'true-fix'd and resting quality,' but its quality and glory stand out only against a darkened sky."[1] The surrounding confusion, which Norman Sanders extends to his discussion of shifting power in the course of the play, is only quelled when another single figure (Octavius) takes control. Although Antony speaks Brutus's epitaph, Sanders asserts:

> it is Octavius who realizes that the body of the idealist among the conspirators is a valuable political property now the life is fled. Thus Brutus' bones shall be used according to his virtue, with all respect, and lie within Octavius' tent. The cycle of control-opposition-chaos-control has worked itself out, echoing the pattern of every political change. And, as with such patterns in life, the emerging figure who exemplifies the final control is

---

8. See G. Wilson Knight's essay, 181–88 in this volume.
9. See John W. Velz's essay, 189–98 in this volume.
1. See Blits's fuller commentary on pp. 199–210.

powerful and enigmatic, and one whose possibilities lie still
within the womb of time.[2]

Many further areas of interest stand out amid the sea of excellent
critical writings on the play, and many more insights can be drawn
from the sources listed in the bibliography. One of these—a discussion of Shakespeare's use of numbers, time, and order—is exempli-
fied in Thomas McAlindon's chapter on *Julius Caesar* in *Shakespeare's
Tragic Cosmos*.[3] Tracing the numerological patterns in the play,
McAlindon notes that four main characters (Caesar, Brutus, Cassius, and Antony) are "broadly identifiable" with what would have
been the four humoural types identified by physicians of the
time—the melancholic (Brutus), the choleric (Cassius), the phleg-
matic (Caesar), and the sanguine (Antony). Taken together, these
types were understood to comprise all of humanity. As McAlindon
observes, the "humours of the four leaders have become 'ill-
temper'd'. . . . and so have contributed to the 'falling sickness that
afflicts the whole body politic.'" The number four, moreover, would
have been thought to be symbolic of "opposites reconciled" and ultimately of "natural unity," which is lacking in Rome at the opening of
the play. However, the unity of oneness, which Rome needs to pros-
per, is found in the ultimate authority of Julius Caesar and in
Octavius who emerges at the play's end.[4] Complementary group-
ings of four are used later in the play as well. There are, for instance,
the two marriages, the four plebeians who speak during the rhetorical contest between Brutus and Antony, and the four plebeians who
murder Cinna the poet.[5] The division of four, into two sets of two
each, is represented in another "symbolic dualism of great significance" according to McAlindon—that of hand and heart.[6] But
placed against the pattern of two and four is the triumvirate that
ascends in the last two acts, a reminder that the number three, being
uneven by definition, is also in danger of becoming unbalanced at
any time. Within a group of three there is a perpetual threat of two
characters forming an alliance against the third. Consequently, the
way in which the numbers and alliances form within the course of
the play (along with the consistent punnng on the word "fourth/
forth") are telling. Such a pattern "gives the time design its special
character and force," McAlindon points out. "The conspiracy consists
of eight men who strike for justice's sake and in order to revive Rome's

2. Norman Sanders, "The Shift of Power in *Julius Caesar*," *RES* 5 (1964): 24–35. This quo-
    tation is from p. 35.
3. (Cambridge: Cambridge University Press, 1991), 76–101.
4. McAlindon, 79.
5. McAlindon, 80–84.
6. McAlindon, 84–85.

'mortified' spirit, but it is Octavius alone who is destined to accomplish what that number signifies."[7]

A final area of critical thinking that deserves mention focuses on the use of ritual in the play. This topic is considered by Naomi Conn Liebler who in *Shakespeare's Festive Tragedy* reminds readers that *Julius Caesar* "begins at the Feast of the Lupercal, the Roman celebration on from February 13 to 15, which later became St. Valentine's day and often coincides in the Christian calendar with Mardi Gras and the Carnival season." And, she adds, it also "passes quickly into history's most famous *ides* of March."[8] Furthermore, the Lupercalia "were the oldest and most sacred rites of purgation and fertility in the ancient Roman calendar. . . . Their association with the figure of Romulus situates them within the foundation myth of Roman civilization. Much of Plutarch's later narrative of Caesar's death echoes that of Romulus."[9] Additionally, as Liebler writes, for Brutus "the language of politics is simultaneously the language of religious ritual. The play's opening upon the Lupercal prepares a way for us to see Brutus' ritualistic coloring of the assassination as something other than naïve or evil. It is not a design he has simply made up, but rather one which the transitional atmosphere that hangs over Rome allows him to construct as credible."[1] There were, as well, many other parallels between the Lupercalian rites and the homegown English rituals of Shakespeare's time. Therefore, the theatrical references that suffuse the play text are not only those related to personal role-playing; they are also, more generally, part of the fabric of the play. Owing to the parallels between the Roman and English rituals, as Liebler explains, "the audience . . . receives the play on, as it were, a two-tiered stage."[2]

Performance History

It is impossible to date the first performance of *Julius Caesar* with any precision; however, Thomas Platter, a Swiss traveler, who visited England from mid-September to mid-October 1599, noted that he went to the Globe to see the play:

> After dinner on the 21st of September, at about two o'clock, I went with my companions over the water, and in the strewn roof-house saw the tragedy of the first Emperor Julius with at

7. McAlindon, 97.
8. Naomi Conn Liebler, *Shakespeare's Festive Tragedy: The Ritual Foundations of Genre* (London and NY: Routledge, 1995), 88.
9. Liebler, 90.
1. Liebler, 92.
2. Liebler, 111.

least fifteen characters very well acted. At the end of the comedy they danced according to their custom with extreme ele-
gance. Two in men's clothes and two in women's gave this
performance, in wonderful combination with each other.[3]

This performance, which probably took place shortly after the new
playhouse opened, would have been one of the plays—along with
Shakespeare's *Henry V*—that were mounted to showcase the lead
actors of Lord Chamberlain's Men. From the beginning the actor
who performed Brutus (in this case, probably Richard Burbage, who
had formerly memorialized such roles as Romeo and Prince Hal)
was preeminent, speaking the majority of the lines. The next largest
role went to Cassius, who speaks the second greatest number of
lines. Julius Caesar, after whom the play is named, had many fewer
lines, and it would not be for several centuries to follow that the
actor who performed the role would be brought further to the fore-
front of productions. Other elements of Platter's description convey
typical aspects of theatrical performance during the period when
Shakespeare wrote and acted. Performances took place in the after-
noon, women's roles were performed by boys (and hence, were kept to
a minimum), and the audience was often treated to a post-performance
entertainment in the form of a dance. (Platter's term "comedy" is
simply a synonym for a play.) Other productions of *Julius Caesar*,
staged during the period, include three court performances in
1611–12 (at Whitehall) and in January and November, 1636 (at St.
James's and the Cockpit). (Leonard Digges's poem, contributed to
the First Folio of Shakespeare's plays (1623), mentions *Julius Caesar*
specifically as one of the highlights of the collection, an assessment
that Digges expanded upon even more in his verses for the 1640 re-
printing of the plays.) Borrowings from Shakespeare's lines and some
allusions to incidents in the play appeared in the work of contemporary playwrights almost from the moment *Julius Caesar* appeared,
indicating the degree to which popular culture of the time had
absorbed it.

After the closing of the theatres, in the mid-seventeenth century,
Julius Caesar was revived and, even then, remained popular. Six
major performances are recorded between 1660 and 1700, and in the
eighty years following, over 120 performances occurred, mounted at
different London venues, including the pre-eminent theatres at
Drury Lane, Covent Garden, Lincoln's Inn Fields, and Goodman's

---

3. E. K. Chambers, *The Elizabethan Stage* (Oxford: Clarendon Press, 1923), 4 vols., 2: 365.
   As do other editors and critics, I owe an enormous debt to the most definitive book on the
   performance history of the play: John Ripley, *"Julius Caesar" on Stage in England and
   America, 1599–1973* (Cambridge and New York: Cambridge University Press, 1980).

Fields.[4] Yet the cultural climate and aesthetic tastes differed from what they were when the play was first written. Shakespeare's text was streamlined by removing shorter scenes, such as the death of the poet Cinna (3.3), and some minor characters were excised or merged with other characters. Additionally, actors and directors, finding the play to be too episodic, relied upon characterization to create a through-line. Consequently, Brutus was interpreted (and performed) as the penultimate noble Roman (Caesar being first), who, being too philosophical for his own good, was the actual hero of the play. By contrast, Cassius was depicted simply as an envious conspirator with a volatile temperament.

Two landmark productions of this period stand out. The earlier, preserved in an acting edition (published in 1684), appears to have been played from 1669 onward by the king's company, which, by royal warrant was granted exclusive right of performance. Thomas Betterton, the distinguished actor-manager, known particularly for the excellent quality of his voice, played Brutus as a hero, but not as wholly restrained. Rather, one commentator, recalling Betterton's talents, spoke of his ability to produce an inner passion tempered by dignity. Only in the quarrel scene with Cassius (4.3) did Betterton allow his anger to open "into that Warmth which becomes a Man of Virtue."[5]

The second production, preserved in an acting edition (and printed in 1719), is now known as the Dryden-Davenant version. This text probably preserves the version of the play performed in the first two decades of the eighteenth century. Most notably, the number of speaking parts was severely reduced. All sexual language was cut and Portia wounded herself in the arm (as opposed to the thigh). References to the supernatural, which clashed with the cultural climate of the time, were likewise severely reduced. Moreover, all humane elements of Brutus's character were eliminated, including the moment in 2.1 when Brutus, left alone following the departure of the conspirators, speaks over the sleeping Lucius. In combination with similar cuts, this streamlining "inititate[d] a trend towards a straight-line interpretation of Brutus as a cold-blooded idealist."[6] Some scenes— for example, the Cinna the Poet scene—were removed to hasten the action and to allow the plot to move directly to the meeting of the triumvirate. The Dryden-Davenant version set the tone for productions to follow, with its spotlight on the high-minded Brutus to the exclusion of much else in the play. In short, actors and directors of the eighteenth century interpreted Shakespeare's text as a battle cry

---

4. For a fuller record of particular performance patterns, see Ripley's detailed chronology, 287–311.
5. Quoted by Ripley, 20.
6. Ripley, 27.

for liberty and as a patriotic play that argued for republican ideals. They prized *Julius Caesar* for its rhetorical eloquence and classical sentiments. As such, the tendency to streamline all characters, events, and language that did not contribute to this effect was common throughout productions of the period.

The early nineteenth century experienced a resurgence of interest in the play, one sparked largely by the 1812 production created by the actor-director John Philip Kemble. For over a dozen years Kemble concentrated his energies on reviving Shakespeare's plays, and of these, *Julius Caesar* was the most successful. Instead of yielding to the tendencies of former directors, who attempted to project the plainness of the Roman characters and setting, Kemble's settings were marked by the extravagance of the imperial city following Caesar's Republic. Grand processions, large groups of actors (more than eighty-five supernumeraries) who performed the parts of citizens at the outset and soldiers in the final battle scene, some consideration of historical costuming, and a careful positioning of groups of characters on the stage all came together to represent what Kemble thought an "ancient atmosphere." (An example of the typical opulence displayed by nineteenth-century stages set can be seen in Illustration 3.) To mention one example, Caesar entered in 1.1 through a large triumphal arch. His train consisted of twenty-one characters or groups of characters, including six senators, twelve guards, two actors carrying "silver eagles," two carrying "golden eagles," one carrying a star, and two carrying SPQR banners ("Senatus Populusque Romanus," i.e., "The Senate and People of Rome"). When the group divided in half, each part occupying a different side of the stage, those displaying the symbolic magnificence of Rome, along with the senators and guards, were located stage left. Caesar stood in the middle front of the stage with Cassius on one side (stage right) and Antony with Lepidus on the other (stage left). Brutus, Casca, Decius, Metellus, with others were stretched in a line from front to back, stage right, facing off against the patriotic symbols denoting the power and glory of Rome. In other ways Kemble paid strict attention to stage placement. Just before the assassination in Act 3, Caesar sat enthroned with the same republican symbols backing him. He was also flanked by priests. Cassius, Brutus, and Casca were isolated as a group, stage left, while Pompey's statue was placed downstage right. The directions for the actual killing of Caesar were detailed and depicted Caesar as a fighter. Casca stabbed Caesar over the left shoulder, following which Caesar started out of the throne. Thereafter he tried to stab two of the conspirators, who avoided his blows, and when he dropped his dagger and was afterward stabbed ferociously by Cassius, he continued to stagger around the stage until Brutus finally delivered the fatal blow. When he died, Caesar fell far downstage near the audience. The tableau briefly foreshadowed the Forum scene in which Caesar's body is used by Antony as a prop to underscore the savagery of the killing and as a means through which he curries sympathy for the fallen leader. At the time some commentators thought that the concept for Kemble's carefully worked production lent itself to an unnatural "staginess," the kind of action that looked so unreal that it worked against any impression of humanity. Certainly Brutus, performed by Kemble, was considered to be the center of the play, but Antony (played memorably by Kemble's son Charles), Cassius, and Caesar were all allowed to claim a piece of the action in some significant way. Most of all, the decisions that Kemble made in placing Caesar as the focal point of magnificent processions and at the center of the assassination began a movement that called for a more serious consideration of the title character's importance in the play, and of the murder scene as major evidence of it. In fact, so stunning was Kemble's creation that virtually all subsequent productions in the nineteenth century were indebted to it.

During the American Revolution *Julius Caesar*, viewed as a vehicle for libertarian attitudes, was performed in Philadelphia and Charleston, South Carolina. After the liberation from English rule, productions occurred in New York. Thereafter, thousands of performances were mounted, and the play seems to have enjoyed an unprecedented popularity to the end of the nineteenth century. Of these, the most notorious production is that of 1864 at New York's Winter Garden in which Edwin Booth first appeared as Brutus. His brothers, Junius Brutus, and John Wilkes (who, a few months later, assassinated Abraham Lincoln), performed the roles of Cassius and Antony, respectively.[7]

Back in London, a visit from the German acting company patronized by the Duke of Saxe-Meiningen, showcased the Forum scene and Mark Antony, thus causing the eminent English director, Herbert Beerbohm Tree to abandon the long-standing tradition that placed Brutus at the center of the play. Instead Tree decided that the Roman mob was significant as well, so much so that Tree's plebeians staged a tableau of everyday life, an historically "accurate" street scene—against a stage set that featured a large bronze statue of Caesar, the roof of the Temple of Jupiter, and a fountain—before the opening of 1.1. Within the context of such theatrical literalism, historians detect a momentous trend, one that ultimately opened up Shakespeare's text in all ways. Before long, many roles (Brutus, Antony, Cassius, Caesar, the crowd) would be seen as critical; many scenes (the assassination, the Forum scene, the murder of Cinna

7. Ripley, 100–14.

the poet, the Brutus-Cassius quarrel, the proscription scene (4.1), even Brutus's suicide) would be thought "central" to the action. And performing the fullness of Shakespeare's text would come back into fashion, bringing with it new light on the character of Cicero, the relationship between Brutus and Portia, or between Brutus and his servant Lucius.[8]

So many fascinating productions were mounted during the twentieth century that they could easily form an entire study on their own. But of these the Orson Welles's production, staged in 1937 at the Mercury Theater in New York City, remains one of the most noteworthy, in part because the production emphasized the parallel between the mindless Roman mob and the forces of Fascism in Hitler's Germany. In order to break with former stage traditions Welles subtitled the play "Death of a Dictator." The text, focused on Caesar, Brutus, and the mob, was cut to its bare bones, allowing the director to dispense with the usual act/scene divisions. (The radical cutting resulted in a production that seemed more like a contemporary filmed newsreel, such as might be shown at the cinema, and less like a play.)[9] In support of Welles's concept, the actors were dressed in dark Nazi-like uniforms (for the senators) and modern street clothes, "dominated by military garb" (for the mob); Caesar, played by Joseph Holland and attired in a green uniform (looking, to some spectators, a bit like Mussolini), was the consummate dictator, appearing overly confident, capable of high-handedness, and threatening. Holland portrayed a Caesar who was "meant to be more of a symbol than a man." Casca, Decius Brutus, Legarius, and Trebonius, the lesser conspirators, were dressed as "modern day racketeers with turned-up collars and black hats pulled low around their ears." Mark Antony and Publius, officers of the state, were dressed in soldiers' tunics, while Brutus, played by Welles, had on "a formal kind of mufti."[1] Welles, as a quiet and thoughtful Brutus, was the center of the action.[2]

Several scenes are memorable for the innovation shown by Welles. Chief among these was the staging of the assassination (3.1), in which the conspirators stood in a diagonal line across the stage:

> Caesar, rolling from one to another in a kind of broken field-run, was, in turn, stabbed by each of them. Finally, as Caesar reached downstage there was only one person left to run to—Brutus, standing like a column against the proscenium wall. His knees buckling, Caesar turned to him as his final haven of

8. Ripley, 147–75.
9. Ripley, 223.
1. Richard France, "Orson Welles's Anti-Fascist Production of 'Julius Caesar,'" *Forum Modernes Theater* 15.2 (2000): 145–61. These references are from pp. 149 and 150.
2. Ripley, 230.

safety. Without a word Brutus' hand came out of his overcoat pocket, and he stood there clutching a knife while Caesar clung to his lapels.[3]

Following this, when it was clear that Brutus would not alter his course, Caesar's "Et tu Brute?" was spoken in resignation. Brutus then stabbed Caesar in virtual silence, a gesture that was "more climactic than the most piercing scream."[4]

Underscoring the recklessness of the Roman mob, Welles decided that the murder of Cinna (3.3) should be performed using the full text, and Cinna was killed onstage, in full sight.[5] Concurrently, the mob was energized by "whispers, murmurs, shouts, chants, and screams" during Antony's oration (3.2).[6] Here, searchlights swept over Antony, suggesting a Nazi rally, while conspirators greeted each other with Fascist salutes. Heightening the terror, instead of the actors exiting in ways that were visible to the audience, they were visualized against a dark background using spotlights, and when they were no longer significant they were "blotted out by darkness."[7] Given Welles's ability to bring *Julius Caesar* in line with the historical atmosphere of the time, it is perhaps not surprising that the production enjoyed 157 performances, making it the longest run on record. Nevertheless Welles's production has drawn a fair amount of negative criticism, both in its own time and later, from commentators who see it as no more than a piece of clever propaganda. John Ripley concludes, "In theory Welles's innovations should have given *Caesar* a new lease on life; but the facts are otherwise. The vitality, freshness, and relevance of the Mercury production in the long run did more harm than good."[8] By contrast, Richard France defends Welles's effort as a landmark in production history: "The highest form of propaganda utilizes the emotive and connotative power of imagery and symbols. It is in this sense that Welles created his own *Caesar*."[9]

In the years immediately following 1937, Welles's work set the tone for other productions, all of which sought to bring out the play's modern political edge. In addition to subsequent productions, staged very much in imitation of Welles's Fascist setting, Caesar has been played as a South American dictator and as Fidel Castro. By contrast, however, most directors have worked to retain more of the play text, and many have allowed Caesar to return at the center of

3. France, 153.
4. France, 153.
5. For a more detailed description of the scene, see France, 154–56.
6. Ripley, 228.
7. France, 146.
8. Ripley, 232.
9. France, 145.

the play in order to underscore the tragic elements, rather than allowing contemporary political parallels to swamp other elements of the text. In this, some directors have altered the scale of Caesar as a character, a few conceiving of him as overwhelming and iconic. (One example was John Schlesinger's 1977 production at the National Theatre, London, in which John Gielgud exuded an effortless authority.[1]) By contrast, some directors (for instance, John Wood, in his 1978 production at the Stratford Festival, Canada) have preferred a less iconic Caesar, one conceived as more ordinary in size.[2] In more recent times, the latter impulse has found its way into Edward Hall's production (2001) at Stratford-upon-Avon, in which the conversation between Caesar and Calphurnia at the opening of 2.2 was conducted in the intimacy of a household bath (see Illustration on p. xxxix).

Fifteen years after Welles's Mercury Theater production caused such a stir came Joseph L. Mankiewicz's 1953 film version, which stands out as a pioneering effort in the production history of *Julius Caesar*.[3] Interestingly, both versions were produced by the actor-director John Houseman (who assisted Welles in founding the Mercury Theater). Houseman's extended commentary on that production optimistically pointed out two assets: the historical climate, just after the close of World War II, was favorable to a highly politicized interpretation; and also, since we are discussing the first filmed version of the play, there was no "hardened tradition of Shakespearean production" to inhibit the filmmakers.[4] One of the first decisions, Houseman writes, was to film the production in black and white in order to diminish the sense of spectacle and emphasize instead "the interplay and conflict of character and personality expressed through the words in the mouths of individual actors." For the film's creators it was a matter of "powerful simplicity," rather than economics.[5] In keeping with these dictates the costumes were Republican-Roman in style, and the set designs were fittingly "solid and architectural."[6] There was a marked contrast between the "official magnificence of the Capitol and the sweaty congestion of our Roman slums."[7] Most

1. J. C. Trewin, "Shakespeare in Britain," *Shakespeare Quarterly* 19.2 (1968): 217.
2. Ralph Berry, "Stratford Festival Canada," *Shakespeare Quarterly* 30.2 (1979): 170.
3. For a survey of film versions of the play, related films, and audio records, see the Film Bibliography in this volume, 245.
4. John Houseman, *Entertainers and the Entertained* (New York: Simon and Schuster, 1986), 85.
5. Houseman, 86.
6. Houseman, 87. P. M. Pasinetti discusses the decisions he participated in as technical advisor to the film. Rome was "to be imagined as a 'lived in' place. . . . it reflected an oligarchy of nobles-magistrates on one side, engaged in violent and often vicious struggles for power and office, and on the other by common people. . . . The aristocratic dwelling and the slum could be close to one another." (See "The Role of the Technical Advisor" in *Focus on Shakespearean Films*, ed. Charles W. Eckert (Englewood Cliffs, N.J.: Prentice-Hall, Inc., 1972), 103–04.
7. Houseman, 88.

notable, perhaps, was the cast, which included James Mason as Brutus, who appeared to be "less of an 'antique Roman' and more of a modern man whose nobility lies not in grandiose sentiment but in the sincerity of his thinking and living." John Gielgud was cast as Cassius. He performed the role as "no common conspirator . . . for Cassius is a man who hates himself no less than he does Caesar. . . . [He] is the first and surest victim of his own discontent."[8] Not least of all, the riskiest casting choice lay in Mankiewicz's decision to have Marlon Brando—known primarily for his role as Stanley Kowalski in the 1951 film *A Streetcar Named Desire*—perform Mark Antony. Houseman notes that Brando was chosen because he could best project the qualities of brilliance and power that distinguish Caesar's cavalry leader. Additionally, Mankiewicz thought that Brando could project his lines with a magnificent, muscular voice. But shaping the character of Antony in this direction was more difficult than it initially appeared. The Forum scene, Antony's showcase, as Houseman points out, is much more than an exercise in virtuoso delivery. Antony "works on them [the mob] as best he can, using every trick he knows to sway them. . . . For twelve and a half minutes the Roman mob in the Forum and the spectator, in the darkness of the theater, should become one."[9] In his summary Houseman gives enormous credit to Gielgud for inspiring the entire cast with his own skill in speaking Elizabethan dramatic verse.[1] Not least of those in his debt was Brando who, according to Houseman, on the day that the Forum scene was filmed, was met by thunderous applause. "When Brando finished his speech . . . nine hundred extras applauded—and John Gielgud, who was not working that day, was leading them!"[2]

Occasionally, in recent years, actors have written at length about their experiences portraying specific roles. In "Brutus in *Julius Caesar*" John Nettles explores the central ambiguities of the character Shakespeare created. The Brutus that the audience sees initially is "depressed and withdrawn," Nettles observes, "far removed from his normal gentleness and affability. . . . It is plain that he is deeply troubled, but he will not be explicit about what precisely it is that is troubling him."[3] Following this, Nettles points out, "it is Cassius

8. Houseman, 94–95.
9. Houseman, 96.
1. Houseman, 94.
2. Houseman, 97. For more commentary on the Welles and Mankiewicz productions, see Jean Chothia, "*Julius Caesar* in Interesting Times" in *Remaking Shakespeare: Performances across Media. Genres and Cultures*, ed. Pascale Aebischer, Edward J. Esche, and Nigel Wheale (Houndsmills and Basingstoke, Hampshire: Palgrave Macmillan, 2003).
3. John Nettles, "Brutus in *Julius Caesar*" in Robert Smallwood, ed., *Players of Shakespeare 4* (Cambridge: Cambridge University Press, 1998), 177–92; this reference is from pp. 177–78. Excerpts can be found on pp. 232–40 of this edition.

Cassius (Julian Glover) attempts to convince Brutus (John Nettles) in Act 1, Scene 2 of the 1995 Royal Shakespeare Company production directed by Sir Peter Hall. Malcolm Davies Collection. © Shakespeare Birthplace Trust.

that has pushed Brutus from melancholic but passive observation of the political scene towards action of an extreme kind," action based upon "jealousy, unalloyed and deadly"[4] (Illustration 4). Later in the play, Brutus convinces himself—through a gross distortion of reality—that he, and the other conspirators, are justified in murdering Caesar. Although he continually misconstrues the reality around him, "he seems to learn nothing along the way. There appears very little development in Brutus' character from the orchard to Philippi."[5] Moreover, Brutus's Forum speech "appears not a little arrogant in its brevity and lack of substance."[6] But how, we might ask, does the audience's sense of Brutus change from that of a steely, misinformed killer, to that of a "noble Roman"? "Here," Nettles points out, "is the main problem with playing the character Brutus. The reputation, and the expectations we have of the man, are destroyed in the course of the play."[7] Yet, at the same time, "we must try to make him a human being and not a one-dimensional-caricature of bad political thinking."[8] As his subsequent commentary tells us, Nettles finds that playing the contradictions within the character creates the most

4. Nettles, 181.
5. Nettles, 183.
6. Nettles, 184.
7. Nettles, 186.
8. Nettles, 187.

satisfying portrayal of Brutus. Several interactions between Brutus and other characters produce the complex character Nettles seeks. These exist in Brutus's argument and reconciliation with Cassius in the Quarrel Scene (4.3), in his gentle management of his young servant Lucius (4.3), and in the reflection of his better qualities that Portia seeks to unearth in her confrontation with him (2.1). But finally, does Brutus ever gain personal enlightenment from what he experiences? Nettles concludes that Brutus's tragedy lies in the fact that he remains a character who is forever baffled. "The better option is to present him at the end as in the orchard," he writes, "a man who does not know himself, a man who deceives himself and cannot develop or grow because of these flaws in his nature." In the last moments the audience is told that "his life was gentle," but in the course of the play he "casts himself in the role of noble hero and the savior of Rome and thereby is o'erparted to a tragic degree."[9] In Nettles's interpretation the roles Brutus takes on are simply too difficult for him, and he fails in the attempt to play them.

Elements of Production

As is the case in all of Shakespeare's dramatic works, each production takes on a life of its own. Nevertheless, there are particular places in the text of *Julius Caesar* that have, over time, become significant "pulse points" in producing the play. At first glance it might seem that the staging would be fairly straightforward. In many ways, the play is like the string of history plays that preceded it during the 1590s. To begin with, *Julius Caesar* is relatively static, being more "talk" than action, and where there is action it is often related either to triumphal processions or to killing. Of course, elements such as processions (which feature trumpet-and-drum entries and the carrying of standards), ghosts (such as appear toward the end of *Richard III*), naked violence (as in *1 Henry VI* and many other plays), assassinations (as in *Richard II*), dead bodies on stage (as in *1 Henry IV*), tent scenes (as in *Richard III*), letters or other kinds of documents (as in *1 Henry IV* and *Richard III*), battle scenes (as in *1 Henry IV* and *Richard III*), the symbolic use of stage position (whether at the center of the platform or above/below), music (as in *Richard II*), and soliloquies are all feature in Shakespeare's early histories. Yet the orchestration of these familiar elements plays out differently in *Julius Caesar* than it does in the earlier plays; and to these Shakespeare added less familiar elements, including the use of handshakes

9. Nettles, 192.

and special props (statues, a pulpit, a lute, and some often-noted anachronistic items such as a nightcap, dressing gown, and a clock). Moreover, there is debate as to whether stage blood was used in the assassination of Caesar and, if so, what it consisted of and how the actors dealt with the problem of cleaning the costumes.[1]

Initially it is important to note that, in comparison with Shakespeare's earliest histories, the cast size of *Julius Caesar* seems average. *1, 2, 3 Henry VI*, and *Richard III* are all large-cast plays; however, those that followed—*Richard II, King* John, and *1 and 2 Henry IV*—featured smaller casts. There are over thirty-five speaking parts, divided among a company that consisted of twelve actors and a few boy players, as historians conclude. Traditionally the women's roles were performed by boys, and there is some evidence that "boy" players were occasionally as old as eighteen to twenty years of age. Because neither Portia nor Calphurnia was on stage at the same times the company could easily have gotten by with a single actor performing both roles. Further, the scenes in which the women appear are short and all occur within the first three acts, liberating the actor(s) who performed these roles to assume other parts later in the play. (A second young boy was obviously needed to play Lucius, Brutus's servant.) The doubling and tripling of roles must have been typical; and also, unless extras were hired (which was known to have occurred periodically, but which reduced the company's profits), battle scenes and mobs were represented by only a few players instead of the hundreds that modern viewers are used to seeing in large-budget films.

As was the custom within the Elizabethan theatre, only the lead actors(s) would probably have been costumed specially for the production. Actors performing supporting roles would have dressed in whatever costumes were stored in the tiring house at the Globe and would not necessarily have been wearing clothes that were designed to be compatible with an ancient Roman setting, although it is probably the case that the Elizabethan tailors would have been familiar with the elements of Roman style, including traditional articles of clothing such as the toga. In the case of *Julius Caesar* the white senatorial togas would have contrasted with the darker colors worn by the plebeians, and the soothsayer might potentially have been wearing something different that would have allowed Brutus to identify him in the crowd ("A soothsayer bids you beware the ides of March." [1.2.19]). In recent times Caesar's toga is often edged in purple, an honor granted him by his rank; and he often wears a wreath of laurel leaves on his head, a privilege accorded

---

1. Of course, some of these same elements occur in Shakespeare's early Roman tragedy, *Titus Andronicus*.

him by his position as Pontifex Maximus of Rome. Interestingly, Plutarch mentions that Caesar's vanity inspired him to wear this in public to cover up his growing baldness; but, as a crownlike symbol, the decoration anticipates the moment when Casca reports to Brutus and Cassius that Mark Antony offered Caesar a coronet (1.2.235ff.)[2] Furthermore, the regal object creates an interesting visual association when considered alongside the decorations that the citizens are placing on Caesar's statues at the opening of the play. While Plutarch suggests that these were "diadems" (i.e., crowns), Flavius's command to "disrobe" the statues suggests that these could have been ornamental draperies. (The image has been annotated both as "crowns" and "draperies" by various editors.) If the director decides that the citizens are draping the statues, then this decision might be reinforced visually later during the assassination when Caesar falls down compassed round by senators and pulls his cloak over his face. In any event, whether the director decides to use garlands or coronets in 1.1, the citizens' act of draping the statues returns in other visual quotations later in the play. The many statues and allusions to statues in the play themselves comprise a motif. (In some productions related objects, such as masks, seen onstage early in the play, turn into death masks later.[3]) An arresting example, illustrating the value of stage symbols surrounding Caesar, can be seen in Illustration 5, which captures the opening of 2.2 in the Royal Shakespeare Company's July 2001 production of the play at Stratford-upon-Avon. Here, we see Caesar in the privacy of his bath, in the moment just before he engages in an intimate conversation with Calphurnia. In the background sits a statue of the young conquering hero, in the prime of his life and virility; in the foreground sits the older statesman, in all of his aging humanity, showing the mortality that will be hacked to death just a few scenes later.

Moreover, among the necessary group of costumes would have been Caesar's bloodied toga, presented by Antony to the mob (3.2.165ff.) and presumably worn by Caesar later when he appears to Brutus as a ghost. The performance also calls for a dressing gown, worn by Caesar in 2.2 and later by Brutus in 4.3. A "cloak" is referred to several times in the course of the play. The conspirators enter with their "hats plucked about their ears" while Caius Ligarus arrives at Brutus's house disguised by a "kerchief" or bandage wrapped around his head (2.1.315). Brutus and Cassius might have been wearing breastplate armor in the later battle scenes, and the soldiers would

---

2. An aging, world-weary Caesar appears in the drawing (c. 1520–21), by Andrea del Sarto, the early sixteenth-century Italian artist, on the cover illustration of this volume.

3. For more on this topic see the excerpt in this volume from Robert F. Willson, Jr., *Shakespeare in Hollywood, 1929–1956* (Madison, N.J.: Fairleigh Dickinson University Press, 2000), pp. 241–44.

Julius Caesar (Ian Hogg) at the opening of Act 2, Scene 2 of the Royal Shakespeare Company production directed by Edward Hall. Malcolm Davies Collection. © Shakespeare Birthplace Trust.

all have been costumed with swords and perhaps helmets. There is also the indication that a traditional Roman standard decorated with a wreath and golden eagles would have been carried by the victors in the final scene of the play and perhaps earlier when Caesar appears in processions.

The issue of stage blood has vexed many editors of *Julius Caesar*. Some have decided that Elizabethan actors were using the blood of animals, collected from local butchers' shops, while others have concluded that actors would have shied away from using anything because of potential damage to costumes. It is clear from the research of theatre historians that some makeup was used on the early modern stage, primarily for the men who performed women's roles. *Julius Caesar* utilizes two prominent female roles, but there is further opportunity for use of makeup on the actor performing Caesar when he returns as a ghost. Moreover, the play seems, both figuratively and literally, steeped in blood, and it is difficult to imagine that the actors would have bypassed the opportunity to include the spectacle created by stage blood in early productions.[4] This is not to say that the players used actual blood in their representations, but that other more readily soluble substances might well have been invented to

4. An interesting discussion of stage blood and theatrical spectacle can be found in Leo Kirschbaum, "Shakespeare's Stage Blood and Its Critical Significance," *PMLA* 64 (1949): 517–24.

resemble blood. And in any event, some common household manuals of the period offered simple procedures for the removal of stains and for bleaching fabrics.

Consistent with the simplicity of costumes, props are minimal in the play; they are used, however, with specific purpose. In 2.1 Brutus opens a letter, thrown through one of his windows, and then consults a calendar. In the opening lines of 3.1 Artimedorus tries in vain to get Caesar to read the letter he wrote earlier in 2.3. Other documents include the list of those marked for execution, penned by Antony at the opening of 4.1, along with the quill and ink with which he damns Lepidus's brother. Candles and lanterns, carried by the actors, would have suggested the darkness of night. Some kind of drapery was used in Acts 4 and 5 to represent Brutus's tent. During 4.3 Brutus mentions a book and asks that his servant play to him on a lute. Not least of all, when Caesar is slain he falls at the base of Pompey's statue, and Mark Antony enters with Caesar's body in 3.2—very much another icon. (But whether it was a prop or the actual actor is open to some debate.) Simple stage furniture would probably have been used to suggest the interior of Caesar's and Brutus's house (2.2., 3.2), and some stage decoration would have indicated that Brutus was in his orchard when the conspirators visit him in 2.1.

Stage geography is used interestingly in *Julius Caesar*. Cassius says that he is on his way to meet other "of the noblest minded Roman" at Pompey's porch (1.3.126) when the conspiracy is gathering momentum. The reference, to the porch of a theatre built by Pompey in 55 BCE, alerts us to a monument constructed by, and associated with, Caesar's immediate predecessor, who was murdered by Caesar's faction. The conspirators gather in Brutus's orchard, a patrician setting, as opposed to the streets where the plebeians congregate. Here, symbolically, they enter a fallen Eden, despite the fact that Brutus characterizes Caesar as a serpent that must be crushed before it is hatched (2.1.32–34). When Lepidus and Octavius first arrive in Rome they go to Caesar's house (3.2.260)—symbolically suggesting themselves as Caesar's successors while, at the same time, Brutus and Cassius are said to be fleeing "like madmen" on horseback through the gates of the city (3.2.263), forsaking their homes. As the conspirator's faction begins to fall apart, the verbal conflict between Brutus and Cassius takes place appropriately in a tent on the battlefield before they both commit suicide. Later in the same scene Caesar's ghost appears to Brutus here, i.e., at Philippi.

Ghosts were popular spectacles in the plays of Shakespeare's time, but different directors have treated Caesar's ghost differently. Some, thinking that modern audiences might respond adversely to the play's supernatural elements, choose to de-emphasize these. In such productions the ghost might be represented by a moving spotlight accompanied by a voice-over. Speeches that accentuate super-natural elements, such as the discussion between Cassius and Casca regarding the portents of thunder and lightning (1.3.3ff), are occasionally cut from the text. Likewise the soothsayer is rendered inconspicuous through costuming so that he fades into the crowd. The same is true in productions that seize the opportunity to represent Caesar's ghost on stage. In the two Folger Library illustrations presented in this volume the ghost is represented, alternatively, as a benign or glowering presence, depending upon whether the director chose to treat the ghost as simply the voice of prophecy or as a more satanic presence, with horn-like crown and menacing gaze (see illustrations following this page).

Among the many decisions that go into a full-scale production, directors pay special attention to blocking, or the stage position and the placement of groups of characters. Caesar is almost always at the center of the stage, emphasizing his charisma and power, and reminding the audience of the way in which he single-handedly seems to hold Rome together. When he is killed, therefore, the entirety of Rome is "de-centered" and turned over to an unruly mob—to chaos. When Mark Antony has Caesar's body brought to the Forum, he returns Caesar to a central position in order to use him as a prop, to stir up the mob's sympathy, and to underscore the fact that even in death Caesar is a potent force. Moreover, with the mob standing between the body and the audience, spectators are invited to think of themselves as part of the mob. Central placement would work well also in 3.3 when the mob surrounds Cinna the poet, savaging him like a pack of wild animals because they mistake him for Cinna the conspirator. In contrast to the power indicated by Caesar's centrality, the servant Lucius falls asleep at the periphery of the stage in 2.1. Customarily, the victors enter the stage from the audience's right, and the losers from the left. In keeping with such symbolism during the final moments of the play Octavius and his band enter from the audience's right; Brutus's tent would probably be pitched on the audience's left. Finally, in depicting the confusion of battlefield maneuvers the use of the balcony or "above" space at 5.3.26 is meant to signify that Pindarus is on higher ground, reporting what he sees to Cassius; but ironically his privileged position causes him to misinterpret everything, announcing that Titinius has been captured when in fact he is surrounded by cheering soldiers.

Acts of greeting, specifically handshakes, which occur throughout the play from beginning to end, serve as opportunities to display great loyalty between characters, and as the play unfolds, some of these are moments that presage treason and disloyalty. In 2.1 the conspirators shake hands to underscore their resolution to assassinate Caesar, a moment that is mirrored in 2.2 when the same men

JULIUS CÆSAR.

Act IV.

E. Edwards del.   *J. Basire sculp.*

I am thy Evil Genius Brutus.

Illustration showing the moment in Act 4, Scene 3 when the ghost of Caesar visits Brutus before the final battle. Note the drapery flowing around Caesar (referred to at 1.1.70). Reproduced by permission of the Folger Shakespeare Library (Washington, DC).

Act IV. JULIUS CÆSAR. Sc.III.

Fuseli Delt. C. Warren sc.

Br. — *Why com'st thou?*
Ghost. *To tell thee, thou shalt see me at Phillippi.*

Engraving (1804) showing the moment in Act 4, Scene 3 when the ghost of Caesar—who appears as a menacing force—visits Brutus before the final battle. Reproduced by permission of the Folger Shakespeare Library (Washington, DC).

arrive in Caesar's house and are greeted there. At 3.1.54 Brutus kisses Caesar's hand in reverence, following which the ruler is slain and the murderers smear their hands in his blood (3.1.106–07). Soon afterward, the gesture is repeated when Antony enters the scene and shakes the conspirators' bloody hands (3.1. 186–90); but although the senators interpret this action as a gesture of solidarity with their cause, Antony quickly begins to speak of revenge once they have left the scene of the crime. Lastly, Cassius and Brutus shake hands as a gesture of reconciliation following their dispute in the tent scene (4.3.117). Other images that form visual motifs in the play include kneeling, opening the shirt in order to expose the chest to a dagger, bodies falling upon the stage (Caesar's, Cinna's, Cassius's, Titinius's, and Brutus's), and the filing of stately processions that play off scenes depicting the Roman mob behaving chaotically. Some of these are attended by violence while others are not; but often, even in the scenes in which violence is suppressed, the veiled threat of violence creates dramatic tension.

Music and a variety of sound effects function interestingly throughout the play in order to signal danger and discord. These include thunder and lightning (at 1.3 and 2.1), the knocking of the conspirators at Brutus's door (2.1), and the sounds of drums and trumpets that accompany Caesar in procession. The chiming of a clock at 3 A.M. cuts short the conspirators' conversation, reminding them that dawn and the day for Caesar's murder is drawing near. Moving toward the final encounter, as Brutus finds the bodies of Cassius and Titinius he notes that it is 3 P.M. (5.4.109). In addition to raising the anxiety level of the plotters (Brutus: "Peace! Count the clock!") the reference to time is reminiscent of famous clocks in other tragedies of the period; for example, that at the end of Christopher Marlowe's *Doctor Faustus* where the final minutes of Faustus's life are counted down. Readers will also note that just prior to the moment when Brutus is visited by Caesar's ghost (4.3.254ff.), he asks his servant Lucius to play the lute for him in order to calm his nerves. The boy falls asleep after a stage direction found in the First Folio (1623) indicates that there is "Music, and a song." It is unclear what sort of song the boy played here, although the tone of the scene would call for something quiet. The boy then falls asleep, and when the ghost exits, Brutus wakes him with his cries. Lucius, picking up from where he had fallen asleep but still somewhat groggy, remarks, "The strings, my lord, are false" (i.e., out of tune), another warning sign that Brutus and his party are moving toward the tragic failure that will play out in the final act.

Because the First Folio text of *Julius Caesar* (1623) is so straightforward there are only a few points at which a director needs to rework the text in production. Such a moment occurs at the very end of 4.2 where, at lines. 48–49, Cassius orders Pindarus to "Bid our commanders lead their charges [i.e., troops] off/ A little from this ground." Here, Brutus adds, "Lucius, do you the like" (l. 50). But the Folio text seems mistaken. Clearly, Brutus's order is meant for Lucilius, an officer, rather than for Brutus's adolescent servant. Another textual problem in the Folio occurs at 4.3.188 where Brutus recounts the death of Portia for a second time, a passage that is occasionally omitted. Apart from these few dramatic moments, the text of the play generally offers clear indications for stage action. Where it does not and actors have to sort out the staging—such as in the occasional unmarked exit or the removal of a body from the stage—solutions are not difficult.

Not least of all, as in *Hamlet*, which follows *Julius Caesar* closely in the chronology of Shakespeare's plays, theatrical metaphors bring the critical world of the play and its life on stage together. In *Shakespeare's Theater of Presence* Sidney Homan has argued that *Julius Caesar* is a combination of two incompatible plays. One, he observes, is "grounded in the facts, depicting a political world in which males confidently, for a time 'read' events in terms of their own prescriptive standards." The other, "one that will prove dominant, includes but goes beyond this secular drama, enacting a mystical, timeless world to which the women, Portia and Calphurnia, prove especially sensitive, one mocking the conspirators' progressive, cause-and-effect mentality with its own cyclical, and therefore cynical 'history.'"[5] In conceptualizing productions Homan makes a case for Brutus remaining at the center of the play since he, like the playwright, attempts to "'fashion' the present, . . . to 'play' with it for a desired end." But, Homan reminds us, "Brutus fails to produce the very play he would fashion."[6] Antony, Homan suggests, is a compromise between the extremes represented by Brutus and Cassius.[7] "Nevertheless," he concludes, "when the play metaphor surfaces most graphically, it is a male speaker who imagines a production that will never exist, a *Julius Caesar* having little in common with the complex play world that the speaker himself presently inhabits. . . . To be more accurate, the laudatory play [Brutus and Cassius] envision never comes from Shakespeare's pen."[8]

---

5. Sidney Homan, *Shakespeare's Theater of Presence: Language, Spectacle, and the Audience* (Lewisburg, PA: Bucknell University Press, 1986), 87.
6. Homan, p. 98 (see excerpt, pp. 223–32).
7. Homan, p. 99.
8. Homan, p. 100.

Acknowledgments

Support for this project came from many different places. I would like to thank Helen Hargast of the Shakespeare Centre Photograph Archive in Stratford-upon-Avon for her assistance in finding photographs and offering advice on reproductions. The librarians and staff of the Folger Shakespeare Library were likewise invaluable in locating appropriate images from their collection. Deborah Whitman of Whitman Studios in Norwich, New York, drew the two maps of Rome included in this volume; her collaboration on this project is deeply appreciated. The members of the library staff at Colgate University have been ready to assist with this project in whatever way they could. Patricia Ryan played a vital role in helping to prepare the files of supplementary readings. I could not have done without her steady hand in this part of the book.

Albert J. Ammerman was generous in his knowledge of ancient Rome, while Charles R. Forker, ever a friend and scholar, looked over my shoulder in matters editorial. Funds provided by the Edgar W. B. Fairchild Professorship were central in completing various aspects of research for this project. The editors and staff at W. W. Norton have been lovely to work with at every stage.

Many friends, too many to list here, have been instrumental in simply standing by to provide insight and, at times, humor.

Not least of all, this volume is dedicated to my nephew Michael Berkowitz-Cerasano, for whom Julius Caesar—whether considered in his mythological or historical context—is very real indeed.

S. P. CERASANO

A Note on the Text

The text of *Julius Caesar* was printed originally in the First Folio (1623) of Shakespeare's plays, compiled by John Heminges and Henry Condell, two of Shakespeare's fellow actors who hoped to produce good reading versions of the plays. They organized the volume according to three categories of plays that remain with us today: comedies, tragedies, and histories. *Julius Caesar* was included in the group of tragedies, along with *Hamlet, King Lear*, and the other Roman plays: *Titus Andronicus, Antony and Cleopatra*, and *Coriolanus*.

As even a glance at the list of variants indicates the First Folio version of *Julius Caesar* is a remarkably clean text. It is used here as a copy text and most variants are relatively minor. The best known textual crux of the play centers on the word *lane* in 3.1.39. In the Folio text the passage, spoken by Caesar, reads:

> These couchings and these lowly courtesies
> Might fire the blood of ordinary men,
> And turn pre-ordinance and first decree
> Into the lane of children.
>
> (lines 36–39)

The word *lane* is uncorrected in the second and third Folios. If we accept the line as printed in 1623 the sense is that significant matters (if overacted) could become disparaged by turning them into children's games (that are played outdoors, in the "lane"), This childishness can then be associated with Caesar's next comment ("Be not fond / To think that Caesar bears such rebel blood . . ."), in which he disavows any "fondness"—that is, foolishness, childishness. By contrast, some editions alter *lane* to "law," emphasizing the rules of children's games. In this case the change contrasts the whimsical laws of children with the "preordinance and first decree" in line 38—that is, "the socially-binding judicial rulings (proclaimed over time by the courts) that hold society together."

The table presented here records the significant changes between this text and the version of the play printed in the First Folio. It does not record variants that are obvious typographical errors or changes in lineation. Nor does it provide the historical variants in the first

xlvii

three Folios or in subsequent noteworthy editions of the eighteenth and nineteenth centuries. In the text presented here spelling and punctuation have been modernized. Any additions to the text, including stage directions, are noted with square brackets. The following table uses abbreviations to designate the First Folio (*F*), and variations in stage directions (*SD*) or speech prefixes (*SP*). Readings adopted in this text are printed first in each line, in boldface, with the readings from the First Folio following in regular typeface.

1.1.38 **Pompey? Many**	(F) *Pompey* many
1.1.40 **windows, yea**	(F) windows? Yea
1.2.9 **remember:**	(F) remember,
1.2.165 **not (so**	(F) not so (
1.2.242 **hooted**	(F) howted
1.2.251 **like, he**	(F) like he
1.3.10 **tempest dropping fire**	(F) tempest-dropping-fire
1.3.109 **offal,**	(F) offal?
1.3.125 **this**	(F) this,
1.3.129 **In favor's**	(F) Is favors,
2.1.13 **question.**	(F) question?
2.1.40 **Ides**	(F) first
2.1.67 **of man**	(F) of a man
2.1.122 **women,**	(F) women.
2.1.136 **oath,**	(F) oath.
2.1.178 **envious,**	(F) Envious.
2.1.213 **eighth**	(F) eight
2.1.227 SD. *Exeunt* [*all but*] BRUTUS.	(F) *Exeunt. / Manet Brutus.*
2.1.274 **half,**	(F) half
2.1.312 SD.———	(F) S.D. occurs earlier, following *Exit Portia.*
2.1.313 SP. LIGARIUS (to end of scene)	(F) Cai.
2.2.46 **are**	(F) heare
3.1.113 **states**	(F) state
3.1.115 **lies**	(F) lie
3.1.198 **foes—**	(F) foes?
3.1.199 **noble— . . . corse**	(F) noble, . . . coarse,
3.1.209 **strucken**	(F) stroken
3.1.253 SD. *Exeunt* [*all but* ANTONY].	(F) *Exeunt. / Manet Antony.*
3.1.283 **catching, for**	(F) catching from

3.2. SD. *Enter* BRUTUS *and* CASSIUS *with the* PLEBEIANS.

(F) *Enter Brutus and goes into the Pulpit, and Cassius, with The Plebeians.*

3.2.1 SP. ALL

(F) *Ple.*

3.2.1 satisfied! Let . . . satisfied!

(F) satisfied: let . . . satisfied.

3.2.7, 10 renderèd

(F) rendred

3.2.108 Marked

Mark'd

3.2.216 wit

(F) writ

3.2.255 SD.———

(F) SD. occurs one line earlier

4.2.34 SP.———

(F) SP omitted

4.2.35 SP.———

(F) SP omitted

4.2.36 SP.———

(F) SP omitted

4.2.52 SD. *Exeunt* [*all but*] BRUTUS *and* CASSIUS.

(F) *Exeunt /Manet Brutus and Cassius.*

4.3.116 ill-tempered

(F) ill remper'd

4.3.156 SD. BOY [LUCIUS] *with wine*

(F) *Boy with wine,*

4.3.230 SD. *Enter* LUCIUS.

(F) SD. occurs one line earlier.

4.3.249 will not have it so

(F) will it not have it so.

4.3.266 slumber,

(F) Slumbler!

4.3.273 SD.———

(F) SD. occurs one line earlier.

4.3.292 Lucius

(F) Lucus, awake!

5.1.41 teeth

(F) teethes

5.1.83 steads

(F) steeds

5.3.72 Pindarus!

(F) Pindarus?

5.3.101 more

(F) ho

5.3.104 Thasos

(F) Tharsus

5.4.8 SD.———

(F) SD. not in Folio

5.4.17 the news

(F) thee newes

5.5.71 He only,

(F) He, only

The Text of
JULIUS CAESAR

The Tragedy of Julius Caesar

Dramatis Personae

JULIUS CAESAR

MARCUS BRUTUS
CAIUS CASSIUS
CASCA
DECIUS BRUTUS
CINNA　　　　　　　　　　*conspirators against Julius Caesar*
METELLUS CIMBER
TREBONIUS
CAIUS LIGARIUS

CICERO
PUBLIUS　　　　　　　　*senators*
POPILLIUS LENA

OCTAVIUS CAESAR
MARK ANTONY　　　　　*triumvirs ruling Rome after the death*
LEPIDUS　　　　　　　　*of Caesar*

CALPHURNIA,　　　　　*wife of Caesar*
PORTIA,　　　　　　　　*wife of Brutus*
LUCIUS,　　　　　　　　*servant to Brutus*

LUCILIUS
TITINIUS
MESSALA　　　　　　　　*friends and soldiers with Brutus*
YOUNG CATO　　　　　　*and Cassius*
VOLUMNIUS
STATILIUS (non-speaking)

FLAVIUS (non-speaking)
LABEO (non-speaking)
VARRUS
CLAUDIO
CLITUS　　　　　　　　　*officers/servants to Brutus*
STRATO
LUCIUS
DARDANUS

FLAVIUS
MURELLUS } *tribunes*

ARTEMIDORUS OF CNIDOS, *a Doctor of Rhetoric*
SOOTHSAYER
CINNA THE POET
ANOTHER POET
PINDARUS, *servant to Cassius*
COMMONERS (*including a* CARPENTER *and a* COBBLER), CITIZENS,
  PLEBEIANS, SENATORS, MESSENGERS, SERVANTS (*to Caesar, Antony,
  Octavius*), SOLDIERS

A Note on Characters

It is not uncommon for the names of historical characters in Shake-speare's texts to be slightly different from those in his original sources. Consequently the names in the list printed here sometimes vary from their antecedents in Plutarch's *Lives* and North's translation of Plutarch's work. To cite one well-known example, Plutarch and North both identified "Decius" Brutus as "Decimus" Brutus. Moreover, although the spellings of names in this edition generally follow those in the text of the First Folio, in a few cases the spellings have been updated. Therefore *Caska* becomes "Casca" and *Porcia* is altered to "Portia," both more Latinate than the Folio spellings. In accordance with many other editions, I have retained *Calphurnia* (probably pronounced without the "h"), *Murellus, Claudio,* and *Varrus,* which are spellings that appear in the First Folio. Finally, it is useful to note that Shakespeare simply invented some characters that do not have speaking parts and others that do not appear anywhere in his source material, among which is Brutus's servant Lucius.

The Tragedy of Julius Caesar

[Act 1. Scene 1. *Rome. A Street.*]

> *Enter* FLAVIUS, MURELLUS, *and certain* COMMONERS *over the stage.*

FLAVIUS   Hence! Home, you idle creatures, get you home!
  Is this a holiday? What, know you not,
  Being mechanical, you ought not walk

---

3. **mechanical:** of the artisan class, common workers.

Upon a laboring day without the sign
Of your profession? Speak, what trade art thou?   5
CARPENTER   Why, sir, a carpenter.
MURELLUS   Where is thy leather apron and thy rule?
What dost thou with thy best apparel on?
You, sir, what trade are you?
COBBLER   Truly, sir, in respect of a fine workman, I am but, as   10
you would say, a cobbler.
MURELLUS   But what trade art thou? Answer me directly.
COBBLER   A trade, sir, that I hope I may use with a safe con-
science, which is indeed, sir, a mender of bad soles.
FLAVIUS   What trade art thou, knave? Thou naughty knave,   15
what trade?
COBBLER   Nay, I beseech you, sir, be not out with me; yet if you
be out, sir, I can mend you.
MURELLUS   What mean'st thou by that? Mend me, thou saucy
fellow?   20
COBBLER   Why, sir, cobble you.
FLAVIUS   Thou art a cobbler, art thou?
COBBLER   Truly, sir, all that I live by is with the awl. I meddle
with no tradesman's matters, nor women's matters; but withal
I am indeed, sir, a surgeon to old shoes; when they are in great   25
danger I recover them. As proper men as ever trod upon neat's
leather have gone upon my handiwork.
FLAVIUS   But wherefore art not in thy shop today?
Why dost thou lead these men about the streets?
COBBLER   Truly, sir, to wear out their shoes, to get myself into   30
more work. But indeed, sir, we make holiday to see Caesar and
to rejoice in his triumph.
MURELLUS   Wherefore rejoice? What conquest brings he home?
What tributaries follow him to Rome
To grace in captive bonds his chariot wheels?   35

4–5. **sign . . . profession:** clothes or insignia indicating particular trades.
5. **thou:** the familiar pronoun, here used with some contempt.
10. **in respect of:** in comparison with.
11. **cobbler:** shoemaker, bungler (with a pun on *soles,* i.e., "souls" at line 14).
12. **directly:** straightforwardly.
15. **naughty:** impertinent, wicked.
17. **out with:** angry with.
23. **meddle:** busy oneself (with sexual innuendo).
24. **withal:** nevertheless.
26. **recover:** cure, mend; **proper:** fine, respectable; **neat's leather:** cowhide.
32. **triumph:** triumphal procession (in honor of Caesar's victory over Pompey's sons, his
    political opponents).
34. **tributaries:** those paying tribute, i.e., taxes exacted by a conquerer.

You blocks, you stones, you worse than senseless things!
O you hard hearts, you cruel men of Rome,
Knew you not Pompey? Many a time and oft
Have you climbed up to walls and battlements,
To towers and windows, yea, to chimney tops,   40
Your infants in your arms, and there have sat
The livelong day, with patient expectation,
To see great Pompey pass the streets of Rome.
And when you saw his chariot but appear,
Have you not made an universal shout,   45
That Tiber trembled underneath her banks
To hear the replication of your sounds
Made in her concave shores?
And do you now put on your best attire?
And do you now cull out a holiday?   50
And do you now strew flowers in his way,
That comes in triumph over Pompey's blood?
Be gone!
Run to your houses, fall upon your knees,
Pray to the gods to intermit the plague   55
That needs must light on this ingratitude.
FLAVIUS   Go, go, good countrymen, and for this fault
Assemble all the poor men of your sort;
Draw them to Tiber banks, and weep your tears
Into the channel till the lowest stream   60
Do kiss the most exalted shores of all.
                                   Exeunt all the COMMONERS.
See where their basest metal be not moved:
They vanish tongue-tied in their guiltiness.
Go you down that way towards the Capitol.
This way will I. Disrobe the images   65

---

36. **senseless:** incapable of perception.
38. **Pompey:** Gnaeus Pompeius, (106–48 B.C.E.), later known as "the Great," was
    formerly allied with Caesar and Crassus during the First Triumvirate. Later,
    Caesar defeated him in battle at Pharsalus. The victim of a treacherous plot
    concocted by the young king Ptolemy XIII, Pompey was stabbed to death on his
    flight into Egypt in 40 B.C.E. His head and signet ring were presented as gifts to
    Caesar, who arrived in Egypt shortly thereafter; but Caesar sent Pompey's ashes
    to Cornelia, Pompey's sister, for burial.
46. **Tiber:** the historic river flowing through Rome.
47. **replication:** echo.
50. **cull out:** pick out, choose.
52. **Pompey's blood:** offspring, sons.
55. **intermit:** put off (the plague that is inevitable).
58. **sort:** rank.
60–61. **till . . . all:** i.e., until the lowest stream rises to the highest point.
62. **where:** sometimes emended by editors as "whe're" (i.e., "whether").
64. **Capitol:** a monumental temple dedicated to Jupiter that overlooked the Forum.
65. **images:** statues.

If you do find them decked with ceremonies.
MURELLUS   May we do so?
  You know it is the feast of Lupercal.
FLAVIUS   It is no matter; let no images
  Be hung with Caesar's trophies. I'll about   70
  And drive away the vulgar from the streets;
  So do you too, where you perceive them thick.
  These growing feathers plucked from Caesar's wing
  Will make him fly an ordinary pitch,
  Who else would soar above the view of men   75
  And keep us all in servile fearfulness.

                                              Exeunt.

[Act 1. Scene 2. *Rome. A Public Place.*]

Enter CAESAR, ANTONY *for the course,* CALPHURNIA, PORTIA,
DECIUS, CICERO, BRUTUS, CASSIUS, CASCA, *a* SOOTHSAYER; *after
them* MURELLUS *and* FLAVIUS.

CAESAR   Calphurnia.
CASCA   Peace ho! Caesar speaks.
CAESAR   Calphurnia.
CALPHURNIA   Here, my lord.
CAESAR   Stand you directly in Antonio's way
  When he doth run his course. Antonio.
ANTONY   Caesar, my lord.   5
CAESAR   Forget not in your speed, Antonio,
  To touch Calphurnia, for our elders say
  The barren, touched in this holy chase,
  Shake off their sterile curse.
ANTONY   I shall remember:
  When Caesar says, "Do this," it is performed.   10
CAESAR   Set on, and leave no ceremony out.
SOOTHSAYER   Caesar!
CAESAR   Ha! Who calls?
CASCA   Bid every noise be still—peace yet again!

---

66. **ceremonies:** tokens denoting religious observance
68. **Lupercal:** February 15, a Roman festival celebrating Pan, one of the gods associated
    with fertility.
70. **trophies:** ornaments.
71. **vulgar:** commoners.
72. **thick:** gathered together, i.e., in groups.
74. **pitch:** height (a term from falconry).
 1. SD. *course:* race.
 8. **holy chase:** sacred race, sacred course.
11. **set on:** proceed.

CAESAR   Who is it in the press that calls on me?   15
    I hear a tongue shriller than all the music
    Cry "Caesar!" Speak. Caesar is turned to hear.
SOOTHSAYER   Beware the Ides of March.
CAESAR   What man is that?
BRUTUS   A soothsayer bids you beware the Ides of March.
CAESAR   Set him before me; let me see his face.   20
CASSIUS   Fellow, come from the throng; look upon Caesar.
CAESAR   What say'st thou to me now? Speak once again.
SOOTHSAYER   Beware the Ides of March.
CAESAR   He is a dreamer. Let us leave him. Pass!
                    Sennet. Exeunt [all but] BRUTUS *and* CASSIUS.
CASSIUS   Will you go see the order of the course?   25
BRUTUS   Not I.
CASSIUS   I pray you, do.
BRUTUS   I am not gamesome. I do lack some part
    Of that quick spirit that is in Antony.
    Let me not hinder, Cassius, your desires;   30
    I'll leave you.
CASSIUS   Brutus, I do observe you now of late.
    I have not from your eyes that gentleness
    And show of love as I was wont to have.
    You bear too stubborn and too strange a hand   35
    Over your friend that loves you.
BRUTUS   Cassius,
    Be not deceived. If I have veiled my look,
    I turn the trouble of my countenance
    Merely upon myself. Vexèd I am
    Of late with passions of some difference,   40
    Conceptions only proper to myself,
    Which give some soil, perhaps, to my behaviors.
    But let not therefore my good friends be grieved
    (Among which number, Cassius, be you one)
    Nor construe any further my neglect   45

---

15. **press:** crowd.
19. **Ides of March:** March 15, later associated in popular culture with Caesar's murder.
24. **SD.** *Sennet:* trumpet flourish.
25. **order of the course:** the path that the race will cover.
28. **gamesome:** fond of sports.
34. **was wont:** accustomed.
35. **strange a hand:** i.e., too unfriendly a hand (an image from horsemanship).
39. **merely:** entirely, exclusively.
40. **passions . . . difference:** conflicting feelings.
41. **proper:** fitting, suitable.
42. **soil:** blemish.
45. **construe:** interpret.

Than that poor Brutus, with himself at war,
Forgets the shows of love to other men.

CASSIUS   Then, Brutus, I have much mistook your passion,
By means whereof this breast of mine hath buried
Thoughts of great value, worthy cogitations.   50
Tell me, good Brutus, can you see your face?

BRUTUS   No, Cassius, for the eye sees not itself
But by reflection, by some other things.

CASSIUS   'Tis just,
And it is very much lamented, Brutus,   55
That you have no such mirrors as will turn
Your hidden worthiness into your eye
That you might see your shadow. I have heard
Where many of the best respect in Rome—
Except immortal Caesar—speaking of Brutus   60
And groaning underneath this age's yoke,
Have wished that noble Brutus had his eyes.

BRUTUS   Into what dangers would you lead me, Cassius,
That you would have me seek into myself
For that which is not in me?   65

CASSIUS   Therefore, good Brutus, be prepared to hear.
And since you know you cannot see yourself
So well as by reflection, I, your glass,
Will modestly discover to yourself
That of yourself which you yet know not of.   70
And be not jealous on me, gentle Brutus,
Were I a common laughter, or did use
To stale with ordinary oaths my love
To every new protester. If you know
That I do fawn on men and hug them hard   75
And after scandal them, or if you know
That I profess myself in banqueting
To all the rout, then hold me dangerous.
        Flourish, and shout.

48. **passion:** feelings.
54. **just:** true.
58. **shadow:** reflection, image.
59. **respect:** reputation.
66. **Therefore:** concerning that.
68. **glass:** mirror.
69. **discover:** reveal.
71. **jealous on:** distrustful, suspicious.
72. **laughter:** laughingstock.
73. **stale:** cheapen.
74. **protester:** one claiming friendship.
76. **scandal:** defame.
77. **profess myself:** profess (i.e., claim) friendship.
78. **rout:** common people (with associations of vulgarity).

BRUTUS   What means this shouting? I do fear the people
  Choose Caesar for their king.
CASSIUS   Ay, do you fear it?   80
  Then must I think you would not have it so.
BRUTUS   I would not, Cassius, yet I love him well.
  But wherefore do you hold me here so long?
  What is it that you would impart to me?
  If it be aught toward the general good,   85
  Set honor in one eye and death i'th'other,
  And I will look on both indifferently.
  For let the gods so speed me as I love
  The name of honor more than I fear death.
CASSIUS   I know that virtue to be in you, Brutus,   90
  As well as I do know your outward favor.
  Well, honor is the subject of my story.
  I cannot tell what you and other men
  Think of this life, but for my single self
  I had as lief not be as live to be   95
  In awe of such a thing as I myself.
  I was born free as Caesar, so were you;
  We both have fed as well, and we can both
  Endure the winter's cold as well as he.
  For once, upon a raw and gusty day,   100
  The troubled Tiber chafing with her shores,
  Caesar said to me, "Dar'st thou, Cassius, now
  Leap in with me into this angry flood
  And swim to yonder point?" Upon the word,
  Accoutred as I was, I plungèd in   105
  And bade him follow; so indeed he did.
  The torrent roared, and we did buffet it
  With lusty sinews, throwing it aside
  And stemming it with hearts of controversy.
  But ere we could arrive the point proposed,   110
  Caesar cried, "Help me, Cassius, or I sink!"
  I, as Aeneas, our great ancestor,
  Did from the flames of Troy upon his shoulder
  The old Anchises bear, so from the waves of Tiber
  Did I the tired Caesar. And this man   115

---

87. **indifferently:** impartially.
88. **speed me:** i.e., help me to succeed.
91. **favor:** appearance.
95. **I . . . be:** I would rather not live.
101. **chafing with:** raging against.
105. **Accoutred:** dressed.
109. **stemming . . . controversy:** making headway with fierce competition.
112. **Ay:** F1 reading

Is now become a god, and Cassius is
A wretched creature and must bend his body
If Caesar carelessly but nod on him.
He had a fever when he was in Spain,
And when the fit was on him I did mark   120
How he did shake. 'Tis true, this god did shake:
His coward lips did from their color fly,
And that same eye whose bend doth awe the world
Did lose his luster. I did hear him groan,
Ay, and that tongue of his that bade the Romans   125
Mark him, and write his speeches in their books,
"Alas," it cried, "give me some drink, Titinius,"
As a sick girl. Ye gods, it doth amaze me
A man of such a feeble temper should
So get the start of the majestic world   130
And bear the palm alone.
          Shout. Flourish.
BRUTUS   Another general shout!
   I do believe that these applauses are
   For some new honors that are heaped on Caesar.
CASSIUS   Why, man, he doth bestride the narrow world
   Like a colossus, and we petty men   135
   Walk under his huge legs and peep about
   To find ourselves dishonorable graves.
   Men at some time are masters of their fates.
   The fault, dear Brutus, is not in our stars
   But in ourselves, that we are underlings.   140
   "Brutus" and "Caesar": what should be in that "Caesar"?
   Why should that name be sounded more than yours?
   Write them together, yours is as fair a name;
   Sound them, it doth become the mouth as well;
   Weigh them, it is as heavy; conjure with 'em,   145
   "Brutus" will start a spirit as soon as "Caesar."
   Now in the names of all the gods at once,
   Upon what meat doth this our Caesar feed
   That he is grown so great? Age, thou art shamed!
   Rome, thou hast lost the breed of noble bloods!   150

---

117. **bend his body:** bow.
123. **bend:** glance.
129. **temper:** constitution.
130. **get the start of:** gain an advantage over.
131. **palm:** victory, triumph.
135. **Colossus:** a bronze statue of Apollo that according to legend straddled the harbor at Rhodes.
149. **Age:** i.e., current era.

When went there by an age, since the great flood,
But it was famed with more than with one man?
When could they say, till now, that talked of Rome,
That her wide walks encompassed but one man?
Now is it Rome indeed, and room enough   155
When there is in it but one only man.
O, you and I have heard our fathers say
There was a Brutus once that would have brooked
Th'eternal devil to keep his state in Rome
As easily as a king.   160
BRUTUS   That you do love me, I am nothing jealous;
What you would work me to, I have some aim.
How I have thought of this, and of these times,
I shall recount hereafter. For this present,
I would not (so with love I might entreat you) 165
Be any further moved. What you have said
I will consider; what you have to say
I will with patience hear, and find a time
Both meet to hear and answer such high things.
Till then, my noble friend, chew upon this: 170
Brutus had rather be a villager
Than to repute himself a son of Rome
Under these hard conditions as this time
Is like to lay upon us.
CASSIUS   I am glad that my weak words   175
Have struck but thus much show of fire from Brutus.
        Enter CAESAR *and his train.*
BRUTUS   The games are done, and Caesar is returning.
CASSIUS   As they pass by, pluck Casca by the sleeve
And he will, after his sour fashion, tell you
What hath proceeded worthy note today.   180
BRUTUS   I will do so. But look you, Cassius,
The angry spot doth glow on Caesar's brow
And all the rest look like a chidden train:
Calphurnia's cheek is pale, and Cicero

---

152. **famed with:** famous for.
155. **Rome . . . room:** These words probably rhymed in Shakespeare's time.
158. **Brutus:** a reference to an earlier figure—Lucius Junius Brutus—who founded the Roman Republic (6th century B.C.E.); **brooked:** tolerated.
159. **keep his state:** i.e., retain his position.
161. **am nothing jealous:** I have no doubt.
162. **work:** persuade; **aim:** idea.
166. **moved:** urged to believe.
169. **meet:** suitable.
183. **chidden:** scolded.

Looks with such ferret and such fiery eyes   185
As we have seen him in the Capitol,
Being crossed in conference by some senators.

CASSIUS   Casca will tell us what the matter is.

CAESAR   Antonio.

ANTONY   Caesar.   190

CAESAR   Let me have men about me that are fat,
  Sleek-headed men and such as sleep a-nights.
  Yond Cassius has a lean and hungry look,
  He thinks too much: such men are dangerous.

ANTONY   Fear him not, Caesar, he's not dangerous,   195
  He is a noble Roman, and well given.

CAESAR   Would he were fatter! But I fear him not.
  Yet if my name were liable to fear
  I do not know the man I should avoid
  So soon as that spare Cassius. He reads much,   200
  He is a great observer, and he looks
  Quite through the deeds of men. He loves no plays,
  As thou dost, Antony; he hears no music;
  Seldom he smiles, and smiles in such a sort
  As if he mocked himself and scorned his spirit   205
  That could be moved to smile at anything.
  Such men as he be never at heart's ease
  Whiles they behold a greater than themselves,
  And therefore are they very dangerous.
  I rather tell thee what is to be feared   210
  Than what I fear: for always I am Caesar.
  Come on my right hand, for this ear is deaf,
  And tell me truly what thou think'st of him.

               Sennet. Exeunt CAESAR *and his train.*

CASCA   You pulled me by the cloak. Would you speak with
me?   215

BRUTUS   Ay, Casca, tell us what hath chanced today
That Caesar looks so sad.

CASCA   Why, you were with him, were you not?

BRUTUS   I should not then ask, Casca, what had chanced.

CASCA   Why, there was a crown offered him; and being offered 220
him he put it by with the back of his hand, thus, and then the
people fell a-shouting.

---

185. **ferret**: ferretlike (i.e., having small, red darting eyes, like a ferret, and therefore a
    threatening look).
196. **given**: disposed.
204. **sort**: manner.
214. **pulled by the cloak**: pulled me aside.

BRUTUS   What was the second noise for?

CASCA   Why, for that too.

CASSIUS   They shouted thrice. What was the last cry for?   225

CASCA   Why, for that too.

BRUTUS   Was the crown offered him thrice?

CASCA   Ay, marry, was't, and he put it by thrice, every time
gentler than other; and at every putting-by mine honest
neighbors shouted.   230

CASSIUS   Who offered him the crown?

CASCA   Why, Antony.

BRUTUS   Tell us the manner of it, gentle Casca.

CASCA   I can as well be hanged as tell the manner of it. It was
mere foolery, I did not mark it. I saw Mark Antony offer him 235
a crown—yet 'twas not a crown neither, 'twas one of these
coronets—and, as I told you, he put it by once; but for all that,
to my thinking he would fain have had it. Then he offered it to
him again; then he put it by again; but to my thinking he was
very loath to lay his fingers off it. And then he offered it the 240
third time; he put it the third time by, and still as he refused
it the rabblement hooted, and clapped their chopped hands,
and threw up their sweaty nightcaps, and uttered such a deal
of stinking breath because Caesar refused the crown that it
had almost choked Caesar, for he swooned and fell down at it. 245
And for mine own part I durst not laugh for fear of opening my
lips and receiving the bad air.

CASSIUS   But soft, I pray you; what, did Caesar swoon?

CASCA   He fell down in the market-place, and foamed at the
mouth, and was speechless.   250

BRUTUS   'Tis very like, he hath the falling sickness.

CASSIUS   No, Caesar hath it not, but you, and I,
And honest Casca, we have the falling sickness.

CASCA   I know not what you mean by that, but I am sure Caesar
fell down. If the tag-rag people did not clap him and hiss him, 255
according as he pleased and displeased them, as they use to do
the players in the theater, I am no true man.

BRUTUS   What said he when he came unto himself?

---

228. **marry:** indeed.
233. **gentle:** noble.
235. **mere foolery:** simply ridiculous.
237. **coronets:** a small crown, worn by those who was inferior to the sovereign.
238. **fain:** gladly.
242. **chopped:** chapped.
251. **falling sickness:** epilepsy.

CASCA Marry, before he fell down, when he perceived the com-
    mon herd was glad he refused the crown, he plucked me ope 260
    his doublet and offered them his throat to cut. An I had been
    a man of any occupation, if I would not have taken him at a
    word, I would I might go to hell among the rogues. And so he
    fell. When he came to himself again, he said if he had done or
    said anything amiss, he desired their worships to think it was 265
    his infirmity. Three or four wenches where I stood cried,
    "Alas, good soul!" and forgave him with all their hearts. But
    there's no heed to be taken of them; if Caesar had stabbed
    their mothers they would have done no less.
BRUTUS And after that he came thus sad away?   270
CASCA Ay.
CASSIUS Did Cicero say anything?
CASCA Ay, he spoke Greek.
CASSIUS To what effect?
CASCA Nay, and I tell you that, I'll ne'er look you i'th'face 275
    again. But those that understood him smiled at one another
    and shook their heads; but for mine own part, it was Greek to
    me. I could tell you more news too: Murellus and Flavius, for
    pulling scarves off Caesar's images, are put to silence. Fare
    you well. There was more foolery yet, if I could remember it. 280
CASSIUS Will you sup with me tonight, Casca?
CASCA No, I am promised forth.
CASSIUS Will you dine with me tomorrow?
CASCA Ay, if I be alive, and your mind hold, and your dinner
    worth the eating.   285
CASSIUS Good. I will expect you.
CASCA Do so. Farewell, both.   *Exit.*
BRUTUS What a blunt fellow is this grown to be!
    He was quick mettle when he went to school.
CASSIUS So is he now in execution   290
    Of any bold or noble enterprise,
    However he puts on this tardy form.
    Thus rudeness is a sauce to his good wit,
    Which gives men stomach to digest his words
    With better appetite.   295
BRUTUS And so it is. For this time I will leave you.

261. **An:** if.
279. **put to silence:** removed from their offices.
282. **forth:** elsewhere.
289. **quick mettle:** of lively, feisty temperament.
292. **However . . . form:** Although he pretends to be slow, sluggish.
295. **appetite:** relish, inclination.

Tomorrow if you please to speak with me,
I will come home to you; or if you will,
Come home to me and I will wait for you.
CASSIUS   I will do so. Till then, think of the world.   300

                                                Exit BRUTUS.

Well, Brutus, thou art noble; yet I see
Thy honorable metal may be wrought
From that it is disposed. Therefore it is meet
That noble minds keep ever with their likes;
For who so firm that cannot be seduced?   '   305
Caesar doth bear me hard, but he loves Brutus.
If I were Brutus now and he were Cassius,
He should not humor me. I will this night,
In several hands, in at his windows throw,
As if they came from several citizens,   310
Writings, all tending to the great opinion
That Rome holds of his name, wherein obscurely
Caesar's ambition shall be glancèd at.
And after this let Caesar seat him sure,
For we will shake him, or worse days endure.   *Exit.* 315

[Act 1. Scene 3. *Rome. A Street.*]

Thunder and lightning. Enter [from opposite sides] CASCA *and*
        CICERO.
CICERO   Good even, Casca. Brought you Caesar home?
Why are you breathless, and why stare you so?
CASCA   Are not you moved when all the sway of earth
Shakes like a thing unfirm? O Cicero,
I have seen tempests when the scolding winds   5
Have rived the knotty oaks, and I have seen
Th'ambitious ocean swell, and rage, and foam,
To be exalted with the threatening clouds;
But never till tonight, never till now,

302–03. wrought . . . disposed: turned from the direction to which it would naturally
          incline.
   303. meet: appropriate.
   306. bear me hard: resents me.
   308. humor: influence.
   309. hands: handwriting.
   311. tending to: intimating.
   313. glancèd at: mentioned.
   314. seat him sure: establish himself securely.
     8. exalted: raised.

Did I go through a tempest dropping fire.   10
Either there is a civil strife in heaven,
Or else the world, too saucy with the gods,
Incenses them to send destruction.
CICERO   Why, saw you anything more wonderful?
CASCA   A common slave—you know him well by sight—   15
Held up his left hand, which did flame and burn
Like twenty torches joined, and yet his hand,
Not sensible of fire, remained unscorched.
Besides—I ha' not since put up my sword—
Against the Capitol I met a lion   20
Who glazed upon me and went surly by
Without annoying me. And there were drawn
Upon a heap a hundred ghastly women,
Transformèd with their fear, who swore they saw
Men, all in fire, walk up and down the streets.   25
And yesterday the bird of night did sit
Even at noon-day upon the market-place,
Hooting and shrieking. When these prodigies
Do so conjointly meet, let not men say,
"These are their reasons, they are natural,"   30
For I believe they are portentous things
Unto the climate that they point upon.
CICERO   Indeed, it is a strange-disposèd time.
But men may construe things after their fashion
Clean from the purpose of the things themselves.   35
Comes Caesar to the Capitol tomorrow?
CASCA   He doth, for he did bid Antonio
Send word to you he would be there tomorrow.
CICERO   Good night then, Casca. This disturbèd sky
Is not to walk in.
CASCA   Farewell, Cicero.   *Exit* CICERO.   40
         Enter CASSIUS.
CASSIUS   Who's there?
CASCA   A Roman.
CASSIUS   Casca, by your voice.

---

    12. **saucy:** insolent, rude.
    14. **wonderful:** amazing.
    20. **Against:** near.
    21. **glazed:** stared.
22–23. **drawn . . . heap:** collected together into a group.
    26. **bird of night:** screech owl.
    28. **prodigies:** unusual events, omens.
    32. **climate:** region.
    35. **Clean . . . of:** i.e., quite differently from the meaning of.

CASCA   Your ear is good. Cassius, what night is this?

CASSIUS   A very pleasing night to honest men.

CASCA   Who ever knew the heavens menace so?

CASSIUS   Those that have known the earth so full of faults.   45
 For my part I have walked about the streets,
 Submitting me unto the perilous night,
 And, thus unbracèd, Casca, as you see,
 Have bared my bosom to the thunder-stone;
 And when the cross blue lightning seemed to open   50
 The breast of heaven, I did present myself
 Even in the aim and very flash of it.

CASCA   But wherefore did you so much tempt the heavens?
 It is the part of men to fear and tremble
 When the most mighty gods by tokens send   55
 Such dreadful heralds to astonish us.

CASSIUS   You are dull, Casca, and those sparks of life
 That should be in a Roman you do want,
 Or else you use not. You look pale, and gaze,
 And put on fear, and cast yourself in wonder   60
 To see the strange impatience of the heavens.
 But if you would consider the true cause
 Why all these fires, why all these gliding ghosts,
 Why birds and beasts from quality and kind,
 Why old men, fools, and children calculate,   65
 Why all these things change from their ordinance,
 Their natures, and preformèd faculties,
 To monstrous quality—why, you shall find
 That heaven hath infused them with these spirits
 To make them instruments of fear and warning   70
 Unto some monstrous state.
 Now could I, Casca, name to thee a man
 Most like this dreadful night,
 That thunders, lightens, opens graves, and roars
 As doth the lion in the Capitol—   75
 A man no mightier than thyself, or me,
 In personal action, yet prodigious grown
 And fearful, as these strange eruptions are.

---

48. unbracèd: with part of his dress open (i.e., the laces loosened).
49. thunder-stone: thunderbolt.
50. cross: crisscrossing.
56. astonish: terrify.
58. want: lack.
64. quality and kind: i.e., disposition, nature.
66. ordinance: appointed place or condition.
77. prodigious: abnormal, portentous.
78. fearful: frightening.

CASCA   'Tis Caesar that you mean. Is it not, Cassius?
CASSIUS   Let it be who it is, for Romans now   80
Have thews and limbs like to their ancestors.
But woe the while, our fathers' minds are dead
And we are governed with our mothers' spirits.
Our yoke and sufferance show us womanish.
CASCA   Indeed, they say the senators tomorrow   85
Mean to establish Caesar as a king,
And he shall wear his crown by sea and land,
In every place save here in Italy.
CASSIUS   I know where I will wear this dagger then:
Cassius from bondage will deliver Cassius.   90
Therein, ye gods, ye make the weak most strong;
Therein, ye gods, you tyrants do defeat.
Nor stony tower, nor walls of beaten brass,
Nor airless dungeon, nor strong links of iron,
Can be retentive to the strength of spirit;   95
But life, being weary of these worldly bars,
Never lacks power to dismiss itself.
If I know this, know all the world besides,
That part of tyranny that I do bear
I can shake off at pleasure.
        Thunder still.
CASCA   So can I,   100
So every bondman in his own hand bears
The power to cancel his captivity.
CASSIUS   And why should Caesar be a tyrant then?
Poor man, I know he would not be a wolf
But that he sees the Romans are but sheep.   105
He were no lion, were not Romans hinds.
Those that with haste will make a mighty fire
Begin it with weak straws. What trash is Rome,
What rubbish and what offal, when it serves
For the base matter to illuminate   110
So vile a thing as Caesar? But, O grief,
Where hast thou led me? I perhaps speak this
Before a willing bondman, then I know
My answer must be made. But I am armed,
And dangers are to me indifferent.   115

81. **thews:** sinews.
84. **sufferance:** submission to the yoke, i.e., servitude.
96. **bars:** barriers.
101. **bondman:** slave.
106. **hinds:** deer.
109. **offal:** residue, cast-off products.

CASCA   You speak to Casca, and to such a man
    That is no fleering tell-tale. Hold, my hand.
    Be factious for redress of all these griefs,
    And I will set this foot of mine as far
    As who goes farthest.
CASSIUS   There's a bargain made.   120
    Now know you, Casca, I have moved already
    Some certain of the noblest-minded Romans
    To undergo with me an enterprise
    Of honorable dangerous consequence.
    And I do know by this they stay for me   125
    In Pompey's Porch. For now, this fearful night,
    There is no stir or walking in the streets,
    And the complexion of the element
    In favor's like the work we have in hand,
    Most bloody, fiery, and most terrible.   130
        Enter CINNA.
CASCA   Stand close a while, for here comes one in haste.
CASSIUS   'Tis Cinna, I do know him by his gait.
    He is a friend. Cinna, where haste you so?
CINNA   To find out you. Who's that? Metellus Cimber?
CASSIUS   No, it is Casca, one incorporate   135
    To our attempts. Am I not stayed for, Cinna?
CINNA   I am glad on't. What a fearful night is this!
    There's two or three of us have seen strange sights.
CASSIUS   Am I not stayed for? Tell me.
CINNA   Yes, you are.
    O Cassius, if you could   140
    But win the noble Brutus to our party—
CASSIUS   Be you content. Good Cinna, take this paper
    And look you lay it in the praetor's chair,
    Where Brutus may but find it; and throw this
    In at his window; set this up with wax   145
    Upon old Brutus' statue. All this done,
    Repair to Pompey's Porch, where you shall find us.

117. **fleering:** smiling obsequiously, sneering; **Hold:** take.
118. **factious:** active within the faction (opposing Caesar).
120. **who:** i.e., anyone who.
126. **Pompey's Porch:** the portico built near Pompey's Theater to shelter spectators during inclement weather.
128. **element:** sky.
131. **close:** hidden.
135. **incorporate:** united.
139. **stayed for:** waited for.
143. **praetor's:** magistrate's (Brutus was made *praetor urbanus* by Caesar in 44 B.C.E.).

Is Decius Brutus and Trebonius there?
CINNA   All but Metellus Cimber, and he's gone
  To seek you at your house. Well, I will hie,   150
  And so bestow these papers as you bade me.
CASSIUS   That done, repair to Pompey's Theatre.

                                        Exit CINNA.

  Come, Casca, you and I will yet, ere day,
  See Brutus at his house. Three parts of him
  Is ours already, and the man entire   155
  Upon the next encounter yields him ours.
CASCA   O, he sits high in all the people's hearts,
  And that which would appear offence in us
  His countenance, like richest alchemy,
  Will change to virtue and to worthiness.   160
CASSIUS   Him and his worth and our great need of him
  You have right well conceited. Let us go,
  For it is after midnight, and ere day
  We will awake him and be sure of him.

                                        Exeunt.

[Act 2. Scene 1. *Rome. Brutus' House.*]

      Enter BRUTUS *in his orchard.*
BRUTUS   What, Lucius, ho!
  I cannot by the progress of the stars
  Give guess how near to day. Lucius, I say!
  I would it were my fault to sleep so soundly.
  When, Lucius, when? Awake, I say! What, Lucius!   5
      Enter LUCIUS.
LUCIUS   Called you, my lord?
BRUTUS   Get me a taper in my study, Lucius.
  When it is lighted, come and call me here.
LUCIUS   I will, my lord.   *Exit.*
BRUTUS   It must be by his death. And for my part   10
  I know no personal cause to spurn at him

---

148. **Decius:** probably Decimus Brutus, an ally of Caesar and his heir (as identified by
     Plutarch).
150. **hie:** go swiftly.
152. **repair:** go.
154. **Three parts:** three quarters.
159. **countenance:** appearance.
162. **conceited:** understood.
 10. **his:** i.e., Caesar's.
 11. **spurn:** kick.
 12. **general:** the public (good).

But for the general. He would be crowned:
How that might change his nature, there's the question.
It is the bright day that brings forth the adder
And that craves wary walking. Crown him that,   15
And then I grant we put a sting in him
That at his will he may do danger with.
Th'abuse of greatness is when it disjoins
Remorse from power. And to speak truth of Caesar,
I have not known when his affections swayed   20
More than his reason. But 'tis a common proof
That lowliness is young ambition's ladder,
Whereto the climber-upward turns his face;
But when he once attains the upmost round
He then unto the ladder turns his back,   25
Looks in the clouds, scorning the base degrees
By which he did ascend. So Caesar may.
Then lest he may, prevent. And since the quarrel
Will bear no color for the thing he is,
Fashion it thus: that what he is, augmented,   30
Would run to these and these extremities.
And therefore think him as a serpent's egg,
Which, hatched, would as his kind grow mischievous,
And kill him in the shell.
                Enter LUCIUS.
LUCIUS   The taper burneth in your closet, sir.   35
Searching the window for a flint, I found
This paper, thus sealed up, and I am sure
It did not lie there when I went to bed.
                Gives him the letter.
BRUTUS   Get you to bed again; it is not day.
Is not tomorrow, boy, the Ides of March?   40
LUCIUS   I know not, sir.
BRUTUS   Look in the calendar and bring me word.
LUCIUS   I will, sir.   *Exit.*
BRUTUS   The exhalations whizzing in the air

---

15. **craves:** calls for.
19. **Remorse:** scruples, conscience.
20. **affections swayed:** emotions influenced, ruled (held sway).
21. **proof:** experience.
22. **lowliness:** humility.
24. **upmost round:** top rung of a ladder.
26. **base degrees:** i.e., lower rungs.
28–29. **since . . . is:** because the argument cannot be grounded in his present conduct.
30. **Fashion:** describe.
33. **kind:** nature; **mischievous:** harmful.
35. **closet:** private room.
44. **exhalations:** meteors.

Give so much light that I may read by them.   45
    [*He*] *opens the letter and reads.*
"Brutus, thou sleep'st. Awake, and see thy self!
Shall Rome, etc. Speak, strike, redress!"
"Brutus, thou sleep'st. Awake!"
Such instigations have been often dropped
Where I have took them up.   50
"Shall Rome, etc." Thus must I piece it out:
Shall Rome stand under one man's awe? What, Rome?
My ancestors did from the streets of Rome
The Tarquin drive when he was called a king.
"Speak, strike, redress!" Am I entreated   55
To speak and strike? O Rome, I make thee promise,
If the redress will follow, thou receivest
Thy full petition at the hand of Brutus.
    Enter LUCIUS.
LUCIUS   Sir, March is wasted fifteen days.
    Knock within.
BRUTUS   'Tis good. Go to the gate, somebody knocks.   60
                           [*Exit* LUCIUS.]

Since Cassius first did whet me against Caesar
I have not slept.
Between the acting of a dreadful thing
And the first motion, all the interim is
Like a phantasma or a hideous dream.   65
The genius and the mortal instruments
Are then in council, and the state of man,
Like to a little kingdom, suffers then
The nature of an insurrection.
    Enter LUCIUS.
LUCIUS   Sir, 'tis your brother Cassius at the door,   70
Who doth desire to see you.
BRUTUS   Is he alone?
LUCIUS   No, sir, there are moe with him.
BRUTUS   Do you know them?
LUCIUS   No, sir, their hats are plucked about their ears
And half their faces buried in their cloaks,
That by no means I may discover them   75

54. **Tarquin:** Tarquinius Superbus, in legend the last king of Rome.
58. **full petition:** i.e., all that has been asked (by the citizens).
61. **whet:** incite.
64. **motion:** impulse.
66. **genius:** inward spirit; **instruments:** bodily parts.
70. **brother:** i.e., brother-in-law.
72. **moe:** more.
73. **plucked about:** i.e., pulled (down) around.
75. **discover:** identify.

By any mark of favor.

BRUTUS   Let 'em enter.

                                        [*Exit* LUCIUS.]

They are the faction. O conspiracy,
Sham'st thou to show thy dang'rous brow by night,
When evils are most free? O then by day
Where wilt thou find a cavern dark enough   80
To mask thy monstrous visage? Seek none, conspiracy:
Hide it in smiles and affability;
For if thou path, thy native semblance on,
Not Erebus itself were dim enough
To hide thee from prevention.   85

      Enter the conspirators, CASSIUS, CASCA, DECIUS, CINNA,
      METELLUS, *and* TREBONIUS

CASSIUS   I think we are too bold upon your rest.
Good morrow, Brutus. Do we trouble you?

BRUTUS   I have been up this hour, awake all night.
Know I these men that come along with you?

CASSIUS   Yes, every man of them; and no man here   90
But honors you, and every one doth wish
You had but that opinion of yourself
Which every noble Roman bears of you.
This is Trebonius.

BRUTUS   He is welcome hither.

CASSIUS   This, Decius Brutus.

BRUTUS   He is welcome too.   95

CASSIUS   This, Casca; this, Cinna; and this, Metellus Cimber.

BRUTUS   They are all welcome.
What watchful cares do interpose themselves
Betwixt your eyes and night?

CASSIUS   Shall I entreat a word?   100

      They whisper.

DECIUS   Here lies the east. Doth not the day break here?

CASCA   No.

CINNA   O, pardon, sir, it doth, and yon grey lines
That fret the clouds are messengers of day.

CASCA   You shall confess that you are both deceived.   105
Here, as I point my sword, the sun arises,

---

76. **mark of favor:** distinguishing physical feature.
83. **path . . . on:** i.e., if you pursue your course without a disguise.
84. **Erebus:** a god symbolizing the dark underworld.
85. **prevention:** being forestalled, hindered.
86. **bold upon:** bold (in intruding) upon.
98. **watchful cares:** cares that keep you awake.
104. **fret:** interlace with.

Which is a great way growing on the south,
Weighing the youthful season of the year.
Some two months hence, up higher toward the north
He first presents his fire, and the high east   110
Stands, as the Capitol, directly here.

BRUTUS   [*Coming forward with* CASSIUS.]
Give me your hands all over, one by one.

CASSIUS   And let us swear our resolution.

BRUTUS   No, not an oath! If not the face of men,
The sufferance of our souls, the time's abuse—   115
If these be motives weak, break off betimes,
And every man hence to his idle bed;
So let high-sighted tyranny range on,
Till each man drop by lottery. But if these
(As I am sure they do) bear fire enough   120
To kindle cowards and to steel with valor
The melting spirits of women, then, countrymen,
What need we any spur but our own cause
To prick us to redress? What other bond
Than secret Romans that have spoke the word   125
And will not palter? And what other oath
Than honesty to honesty engaged
That this shall be or we will fall for it?
Swear priests and cowards and men cautelous,
Old feeble carrions, and such suffering souls   130
That welcome wrongs; unto bad causes swear
Such creatures as men doubt. But do not stain
The even virtue of our enterprise,
Nor th'insuppressive mettle of our spirits,
To think that or our cause or our performance   135
Did need an oath, when every drop of blood

107. **growing on:** advancing on.
108. **weighing:** considering.
110. **high:** due.
112. **all over:** all of you.
114. **face:** (grim) expressions.
115. **sufferance:** suffering.
116. **betimes:** immediately, at once.
117. **idle:** unused.
118. **high-sighted:** arrogant.
119. **drop by lottery:** die by chance (i.e., at the tyrant's whim); **these:** i.e., these motives.
125. **Than:** than that of.
126. **palter:** waver.
129. **Swear:** i.e., let swear; **cautelous:** cautious, wary.
130. **carrions:** carcasses, corpselike men.
132. **doubt:** suspect.
133. **even:** just.
134. **insuppressive:** irrepressible.
135. **or our cause:** either our cause.

That every Roman bears, and nobly bears,
Is guilty of a several bastardy
If he do break the smallest particle
Of any promise that hath passed from him.   140
CASSIUS   But what of Cicero? Shall we sound him?
  I think he will stand very strong with us.
CASCA   Let us not leave him out.
CINNA   No, by no means.
METELLUS   O, let us have him, for his silver hairs
  Will purchase us a good opinion   145
  And buy men's voices to commend our deeds.
  It shall be said his judgment ruled our hands;
  Our youths and wildness shall no whit appear,
  But all be buried in his gravity.
BRUTUS   O, name him not, let us not break with him,   150
  For he will never follow anything
  That other men begin.
CASSIUS   Then, leave him out.
CASCA   Indeed he is not fit.
DECIUS   Shall no man else be touched but only Caesar?
CASSIUS   Decius, well urged. I think it is not meet   155
  Mark Antony, so well beloved of Caesar,
  Should outlive Caesar. We shall find of him
  A shrewd contriver. And, you know, his means,
  If he improve them, may well stretch so far
  As to annoy us all, which to prevent,   160
  Let Antony and Caesar fall together.
BRUTUS   Our course will seem too bloody, Caius Cassius,
  To cut the head off and then hack the limbs—
  Like wrath in death and envy afterwards—
  For Antony is but a limb of Caesar.   165
  Let's be sacrificers, but not butchers, Caius.
  We all stand up against the spirit of Caesar,
  And in the spirit of men there is no blood.
  O, that we then could come by Caesar's spirit
  And not dismember Caesar! But, alas,   170
  Caesar must bleed for it. And, gentle friends,

138. several: separate.
141. sound him: sound him out.
150. break with him: disclose to him (the plans).
155. meet: proper, fitting.
158. shrewd: malicious.
159. improve: make the most of.
160. annoy: harm.
164. envy: malice.
169. come by: obtain.

Let's kill him boldly, but not wrathfully;
Let's carve him as a dish fit for the gods,
Not hew him as a carcass fit for hounds.
And let our hearts, as subtle masters do,   175
Stir up their servants to an act of rage
And after seem to chide 'em. This shall make
Our purpose necessary, and not envious,
Which so appearing to the common eyes,
We shall be called purgers, not murderers.   180
And for Mark Antony, think not of him,
For he can do no more than Caesar's arm
When Caesar's head is off.
CASSIUS   Yet I fear him,
For in the engrafted love he bears to Caesar—
BRUTUS   Alas, good Cassius, do not think of him.   185
If he love Caesar, all that he can do
Is to himself—take thought and die for Caesar;
And that were much he should, for he is given
To sports, to wildness, and much company.
TREBONIUS   There is no fear in him. Let him not die,   190
For he will live and laugh at this hereafter.
        Clock strikes.
BRUTUS   Peace, count the clock.
CASSIUS   The clock hath stricken three.
TREBONIUS   'Tis time to part.
CASSIUS   But it is doubtful yet
Whether Caesar will come forth today or no,
For he is superstitious grown of late,   195
Quite from the main opinion he held once
Of fantasy, of dreams, and ceremonies.
It may be these apparent prodigies,
The unaccustomed terror of this night,
And the persuasion of his augerers   200
May hold him from the Capitol today.
DECIUS   Never fear that. If he be so resolved

---

174. **hew:** chop up.
175. **subtle:** cunning, crafty.
176. **servants:** passions.
178. **envious:** malicious.
184. **engrafted:** deep-rooted.
187. **take thought:** become melancholy.
188. **that . . . should:** that is more than he is likely to perform.
190. **no fear:** nothing to fear.
196. **Quite from:. . .** contrary to.
197. **ceremonies:** omens.
199. **unaccustomed:** unusual.
200. **augurers:** Roman priests.

I can o'ersway him, for he loves to hear
That unicorns may be betrayed with trees,
And bears with glasses, elephants with holes,   205
Lions with toils, and men with flatterers.
But when I tell him he hates flatterers
He says he does, being then most flattered.
Let me work:
For I can give his humor the true bent,   210
And I will bring him to the Capitol.

CASSIUS   Nay, we will all of us be there to fetch him.

BRUTUS   By the eighth hour, is that the uttermost?

CINNA   Be that the uttermost, and fail not then.

METELLUS   Caius Ligarius doth bear Caesar hard,   215
Who rated him for speaking well of Pompey.
I wonder none of you have thought of him.

BRUTUS   Now, good Metellus, go along by him.
He loves me well, and I have given him reasons.
Send him hither and I'll fashion him.   220

CASSIUS   The morning comes upon's. We'll leave you, Brutus,
And, friends, disperse yourselves, but all remember
What you have said and show yourselves true Romans.

BRUTUS   Good gentlemen, look fresh and merrily.
Let not our looks put on our purposes,   225
But bear it as our Roman actors do,
With untired spirits and formal constancy.
And so good morrow to you every one.

                    Exeunt [all but] BRUTUS.

Boy! Lucius! Fast asleep? It is no matter.
Enjoy the honey-heavy dew of slumber.   230
Thou hast no figures nor no fantasies
Which busy care draws in the brains of men,
Therefore thou sleep'st so sound.

          Enter PORTIA.

PORTIA   Brutus, my lord.

BRUTUS   Portia! What mean you? Wherefore rise you now?

---

204. **betrayed with trees:** fooled into impaling themselves on trees.
205. **glasses:** mirrors; **holes:** pitfalls.
206. **toils:** nets.
210. **humor:** disposition; **bent:** direction.
213. **uttermost:** latest.
215. **hard:** ill will, a grudge.
216. **rated:** berated.
218. **by:** to.
220. **fashion:** transform; i.e., convince.
225. **put on:** show, reveal.
227. **formal constancy:** outward resolution.
231. **figures:** imaginings.

It is not for your health thus to commit   235
    Your weak condition to the raw cold morning.
PORTIA   Nor for yours neither. Y'have ungently, Brutus,
    Stole from my bed; and yesternight at supper
    You suddenly arose and walked about,
    Musing and sighing, with your arms across,   240
    And when I asked you what the matter was,
    You stared upon me with ungentle looks.
    I urged you further, then you scratched your head
    And too impatiently stamped with your foot.
    Yet I insisted, yet you answered not,   245
    But with an angry wafture of your hand
    Gave sign for me to leave you. So I did,
    Fearing to strengthen that impatience
    Which seemed too much enkindled, and withal
    Hoping it was but an effect of humor,   250
    Which sometime hath his hour with every man.
    It will not let you eat, nor talk, nor sleep;
    And could it work so much upon your shape
    As it hath much prevailed on your condition,
    I should not know you, Brutus. Dear my lord,   255
    Make me acquainted with your cause of grief.
BRUTUS   I am not well in health, and that is all.
PORTIA   Brutus is wise, and were he not in health
    He would embrace the means to come by it.
BRUTUS   Why, so I do. Good Portia, go to bed.   260
PORTIA   Is Brutus sick? And is it physical
    To walk unbracèd and suck up the humors
    Of the dank morning? What, is Brutus sick?
    And will he steal out of his wholesome bed
    To dare the vile contagion of the night,   265
    And tempt the rheumy and unpurgèd air
    To add unto this sickness? No, my Brutus,
    You have some sick offence within your mind,
    Which by the right and virtue of my place
    I ought to know of. [*Kneels.*] And upon my knees   270

---

237. **ungently:** unkindly.
240. **across:** crossed, folded (indicating melancholy).
246. **wafture:** wave.
251. **his:** i.e., its.
254. **condition:** disposition.
261. **physical:** good for one's health.
262. **unbracèd:** with an unlaced doublet; **humors:** vapors.
266. **rheumy:** moist.
268. **sick offence:** harmful disorder.
269. **virtue:** power (as prerogative).

I charm you, by my once commended beauty,
By all your vows of love, and that great vow
Which did incorporate and make us one,
That you unfold to me, your self, your half,
Why you are heavy, and what men tonight   275
Have had resort to you; for here have been
Some six or seven who did hide their faces
Even from darkness.
BRUTUS   Kneel not, gentle Portia.
PORTIA   I should not need if you were gentle Brutus.
    Within the bond of marriage, tell me, Brutus,   280
    Is it excepted I should know no secrets
    That appertain to you? Am I your self
    But, as it were, in sort or limitation,
    To keep with you at meals, comfort your bed,
    And talk to you sometimes? Dwell I but in the suburbs   285
    Of your good pleasure? If it be no more
    Portia is Brutus' harlot, not his wife.
BRUTUS   You are my true and honorable wife,
    As dear to me as are the ruddy drops
    That visit my sad heart.   290
PORTIA   If this were true, then should I know this secret.
    I grant I am a woman, but withal
    A woman that Lord Brutus took to wife.
    I grant I am a woman, but withal
    A woman well reputed, Cato's daughter.   295
    Think you I am no stronger than my sex,
    Being so fathered and so husbanded?
    Tell me your counsels; I will not disclose 'em.
    I have made strong proof of my constancy,
    Giving myself a voluntary wound   300
    Here, in the thigh. Can I bear that with patience
    And not my husband's secrets?
BRUTUS   O ye gods,
    Render me worthy of this noble wife!
        Knock.
    Hark, hark, one knocks. Portia, go in a while,
    And by and by thy bosom shall partake   305
    The secrets of my heart.
    All my engagements I will construe to thee,

271. **charm:** conjure, entreat.
275. **heavy:** heavyhearted, sad.
285. **suburbs:** outlying areas, fringes.
292. **withal:** still, even yet.
295. **Cato's daughter:** Marcus Porcius Cato was known for his moral rectitude.
298. **counsels:** secrets.

All the charactery of my sad brows.
Leave me with haste.

Exit PORTIA.

                Lucius, who's that knocks?

Enter LUCIUS *and* LIGARIUS.

LUCIUS   Here is a sick man that would speak with you.   310
BRUTUS   Caius Ligarius, that Metellus spake of.
   Boy, stand aside.

[*Exit* LUCIUS.]

                Caius Ligarius, how?
LIGARIUS   Vouchsafe good morrow from a feeble tongue.
BRUTUS   O, what a time have you chose out, brave Caius,
   To wear a kerchief! Would you were not sick!   315
LIGARIUS   I am not sick if Brutus have in hand
   Any exploit worthy the name of honor.
BRUTUS   Such an exploit have I in hand, Ligarius,
   Had you a healthful ear to hear of it.
LIGARIUS   By all the gods that Romans bow before,   320
   I here discard my sickness!
     [*He pulls off his kerchief.*]
                   Soul of Rome,
   Brave son, derived from honorable loins,
   Thou, like an exorcist, hast conjured up
   My mortified spirit. Now bid me run
   And I will strive with things impossible,   325
   Yea, get the better of them. What's to do?
BRUTUS   A piece of work that will make sick men whole.
LIGARIUS   But are not some whole that we must make sick?
BRUTUS   That must we also. What it is, my Caius,
   I shall unfold to thee as we are going   330
   To whom it must be done.
LIGARIUS   Set on your foot,
   And with a heart new-fired I follow you
   To do I know not what; but it sufficeth
   That Brutus leads me on.
     Thunder.
BRUTUS   Follow me then.

Exeunt.

---

307. **engagements:** formal agreements.
308. **charactery:** handwriting, i.e., the meaning behind his serious expression.
312. **how:** an exclamation of surprise.
313. **Vouchsafe:** receive graciously.
315. **kerchief:** a headscarf worn by the sick.
324. **mortified:** deadened.
327. **whole:** healthy.
331. **Set on your foot:** proceed.

[Act 2. Scene 2. *Rome. Caesar's House.*]

Thunder and lightning. Enter JULIUS CAESAR *in his nightgown.*

CAESAR   Nor heaven nor earth have been at peace tonight.
  Thrice hath Calphurnia in her sleep cried out,
    "Help ho, they murder Caesar!" Who's within?

    Enter a SERVANT.

SERVANT   My lord?

CAESAR   Go bid the priests do present sacrifice   5
  And bring me their opinions of success.

SERVANT   I will, my lord.

                                        Exit.

    Enter CALPHURNIA.

CALPHURNIA   What mean you, Caesar? Think you to walk forth?
  You shall not stir out of your house today.

CAESAR   Caesar shall forth. The things that threatened me   10
  Ne'er looked but on my back; when they shall see
  The face of Caesar, they are vanishèd.

CALPHURNIA   Caesar, I never stood on ceremonies,
  Yet now they fright me. There is one within,
  Besides the things that we have heard and seen,   15
  Recounts most horrid sights seen by the watch.
  A lioness hath whelpèd in the streets,
  And graves have yawned and yielded up their dead;
  Fierce fiery warriors fight upon the clouds
  In ranks and squadrons and right form of war,   20
  Which drizzled blood upon the Capitol;
  The noise of battle hurtled in the air,
  Horses did neigh and dying men did groan,
  And ghosts did shriek and squeal about the streets.
  O Caesar, these things are beyond all use,   25
  And I do fear them.

CAESAR   What can be avoided
  Whose end is purposed by the mighty gods?
  Yet Caesar shall go forth, for these predictions
  Are to the world in general as to Caesar.

CALPHURNIA   When beggars die there are no comets seen;   30

---

   1. **SD. *nightgown:*** dressing gown.
   5. **present:** immediate.
   6. **success:** results.
  13. **stood on ceremonies:** believed in omens.
  20. **right form of war:** regular (square) battle ornaments.
  25. **use:** usual experience.
  29. **Are to:** i.e., are as applicable to.

The heavens themselves blaze forth the death of princes.
CAESAR   Cowards die many times before their deaths,
The valiant never taste of death but once.
Of all the wonders that I yet have heard
It seems to me most strange that men should fear,   35
Seeing that death, a necessary end,
Will come when it will come.
> *Enter a* SERVANT.
                                        What say the augurers?
SERVANT   They would not have you stir forth today.
Plucking the entrails of an offering forth,
They could not find a heart within the beast.   40
CAESAR   The gods do this in shame of cowardice.
Caesar should be a beast without a heart
If he should stay at home today for fear.
No, Caesar shall not. Danger knows full well
That Caesar is more dangerous than he: 45
We are two lions littered in one day,
And I the elder and more terrible.
And Caesar shall go forth.
CALPHURNIA   Alas, my lord,
Your wisdom is consumed in confidence.
Do not go forth today. Call it my fear   50
That keeps you in the house, and not your own.
We'll send Mark Antony to the Senate House
And he shall say you are not well today.
Let me, upon my knee, prevail in this.
CAESAR   Mark Antony shall say I am not well,   55
And for thy humor I will stay at home.
> *Enter* DECIUS.
Here's Decius Brutus; he shall tell them so.
DECIUS   Caesar, all hail! Good morrow, worthy Caesar,
I come to fetch you to the Senate House.
CAESAR   And you are come in very happy time   60
To bear my greeting to the senators
And tell them that I will not come today.
Cannot is false; and that I dare not, falser.
I will not come today. Tell them so, Decius.
CALPHURNIA   Say he is sick.
CAESAR   Shall Caesar send a lie?   65
Have I in conquest stretched mine arm so far

31. **blaze forth:** proclaim.
41. **in shame of:** to shame.
49. **confidence:** overconfidence.
60. **happy:** opportune.

To be afeard to tell graybeards the truth?
Decius, go tell them Caesar will not come.
DECIUS   Most mighty Caesar, let me know some cause,
   Lest I be laughed at when I tell them so.   70
CAESAR   The cause is in my will. I will not come:
   That is enough to satisfy the Senate.
   But for your private satisfaction,
   Because I love you, I will let you know.
   Calphurnia here, my wife, stays me at home.   75
   She dreamt tonight she saw my statue,
   Which like a fountain with an hundred spouts
   Did run pure blood, and many lusty Romans
   Came smiling and did bathe their hands in it.
   And these does she apply for warnings and portents   80
   And evils imminent, and on her knee
   Hath begged that I will stay at home today.
DECIUS   This dream is all amiss interpreted;
   It was a vision fair and fortunate.
   Your statue spouting blood in many pipes,   85
   In which so many smiling Romans bathed,
   Signifies that from you great Rome shall suck
   Reviving blood and that great men shall press
   For tinctures, stains, relics, and cognizance.
   This by Calphurnia's dream is signified.   90
CAESAR   And this way have you well expounded it.
DECIUS   I have, when you have heard what I can say.
   And know it now: the Senate have concluded
   To give this day a crown to mighty Caesar.
   If you shall send them word you will not come,   95
   Their minds may change. Besides, it were a mock
   Apt to be rendered for someone to say,
   "Break up the Senate till another time,
   When Caesar's wife shall meet with better dreams."
   If Caesar hide himself, shall they not whisper,   100
   "Lo, Caesar is afraid"?
   Pardon me, Caesar, for my dear dear love
   To your proceeding bids me tell you this,

---

67. **graybeards:** old men (slang).
75. **stays:** keeps.
76. **tonight:** last night.
78. **lusty:** joyful.
80. **apply for:** interpret as.
89. **tinctures . . . cognizance:** items associated with both the magical powers of saints
    and/or martyrs (tinctures, stains, relics) and the armorial heraldry of great nobles
    (cognizance).
103. **proceeding:** advancement, prospering.

And reason to my love is liable.

CAESAR   How foolish do your fears seem now, Calphurnia!   105
I am ashamèd I did yield to them.
Give me my robe, for I will go.

> *Enter* BRUTUS, LIGARIUS, METELLUS, CASCA, TREBONIUS, CINNA,
> *and* PUBLIUS.

And look where Publius is come to fetch me.

PUBLIUS   Good morrow, Caesar.

CAESAR   Welcome, Publius.
What, Brutus, are you stirred so early too?   110
Good morrow, Casca. Caius Ligarius,
Caesar was ne'er so much your enemy
As that same ague which hath made you lean.
What is't o'clock?

BRUTUS   Caesar, 'tis strucken eight.

CAESAR   I thank you for your pains and courtesy.   115

> *Enter* ANTONY.

See, Antony, that revels long a-nights,
Is notwithstanding up. Good morrow, Antony.

ANTONY   So to most noble Caesar.

CAESAR   [*To* CALPHURNIA.]   Bid them prepare within,
> [*Exit* CALPHURNIA.]

I am to blame to be thus waited for.
Now, Cinna, now, Metellus. What, Trebonius,   120
I have an hour's talk in store for you.
Remember that you call on me today;
Be near me that I may remember you.

TREBONIUS   Caesar, I will. [*Aside.*] And so near will I be
That your best friends shall wish I had been further.   125

CAESAR   Good friends, go in and taste some wine with me,
And we, like friends, will straightway go together.

BRUTUS   [*Aside.*] That every like is not the same, O Caesar,
The heart of Brutus earns to think upon.

                                        Exeunt.

---

104. **liable:** subordinate.
112. **enemy:** Ligarius had previously supported Pompey against Caesar.
113. **ague:** fever.
129. **earns:** grieves.

[Act 2. Scene 3. *Rome. A Street.*]

Enter ARTEMIDORUS [*reading a paper.*]
ARTEMIDORUS   "Caesar, beware of Brutus. Take heed of Cassius. Come not near Casca. Have an eye to Cinna. Trust not
Trebonius. Mark well Metellus Cimber. Decius Brutus loves
thee not. Thou hast wronged Caius Ligarius. There is but one
mind in all these men, and it is bent against Caesar. If thou   5
beest not immortal look about you. Security gives way to con-
spiracy. The mighty gods defend thee.
                                        Thy lover, Artemidorus."
Here will I stand till Caesar pass along,
And as a suitor will I give him this.   10
My heart laments that virtue cannot live
Out of the teeth of emulation.
If thou read this, O Caesar, thou mayst live;
If not, the fates with traitors do contrive."
                                                          Exit.

[Act 2. Scene 4. *Rome. Brutus' House.*]

Enter PORTIA *and* LUCIUS.
PORTIA   I prithee, boy, run to the Senate House.
Stay not to answer me, but get thee gone.
Why dost thou stay?
LUCIUS   To know my errand, madam.
PORTIA   I would have had thee there and here again
Ere I can tell thee what thou shouldst do there.   5
[*Aside*] O constancy, be strong upon my side;
Set a huge mountain 'tween my heart and tongue.
I have a man's mind, but a woman's might.
How hard it is for women to keep counsel!—
[*To* LUCIUS.] Art thou here yet?
LUCIUS   Madam, what should I do?   10
Run to the Capitol, and nothing else?
And so return to you, and nothing else?

---

  6. **Security:** overconfidence.
  8. **lover:** devoted friend.
 10. **suitor:** petitioner.
 12. **Out . . . emulation:** beyond the reach of envious people.
  9. **keep counsel:** keep a secret.

PORTIA   Yes, bring me word, boy, if thy lord look well,
       For he went sickly forth, and take good note
       What Caesar doth, what suitors press to him.   15
       Hark, boy, what noise is that?
LUCIUS   I hear none, Madam.
PORTIA   Prithee listen well:
       I heard a bustling rumor, like a fray,
       And the wind brings it from the Capitol.
LUCIUS   Sooth, madam, I hear nothing.   20
           Enter the SOOTHSAYER.
PORTIA   Come hither, fellow, which way hast thou been?
SOOTHSAYER   At mine own house, good lady.
PORTIA   What is't o'clock?
SOOTHSAYER   About the ninth hour, lady.
PORTIA   Is Caesar yet gone to the Capitol?
SOOTHSAYER   Madam, not yet. I go to take my stand   25
       To see him pass on to the Capitol.
PORTIA   Thou hast some suit to Caesar, hast thou not?
SOOTHSAYER   That I have, lady, if it will please Caesar
       To be so good to Caesar as to hear me:
       I shall beseech him to befriend himself.   30
PORTIA   Why, know'st thou any harm's intended towards him?
SOOTHSAYER   None that I know will be, much that I fear may
           chance.
       Good morrow to you. Here the street is narrow:
       The throng that follows Caesar at the heels,
       Of senators, of praetors, common suitors,   35
       Will crowd a feeble man almost to death.
       I'll get me to a place more void, and there
       Speak to great Caesar as he comes along.
                                                            Exit.
PORTIA   I must go in. [*Aside*] Ay me, how weak a thing
       The heart of woman is! O Brutus,   40
       The heavens speed thee in thine enterprise!
       Sure the boy heard me. [*To* LUCIUS.] Brutus hath a suit
       That Caesar will not grant. [*Aside*] O, I grow faint.—
       [*To* LUCIUS.] Run, Lucius, and commend me to my lord,

16. **Hark:** listen.
18. **rumor:** noise, clamor.
20. **Sooth:** in truth.
20. **SD.** *Soothsayer:* prophet (who earlier warned Caesar in Act 1, scene 2).
25. **stand:** place, position.
35. **praetors:** judges.
37. **a place more void:** a more open place, less crowded.
44. **commend me:** remember me.

Say I am merry. Come to me again   45
And bring me word what he doth say to thee.
                                 Exeunt [through separate doors].

[Act 3. Scene 1. *Rome. The Capitol.*]

Flourish. Enter CAESAR, BRUTUS, CASSIUS, CASCA, DECIUS,
METELLUS, TREBONIUS, CINNA, ANTONY, LEPIDUS, ARTEMI-
DORUS, PUBLIUS, [POPILLIUS, LIGARIUS,] *and the* SOOTHSAYER.

CAESAR   The Ides of March are come.
SOOTHSAYER   Ay, Caesar, but not gone.
ARTEMIDORUS   Hail, Caesar! Read this schedule.
DECIUS   Trebonius doth desire you to o'er-read
  (At your best leisure) this his humble suit.   5
ARTEMIDORUS   O Caesar, read mine first, for mine's a suit
  That touches Caesar nearer. Read it, great Caesar.
CAESAR   What touches us ourself shall be last served.
ARTEMIDORUS   Delay not, Caesar, read it instantly.
CAESAR   What, is the fellow mad?
PUBLIUS   Sirrah, give place.   10
CASSIUS   What, urge you your petitions in the street?
  Come to the Capitol.
      [CAESAR *moves forward on the stage, the rest following.*]
POPILLIUS   [*Aside, to* CASSIUS] I wish your enterprise today may
      thrive.
CASSIUS   What enterprise, Popillius?
POPILLIUS   Fare you well.
      [*Moves to join Caesar's followers.*]
BRUTUS   What said Popillius Lena?   15
CASSIUS   He wished today our enterprise might thrive.
  I fear our purpose is discovered.
BRUTUS   Look how he makes to Caesar. Mark him.
CASSIUS   Casca, be sudden, for we fear prevention.
  Brutus, what shall be done? If this be known   20
  Cassius or Caesar never shall turn back,

---

45. **merry:** in good spirits.
  3. **schedule:** paper, document.
  7. **touches:** concerns.
  8. **served:** addressed, attended to.
10. **give place:** move away.
18. **makes to:** moves toward.
19. **sudden:** quick; **prevention:** being forestalled.
21. **turn back:** return (alive).

For I will slay myself.
BRUTUS   Cassius, be constant.
  Popillius Lena speaks not of our purposes,
  For look, he smiles, and Caesar doth not change.
CASSIUS   Trebonius knows his time, for look you, Brutus,   25
  He draws Mark Antony out of the way.
                        [*Exeunt* ANTONY *and* TREBONIUS.]
DECIUS   Where is Metellus Cimber? Let him go
  And presently prefer his suit to Caesar.
BRUTUS   He is addressed; press near and second him.
CINNA   Casca, you are the first that rears your hand.   30
CAESAR   Are we all ready? What is now amiss
  That Caesar and his Senate must redress?
METELLUS   [*Kneeling.*] Most high, most mighty, and most puissant
    Caesar,
  Metellus Cimber throws before thy seat
  An humble heart.
CAESAR   I must prevent thee, Cimber.   35
  These couchings and these lowly courtesies
  Might fire the blood of ordinary men
  And turn preordinance and first decree
  Into the lane of children. Be not fond
  To think that Caesar bears such rebel blood   40
  That will be thawed from the true quality
  With that which melteth fools—I mean sweet words,
  Low-crookèd curtsies, and base spaniel fawning.
  Thy brother by decree is banished.
  If thou dost bend, and pray, and fawn for him,   45
  I spurn thee like a cur out of my way.
  Know Caesar doth not wrong, nor without cause
  Will he be satisfied.
METELLUS   Is there no voice more worthy than my own
  To sound more sweetly in great Caesar's ear   50
  For the repealing of my banished brother?
BRUTUS   I kiss thy hand, but not in flattery, Caesar,

22. **constant:** determined.
24. **Caesar:** Caesar's expression.
28. **presently prefer:** immediately put forward.
29. **addressed:** ready.
30. **are:** will be.
35. **prevent:** thwart.
36. **couchings:** reverent bows; **courtesies:** subservient curtsies.
38. **preordinance and first decree:** precedent and former judicial rulings.
39. **lane of children:** childlike whimsy; **fond:** foolish.
43. **Low-crookèd:** obsequious.
46. **spurn:** kick
47. **doth not wrong:** does not act unjustly; i.e., acts justly.

Desiring thee that Publius Cimber may
Have an immediate freedom of repeal.
CAESAR   What, Brutus?
CASSIUS   Pardon, Caesar; Caesar, pardon.   55
As low as to thy foot doth Cassius fall
To beg enfranchisement for Publius Cimber.
CAESAR   I could be well moved, if I were as you;
If I could pray to move, prayers would move me.
But I am constant as the Northern Star,   60
Of whose true-fixed and resting quality
There is no fellow in the firmament.
The skies are painted with unnumbered sparks,
They are all fire, and every one doth shine;
But there's but one in all doth hold his place.   65
So in the world: 'tis furnished well with men,
And men are flesh and blood, and apprehensive.
Yet in the number I do know but one
That unassailable holds on his rank,
Unshaked of motion, and that I am he   70
Let me a little show it, even in this:
That I was constant Cimber should be banished,
And constant do remain to keep him so.
CINNA   [*Kneeling.*] O Caesar—
CAESAR   Hence! Wilt thou lift up Olympus?
DECIUS   [*Kneeling.*] Great Caesar—
CAESAR   Doth not Brutus bootless
kneel?   75
CASCA   Speak hands for me!
            They stab CAESAR.
CAESAR   *Et tu, Brute?*—Then fall, Caesar!
                                                          Dies[.]
CINNA   Liberty! Freedom! Tyranny is dead!
Run hence, proclaim, cry it about the streets.
CASSIUS   Some to the common pulpits, and cry out,   80
"Liberty, freedom, and enfranchisement!"

---

54. **freedom of repeal:** probably release from banishment.
57. **enfranchisement:** restoration of citizenship.
60. **Northern Star:** the polestar.
62. **fellow:** equal.
63. **unnumbered:** innumerable.
67. **apprehensive:** able to understand.
69. **holds on:** maintains.
74. **Olympus:** Greek mountain where the gods dwelled, i.e., attempt the impossible.
75. **bootless:** uselessly.
77. **Et tu, Brute?:** And you, Brutus? (Latin).
80. **common pulpits:** public platforms (for speeches).
81. **enfranchisement:** citizenship.

BRUTUS   People and senators, be not affrighted.
  Fly not; stand still. Ambition's debt is paid.
CASCA   Go to the pulpit, Brutus.
DECIUS   And Cassius too.
BRUTUS   Where's Publius?   85
CINNA   Here, quite confounded with this mutiny.
METELLUS   Stand fast together lest some friend of Caesar's
  Should chance—
BRUTUS   Talk not of standing. Publius, good cheer,
  There is no harm intended to your person,   90
  Nor to no Roman else. So tell them, Publius.
CASSIUS   And leave us, Publius, lest that the people,
  Rushing on us, should do your age some mischief.
BRUTUS   Do so, and let no man abide this deed
  But we the doers.   95
                         [*Exeunt all but the conspirators.*]
        Enter TREBONIUS.
CASSIUS   Where is Antony?
TREBONIUS   Fled to his house amazed.
  Men, wives, and children stare, cry out, and run
  As it were doomsday.
BRUTUS   Fates, we will know your pleasures.
  That we shall die we know: 'tis but the time,
  And drawing days out, that men stand upon.   100
CASCA   Why, he that cuts off twenty years of life
  Cuts off so many years of fearing death.
BRUTUS   Grant that, and then is death a benefit.
  So are we Caesar's friends, that have abridged
  His time of fearing death. Stoop, Romans, stoop,   105
  And let us bathe our hands in Caesar's blood
  Up to the elbows and besmear our swords.
  Then walk we forth, even to the market-place,
  And waving our red weapons o'er our heads
  Let's all cry, "Peace, freedom, and liberty!"   110
CASSIUS   Stoop then and wash. How many ages hence
  Shall this our lofty scene be acted over
  In states unborn and accents yet unknown!
BRUTUS   How many times shall Caesar bleed in sport,
  That now on Pompey's basis lies along   115

  86. **confounded:** confused; **mutiny:** tumult, chaos.
  93. **mischief:** harm.
  94. **abide:** pay for.
  96. **amazed:** stunned.
  108. **market-place:** i.e., the Forum.
  115. **basis:** base, i.e., pedestal.

No worthier than the dust!
CASSIUS   So oft as that shall be,
  So often shall the knot of us be called
  The men that gave their country liberty.
DECIUS   What, shall we forth?
CASSIUS   Ay, every man away.
  Brutus shall lead, and we will grace his heels   120
  With the most boldest and best hearts of Rome.
    Enter a SERVANT.
BRUTUS   Soft, who comes here? A friend of Antony's.
SERVANT   Thus, Brutus, did my master bid me kneel,
  Thus did Mark Antony bid me fall down,
  And, being prostrate, thus he bade me say: 125
  Brutus is noble, wise, valiant, and honest;
  Caesar was mighty, bold, royal, and loving.
  Say I love Brutus, and I honor him;
  Say I feared Caesar, honored him, and loved him.
  If Brutus will vouchsafe that Antony   130
  May safely come to him and be resolved
  How Caesar hath deserved to lie in death,
  Mark Antony shall not love Caesar dead
  So well as Brutus living, but will follow
  The fortunes and affairs of noble Brutus   135
  Thorough the hazards of this untrod state
  With all true faith. So says my master Antony.
BRUTUS   Thy master is a wise and valiant Roman;
  I never thought him worse.
  Tell him, so please him come unto this place,   140
  He shall be satisfied, and by my honor
  Depart untouched.
SERVANT   I'll fetch him presently.
                           Exit [SERVANT].
BRUTUS   I know that we shall have him well to friend.
CASSIUS   I wish we may. But yet have I a mind
  That fears him much, and my misgiving still   145
  Falls shrewdly to the purpose.
    Enter ANTONY.
BRUTUS   But here comes Antony. Welcome, Mark Antony!

117. **knot:** crowd, group.
122. **Soft:** wait.
130. **vouchsafe:** allow.
131. **resolved:** convinced.
136. **Thorough:** through.
140. **so:** if.
142. **presently:** immediately.
143. **to friend:** as our friend.

ANTONY   O mighty Caesar! Dost thou lie so low?
  Are all thy conquests, glories, triumphs, spoils,
  Shrunk to this little measure? Fare thee well!   150
  I know not, gentlemen, what you intend,
  Who else must be let blood, who else is rank.
  If I myself, there is no hour so fit
  As Caesar's death's hour, nor no instrument
  Of half that worth as those your swords, made rich   155
  With the most noble blood of all this world.
  I do beseech ye, if you bear me hard,
  Now, whilst your purpled hands do reek and smoke,
  Fulfil your pleasure. Live a thousand years,
  I shall not find myself so apt to die.   160
  No place will please me so, no mean of death,
  As here by Caesar, and by you cut off,
  The choice and master spirits of this age.
BRUTUS   O Antony, beg not your death of us.
  Though now we must appear bloody and cruel,   165
  As by our hands and this our present act
  You see we do, yet see you but our hands
  And this the bleeding business they have done.
  Our hearts you see not; they are pitiful.
  And pity to the general wrong of Rome—   170
  As fire drives out fire, so pity pity—
  Hath done this deed on Caesar. For your part,
  To you our swords have leaden points, Mark Antony.
  Our arms in strength of malice, and our hearts
  Of brothers' temper, do receive you in   175
  With all kind love, good thoughts, and reverence.
CASSIUS   Your voice shall be as strong as any man's
  In the disposing of new dignities.
BRUTUS   Only be patient till we have appeased
  The multitude, beside themselves with fear,   180
  And then we will deliver you the cause
  Why I, that did love Caesar when I struck him,
  Have thus proceeded.
ANTONY   I doubt not of your wisdom.
  Let each man render me his bloody hand.

---

152. **let blood:** bled (i.e., killed); **rank:** swollen (with blood).
157. **beseech:** implore; **bear me hard:** hold a grudge against me.
158. **purpled:** bloody.
159. **Live:** i.e., if I live.
160. **apt:** ready.
161. **mean:** means.
169. **pitiful:** full of pity.
173. **leaden:** made of lead, i.e., blunt.

First, Marcus Brutus, will I shake with you;   185
Next, Caius Cassius, do I take your hand;
Now, Decius Brutus, yours. Now yours, Metellus.
Yours, Cinna; and, my valiant Casca, yours.
Though last, not least in love, yours, good Trebonius.
Gentlemen all—alas, what shall I say?   190
My credit now stands on such slippery ground
That one of two bad ways you must conceit me,
Either a coward or a flatterer.
That I did love thee, Caesar, O 'tis true.
If then thy spirit look upon us now,   195
Shall it not grieve thee dearer than thy death
To see thy Antony making his peace,
Shaking the bloody fingers of thy foes—
Most noble—in the presence of thy corse?
Had I as many eyes as thou hast wounds,   200
Weeping as fast as they stream forth thy blood,
It would become me better than to close
In terms of friendship with thine enemies.
Pardon me, Julius! Here wast thou bayed, brave hart.
Here didst thou fall, and here thy hunters stand,   205
Signed in thy spoil and crimsoned in thy Lethe.
O world! Thou wast the forest to this hart,
And this indeed, O world, the heart of thee.
How like a deer strucken by many princes
Dost thou here lie!   210
CASSIUS   Mark Antony—
ANTONY   Pardon me, Caius Cassius,
The enemies of Caesar shall say this;
Then, in a friend, it is cold modesty.
CASSIUS   I blame you not for praising Caesar so,
But what compact mean you to have with us?   215
Will you be pricked in number of our friends,
Or shall we on and not depend on you?
ANTONY   Therefore I took your hands, but was indeed
Swayed from the point by looking down on Caesar.
Friends am I with you all, and love you all,   220

192. **conceit**: judge.
199. **corse**: corpse.
202. **close**: agree.
204. **bayed**: brought to bay, cornered; **hart**: stag.
206. **Signed**: marked; **spoil**: slaughter; **Lethe**: the river in Hades whose waters caused
      forgetfulness.
213. **modesty**: moderation.
215. **compact**: agreement.
216. **pricked**: marked, i.e., counted among.

Upon this hope, that you shall give me reasons
Why and wherein Caesar was dangerous.
BRUTUS   Or else were this a savage spectacle.
Our reasons are so full of good regard
That were you, Antony, the son of Caesar   225
You should be satisfied.
ANTONY   That's all I seek,
And am, moreover, suitor that I may
Produce his body to the market-place,
And in the pulpit, as becomes a friend,
Speak in the order of his funeral.   230
BRUTUS   You shall, Mark Antony.
CASSIUS   Brutus, a word with you.
[*Aside, to* BRUTUS] You know not what you do. Do not consent
That Antony speak in his funeral.
Know you how much the people may be moved
By that which he will utter?
BRUTUS   [*Aside, to* CASSIUS] By your pardon,   235
I will myself into the pulpit first
And show the reason of our Caesar's death.
What Antony shall speak, I will protest
He speaks by leave and by permission,
And that we are contented Caesar shall   240
Have all true rites and lawful ceremonies.
It shall advantage more than do us wrong.
CASSIUS   [*Aside, to* BRUTUS] I know not what may fall. I like it
    not.
BRUTUS   Mark Antony, here, take you Caesar's body.
You shall not in your funeral speech blame us,   245
But speak all good you can devise of Caesar
And say you do't by our permission,
Else shall you not have any hand at all
About his funeral. And you shall speak
In the same pulpit whereto I am going,   250
After my speech is ended.
ANTONY   Be it so.
I do desire no more.
BRUTUS   Prepare the body, then, and follow us.
                              Exeunt [*all but* ANTONY].
ANTONY   O, pardon me, thou bleeding piece of earth,
That I am meek and gentle with these butchers.   255

230. **order:** ceremony.
238. **protest:** assert.
243. **fall:** befall, happen.
249. **About:** in.

Thou art the ruins of the noblest man
That ever livèd in the tide of times.
Woe to the hand that shed this costly blood.
Over thy wounds now do I prophesy—
Which like dumb mouths do ope their ruby lips   260
To beg the voice and utterance of my tongue—
A curse shall light upon the limbs of men:
Domestic fury and fierce civil strife
Shall cumber all the parts of Italy;
Blood and destruction shall be so in use,   265
And dreadful objects so familiar,
That mothers shall but smile when they behold
Their infants quartered with the hands of war,
All pity choked with custom of fell deeds;
And Caesar's spirit, ranging for revenge,   270
With Ate by his side come hot from hell,
Shall in these confines with a monarch's voice
Cry havoc and let slip the dogs of war,
That this foul deed shall smell above the earth
With carrion men, groaning for burial.   275
     Enter Octavius' SERVANT.
You serve Octavius Caesar, do you not?
SERVANT   I do, Mark Antony.
ANTONY   Caesar did write for him to come to Rome.
SERVANT   He did receive his letters, and is coming,
  And bid me say to you by word of mouth—   280
    [*Seeing the body.*]
  O Caesar!
ANTONY   Thy heart is big, get thee apart and weep.
  Passion, I see, is catching, for mine eyes,
  Seeing those beads of sorrow stand in thine,
  Begin to water. Is thy master coming?   285
SERVANT   He lies tonight within seven leagues of Rome.
ANTONY   Post back with speed and tell him what hath chanced.
  Here is a mourning Rome, a dangerous Rome,
  No Rome of safety for Octavius yet—
  Hie hence and tell him so. Yet stay awhile;   290
  Thou shalt not back till I have borne this corse

---

264. **cumber:** overwhelm.
268. **quartered:** cut into pieces.
269. **fell:** cruel.
271. **Ate:** goddess of discord; chaos.
273. **havoc:** destruction! (a military order to commence slaughter); **let slip:** unleash.
290. **Hie:** go.
291. **corse:** corpse.

Into the market-place. There shall I try
In my oration how the people take
The cruel issue of these bloody men,
According to the which thou shalt discourse   295
To young Octavius of the state of things.
Lend me your hand.

                         Exeunt [*with* CAESAR'*s body*].

[Act 3. Scene 2. *Rome. The Forum.*]

      Enter BRUTUS *and* CASSIUS *with the* PLEBEIANS.
ALL   We will be satisfied! Let us be satisfied!
BRUTUS   Then follow me and give me audience, friends.
  Cassius, go you into the other street
  And part the numbers.
  Those that will hear me speak, let 'em stay here.   5
  Those that will follow Cassius, go with him
  And public reasons shall be renderèd
  Of Caesar's death.   [BRUTUS *goes into the pulpit.*]
1 PLEBEIAN   I will hear Brutus speak.
2 PLEBEIAN   I will hear Cassius and compare their reasons
  When severally we hear them renderèd.   10
        [*Exit* CASSIUS, *some of the* PLEBEIANS *following.*]
3 PLEBEIAN   The noble Brutus is ascended. Silence.
BRUTUS   Be patient till the last.
  Romans, countrymen, and lovers, hear me for my cause, and
  be silent that you may hear. Believe me for mine honor, and
  have respect to mine honor that you may believe. Censure me   15
  in your wisdom, and awake your senses that you may the better judge. If there be any in this assembly, any dear friend of
  Caesar's, to him I say that Brutus' love to Caesar was no less
  than his. If then that friend demand why Brutus rose against
  Caesar, this is my answer: not that I loved Caesar less, but   20
  that I loved Rome more. Had you rather Caesar were living,
  and die all slaves, than that Caesar were dead, to live all free-
  men? As Caesar loved me, I weep for him; as he was fortunate,
  I rejoice at it; as he was valiant, I honor him; but as he was
  ambitious, I slew him. There is tears for his love, joy for his   25

---

294. **issue:** result.
  4. **part the numbers:** divide the crowd.
 10. **severally:** separately.
 13. **lovers:** friends.
 15. **have respect to:** consider, regard; **Censure:** judge.
 16. **senses:** wits, reason.

fortune, honor for his valor, and death for his ambition. Who
is here so base that would be a bondman? If any, speak, for
him have I offended. Who is here so rude that would not be a
Roman? If any, speak, for him have I offended. Who is here so
vile that will not love his country? If any, speak, for him have   30
I offended. I pause for a reply.

ALL   None, Brutus, none.

BRUTUS   Then none have I offended. I have done no more to
Caesar than you shall do to Brutus. The question of his death
is enrolled in the Capitol: his glory not extenuated wherein he   35
was worthy, nor his offences enforced for which he suffered
death.

     Enter MARK ANTONY, *with Caesar's body.*

Here comes his body, mourned by Mark Antony, who, though he
had no hand in his death, shall receive the benefit of his dying,
a place in the commonwealth, as which of you shall not? With   40
this I depart: that, as I slew my best lover for the good of Rome,
I have the same dagger for myself when it shall please my country to need my death.

     [*Comes down.*]

ALL   Live, Brutus, live, live!

1 PLEBEIAN   Bring him with triumph home unto his house.   45

2 PLEBEIAN   Give him a statue with his ancestors.

3 PLEBEIAN   Let him be Caesar.

4 PLEBEIAN   Caesar's better parts
Shall be crowned in Brutus.

1 PLEBEIAN   We'll bring him to his house
With shouts and clamors.

BRUTUS   My countrymen—

2 PLEBEIAN   Peace, silence, Brutus speaks!

1 PLEBEIAN   Peace ho!   50

BRUTUS   Good countrymen, let me depart alone,
And, for my sake, stay here with Antony.
Do grace to Caesar's corpse, and grace his speech
Tending to Caesar's glories, which Mark Antony
(By our permission) is allowed to make.   55
I do entreat you, not a man depart,

27. **bondman:** slave.
28. **offended:** wronged; **rude:** crude.
35. **enrolled:** written (officially), i.e., written on a parchment roll.
36. **enforced:** emphasized.
41. **lover:** friend.
47. **parts:** qualities, characteristics.
53. **Do grace to:** respect; **grace:** listen respectfully to.
54. **Tending to:** regarding.

Save I alone, till Antony have spoke.

Exit.

1 PLEBEIAN   Stay ho, and let us hear Mark Antony.

3 PLEBEIAN   Let him go up into the public chair,
  We'll hear him. Noble Antony, go up.   60

ANTONY   For Brutus' sake, I am beholding to you.
      [*He goes into the pulpit.*]

4 PLEBEIAN   What does he say of Brutus?

3 PLEBEIAN   He says, for Brutus' sake
  He finds himself beholding to us all.

4 PLEBEIAN   'Twere best he speak no harm of Brutus here.

1 PLEBEIAN   This Caesar was a tyrant.

3 PLEBEIAN   Nay, that's certain.   65
  We are blest that Rome is rid of him.

2 PLEBEIAN   Peace, let us hear what Antony can say.

ANTONY   You gentle Romans—

ALL   Peace ho! Let us hear him.

ANTONY   Friends, Romans, countrymen, lend me your ears.
  I come to bury Caesar, not to praise him.   70
  The evil that men do lives after them,
  The good is oft interrèd with their bones.
  So let it be with Caesar. The noble Brutus
  Hath told you Caesar was ambitious;
  If it were so, it was a grievous fault,   75
  And grievously hath Caesar answered it.
  Here, under the leave of Brutus and the rest—
  For Brutus is an honorable man,
  So are they all, all honorable men—
  Come I to speak in Caesar's funeral.   80
  He was my friend, faithful and just to me,
  But Brutus says he was ambitious,
  And Brutus is an honorable man.
  He hath brought many captives home to Rome,
  Whose ransoms did the general coffers fill.   85
  Did this in Caesar seem ambitious?
  When that the poor have cried, Caesar hath wept.
  Ambition should be made of sterner stuff.
  Yet Brutus says he was ambitious,
  And Brutus is an honorable man.   90
  You all did see that on the Lupercal
  I thrice presented him a kingly crown,

61. **beholding:** beholden.
76. **answered:** paid for.
77. **under the leave of:** with the permission of.

Which he did thrice refuse. Was this ambition?
Yet Brutus says he was ambitious,
And sure he is an honorable man.   95
I speak not to disprove what Brutus spoke,
But here I am to speak what I do know.
You all did love him once, not without cause;
What cause withholds you then to mourn for him?
O judgment, thou art fled to brutish beasts,   100
And men have lost their reason! Bear with me.
My heart is in the coffin there with Caesar,
And I must pause till it come back to me.

1 PLEBEIAN   Methinks there is much reason in his sayings.
2 PLEBEIAN   If thou consider rightly of the matter,   105
Caesar has had great wrong.
3 PLEBEIAN   Has he, masters?
I fear there will a worse come in his place.
4 PLEBEIAN   Marked ye his words? He would not take the
     crown;
Therefore 'tis certain he was not ambitious.
1 PLEBEIAN   If it be found so, some will dear abide it.   110
2 PLEBEIAN   Poor soul, his eyes are red as fire with weeping.
3 PLEBEIAN   There's not a nobler man in Rome than Antony.
4 PLEBEIAN   Now mark him, he begins again to speak.
ANTONY   But yesterday the word of Caesar might
Have stood against the world; now lies he there,   115
And none so poor to do him reverence.
O masters, if I were disposed to stir
Your hearts and minds to mutiny and rage,
I should do Brutus wrong and Cassius wrong,
Who (you all know) are honorable men.   120
I will not do them wrong; I rather choose
To wrong the dead, to wrong myself and you,
Than I will wrong such honorable men.
But here's a parchment with the seal of Caesar,
I found it in his closet. 'Tis his will.   125
Let but the commons hear this testament—
Which, pardon me, I do not mean to read—
And they would go and kiss dead Caesar's wounds
And dip their napkins in his sacred blood,

---

110. **dear abide:** pay dearly (for).
114. **But:** only.
116. **none . . . reverence:** no one is so lowly that they owe him deference.
125. **closet:** private room.
126. **commons:** common people, i.e., the people.
129. **napkins:** handkerchiefs.

Yea, beg a hair of him for memory,   130
And, dying, mention it within their wills,
Bequeathing it as a rich legacy
Unto their issue.
4 PLEBEIAN   We'll hear the will. Read it, Mark Antony.
ALL   The will, the will. We will hear Caesar's will!   135
ANTONY   Have patience, gentle friends, I must not read it.
   It is not meet you know how Caesar loved you:
   You are not wood, you are not stones, but men.
   And, being men, hearing the will of Caesar,
   It will inflame you, it will make you mad.   140
   'Tis good you know not that you are his heirs,
   For if you should, O, what would come of it?
4 PLEBEIAN   Read the will. We'll hear it, Antony.
   You shall read us the will, Caesar's will!
ANTONY   Will you be patient? Will you stay awhile?   145
   I have o'ershot myself to tell you of it.
   I fear I wrong the honorable men
   Whose daggers have stabbed Caesar. I do fear it.
4 PLEBEIAN   They were traitors. Honorable men?
ALL   The will! The testament!   150
2 PLEBEIAN   They were villains, murderers! The will, read the
   will!
ANTONY   You will compel me then to read the will?
   Then make a ring about the corpse of Caesar
   And let me show you him that made the will.   155
   Shall I descend? And will you give me leave?
ALL   Come down.
2 PLEBEIAN   Descend.
3 PLEBEIAN   You shall have leave.
   [ANTONY *comes down from the pulpit.*]
4 PLEBEIAN   A ring, stand round.   160
I PLEBEIAN   Stand from the hearse, stand from the body.
2 PLEBEIAN   Room for Antony, most noble Antony.
ANTONY   Nay, press not so upon me. Stand far off.
ALL   Stand back. Room, bear back.
ANTONY   If you have tears, prepare to shed them now.   165
   You all do know this mantle. I remember
   The first time ever Caesar put it on.
   'Twas on a summer's evening, in his tent,

---

133. **issue:** heirs.
137. **meet:** appropriate.
146. **o'ershot myself:** gone too far.
161. **hearse:** bier.
163. **far:** farther.

That day he over came the Nervii.
Look, in this place ran Cassius' dagger through.   170
See what a rent the envious Casca made.
Through this the well-belovèd Brutus stabbed,
And as he plucked his cursèd steel away,
Mark how the blood of Caesar followed it,
As rushing out of doors to be resolved   175
If Brutus so unkindly knocked or no,
For Brutus, as you know, was Caesar's angel.
Judge, O you gods, how dearly Caesar loved him!
This was the most unkindest cut of all.
For when the noble Caesar saw him stab,   180
Ingratitude, more strong than traitors' arms,
Quite vanquished him. Then burst his mighty heart,
And, in his mantle muffling up his face,
Even at the base of Pompey's statue
(Which all the while ran blood) great Caesar fell.   185
O, what a fall was there, my countrymen!
Then I, and you, and all of us fell down,
Whilst bloody treason flourished over us.
O, now you weep, and I perceive you feel
The dint of pity. These are gracious drops.   190
Kind souls, what weep you when you but behold
Our Caesar's vesture wounded? Look you here,
Here is himself, marred as you see with traitors.

1 PLEBEIAN   O piteous spectacle!
2 PLEBEIAN   O noble Caesar!   195
3 PLEBEIAN   O woeful day!
4 PLEBEIAN   O traitors, villains!
1 PLEBEIAN   O most bloody sight!
2 PLEBEIAN   We will be revenged!
ALL   Revenge! About! Seek! Burn! Fire! Kill! Slay!   200
      Let not a traitor live!
ANTONY   Stay, countrymen!
1 PLEBEIAN   Peace there, hear the noble Antony.

---

169. **Nervii:** a Gallic tribe whose defeat by Caesar in 57 B.C.E. brought enormous cele-
    bration to the Romans.
171. **rent:** tear; **envious:** malicious.
175. **As:** as if; **resolved:** convinced.
176. **unkindly:** unnaturally (therefore, cruelly).
177. **angel:** more beloved friend.
182. **Quite:** absolutely.
188. **flourished:** triumphed.
190. **dint:** blow.
192. **vesture:** garment.
200. **About!:** go to work!

2 PLEBEIAN   We'll hear him, we'll follow him, we'll die with him.
ANTONY   Good friends, sweet friends, let me not stir you up   205
  To such a sudden flood of mutiny.
  They that have done this deed are honorable.
  What private griefs they have, alas, I know not,
  That made them do it. They are wise and honorable,
  And will no doubt with reasons answer you.   210
  I come not, friends, to steal away your hearts.
  I am no orator, as Brutus is,
  But—as you know me all—a plain blunt man
  That love my friend, and that they know full well
  That gave me public leave to speak of him.   215
  For I have neither wit, nor words, nor worth,
  Action, nor utterance, nor the power of speech
  To stir men's blood. I only speak right on.
  I tell you that which you yourselves do know,
  Show you sweet Caesar's wounds, poor poor dumb mouths,   220
  And bid them speak for me. But were I Brutus,
  And Brutus Antony, there were an Antony
  Would ruffle up your spirits and put a tongue
  In every wound of Caesar, that should move
  The stones of Rome to rise and mutiny.   225
ALL   We'll mutiny.
1 PLEBEIAN   We'll burn the house of Brutus.
3 PLEBEIAN   Away then. Come, seek the conspirators.
ANTONY   Yet hear me, countrymen, yet hear me speak.
ALL   Peace ho. Hear Antony, most noble Antony.   230
ANTONY   Why, friends, you go to do you know not what.
  Wherein hath Caesar thus deserved your loves?
  Alas, you know not. I must tell you then.
  You have forgot the will I told you of.
ALL   Most true. The will. Let's stay and hear the will.   235
ANTONY   Here is the will, and under Caesar's seal.
  To every Roman citizen he gives,
  To every several man, seventy-five drachmas.
2 PLEBEIAN   Most noble Caesar! We'll revenge his death!
3 PLEBEIAN   O royal Caesar!   240
ANTONY   Hear me with patience.

---

208. **griefs:** grievances.
215. **public leave:** permission to speak publicly.
216. **wit:** intelligence; **worth:** social stature.
217. **Action:** gesture.
218. **right on:** plainly.
223. **ruffle up:** stir up (to rage).
238. **drachmas:** silver coins.

ALL   Peace, ho!
ANTONY   Moreover, he hath left you all his walks,
   His private arbors and new-planted orchards,
   On this side Tiber. He hath left them you   245
   And to your heirs for ever—common pleasures,
   To walk abroad and recreate yourselves.
   Here was a Caesar! When comes such another?
1 PLEBEIAN   Never, never! Come, away, away!
   We'll burn his body in the holy place   250
   And with the brands fire the traitors' houses.
   Take up the body.
2 PLEBEIAN   Go fetch fire!
2 PLEBEIAN   Pluck down benches!
4 PLEBEIAN   Pluck down forms, windows, anything!   255
                        Exeunt PLEBEIANS [*with the body*].
ANTONY   Now let it work. Mischief, thou art afoot.
   Take thou what course thou wilt.
                        Enter SERVANT.
                                   How now, fellow?
SERVANT   Sir, Octavius is already come to Rome.
ANTONY   Where is he?
SERVANT   He and Lepidus are at Caesar's house.   260
ANTONY   And thither will I straight to visit him.
   He comes upon a wish. Fortune is merry,
   And in this mood will give us anything.
SERVANT   I heard him say Brutus and Cassius
   Are rid like madmen through the gates of Rome.   265
ANTONY   Belike they had some notice of the people,
   How I had moved them. Bring me to Octavius.
                                   Exeunt.

[Act 3. Scene 3. *Rome. A Street.*]

Enter CINNA THE POET, *and after him the* PLEBEIANS.
CINNA THE POET   I dreamt tonight that I did feast with Caesar,
   And things unluckily charge my fantasy.

---

244. **orchards:** gardens.
246. **common pleasures:** pleasure gardens, i.e., public gardens.
251. **brands:** firebrands.
255. **forms:** benches; **windows:** probably shutters.
262. **upon a wish:** just as I had wished, i.e., at an opportune moment.
265. **Are rid:** have ridden.
266. **Belike:** probably.
   1. **tonight:** last night.
   2. **things . . . fantasy:** bad omens burden my imagination.

I have no will to wander forth of doors,
Yet something leads me forth.

1 PLEBEIAN   What is your name?   5
2 PLEBEIAN   Whither are you going?
3 PLEBEIAN   Where do you dwell?
4 PLEBEIAN   Are you a married man or a bachelor?
2 PLEBEIAN   Answer every man directly.
1 PLEBEIAN   Ay, and briefly.   10
4 PLEBEIAN   Ay, and wisely.
3 PLEBEIAN   Ay, and truly, you were best.
CINNA THE POET   What is my name? Whither am I going? Where
     do I dwell? Am I am married man or a bachelor? Then to
     answer every man directly and briefly, wisely and truly. Wisely   15
     I say, I am a bachelor.
2 PLEBEIAN   That's as much as to say they are fools that marry.
     You'll bear me a bang for that, I fear. Proceed directly.
CINNA THE POET   Directly I am going to Caesar's funeral.
1 PLEBEIAN   As a friend or an enemy?   20
CINNA THE POET   As a friend.
2 PLEBEIAN   That matter is answered directly.
4 PLEBEIAN   For your dwelling—briefly.
CINNA THE POET   Briefly, I dwell by the Capitol.
3 PLEBEIAN   Your name, sir, truly.   25
CINNA THE POET   Truly, my name is Cinna.
1 PLEBEIAN   Tear him to pieces! He's a conspirator.
CINNA THE POET   I am Cinna the poet, I am Cinna the poet.
4 PLEBEIAN   Tear him to pieces for his bad verses, tear him for
     his bad verses.   30
CINNA THE POET   I am not Cinna the conspirator.
4 PLEBEIAN   It is no matter, his name's Cinna. Pluck but his
     name out of his heart and turn him going.
3 PLEBEIAN   Tear him, tear him! Come, brands, ho, firebrands!
     To Brutus', to Cassius'! Burn all! Some to Decius' house, and   35
     some to Casca's, some to Ligarius'! Away, go!

                    Exeunt all the PLEBEIANS [*with* CINNA].

---

3. **forth of doors:** out of doors
12. **you were best:** i.e., if you know what's good for you.
18. **bear me a bang:** get a blow from me.
33. **turn him going:** send him away.

[Act 4. Scene 1. *Rome. Antony's house.*]

Enter ANTONY, OCTAVIUS, *and* LEPIDUS.

ANTONY   These many then shall die; their names are pricked.
OCTAVIUS   Your brother too must die; consent you, Lepidus?
LEPIDUS   I do consent.
OCTAVIUS   Prick him down, Antony.
LEPIDUS   Upon condition Publius shall not live,
   Who is your sister's son, Mark Antony.   5
ANTONY   He shall not live—look, with a spot I damn him.
   But, Lepidus, go you to Caesar's house,
   Fetch the will hither, and we shall determine
   How to cut off some charge in legacies.
LEPIDUS   What, shall I find you here?   10
OCTAVIUS   Or here or at the Capitol.

                               Exit LEPIDUS.

ANTONY   This is a slight, unmeritable man,
   Meet to be sent on errands; is it fit,
   The threefold world divided, he should stand
   One of the three to share it?
OCTAVIUS   So you thought him   15
   And took his voice who should be pricked to die
   In our black sentence and proscription.
ANTONY   Octavius, I have seen more days than you,
   And though we lay these honors on this man
   To ease ourselves of divers slanderous loads,   20
   He shall but bear them as the ass bears gold,
   To groan and sweat under the business,
   Either led or driven, as we point the way;
   And having brought our treasure where we will,
   Then take we down his load and turn him off   25
   (Like to the empty ass) to shake his ears
   And graze in commons.

---

  1. **pricked:** marked.
  6. **spot:** mark.
  9. **charge:** outlay, cost.
11. **Or:** either.
13. **Meet:** suitable.
14. **threefold world divided:** i.e., the world, described in geographical terms, consisted of Europe, Asia, and Africa; also, the Roman Empire, was divided among Antony, Octavius, and Lepidus.
16. **voice:** vote, designation.
17. **black sentence and proscription:** i.e., death sentence.
20. **divers slanderous loads:** weight of reproach, i.e., the blame.
26. **empty:** unladen.
27. **commons:** public lands.

OCTAVIUS   You may do your will,
     But he's a tried and valiant soldier.
ANTONY   So is my horse, Octavius, and for that
     I do appoint him store of provender.   30
     It is a creature that I teach to fight,
     To wind, to stop, to run directly on,
     His corporal motion governed by my spirit.
     And, in some taste, is Lepidus but so.
     He must be taught and trained and bid go forth—   35
     A barren-spirited fellow, one that feeds
     On objects, arts, and imitations,
     Which, out of use and staled by other men,
     Begin his fashion. Do not talk of him
     But as a property. And now, Octavius,   40
     Listen great things. Brutus and Cassius
     Are levying powers. We must straight make head.
     Therefore let our alliance be combined,
     Our best friends made, our means stretched,
     And let us presently go sit in counsel,   45
     How covert matters may be best disclosed
     And open perils surest answered.
OCTAVIUS   Let us do so, for we are at the stake
     And bayed about with many enemies,
     And some that smile have in their hearts, I fear,   50
     Millions of mischiefs.

                                                   Exeunt.

[Act 4. Scene 2. *A Camp near Sardis. Brutus' Tent.*]

> *Drum. Enter* BRUTUS, LUCILIUS, [LUCIUS,] *and the* army.
> TITINIUS *and* PINDARUS *meet them.*

BRUTUS   Stand ho!
LUCILIUS   Give the word, ho, and stand!

----

   30. **appoint**: give formally; **store**: a supply.
   32. **wind**: turn.
   34. **taste**: degree.
   38. **staled**: deemed uninteresting (and therefore out of fashion).
   39. **fashion**: custom.
   40. **property**: tool, means to an end.
   41. **Listen**: i.e., listen to.
   42. **make head**: advance; raise a force.
   44. **made**: gathered.
   47. **answered**: countered, confronted.
48–49. **stake ... enemies**: the image is of bearbaiting in which a bear was baited by
          dogs.
   51. **mischiefs**: dangers.
    2. **Give ... stand!**: i.e., pass the word and halt!

BRUTUS   What now, Lucilius, is Cassius near?

LUCILIUS   He is at hand, and Pindarus is come
To do you salutation from his master.   5

BRUTUS   He greets me well. Your master, Pindarus,
In his own change or by ill officers,
Hath given me some worthy cause to wish
Things done undone, but if he be at hand
I shall be satisfied.

PINDARUS   I do not doubt   10
But that my noble master will appear
Such as he is, full of regard and honor.

BRUTUS   He is not doubted.
     [BRUTUS *and* LUCILIUS *draw apart.*]
                              A word, Lucilius,
How he received you; let me be resolved.

LUCILIUS   With courtesy and with respect enough,   15
But not with such familiar instances,
Nor with such free and friendly conference,
As he hath used of old.

BRUTUS   Thou hast described
A hot friend cooling. Ever note, Lucilius,
When love begins to sicken and decay   20
It useth an enforcèd ceremony.
There are no tricks in plain and simple faith,
But hollow men, like horses hot at hand,
Make gallant show and promise of their mettle.
     Low march within.
But when they should endure the bloody spur   25
They fall their crests, and like deceitful jades
Sink in the trial. Comes his army on?

LUCILIUS   They mean this night in Sardis to be quartered.
The greater part, the horse in general,
Are come with Cassius.
     Enter CASSIUS *and his powers.*

BRUTUS   Hark, he is arrived.   30
March gently on to meet him.

---

7. **change:** i.e., changed opinion.
8. **worthy:** justifiable.
14. **resolved:** informed.
16. **familiar instances:** evidence of friendship.
17. **conference:** conversation.
21. **enforcèd:** strained.
23. **hollow:** disingenuous; **hot at hand:** eager at the start.
26. **fall their crests:** lower their necks; **jades:** nags.
29. **in general:** all together.
31. **gently:** with dignity.

CASSIUS   Stand ho!
BRUTUS   Stand ho. Speak the word along.
1 SOLDIER   Stand!
2 SOLDIER   Stand!   35
3 SOLDIER   Stand!
CASSIUS   Most noble brother, you have done me wrong.
BRUTUS   Judge me, you gods! Wrong I mine enemies?
  And if not so, how should I wrong a brother?
CASSIUS   Brutus, this sober form of yours hides wrongs,   40
  And when you do them—
BRUTUS   Cassius, be content,
  Speak your griefs softly. I do know you well.
  Before the eyes of both our armies here—
  Which should perceive nothing but love from us—
  Let us not wrangle. Bid them move away.   45
  Then in my tent, Cassius, enlarge your griefs
  And I will give you audience.
CASSIUS   Pindarus,
  Bid our commanders lead their charges off
  A little from this ground.
BRUTUS   Lucilius, do you the like, and let no man   50
  Come to our tent till we have done our conference.
  Let Lucius and Titinius guard our door.
                    Exeunt [all but] BRUTUS *and* CASSIUS.

[Act 4. Scene 3. *A Camp near Sardis. Brutus' Tent.*]

CASSIUS   That you have wronged me doth appear in this:
  You have condemned and noted Lucius Pella
  For taking bribes here of the Sardians,
  Wherein my letters, praying on his side,
  Because I knew the man, was slighted off.   5
BRUTUS   You wronged yourself to write in such a case.
CASSIUS   In such a time as this it is not meet
  That every nice offence should bear his comment.
BRUTUS   Let me tell you, Cassius, you yourself
  Are much condemned to have an itching palm,   10

42. **griefs**: grievances.
46. **enlarge**: expound upon.
 2. **noted**: publicly disgraced.
 4. **letters**: i.e., letter (always plural in Latin); **praying on**: defending.
 5. **slighted off**: dismissed; ignored.
 8. **nice**: small; **his**: its.
10. **to have**: for having.

 To sell and mart your offices for gold
 To underservers.
CASSIUS   I, an itching palm?
 You know that you are Brutus that speaks this,
 Or, by the gods, this speech were else your last.
BRUTUS   The name of Cassius honors this corruption,   15
 And chastisement doth therefore hide his head.
CASSIUS   Chastisement?
BRUTUS   Remember March, the Ides of March remember.
 Did not great Julius bleed for justice' sake?
 What villain touched his body, that did stab   20
 And not for justice? What, shall one of us,
 That struck the foremost man of all this world,
 But for supporting robbers, shall we now
 Contaminate our fingers with base bribes
 And sell the mighty space of our large honors   25
 For so much trash as may be grasped thus?
 I had rather be a dog and bay the moon
 Than such a Roman.
CASSIUS   Brutus, bait not me.
 I'll not endure it. You forget yourself
 To hedge me in. I am a soldier, I,   30
 Older in practice, abler than yourself
 To make conditions.
BRUTUS   Go to. You are not, Cassius.
CASSIUS   I am.
BRUTUS   I say you are not.
CASSIUS   Urge me no more. I shall forget myself.   35
 Have mind upon your health. Tempt me no farther.
BRUTUS   Away, slight man!
CASSIUS   Is't possible?
BRUTUS   Hear me, for I will speak.
 Must I give way and room to your rash choler?
 Shall I be frighted when a madman stares?   40
CASSIUS   O ye gods, ye gods, must I endure all this?
BRUTUS   All this? Ay, more. Fret till your proud heart break.
 Go show your slaves how choleric you are,
 And make your bondmen tremble. Must I budge?

---

11. **mart:** traffic in.
15. **honors:** makes honorable.
25. **honors:** reputations.
26. **trash:** i.e., money.
28. **bait:** attack (see 4.1.48–49).
30. **hedge me in:** i.e., limit me.
32. **make conditions:** manage affairs.
39. **choler:** anger.
44. **budge:** flinch.

Must I observe you? Must I stand and crouch   45
Under your testy humor? By the gods,
You shall digest the venom of your spleen
Though it do split you. For, from this day forth,
I'll use you for my mirth, yea, for my laughter,
When you are waspish.
CASSIUS   Is it come to this?   50
BRUTUS   You say you are a better soldier.
  Let it appear so. Make your vaunting true
  And it shall please me well. For mine own part
  I shall be glad to learn of noble men.
CASSIUS   You wrong me every way; you wrong me, Brutus.   55
  I said an elder soldier, not a better.
  Did I say "better"?
BRUTUS   If you did, I care not.
CASSIUS   When Caesar lived, he durst not thus have moved me.
BRUTUS   Peace, peace, you durst not so have tempted him.
CASSIUS   I durst not?   60
BRUTUS   No.
CASSIUS   What? Durst not tempt him?
BRUTUS   For your life, you durst
  not.
CASSIUS   Do not presume too much upon my love.
  I may do that I shall be sorry for.
BRUTUS   You have done that you should be sorry for.   65
  There is no terror, Cassius, in your threats,
  For I am armed so strong in honesty
  That they pass by me as the idle wind,
  Which I respect not. I did send to you
  For certain sums of gold, which you denied me.   70
  For I can raise no money by vile means.
  By heaven, I had rather coin my heart
  And drop my blood for drachmas than to wring
  From the hard hands of peasants their vile trash
  By any indirection. I did send   75
  To you for gold to pay my legions,
  Which you denied me. Was that done like Cassius?
  Should I have answered Caius Cassius so?
  When Marcus Brutus grows so covetous

45. **observe:** show respect for; **crouch:** cringe.
47. **spleen:** anger.
50. **waspish:** stinging, angry, irritated.
52. **vaunting:** boasting.
59. **tempted:** tested.
69. **respect:** regard.
75. **indirection:** devious methods.

To lock such rascal counters from his friends,   80
Be ready, gods, with all your thunderbolts,
Dash him to pieces!
CASSIUS   I denied you not.
BRUTUS   You did.
CASSIUS   I did not. He was but a fool that brought
My answer back. Brutus hath rived my heart.   85
A friend should bear his friend's infirmities,
But Brutus makes mine greater than they are.
BRUTUS   I do not, till you practice them on me.
CASSIUS   You love me not.
BRUTUS   I do not like your faults.
CASSIUS   A friendly eye could never see such faults.   90
BRUTUS   A flatterer's would not, though they do appear
As huge as high Olympus.
CASSIUS   Come, Antony, and young Octavius, come,
Revenge yourselves alone on Cassius,
For Cassius is a-weary of the world: 95
Hated by one he loves, braved by his brother,
Checked like a bondman; all his faults observed,
Set in a notebook, learned, and conned by rote,
To cast into my teeth. O, I could weep
My spirit from mine eyes! There is my dagger   100
And here my naked breast: within, a heart
Dearer than Pluto's mine, richer than gold.
If that thou beest a Roman take it forth.
I that denied thee gold will give my heart.
Strike as thou didst at Caesar. For I know   105
When thou didst hate him worst thou loved'st him better
Than ever thou loved'st Cassius.
BRUTUS   Sheathe your dagger.
Be angry when you will, it shall have scope;
Do what you will, dishonor shall be humour.
O Cassius, you are yokèd with a lamb   110
That carries anger as the flint bears fire,
Who, much enforcèd, shows a hasty spark
And straight is cold again.

---

   80. **rascal:** worthless; **counters:** tokens, i.e., debased, worthless coins.
   96. **braved:** defied.
   97. **Checked:** rebuked.
   98. **conned by rote:** memorized.
   102. **Dearer:** more valuable.
   108. **scope:** room (to vent).
   109. **dishonor . . . humor:** i.e., I will interpret your dishonorable behavior as a bad
        mood.
   112. **enforcèd:** struck upon.

CASSIUS   Hath Cassius lived
  To be but mirth and laughter to his Brutus
  When grief and blood ill-tempered vexeth him?   115
BRUTUS   When I spoke that, I was ill-tempered too.
CASSIUS   Do you confess so much? Give me your hand.
BRUTUS   And my heart too.
CASSIUS   O Brutus!
BRUTUS   What's the matter?
CASSIUS   Have you not love enough to bear with me
  When that rash humour which my mother gave me   120
  Makes me forgetful?
BRUTUS   Yes, Cassius, and from henceforth
  When you are over-earnest with your Brutus,
  He'll think your mother chides, and leave you so.
     Enter a POET, [LUCILIUS, *and* TITINIUS].
POET   Let me go in to see the generals.
  There is some grudge between 'em; 'tis not meet   125
  They be alone.
LUCILIUS   You shall not come to them.
POET   Nothing but death shall stay me.
CASSIUS   How now? What's the matter?
POET   For shame, you generals, what do you mean?
  Love and be friends, as two such men should be,   130
  For I have seen more years, I'm sure, than ye.
CASSIUS   Ha, ha, how vildly doth this cynic rhyme!
BRUTUS   Get you hence, sirrah; saucy fellow, hence!
CASSIUS   Bear with him, Brutus; 'tis his fashion.
BRUTUS   I'll know his humor when he knows his time.   135
  What should the wars do with these jigging fools?
  Companion, hence!
CASSIUS   Away, away, be gone!
                              Exit POET.
BRUTUS   Lucilius and Titinius, bid the commanders
  Prepare to lodge their companies tonight.
CASSIUS   And come yourselves, and bring Messala with you   140
  Immediately to us.
                [*Exeunt* LUCILIUS *and* TITINIUS.]
BRUTUS   [*To* LUCIUS *within.*] Lucius, a bowl of wine.
CASSIUS   I did not think you could have been so angry.

---

115. **ill-tempered:** poorly mixed.
120. **rash humour:** choler (thought to produce anger).
123. **leave you so:** leave you alone.
131. **ye:** you.
132. **vildly:** vilely; **cynic:** scoffer.
133. **sirrah:** form of address (contemptuous).
136. **jigging:** term applied to incompetent poets.

BRUTUS   O Cassius, I am sick of many griefs.
CASSIUS   Of your philosophy you make no use
    If you give place to accidental evils.   145
BRUTUS   No man bears sorrow better. Portia is dead.
CASSIUS   Ha? Portia?
BRUTUS   She is dead.
CASSIUS   How scaped I killing when I crossed you so?
    O insupportable and touching loss!   150
    Upon what sickness?
BRUTUS   Impatient of my absence,
    And grief that young Octavius with Mark Antony
    Have made themselves so strong—for with her death
    That tidings came. With this she fell distract
    And, her attendants absent, swallowed fire.   155
CASSIUS   And died so?
BRUTUS   Even so.
CASSIUS   O ye immortal gods!
    Enter BOY [LUCIUS] *with wine and tapers.*
BRUTUS   Speak no more of her. Give me a bowl of wine.
    In this I bury all unkindness, Cassius. *Drinks.*
CASSIUS   My heart is thirsty for that noble pledge.
    Fill, Lucius, till the wine o'erswell the cup,   160
    I cannot drink too much of Brutus' love. [*Drinks.*]
                                      [*Exit* LUCIUS.]
    Enter TITINIUS *and* MESSALA.
BRUTUS   Come in, Titinius; welcome, good Messala.
    Now we sit close about this taper here
    And call in question our necessities.
CASSIUS   Portia, art thou gone?
BRUTUS   No more, I pray you.   165
    Messala, I have here receivèd letters
    That young Octavius and Mark Antony
    Come down upon us with a mighty power,
    Bending their expedition toward Philippi.
MESSALA   Myself have letters of the selfsame tenor.   170
BRUTUS   With what addition?

---

143. **sick of:** i.e., sickened by.
145. **evils:** misfortunes.
149. **killing:** i.e., being killed.
151. **Impatient of:** unable to tolerate.
155. **fire:** burning embers, i.e., live coals.
160. **o'erswell:** overflow.
164. **call in question:** summon for examination.
169. **Bending their expedition:** moving quickly.

MESSALA   That by proscription and bills of outlawry
  Octavius, Antony, and Lepidus
  Have put to death an hundred senators.
BRUTUS   Therein our letters do not well agree.   175
  Mine speak of seventy senators that died
  By their proscriptions, Cicero being one.
CASSIUS   Cicero one?
MESSALA   Cicero is dead,
  And by that order of proscription.
  Had you your letters from your wife, my lord?   180
BRUTUS   No, Messala.
MESSALA   Nor nothing in your letters writ of her?
BRUTUS   Nothing, Messala.
MESSALA   That, methinks, is strange.
BRUTUS   Why ask you? Hear you aught of her in yours?
MESSALA   No, my lord.   185
BRUTUS   Now as you are a Roman, tell me true.
MESSALA   Then like a Roman bear the truth I tell,
  For certain she is dead, and by strange manner.
BRUTUS   Why, farewell, Portia. We must die, Messala.
  With meditating that she must die once,   190
  I have the patience to endure it now.
MESSALA   Even so, great men great losses should endure.
CASSIUS   I have as much of this in art as you,
  But yet my nature could not bear it so.
BRUTUS   Well, to our work alive. What do you think   195
  Of marching to Philippi presently?
CASSIUS   I do not think it good.
BRUTUS   Your reason?
CASSIUS   This it is:
  'Tis better that the enemy seek us,
  So shall he waste his means, weary his soldiers,
  Doing himself offence, whilst we, lying still,   200
  Are full of rest, defense, and nimbleness.
BRUTUS   Good reasons must of force give place to better:
  The people 'twixt Philippi and this ground
  Do stand but in a forced affection,
  For they have grudged us contribution.   205

---

172. **proscription ... outlawry:** legal measures declaring certain Roman citizens
    outlaws.
190. **once:** in any case.
193. **in art:** i.e., acquired through art (as opposed to Nature).
196. **presently:** immediately.
202. **of force:** perforce, of necessity.
205. **contribution:** monetary support.

The enemy, marching along by them,
By them shall make a fuller number up,
Come on refreshed, new added, and encouraged,
From which advantage shall we cut him off
If at Philippi we do face him there,   210
These people at our back.
CASSIUS   Hear me, good brother.
BRUTUS   Under your pardon. You must note beside
That we have tried the utmost of our friends,
Our legions are brimful, our cause is ripe.
The enemy increaseth every day;   215
We, at the height, are ready to decline.
There is a tide in the affairs of men
Which, taken at the flood, leads on to fortune;
Omitted, all the voyage of their life
Is bound in shallows and in miseries.   220
On such a full sea are we now afloat,
And we must take the current when it serves
Or lose our ventures.
CASSIUS   Then with your will go on.
We'll along ourselves and meet them at Philippi.
BRUTUS   The deep of night is crept upon our talk,   225
And nature must obey necessity,
Which we will niggard with a little rest.
There is no more to say?
CASSIUS   No more. Good night.
Early tomorrow will we rise and hence.
BRUTUS   Lucius!
        Enter LUCIUS.
                    My gown.

                                        [*Exit* LUCIUS.]
                    Farewell, good Messala.   230
Good night, Titinius. Noble, noble Cassius,
Good night and good repose.
CASSIUS   O my dear brother!
This was an ill beginning of the night.
Never came such division 'tween our souls!
Let it not, Brutus.
        Enter LUCIUS *with the gown.*
BRUTUS   Everything is well.   235

208. **new added:** reinforced.
219. **Omitted:** having passed.
223. **ventures:** merchandise (a mercantile term).
227. **niggard:** supplement (a bit).
229. **hence:** go hence.

CASSIUS   Good night, my lord.
BRUTUS   Good night, good brother.
TITINIUS and MESSALA
    Good night, Lord Brutus.
BRUTUS   Farewell, every one.
                              Exeunt [CASSIUS, TITINIUS, MESSALA].
    Give me the gown. Where is thy instrument?
LUCIUS   Here in the tent.
BRUTUS   What, thou speak'st drowsily.
    Poor knave, I blame thee not, thou art o'erwatched.   240
    Call Claudio and some other of my men,
    I'll have them sleep on cushions in my tent.
LUCIUS   Varrus and Claudio!
         Enter VARRUS *and* CLAUDIO.
VARRUS   Calls my lord?
BRUTUS   I pray you, sirs, lie in my tent and sleep,   245
    It may be I shall raise you by and by
    On business to my brother Cassius.
VARRUS   So please you, we will stand and watch your pleasure.
BRUTUS   I will not have it so. Lie down, good sirs,
    It may be I shall otherwise bethink me.   250
                              [VARRUS *and* CLAUDIO *lie down.*]
    Look, Lucius, here's the book I sought for so.
    I put it in the pocket of my gown.
LUCIUS   I was sure your lordship did not give it me.
BRUTUS   Bear with me, good boy, I am much forgetful.
    Canst thou hold up thy heavy eyes awhile   255
    And touch thy instrument a strain or two?
LUCIUS   Ay, my lord, an't please you.
BRUTUS   It does, my boy.
    I trouble thee too much, but thou art willing.
LUCIUS   It is my duty, sir.
BRUTUS   I should not urge thy duty past thy might;   260
    I know young bloods look for a time of rest.
LUCIUS   I have slept, my lord, already.
BRUTUS   It was well done and thou shalt sleep again,
    I will not hold thee long. If I do live,
    I will be good to thee.   265
         Music, and a song.

---

240. **knave:** boy (here, an affectionate term); **o'erwatched:** wearied from too much watching.
246. **raise you:** wake you up.
248. **stand:** i.e., stand watch; **watch:** wait upon, attend to.
256. **touch:** play upon.
257. **an't:** if it.
261. **young bloods:** young persons (figurative).

This is a sleepy tune. O murd'rous slumber,
Layest thou thy leaden mace upon my boy,
That plays thee music? Gentle knave, good night;
I will not do thee so much wrong to wake thee.
If thou dost nod thou break'st thy instrument.   270
I'll take it from thee and, good boy, good night.
Let me see, let me see; is not the leaf turned down
Where I left reading? Here it is, I think.
    Enter the GHOST *of Caesar.*
How ill this taper burns! Ha, who comes here?
I think it is the weakness of mine eyes   275
That shapes this monstrous apparition.
It comes upon me. Art thou any thing?
Art thou some god, some angel, or some devil,
That mak'st my blood cold and my hair to stare?
Speak to me what thou art.   280
GHOST   Thy evil spirit, Brutus.
BRUTUS   Why com'st thou?
GHOST   To tell thee thou shalt see me at Philippi.
BRUTUS   Well, then I shall see thee again?
GHOST   Ay, at Philippi.
BRUTUS   Why, I will see thee at Philippi then.   285
                             [*Exit* GHOST.]
Now I have taken heart thou vanishest.
Ill spirit, I would hold more talk with thee.
Boy, Lucius! Varrus! Claudio! Sirs, awake!
Claudio!
LUCIUS   The strings, my lord, are false.   290
BRUTUS   He thinks he still is at his instrument.
  Lucius, awake!
LUCIUS   My lord?
BRUTUS   Didst thou dream, Lucius, that thou so cried'st out?
LUCIUS   My lord, I do not know that I did cry.   295
BRUTUS   Yes, that thou didst. Didst thou see anything?
LUCIUS   Nothing, my lord.
BRUTUS   Sleep again, Lucius. Sirrah Claudio!
  [*To* VARRUS] Fellow, thou, awake!
VARRUS   My lord?   300
CLAUDIO   My lord?
BRUTUS   Why did you so cry out, sirs, in your sleep?

---

267. **leaden mace:** poetic locution. (The bailiff [slumber] arrests Brutus by touching his
    shoulder with his staff of office.)
272. **leaf:** page.
279. **stare:** stand on end.
290. **false:** out of tune.

BOTH   Did we, my lord?

BRUTUS   Ay. Saw you anything?

VARRUS   No, my lord, I saw nothing.

CLAUDIO   Nor I, my lord.

BRUTUS   Go and commend me to my brother Cassius.   305
  Bid him set on his powers betimes before,
  And we will follow.

BOTH   It shall be done, my lord.

                                        Exeunt.

[Act 5. Scene 1. *Philippi. A Battlefield.*]

Enter OCTAVIUS, ANTONY, *and their army.*

OCTAVIUS   Now, Antony, our hopes are answered.
  You said the enemy would not come down
  But keep the hills and upper regions.
  It proves not so: their battles are at hand,
  They mean to warn us at Philippi here,   5
  Answering before we do demand of them.

ANTONY   Tut, I am in their bosoms, and I know
  Wherefore they do it. They could be content
  To visit other places and come down
  With fearful bravery, thinking by this face   10
  To fasten in our thoughts that they have courage.
  But 'tis not so.

        Enter a MESSENGER.

MESSENGER   Prepare you, generals,
  The enemy comes on in gallant show,
  Their bloody sign of battle is hung out,
  And something to be done immediately.   15

ANTONY   Octavius, lead your battle softly on
  Upon the left hand of the even field.

OCTAVIUS   Upon the right hand I; keep thou the left.

ANTONY   Why do you cross me in this exigent?

OCTAVIUS   I do not cross you, but I will do so.   20
        March.

---

306. **set . . . before:** set off with his army before I do.
  4. **battles:** military forces.
  5. **warn us:** resist.
  9. **come down:** attack.
  10. **fearful:** causing fear; **face:** appearance.
  14. **bloody sign:** red banner.
  16. **softly:** slowly.
  19. **exigent:** critical time.

     Drum. Enter BRUTUS, CASSIUS, *and their army;* [LUCILIUS,
     TITINIUS, MESSALA, *and others*].

BRUTUS   They stand and would have parley.

CASSIUS   Stand fast, Titinius. We must out and talk.

OCTAVIUS   Mark Antony, shall we give sign of battle?

ANTONY   No, Caesar, we will answer on their charge.
   Make forth, the generals would have some words.   25

OCTAVIUS   Stir not until the signal.

BRUTUS   Words before blows; is it so, countrymen?

OCTAVIUS   Not that we love words better, as you do.

BRUTUS   Good words are better than bad strokes, Octavius.

ANTONY   In your bad strokes, Brutus, you give good words.   30
   Witness the hole you made in Caesar's heart,
   Crying, "Long live! Hail, Caesar!"

CASSIUS   Antony,
   The posture of your blows are yet unknown;
   But for your words, they rob the Hybla bees
   And leave them honeyless.

ANTONY   Not stingless too?   35

BRUTUS   O yes, and soundless too,
   For you have stol'n their buzzing, Antony,
   And very wisely threat before you sting.

ANTONY   Villains! You did not so when your vile daggers
   Hacked one another in the sides of Caesar.   40
   You showed your teeth like apes and fawned like hounds,
   And bowed like bondmen, kissing Caesar's feet,
   Whilst damnèd Casca, like a cur, behind
   Struck Caesar on the neck. O you flatterers!

CASSIUS   Flatterers? Now, Brutus, thank yourself.   45
   This tongue had not offended so today
   If Cassius might have ruled.

OCTAVIUS   Come, come, the cause. If arguing make us sweat,
   The proof of it will turn to redder drops.
   Look, I draw a sword against conspirators.   50
   When think you that the sword goes up again?
   Never, till Caesar's three and thirty wounds
   Be well avenged, or till another Caesar
   Have added slaughter to the sword of traitors.

BRUTUS   Caesar, thou canst not die by traitors' hands   55
   Unless thou bring'st them with thee.

---

21. **parley:** conversation.
25. **Make forth:** go forward.
33. **posture:** site, position.
34. **Hybla:** Sicilian town known for the production of honey.
41. **showed your teeth:** smiled (insincerely).
49. **proof:** testing (in battle).

OCTAVIUS   So I hope.
  I was not born to die on Brutus' sword.
BRUTUS   O, if thou wert the noblest of thy strain,
  Young man, thou couldst not die more honorable.
CASSIUS   A peevish schoolboy, worthless of such honor,   60
  Joined with a masker and a reveler!
ANTONY   Old Cassius still!
OCTAVIUS   Come, Antony, away!
  Defiance, traitors, hurl we in your teeth.
  If you dare fight today, come to the field;
  If not, when you have stomachs.   65
               Exeunt OCTAVIUS, ANTONY, *and army*[.]
CASSIUS   Why now blow wind, swell billow, and swim bark!
  The storm is up, and all is on the hazard.
BRUTUS   Ho, Lucilius, hark, a word with you.
     LUCILIUS *and* MESSALA *stand forth.*
LUCILIUS   My lord.
    [BRUTUS *speaks apart to* LUCILIUS.]
CASSIUS   Messala!
MESSALA   What says my general?
CASSIUS   Messala,
  This is my birthday, as this very day   70
  Was Cassius born. Give my thy hand, Messala.
  Be thou my witness that against my will
  (As Pompey was) am I compelled to set
  Upon one battle all our liberties.
  You know that I held Epicurus strong   75
  And his opinion. Now I change my mind
  And partly credit things that do presage.
  Coming from Sardis, on our former ensign
  Two mighty eagles fell, and there they perched,
  Gorging and feeding from our soldiers' hands,   80
  Who to Philippi here consorted us.
  This morning are they fled away and gone,
  And in their steads do ravens, crows, and kites

---

58. **strain:** lineage.
60. **peevish:** silly.
61. **masker and reveler:** i.e., those who engage in entertainments (masques).
65. **stomachs:** inclination.
66. **billow:** a great wave; **bark:** ship.
67. **hazard:** at risk.
70. **as:** on.
75. **Epicurus:** Greek philosopher (341–270 B.C.E.) who was suspicious of the supernatural.
78. **ensign:** standard, banner.
79. **fell:** descended.
81. **consorted:** accompanied.

Fly o'er our heads and downward look on us
As we were sickly prey. Their shadows seem   85
A canopy most fatal, under which
Our army lies, ready to give up the ghost.
MESSALA　Believe not so.
CASSIUS　　　　　　　　　I but believe it partly,
For I am fresh of spirit and resolved
To meet all perils very constantly.   90
BRUTUS [*advancing*]　Even so, Lucilius.
CASSIUS　　　　　　　　　　　　Now, most noble Brutus,
The gods today stand friendly that we may,
Lovers in peace, lead on our days to age!
But since the affairs of men rests still incertain,
Let's reason with the worst that may befall.   95
If we do lose this battle, then is this
The very last time we shall speak together.
What are you then determined to do?
BRUTUS　Even by the rule of that philosophy
By which I did blame Cato for the death   100
Which he did give himself—I know not how,
But I do find it cowardly and vile,
For fear of what might fall, so to prevent
The time of life—arming myself with patience
To stay the providence of some high powers   105
That govern us below.
CASSIUS　　　　　　　　Then if we lose this battle,
You are contented to be led in triumph
Thorough the streets of Rome?
BRUTUS　No, Cassius, no. Think not, thou noble Roman,
That ever Brutus will go bound to Rome.   110
He bears too great a mind. But this same day
Must end that work the Ides of March begun.
And whether we shall meet again I know not.
Therefore our everlasting farewell take:
For ever and for ever, farewell, Cassius!   115
If we do meet again, why, we shall smile.

---

86. **fatal:** ominous, indicative of misfortune.
90. **constantly:** resolutely.
93. **Lovers:** devoted friends.
95. **reason with:** consider.
100. **Cato:** see note at 2.1.295
103. **fall:** befall; **prevent:** forestall.
104. **time:** natural limit.
105. **stay:** wait for.
107. **triumph:** triumphal procession.

If not, why then this parting was well made.
CASSIUS   For ever and for ever, farewell, Brutus!
   If we do meet again, we'll smile indeed;
   If not, 'tis true this parting was well made.   120
BRUTUS   Why then, lead on. O, that a man might know
   The end of this day's business ere it come!
   But it sufficeth that the day will end,
   And then the end is known. Come ho, away!

                                                      Exeunt.

[Act 5. Scene 2. *Philippi. A Battlefield.*]

   Alarum. Enter BRUTUS *and* MESSALA.
BRUTUS   Ride, ride, Messala, ride, and give these bills
   Unto the legions on the other side.
       Loud alarum.
   Let them set on at once, for I perceive
   But cold demeanor in Octavius's wing,
   And sudden push gives them the overthrow.   5
   Ride, ride, Messala. Let them all come down.

                                                      Exeunt.

[Act 5. Scene 3. *Philippi. Another Part of the Battlefield.*]

   Alarums. Enter CASSIUS *and* TITINIUS.
CASSIUS   O, look, Titinius, look, the villains fly!
   Myself have to mine own turned enemy.
   This ensign here of mine was turning back;
   I slew the coward and did take it from him.
TITINIUS   O Cassius, Brutus gave the word too early,   5
   Who, having some advantage on Octavius,
   Took it too eagerly. His soldiers fell to spoil
   Whilst we by Antony are all enclosed.
       Enter PINDARUS.
PINDARUS   Fly further off, my lord, fly further off!
   Mark Antony is in your tents, my lord.   10

---

1. **SD.** *Alarum:* a call to arms, battle cry; **bills:** written orders.
4. **cold demeanor:** lack of spirit.
3. **ensign:** standard bearer.
7. **fell to spoil:** started looting.

Fly therefore, noble Cassius, fly far off.
CASSIUS   This hill is far enough. Look, look, Titinius,
   Are those my tents where I perceive the fire?
TITINIUS   They are, my lord.
CASSIUS   Titinius, if thou lovest me,
   Mount thou my horse and hide thy spurs in him   15
   Till he have brought thee up to yonder troops
   And here again that I may rest assured
   Whether yond troops are friend or enemy.
TITINIUS   I will be here again, even with a thought.

                                                    Exit.

CASSIUS   Go, Pindarus, get higher on that hill.   20
   My sight was ever thick. Regard, Titinius,
   And tell me what thou not'st about the field.
      [PINDARUS *goes up.*]
   This day I breathèd first. Time is come round
   And where I did begin there shall I end.
   My life is run his compass. Sirrah, what news?   25
PINDARUS   [*Above*] O my lord!
CASSIUS   What news?
PINDARUS   Titinius is enclosed round about
   With horsemen that make to him on the spur,
   Yet he spurs on. Now they are almost on him.   30
   Now Titinius—Now some light; O, he lights too.
   He's ta'en.
      [*Shout.*]
                     And hark, they shout for joy.
CASSIUS   Come down, behold no more.
   O, coward that I am to live so long
   To see my best friend ta'en before my face.   35
      Enter PINDARUS [*below*].
   Come hither, sirrah.
   In Parthia did I take thee prisoner,
   And then I swore thee, saving of thy life,
   That whatsoever I did bid thee do
   Thou shouldst attempt it. Come now, keep thine oath.   40
   Now be a freeman, and with this good sword,
   That ran through Caesar's bowels, search this bosom.

---

19. **even with a thought:** as quickly as thought (travels), i.e., instantly.
21. **thick:** weak, bad.
25. **compass:** circuit, limit.
29. **on the spur:** at a gallop, rapidly.
31. **light:** alight.
37. **Parthia:** modern Iran.
42. **search:** penetrate.

Stand not to answer; here, take thou the hilts,
And when my face is covered, as 'tis now,
Guide thou the sword.
    [PINDARUS *stabs him.*]
                         Caesar, thou art revenged   45
Even with the sword that killed thee.
                                        [*Dies.*]

PINDARUS   So I am free, yet would not so have been
Durst I have done my will. O Cassius!
Far from this country Pindarus shall run,
Where never Roman shall take note of him.   50
                                        [*Exit.*]

    Enter TITINIUS *and* MESSALA.
MESSALA   It is but change, Titinius; for Octavius
Is overthrown by noble Brutus' power,
As Cassius' legions are by Antony.
TITINIUS   These tidings will well comfort Cassius.
MESSALA   Where did you leave him?
TITINIUS   All disconsolate,   55
With Pindarus his bondman, on this hill.
MESSALA   Is not that he that lies upon the ground?
TITINIUS   He lies not like the living. O my heart!
MESSALA   Is not that he?
TITINIUS   No, this was he, Messala;
But Cassius is no more. O setting sun,   60
As in thy red rays thou dost sink tonight,
So in his red blood Cassius' day is set.
The sun of Rome is set. Our day is gone;
Clouds, dews, and dangers come. Our deeds are done.
Mistrust of my success hath done this deed.   65
MESSALA   Mistrust of good success hath done this deed.
O hateful Error, Melancholy's child,
Why dost thou show to the apt thoughts of men
The things that are not? O Error, soon conceived,
Thou never com'st unto a happy birth   70
But kill'st the mother that engendered thee.
TITINIUS   What, Pindarus! Where art thou, Pindarus?
MESSALA   Seek him, Titinius, whilst I go to meet

---

43. **hilts:** i.e., handle of the sword.
48. **Durst:** dared.
51. **change:** an even exchange.
65. **Mistrust my success:** doubting the result of my mission.
66. **Mistrust of good success:** fearing the general outcome.
68. **apt:** impressionable.
71. **mother:** i.e., the melancholy person.

The noble Brutus, thrusting this report
Into his ears. I may say "thrusting" it,   75
For piercing steel and darts envenomed
Shall be as welcome to the ears of Brutus
As tidings of this sight.
TITINIUS   Hie you, Messala,
And I will seek for Pindarus the while.

                                    [*Exit* MESSALA.]

Why didst thou send me forth, brave Cassius?   80
Did I not meet thy friends? And did not they
Put on my brows this wreath of victory
And bid me give it thee? Didst thou not hear their shouts?
Alas, thou hast misconstrued everything.
But hold thee, take this garland on thy brow;   85
Thy Brutus bid me give it thee, and I
Will do his bidding. Brutus, come apace,
And see how I regarded Caius Cassius.
By your leave, gods!—This is a Roman's part.
Come, Cassius' sword, and find Titinius' heart.   90
        [*Stabs himself and*] *dies*[.]
        Alarum. Enter BRUTUS, MESSALA, YOUNG CATO, STRATO,
        VOLUMNIUS, *and* LUCILIUS [, LABEO, *and* FLAVIUS].
BRUTUS   Where, where, Messala, doth his body lie?
MESSALA   Lo yonder, and Titinius mourning it.
BRUTUS   Titinius' face is upward.
CATO   He is slain.
BRUTUS   O Julius Caesar, thou art mighty yet,
Thy spirit walks abroad and turns our swords   95
In our own proper entrails.
        Low alarums.
CATO   Brave Titinius!
Look whe'er he have not crowned dead Cassius.
BRUTUS   Are yet two Romans living such as these?
The last of all the Romans, fare thee well!
It is impossible that ever Rome   100
Should breed thy fellow. Friends, I owe more tears
To this dead man than you shall see me pay.
I shall find time, Cassius; I shall find time.
Come therefore and to Thasos send his body;

---

76. **darts:** spears.
87. **apace:** quickly.
88. **regarded:** esteemed.
96. **own proper:** our very own; SD. **low:** soft.
97. **whe'er:** whether.
104. **Thasos:** an island in the Aegean, near Philippi.

His funerals shall not be in our camp   105
Lest it discomfort us. Lucilius, come,
And come, young Cato, let us to the field.
Labeo and Flavio, set our battles on.
'Tis three o'clock, and, Romans, yet ere night,
We shall try fortune in a second fight.   110
                              Exeunt [*bearing out the bodies*].

[Act 5. Scene 4. *Philippi. Another Part of the Battlefield.*]

    Alarum. Enter BRUTUS, MESSALA, [*Young*] CATO, LUCILIUS, *and*
    FLAVIUS [, LABEO].

BRUTUS   Yet, countrymen, O yet hold up your heads!
            [*Exit with* MESSALA, FLAVIUS, *and* LABEO.]
CATO   What bastard doth not? Who will go with me?
  I will proclaim my name about the field.
  I am the son of Marcus Cato, ho!
  A foe to tyrants, and my country's friend.   5
  I am the son of Marcus Cato, ho!
     Enter SOLDIERS *and fight.*
LUCILIUS   And I am Brutus, Marcus Brutus, I!
  Brutus, my country's friend. Know me for Brutus!
     [*Young* CATO *is slain.*]
  O young and noble Cato, art thou down?
  Why, now thou diest as bravely as Titinius   10
  And mayst be honored, being Cato's son.
1 SOLDIER   Yield, or thou diest.
LUCILIUS   Only I yield to die.
  There is so much that thou wilt kill me straight.
  Kill Brutus and be honored in his death.
1 SOLDIER   We must not. A noble prisoner!   15
     Enter ANTONY.
2 SOLDIER   Room ho! Tell Antony, Brutus is ta'en.
1 SOLDIER   I'll tell the news. Here comes the general.
  Brutus is ta'en, Brutus is ta'en, my lord!
ANTONY   Where is he?
LUCILIUS   Safe, Antony; Brutus is safe enough.   20

---

105. **funerals:** i.e., funeral service, sometimes used in the plural form.
106. **discomfort:** dishearten.
108. **battles:** troops in battle gear.
  2. **bastard:** illegitimate (therefore untrue person).
12. **Only I yield:** i.e., I yield only.
13. **straight:** immediately.

I dare assure thee that no enemy
Shall ever take alive the noble Brutus.
The gods defend him from so great a shame!
When you do find him, or alive or dead,
He will be found like Brutus, like himself.   25
ANTONY   This is not Brutus, friend, but, I assure you,
A prize no less in worth. Keep this man safe,
Give him all kindness. I had rather have
Such men my friends than enemies. Go on,
And see whe'er Brutus be alive or dead,   30
And bring us word unto Octavius' tent
How everything is chanced.
                    Exeunt [*in two groups, through different doors*].

[Act 5. Scene 5. *Philippi. Another Part of the Battlefield.*]

Enter BRUTUS, DARDANIUS, CLITUS, STRATO, *and* VOLUMNIUS.
BRUTUS   Come, poor remains of friends, rest on this rock.
       [STRATO *falls asleep.*]
CLITUS   Statilius showed the torchlight but, my lord,
   He came not back. He is or ta'en or slain.
BRUTUS   Sit thee down, Clitus. Slaying is the word,
   It is a deed in fashion. Hark thee, Clitus. [*Whispers.*]   5
CLITUS   What, I, my lord? No, not for all the world.
BRUTUS   Peace then, no words.
CLITUS   I'll rather kill myself.
BRUTUS   Hark thee, Dardanius. [*Whispers.*]
DARDANUS   Shall I do such a deed?
CLITUS   O Dardanus!
DARDANUS   O Clitus!   10
CLITUS   What ill request did Brutus make to thee?
DARDANUS   To kill him, Clitus. Look, he meditates.
CLITUS   Now is that noble vessel full of grief,
   That it runs over even at his eyes.
BRUTUS   Come hither, good Volumnius. List a word.   15
VOLUMNIUS   What says my lord?

24. or . . . or: either . . . or.
25. like himself: true to his character.
32. is chanced: unfolds.
 2. showed the torchlight: signaled.
 3. or . . . or: either . . . or.
15. List: listen to.

BRUTUS   Why, this, Volumnius:
  The ghost of Caesar hath appeared to me
  Two several times by night, at Sardis once
  And this last night here in Philippi fields.
  I know my hour is come.
VOLUMNIUS   Not so, my lord.   20
BRUTUS   Nay, I am sure it is, Volumnius.
  Thou seest the world, Volumnius, how it goes.
  Our enemies have beat us to the pit.
      Low alarums.
  It is more worthy to leap in ourselves
  Than tarry till they push us. Good Volumnius,   25
  Thou know'st that we two went to school together;
  Even for that our love of old, I prithee
  Hold thou my sword-hilts whilst I run on it.
VOLUMNIUS   That's not an office for a friend, my lord.
      Alarum still.
CLITUS   Fly, fly, my lord! There is no tarrying here.   30
BRUTUS   Farewell to you; and you; and you, Volumnius.
  Strato, thou hast been all this while asleep.
      [STRATO *awakes.*]
  Farewell to thee too, Strato. Countrymen,
  My heart doth joy that yet in all my life
  I found no man but he was true to me.   35
  I shall have glory by this losing day
  More than Octavius and Mark Antony
  By this vile conquest shall attain unto.
  So fare you well at once, for Brutus' tongue
  Hath almost ended his life's history.   40
  Night hangs upon mine eyes; my bones would rest,
  That have but labored to attain this hour.
      Alarum. Cry within, "Fly, fly, fly[!]"
CLITUS   Fly, my lord, fly!
BRUTUS   Hence! I will follow.
      [*Exeunt* CLITUS, DARDANIUS, *and* VOLUMNIUS.]
  I prithee, Strato, stay thou by thy lord.
  Thou art a fellow of a good respect,   45
  Thy life hath had some smatch of honor in it.
  Hold then my sword and turn away thy face,

18. **several:** separate.
23. **beat . . . pit:** i.e., driven us into a hole (like animals).
28. **hilts:** handle.
45. **respect:** reputation.
46. **smatch:** flavor, taste.

While I do run upon it. Wilt thou, Strato?

STRATO   Give me your hand first. Fare you well, my lord.

BRUTUS   Farewell, good Strato.
    [*Runs on his sword.*]
                          Caesar, now be still,   50
I killed not thee with half so good a will.

                                                  Dies.

    Alarum. Retreat. Enter ANTONY, OCTAVIUS, MESSALA, LUCILIUS,
    and the army.

OCTAVIUS   What man is that?

MESSALA   My master's man. Strato, where is thy master?

STRATO   Free from the bondage you are in, Messala.
The conquerors can but make a fire of him,   55
For Brutus only overcame himself,
And no man else hath honor by his death.

LUCILIUS   So Brutus should be found. I thank thee, Brutus,
That thou hast proved Lucilius' saying true.

OCTAVIUS   All that served Brutus I will entertain them.   60
Fellow, wilt thou bestow thy time with me?

STRATO   Ay, if Messala will prefer me to you.

OCTAVIUS   Do so, good Messala.

MESSALA   How died my master, Strato?

STRATO   I held the sword and he did run on it.   65

MESSALA   Octavius, then take him to follow thee,
That did the latest service to my master.

ANTONY   This was the noblest Roman of them all.
All the conspirators, save only he,
Did that they did in envy of great Caesar.   70
He only, in a general honest thought
And common good to all, made one of them.
His life was gentle, and the elements
So mixed in him that Nature might stand up
And say to all the world, "This was a man!"   75

OCTAVIUS   According to his virtue let us use him,

---

51. SD. *Retreat*: trumpet call to cease pursuing the enemy.
55. **make . . . him**: burn him (on a funeral pyre).
56. **only**: alone.
60. **entertain them**: take them into service.
61. **bestow**: spend.
62. **prefer**: recommend.
66. **follow**: serve.
67. **latest**: last.
70. **that**: what.
71. **in . . . thought**: moved by virtuous principles.
72. **common good to all**: out of concern for the common good.
73. **gentle**: noble; **elements**: the four humours (bodily fluids) that were thought to determine and affect temperament.
76. **use**: i.e., honor.

With all respect and rites of burial.
Within my tent his bones tonight shall lie,
Most like a soldier, ordered honorably.
So call the field to rest, and let's away   80
To part the glories of this happy day.

Exeunt omnes.

79. **ordered:** treated.
80. **field:** army.
81. **part:** share.

SOURCES AND CONTEXTS

Sources

PLUTARCH

From The Life of Julius Caesar[†]

Pompey and Crassus, two of the greatest personages of the city of
Rome, being at jarre together, Caesar made them frends, and by that
meanes got unto him selfe the power of them both: for, by colour of
that gentle acte and frendshippe of his, he subtilly (unwares to them
all) did greatly alter and change the state of the common wealth. For
it was not the private discord between Pompey and Caesar, as many
men thought, that caused the civill warre: but rather it was their
agreement together, who joined all their powers first to overthrowe
the state of the Senate and nobilitie, and afterwards they fell at
jarre one with an other. * * * But the time of the great armies and
conquests he made afterwards, and of the warre in the which he
subdued al the Gaules: (entering into an other course of life farre
contrarie unto the first) made him to be knowen for as valliant a
souldier and as excellent a Captaine to lead men, as those that afore
him had bene counted the wisest and most valliantest Generalles
that ever were, and that by their valliant deedes had atchieved great
honor. For whosoever would compare the house of the Fabians, of
the Scipioes, of the Metellians, yea those also of his owne time, or
long before him, as Sylla, Marius, the two Lucullians, and Pompey
selfe,

> Whose fame ascendeth up unto the heavens:

it will appeare that Caesars prowes and deedes of armes, did excel
them all together. The one, in the hard contries where he made
warres: an other, in enlarging the realms and contries which he
joined unto the Empire of Rome: an other, in the multitude and
power of his enemies whome he overcame: an other, in the rudenesse

† From *Plutarch's Lives of the Noble Grecians and Romanes*, trans. Sir Thomas North
(London, 1579). Marginal section headings have been removed. Page numbers to this
source appear in square brackets. Except in rare cases, "æ" has been set as "ae."

and austere nature of men with whom he had to doe, whose maners afterwards he softned and made civill: an other, in curtesie and clemencie which he used unto them whome he had conquered: an other in great bountie and liberality bestowed upon them that served under him in those warres: and in fine, he excelled them all in the number of battells he had fought, and in the multitude of his enemies he had slaine in battell. For in lesse then tenne yeares warre in Gaule he tooke by force and assault above eight hundred townes; he conquered three hundred severall nations: and having before him in battell thirty hundred thowsand souldiers, at sundrie times he slue tenne hundred thowsand of them, and tooke as many more prisoners. Furthermore, he was so entirely beloved of his souldiers, that to doe him service (where otherwise they were no more then other men in any private quarrel) if Caesars honor were touched, they were invincible, and would so desperately venter them selves, and with such furie, that no man was able to abide them . . . Nowe Caesars selfe did breede this noble corage and life in them. First, for that he gave them bountifully, and did honor them also, shewing thereby, that he did not heape up riches in the warres to maintaine his life afterwards in wantonnesse and pleasure, but that he did keepe it in store, honorably to reward their valliant service: and that by so much he thought him selfe riche, by howe much he was liberall in rewarding of them that had deserved it. Furthermore, they did not wonder so much as his valliantnesse in putting him selfe at every instant in such manifest daunger, and in taking so extreame paines as he did, knowing that it was his greedie desire of honor that set him a fire, and pricked him forward to doe it: but that he always continued all labour and hardnesse, more then his bodie could beare, that filled them all with admiration. For, concerning the constitucion of his bodie, he was leane, white, and soft skinned, and often subject to headache, and otherwhile to the falling sickenes[1]: (the which tooke him the first time, as it is reported, in Corduba, a citie of Spayne)[2] but yet therefore yielded not to the disease of his bodie,[3] to make it a cloke to cherishe him withal, but contrarily, tooke the paines of warre, as a medicine to cure his sicke bodie fighting always with his disease, traveling continually, living soberly, and commonly lying abroade in the field. For the most nights he slept in his coch or litter, and thereby bestowed his rest, to make him always able to do some thing: and in the day time, he would travel up and downe the contrie to see townes, castels, and strong places. He had always a secretarie with him in his coche, who did still wryte as he

1. See 1.2.251.
2. See 1.2.119.
3. See Cassius' slander, 1.2.119–31.

went by the way, and a souldier behinde him that carried his sword. He made such speede the first time he came from Rome, when he had his office: that in eight dayes, he came to the river of Rhone. He was so excellent a rider of horse from his youth, that holding his handes behinde him, he would galloppe his horse upon the spurre. In his warres in Gaule, he did further exercise him selfe to indite letters as he rode by the way, and did occupie two secretaries at once with as much as they could wryte: and as Oppius wryteth, more then two at a time. And it is reported, that Caesar was the first that devised frendes might talke together by writing ciphers in letters, when he had no leasure to speake with them for his urgent business, and for the great distaunce besides from Rome. How little accompt Caesar made of his dyet, this example doth prove it. Caesar supping one night in Milane with his frende Valerius Leo, there was served sparrage to his bourde, and oyle of perfume put into it in stead of Sallet oyle. He simplie eate it, and found no fault, blaming his frendes that were offended: and told them, that it had bene enough for them to have absteyned to eate of that they misliked, and not to shame their frend, and how that he lacked good manner that found fault with his frend. An other time as he traveled through the con-trie, he was driven by fowle weather on the sodaine to take a poore mans cottage, that had but one little cabin it, and that was so nar-rowe, that one man could but scarce lye in it. Then he sayd to his frendes that were about him: Greatest roomes are meetest for great-est men, and the most necessarie roomes, for the sickest persons. And thereupon he caused Oppius that was sicke to lye there all night: and he him selfe, with the rest of his frendes, lay with out dores, under the easing of the house [pp. 769–71].

* * *

Nowe Caesar had of long time determined to destroy Pompey, and Pompey him also. For Crassus being killed amongst the Parthians, who onely did see, that one of them two must needes fall: nothing kept Caesar from being the greatest person, but because he destroyed not Pompey, that was the greater: neither did any thing let Pompey to withstand that it should not come to passe, but because he did not first overcome Caesar, whom onely he feared. For till then, Pompey had not long feared him, but always before set light by him, thinking it an easie matter for him to put him downe when he would, sithe he had brought him to that greatnes he was come unto. But Caesar contrarily, having had that drift in his head from the beginning, like a wrestler that studieth for trickes to overthrowe his adversary: he went farre from Rome, to exercise him selfe in the warres of Gaule, where he did trayne his armie, and presently by his valiant deedes did increase his fame and honor. By these meanes became Caesar as famous as Pompey in his doings, and lacked no more to put his enterprise in execution, but some occasions of culler, which Pompey partly gave him, and partly also the tyme delivered him, but chiefly, the hard fortune and ill government of that tyme of the common wealth at Rome. For they that made sute for honor and offices, bought the voices of the people with ready money, which they gave out openly to usury, without shame or feare. Thereupon, the common people that had sold their voices for money, came to the market place at the day of election, to fight for him that had hyered them: not with their voices, but with their bowes, slings, and swords. So that the assembly seldom tyme brake up, but that the pulpit for orations was defiled and sprinckled with the bloode of them that were slayne in the market place, the citie remaining all that tyme without government of Magistrate, like a shippe left without a Pilote. Insomuch, as men of deepe judgement and discression seing such furie and madness of the people, thought them selves happy if the common wealth were no worse troubled, then with the absolute state of a Monarchy and soveraine Lord to governe them. Furthermore, there were many that were not afraid to speake it openly, that there was no other help to remedy the troubles of the common wealth, but by the authority of one man only, that should command them all: and that this medicine must be ministred by the hands of him, that was the gentlest Phisition, meaning covertly Pompey. Now Pompey used many fine speeches, making semblance as though he would none of it, and yet cunningly under hand did lay all the yrons in the fire he could, to bring it to passe, that he might be chosen Dictator [pp. 776–77].

*   *   *

Now Caesar having assembled a great and dreadfull power together, went straight where he thought to finde Pompey him selfe. But Pompey tarried not his coming, but fled into the citie of Brundusium, from whence he had sent the two Consuls before with that armie he had, unto Dyrrachium: and he him selfe also went thither afterwards, when he understoode that Caesar was come, as you shall heare more amply hereafter in his life. Caesar lacked no good will to follow him, but wanting shippes to take the seas, he returned forthwith to Rome: So that in lesse then three skore dayes, he was Lord of all Italy, without any blood shed. Who when he was come to Rome, and found it much quieter then he looked for, and many Senatours there also: he courteously intreated them, and prayed them to send unto Pompey, to pacifie all matters betweene them, apon reasonable conditions. But no man did attempt it, eyther because they feared Pompey for that they had forsaken him, or els for that they thought Caesar ment not as he spake, but that they

were wordes of course, to culler his purpose withal. And when
Metellus also, one of the Tribunes, would not suffer him to take any
of the common treasure out of the temple of Saturne, but tolde him
that it was against the lawe: Tushe, sayd he, tyme of warre and lawe
are two thinges. If this that I doe, quoth he, doe offende thee, then
get thee hence for ths tyme: for warre can not abyde this francke and
bolde speeche. But when warres are done, and that we are all quiet
agayne, then thou shalt speake in the pulpit what thou wilt: and yet
I doe tell thee this of favor, impairing so much my right, for thou
art myne, both thou, and all them that have risen against me, and
whom I have in my hands. When he had spoken thus unto Metellus,
he went to the temple dore where the treasure laye: and finding no
keyes there, he caused Smythes to be sent for, and made them breake
open the lockes. Metellus thereupon beganne agayne to withstande
him, and certen men that stoode by praysed him in his doing: but
Caesar at length speaking biggely to him, threatned him he would
kill him presently, if he troubled him any more: and told him furthermore, Younge man, quoth he, thow knowest it is harder for me
to tell it thee, than to doe it. That word made Metellus quake for
feare, that he gotte him away rowndly: and ever after that, Caesar
had all at his commaundement for the warres. From thence he went
into Spayne, to make warre with Petreius and Varro, Pompeys
Lieuetenants: first to gette their armies and provinces into his hands
which they governed, that afterwards he might follow Pompey the
better, leaving never an enemie behinde him. In this jorney he was
oftentimes him selfe in daunger, through the ambushes that were
layde for him in divers straunge sortes and places, and likely also to
have lost all his armie for lacke of vittells. All this notwithstanding,
he never left following of Pompeys Lieuetenants, provoking them to
battell, and intrenching them in: until he had gotten their campe
and armies into his handes, albeit that the Lieuetenants them selves
fled unto Pompey. [pp. 780–81] * * * Then Pompey seeing his
horsemen from the other winge of his battell, so scattered and dis-
persed, flying away: forgate that he was any more Pompey the great
which he had bene before, but rather was like a man whose wittes
the goddess had taken from him, being affrayde and amazed with
the slaughter sent from above, and so retired into his tent speaking
never a worde, and sate there to see the ende of this battell. Untill at
length all his army being overthrowen, and put to flight, the enemies came, and gotte up upon the rampers and defence of his
campe, and fought hande to hande with them that stoode to defende
the same. Then as a man come to him selfe agayne, he spake but
this onely worde: What, even into our campe? So in haste, casting of
his coate armor and apparel of a generall, he shifted him, and put on
such, as became his miserable fortune, and so stale out of his

campe. Furthermore, what he did after this over throwe, and howe he had put him selfe into the handes of the Ægyptians, by whome he was miserably slayne: we have sette it forthe at large in his life. Then Caesar entering into Pompeys campe, and seeing the bodies layed on the grounde that were slayne, and others also that were a killing, sayde, fetching a great sighe: It was their owne doing, and against my will. For Caius Caesar, after he had wonne so many famous conquests, and overcome so many great battells, had beene utterly condemned notwithstanding, if he had departed from his armie. Asinius Pollio writeth, that he spake these wordes then in Latyn, which he afterwards wrote in Greeke, and sayeth further-more, that the moste parte of them which were put to the sworde in the campe, were slaves and bondmen, and that there were not slayne in all at this battell, above six thowsand souldiers. As for them that were taken prisoners, Caesar did put many of them amongst his legions, and did pardon also many men of estimation, amonge whome Brutus was one, that afterwards slue Caesar him selfe: and it is reported, that Caesar was very sory for him, when he could not immediately be founde after the battell, and that he rejoiced againe, when he knewe he was alive, and that he came to yeelde him selfe unto him [p. 785].

* * *

After all these thinges were ended, he was chosen Consul the fourth time, and went into Spayne to make warre with the sonnes of Pompey: who were yet but very young, but had notwithstanding raised a marvelous great army together, and shewed to have had manhoode and corage worthie to commaunde such an armie, inso-much as they put Caesar him selfe in great daunger of his life. The greatest battell that was fought between them in all this warre, was by the citie of Munda. . . . This was the last warre that Caesar made. But the triumphe he made into Rome for the same, did as much offend the Romanes, and more, then any thing that ever he had done before: because he had not overcome Captaines that were straungers, nor barbarous kinges, but had destroyed the sonnes of the noblest man in Rome, whom fortune had overthrowen. And because he had plucked up his race by the rootes, men did not thinke it meete for him to triumphe so, for the calamities of his contrie, rejoicing at a thing for the which he had but one excuse to alleage in his defence, unto the gods and men: that he was compelled to doe that he did. And the rather they thought it not meete, because he had never before sent letters nor messengers unto the common wealth at Rome, for any victorie that he had ever wonne in all the civill warres: but did always for shame refuse the glorie of it. This notwithstanding, the

Romanes inclining to Caesars prosperity, and taking the bit in the mouth, supposing that to be ruled by one man alone, it would be a good meane for them to take breth a little, after so many troubles and miseries as they had abidden in these civill warres: they chose him perpetuall Dictator. This was a plaine tyranny: for to this absolute power of Dictator, they added this, never to be affraied to be deposed. Cicero propounded before the Senate, that they should geve him such honors, as were meete for a man: howbeit others afterwards added to, honors beyonde all reason. For, men striving who shoulde most honor him, they made him hatefull and troublesome to them selves that most favored him, by reason of the unmeasurable greatnes and honors which they gave him. Thereuppon, it is reported, that even they that most hated him, were no lesse favorers and furtherers of his honors, then they that most flattered him: because they might have greater occasions to rise, and that it might appeare they had just cause and colour to attempt that they did against him. And now for him selfe, after he had ended his civill warres, he did so honorably behave him selfe, that there was no fault to be founde in him: and therefore me thinkes, amongst other honors they gave him, he rightly deserved this, that they should builde him a temple of clemency, to thanke him for his curtesie he had used unto them in his victorie. For he pardoned many of them that had borne armes against him, and furthermore, did preferred some of them to honor and office in the common wealth: as amongst others, Cassius and Brutus, both the which were made Praetors. And where Pompeys images had bene throwen downe, he caused them to be set up againe: whereupon Cicero sayd then, that Caesar setting up Pompeys images againe, he made his owne to stand the surer. And when some of his frends did counsel him to have a gard for the safety of his person, and some also did offer them selves to serve him: he would never consent to it, but sayd, it was better to dye once, then always to be affrayed of death. But to win him selfe the love and good will of the people, as the honorablest gard and best safety he could have: he made common feasts againe, and generall distributions of corne. Furthermore, to gratifie the souldiers also, he replenished many cities againe with inhabitants, which before had bene destroyed, and placed them there that had no place to repaire unto: of the which the noblest and chiefest cities were these two, Carthage, and Corinthe, and it chaunced so, that like as aforetime they had bene both taken and destroyed together, even so were they both set a foote againe, and replenished with people, at one selfe time. And as for great personages, he wane them also, promising some of them, to make them Praetors and Consulls in time to come, and unto others, honors and preferrements, but to all men generally good hope, seeking all the wayes he coulde to make everie man contented with his raigne. * * * But the chiefest cause that made him mortally hated, was the covetous desire he had to be called king[4]: which first gave the people just cause, and next his secret enemies, honest colour to beare him ill will. This notwithstanding, they that procured him this honor and dignity, gave it out among the people, that it was written in the Sybilline prophecies, how the Romanes might overcome the Parthians, if they made warre with them, and were led by a king, but otherwise that they were unconquerable. And furthermore they were so bold besides, that Caesar returning to Rome from the citie of Alba, when they came to salute him, they called him king. But the people being offended, and Caesar also angry, he said he was not called king, but Caesar. Then every man keeping silence, he went his way heavy and sorowfull. When they had decreed divers honors for him in the Senate, the Consulls and Praetors accompanied with the whole assembly of the Senate, went unto him in the market place, where he was set by the pulpit for orations, to tell him what honors they had decreed for him in his absence. But he sitting still in his majesty, disdaining to rise up unto them when they came in, as if they had bene private men, aunswered them: that his honors had more neede to be cut of, then enlarged. This did not onely offend the Senate, but the common people also, to see that he should so lightly esteeme of the Magistrates of the common wealth: insomuch as every man that might lawfully goe his way, departed thence very sorrowfully. Thereupon also Caesar rising, departed home to his house, and tearing open his doblet coller,[5] making his necke bare, he cried out alowde to his frendes, that his throte was readie to offer to any man that would come and cut it. Notwithstanding, it is reported, that afterwards to excuse this folly, he imputed it to his disease,[6] saying, that their wittes are not perfit which have his disease of the falling evil, when standing of their feete they speake to the common people, but are soone troubled with a trembling of their body, and a sodaine dimness and guidines. But that was not true. For he would have risen up to the Senate, but Cornelius Balbus one of his frendes (but rather a flatterer) would not let him, saying: What, doe you not remember that you are Caesar, and will you not let them reverence you, and doe their dueties? Besides these occasions and offences, there followed also his shame and reproache, abusing the Tribunes of the people in this sorte. At that time, the feast Lupercalia was celebrated, the which in olde time men say was the feast of sheapheards or heard

---

4. Cf. 1.2.155–60.
5. Cf. 1.2.235–45 when Caesar is offered the crown.
6. See 1.2.263–66.

men, and is much like unto the feast of the Lycaeians in Arcadia. But
howsoever it is, that day there are divers noble mens sonnes, young
men, (and some of them Magistrats them selves that governe then)
which run naked through the city, striking in sport them they meete
in their way, with leather thonges, heare and all on, to make them
geve place. And many noble women, and gentle women also, goe of
purpose to stand in their way,[7] and doe put forth their handes to be
striken, as schollers hold them out to their schoolemaster, to be
striken with the ferula: perswading them selves that being with
childe, they shall have good deliverie, and also being barren, that it
will make them to conceive with child.[8] Caesar sate to beholde that
sport upon the pulpit for orations, in a chayer of gold, apparelled in
triumphing manner. Antonius, who was Consull at that time, was
one of them that ranne this holy course. So when he came into the
market place, the people made a lane for him to runne at libertie,
and he came to Caesar, and presented him a Diadeame wreathed
about with laurell.[9] Whereuppon there rose a certaine crie of rejoicing, not very great, done onely by a few, appointed for the purpose.
But when Caesar refused the Diadeame, then all the people together
made an outcrie of joy. Then Antonius offering it him againe, there
was a second shoute of joy, but yet of a few. But when Caesar refused
it againe the second time, then all the whole people showted.[1] Caesar having made this proofe, found that the people did not like of it,
and thereuppon rose out of his chayer, and commaunded the
crowne to be carried unto Jupiter in the Capitoll. After that, there
were set up images of Caesar in the city with Diadeames upon their
heades, like kinges. Those, the two Tribunes, Flaviuis and Marullus,
went and pulled downe: and furthermore, meeting with them that
first saluted Caesar as king, they committed them to prison. The
people followed them rejoicing at it, and called them Brutes: bicause
of Brutus, who had in old time driven the kings out of Rome, and
that brought the kingdom of one person, unto the government of the
Senate and people. Caesar was so offended withall, that he deprived
Marullus and Flavius of their Tribuneshippes, and accusing them,
he spake also against the people, and called them Bruti, and
Cumani, to witte, beastes, and fooles. Hereuppon the people went
straight unto Marcus Brutus, who from his father came of the first
Brutus, and by his mother, of the house of the Servilians, a noble
house as any was in Rome, and was also nephew and sonne in law of
Marcus Cato. Notwithstanding, the great honors and favor Caesar
shewed unto him, kept him backe that of him selfe alone, he did not

7. See 1.2.3–4.
8. Cf. 1.2.7–9.
9. See 1.2.235–45.
1. This occurs three times in 1.2.241.

conspire nor consent to depose him of his kingdom. For Caesar did not onely save his life, after the battell of Pharsalia when Pompey fled, and did at his request also save many more of his frendes besides: but furthermore, he put a marvelous confidence in him. For he had already preferred him to the Praetorshippe for that yeare, and furthermore was appointed to be Consul, the fourth yeare after that, having through Caesars frendshippe, obtained it before Cassius, who likewise made sute for the same: and Caesar also, as it is reported, sayd in this contention, In deede Cassius hath alleaged best reason, but yet shall not be chosen before Brutus. Some one day accusing Brutus while he practiced this conspiracy, Caesar would not heare of it, but clapping his hande on his bodie, told them, Brutus will looke for this skinne: meaning thereby, that Brutus for his virtue, deserved to rule after him, but yet, that for ambitions sake, he woulde not shewe him selfe unthankefull nor dishonorable. Nowe they that desired change, and wished Brutus only their Prince and Governour above all other: they durst not come to him them selves to tell him what they woulde have him to doe, but in the night did cast sundrie papers into the Praetors seate where he gave audience,[2] and the most of them to this effect: Thou sleepest Brutus, and art not Brutus in deede.[3] Cassius finding Brutus ambition sturred up the more by these seditious billes, did pricke him forwarde, and egge him on the more, for a private quarrel he had conceived against Caesar: the circumstance whereof, we have sette downe more at large in Brutus life. Caesar also had Cassius in great gelouzie, and suspected him much: whereupon he sayd on a time to his frendes, What will Cassius doe, thinke ye? I like not his pale lookes. An other time when Caesars frendes complained unto him of Antonius, and Dolabella, that they pretended some mischiefe towards him: he aunswered them againe, As for those fatte men and smooth comed heades, quoth he, I never reckon of them: but these pale visaged and carian leane people, I feare them most, meaning Brutus and Cassius.[4] Certainly, destenie may easier be foreseene, then avoyded: considering the straunge and wonderfull signes that were sayd to be seene before Caesars death. For, touching the fires in the element, and spirites running up and downe in the night, and also these solitarie birdes to be seene at noone dayes sitting in the great market place: are not all these signes perhappes worth the noting, in such a wonderfull chaunce as happened? But Strabo the Philosopher wryteth, that divers men were seene going up and downe in fire: and furthermore, that there was a slave of the

2. See 1.3.142–46.
3. See 2.1.46.
4. See 1.2.191–94. Brutus is left out.

souldiers, that did cast a marvelous burning flame out of his hande, insomuch as they that saw it, thought he had bene burnt, but when the fire was out, it was found he had no hurt.[5] Caesar self also doing sacrifice unto the goddess, found that one of the beastes which was sacrificed had no hart: and that was a straunge thing in nature, how a beast could live without a hart.[6] Furthermore, there was a certaine Soothsayer that had geven Caesar warning long time affore, to take heede of the day of the Ides of Marche, (which is the fifteenth of the moneth) for on that day he shoulde be in great daunger.[7] That day being come, Caesar going unto the Senate house, and speaking merily to the Soothsayer, tolde him. The Ides of Marche be come: So be they, softly aunswered the Soothsayer, but yet are they not past.[8] And the very day before, Caesar supping with Marcus Lepidus, sealed certaine letters as he was wont to do at the bord; so talke falling out amongst them, reasoning what death was best: he preventing their opinions, cried out alowde, Death unlooked for.[9] Then going to bedde the same night as his manner was, and lying with his wife Calpurnia, all the windowes and dores of his chamber flying open, the noyse awooke him, and made him affrayed when he saw such light[1]: but more, when he heard his wife Calpurnia, being fast a sleepe, weepe and sigh, and put forth many fumbling lamentable speaches. For she dreamed that Caesar was slaine, and that she had him in her armes.[2] Others also doe denie that she had any suche dreams, as amongst other, Titus Livius wryteth, that it was in this sorte. The Senate having set upon the toppe of Caesars house, for an ornament and setting foorth of the same, a certaine pinnacle: Calpurnia dreamed that she sawe it broken downe, and that she thought she lamented and wept for it. Insomuch that Caesar rising in the morning, she prayed him if it were possible, not to goe out of the dores that day, but to adjorne the session of the Senate, untill an other day. And if that he made no reckoning of her dreame, yet that he woulde searche further of the Soothsayers by their sacrifices, to knowe what should happen him that day.[3] Thereby it seemed that Caesar likewise did feare and suspect somewhat, bicause his wife Calpurnia untill that time, was never geven to any feare or supersticion[4]: and then, for that he saw her so troubled in minde with this dreame she had. But much more afterwardes, when the Soothsayers

5. See 1.3.15–18.
6. See 2.2.39–40.
7. See 1.2.15–24.
8. See 3.1.1–2.
9. Cf. 2.2.32–37.
1. This is suggested at 2.2.10–12.
2. Cf. 2.2.1–3.
3. See 2.2.5–9.
4. See 2.2.13–14.

having sacrificed many beastes one after an other, told him that none did like them[5]: then he determined to sende Antonius to adjourne the session of the Senate.[6] But in the meane time came Decius Brutus, surnamed Albinus, in whom Caesar put such confidence, that in his last will and testament he had appointed him to be his next heire, and yet was of the conspiracie with Cassius and Brutus: he fearing that if Caesar did adjorne the session that day, the conspiracie woulde out, laughed the Soothsayers to scorne,[7] and reproved Caesar, saying: that he gave the Senate occasion to mislike with him, and that they might thinke he mocked them, considering that by his commaundement they were assembled, and that they were readie willingly to graunt him all thinges, and to proclaime him king of all the provinces of the Empire of Rome out of Italie, and that he should weare his Diadeame in all other places, both by sea and land.[8] And furthermore, that if any man should tell them from him, they should departe for that present time, and returne againe when Calpurnia shoulde have better dreames: what would his enemies and ill willers say, and how could they like of his frendes wordes? And who could perswade them otherwise, but that they would thinke his dominion a slaverie unto them, and tirannicall in him selfe?[9] And yet if it be so, sayd he, that you utterly mislike of this day, it is better that you goe your selfe in person, and saluting the Senate, to dismisse them till an other time. Therewithall he tooke Caesar by the hand, and brought him out of his house. Caesar was not gone farre from His house, but a bondman, a straunger, did what he could to speake with him: and when he sawe he was put backe by the great prease and multitude of people that followed him, he went straight unto his house, and put him selfe into Calpurniaes handes to be kept, till Caesar came backe againe, telling her that he had great matters to imparte unto him. And one Artemidorus also borne in the Ile of Gnidos, a Doctor of Rethoricke in the Greeke tongue, who by meanes of his profession was verie familiar with certaine of Brutus confederates, and therefore knew the most parte of all their practises against Caesar: came and brought him a litle bill wrytten with his owne hand, of all that he ment to tell him.[1] He marking howe Caesar received all the supplications that were offered him, and that he gave them straight to his men that were about him, pressed neerer to him, and sayed: Caesar, reade this memoriall to your selfe, and that

5. See 2.2.37–40 and following.
6. See 2.2.52–56.
7. See 2.2.57–104.
8. See 2.2.93–96.
9. See 2.2.96–101; 119.
1. See 2.3.

quickely, for they be matters of great waight and touche you neerely.[2]
Caesar tooke it of him, but coulde never reade it, though he many
times attempted it, for the number of people that did salute him: but
holding it still in his hande, keeping it to him selfe, went on withal
into the Senate house.[3] Howbeit other are of opinion, that it was
some man else that gave him that memoriall, and not Artemidorus,
who did what he could all the way as he went to geve it Caesar, but
he was alwayes repulsed by the people. For these things, they may
seeme to come by chaunce: but the place where the murther was
prepared, and where the Senate were assembled, and where also
there stoode up an image of Pompey dedicated by him selfe amongst
other ornamentes which he gave unto the Theater[4]: all these were
manifest proofes that it was the ordinaunce of some god, that made
this treason to be executed, specially in that verie place. It is also
reported, that Cassius (though otherwise he did favour the doctrine
of Epicurus) beholding the image of Pompey, before they entred into
the action of their traiterous enterprise: he did softely call upon it,
to aide him. But the instant daunger of the present time, taking
away his former reason, did sodainly put him into a furious passion,
and made him like a man halfe besides him selfe. Now Antonius,
that was a faithfull frende to Caesar, and a valliant man besides of
his handes, him, Decius Brutus Albinus entertained out of the Senate house, having begon a long tale of set purpose.[5] So Caesar coming into the house, all the Senate stoode up on their feete to doe
him honor. Then parte of Brutus companie and confederates stoode
rounde about Caesars chayer, and parte of them also came towards
him, as though they made sute with Metellus Cimber, to call home
his brother againe from banishment: and thus prosecuting still
their sute, they followed Caesar, till he was set in his chayer. Who,
denying their petitions, and being offended with them one after an
other, bicause the more they were denied, the more they pressed
upon him, and were the earnester with him[6]: Metellus at length, taking his gowne with both his handes, pulled it over his necke, which
was the signe given the confederates to sette apon him. Then Casca[7]
behinde him strake him in the necke with his sword, howbeit the
wounde was not great nor mortall, because it seemed, the feare of
such a develishe attempt did amaze him, and take his strength from
him, that he killed him not at the first blowe. But Caesar turning
straight unto him, caught hold of his sword, and held it hard: and

2. See 3.1.3–7.
3. Cf. 3.1.8–12.
4. This is the place where Caesar was murdered.
5. This is Trebonius at 3.1.25–26.
6. See 3.1.28–75.
7. See 3.1.76.

they both cried out, Caesar in Latin: O vile traitor Casca, what doest
thou? And Casca in Greeke to his brother, Brother, helpe me.[8]
At the beginning of this sturre, they that were present, not knowing of the conspiracie were so amazed with the horrible sight they
sawe: that they had no power to flie, neither to helpe him, not so
much, as once to make any outcrie. They on thother side that had
conspired his death, compassed him in on everie side with their
swords drawen in their handes, that Caesar turned him no where,
but he was striken at by some, and still had naked swords in his face,
and was hacked and mangeled amonge them, as a wilde beaste
taken of hunters.[9] For it was agreed among them, that every man
should geve him a wound, bicause all their partes should be in this
murther: and then Brutus him selfe gave him one wounde about his
privities. Men reporte also, that Caesar did still defende him selfe
against the rest, running everie waye with his bodie: but when he
sawe Brutus with his sworde drawen in his hande, then he pulled
his gowne over his heade, and made no more resistaunce,[1] and was
driven either casually, or purposedly, by the counsell of the conspirators, against the base[2] whereupon Pompeys image stoode,
which ranne all of a goare bloude, till he was slaine. Thus it seemed,
that the image tooke just revenge of Pompeys enemie, being throwen
downe on the ground at his feete, and yelding up his ghost there, for
the number of wounds he had upon him. For it is reported, that he
had three and twenty wounds apon his body: and divers of the conspirators did hurt them selves, striking one body with so many
blowes. When Caesar was slaine, the Senate (though Brutus stood
in the middest amongst them as though he would have sayd somewhat touching this fact) presently ran out of the house, and flying,
filled all the city with marvelous feare and tumult. Insomuch as
some did shut to their dores, others forsooke their shops and ware-
houses, and others ranne to the place to see what the matter was:
and others also that had seene it, ran home to their houses againe.[3]
But Antonius and Lepidus, which were two of Caesars chiefest
frends, secretly conveying them selves away, fled into other mens
houses, and forsooke their owne.[4] Brutus and his confederates on
thother side, being yet hotte with this murther they had committed,
having their swords drawen in their hands, came all in a troupe
together out of the Senate, and went into the market place, not as
men that made countenaunce to flie, but otherwise boldly holding up

8. Cf. 1.2.273–78.
9. See in light of Brutus's wish, 2.1.173–74.
1. See 3.1.77; 3.2.182–85.
2. 3.1.116–17.
3. See 3.1.96–99.
4. Cf. 3.1.96.

their heades like men of corage, and called to the people to defende
their libertie, and stayed to speake with every great personage whome
they met in their way. Of them, some followed this troupe, and went
amongst them, as if they had bene of the conspiracie, and falsely
chalenged parte of the honor with them: among them was Caius
Octavius, and Lentulus Spinther. But both of them were afterwards
put to death, for their vaine covetousnes of honor, by Antonius, and
Octavius Caesar the younger: and yet had no parte of that honor for
the which they were put to death, neither did any man beleve that
they were any of the confederates, or of counsell with them. For
they that did put them to death, tooke revenge rather of the will
they had to offend, then of any fact they had committed. The next
morning, Brutus and his confederates came into the market place to
speake unto the people, who gave them such audience, that it
seemed they neither greatly reproved, nor allowed the fact; for by
their great silence they showed, that they were sory for Caesars
death, and also that they did reverence Brutus.[5] Nowe the Senate
graunted generall pardonne for all that was paste, and to pacifie
every man, ordained besides, that Caesars funeralls shoulde bee
honored as a god, and established all thinges that he had done: and
gave certaine provinces also, and convenient honors unto Brutus
and his confederates, whereby every man thought all things were
brought to good peace and quietnes againe. But when they had
opened Caesars testament,[6] and found a liberall legacie of money,
bequeathed unto every citizen of Rome,[7] and that they saw his body
(which was brought into the market place) al bemangled with gashes
of swordes[8]: then there was no order to keepe the multitude and
common people quiet, but they plucked up formes, tables, and
stooles, and layed them all about the body, and setting them a fire,
burnt the corse. Then when the fire was well kindled, they tooke the
firebrandes, and went unto their houses that had slaine Caesar, to
set them a fire.[9] Other[s] also ranne up and downe the citie to see if
they could meete with any of them, to cut them in peeces: howbeit
they could meete with never a man of them, bicause they had
locked them selves up safely in their houses. There was one of Caesars friends called Cinna, that had a marvelous straunge and terrible
dreame the night before. He dreamed that Caesar bad him to supper, and that he refused, and would not goe: then that Caesar tooke
him by the hand, and led him against his will. Now Cinna hearing
at that time, that they burnt Caesars body in the market place,

5. See 3.2.1–11.
6. Cf. Antony, 3.2.134–247.
7. See 3.2.236–38.
8. See 3.2.174–97; 170–97.
9. Cf. 3.2.250–53.

notwithstanding that he feared his dreame, and had an agew on him besides: he went into the market place to honor his funeralls. When he came thither, one of meane sorte asked what his name was? He was straight called by his name. The first man told it to an other, and that other unto an other, so that it ranne straight through them all, that he was one of them that murdered Caesar: (for in deede one of the traitors to Caesar, was also called Cinna as him selfe) wherefore taking him for Cinna the murderer, they fell upon him with such furie, that they presently dispatched him in the market place. This sturre and furie made Brutus and Cassius more affrayed, then of all that was past, and therefore within fewe dayes after, they departed out of Rome[1]: and touching their doings afterwards, and what calamity they suffered till their deathes, we have wrytten it at large, in the life of Brutus. Caesar dyed at six and fifty yeres of age: and Pompey also lived not passing foure yeares more then he. So he reaped no other frute of all his raigne and dominion, which he had so vehemently desired all his life, and pursued with such extreame daunger: but a vaine name only, and a superficiall glory, that procured him the envy and hatred of his contrie. But his great prosperitie and good fortune that favored him all his life time, did continue afterwards in the revenge of his death, pursuing the murtherers both by sea and land, till they had not left a man more to be executed, of al them that were actors or counsellers in the conspiracy of his death. Furthermore, of all the chaunces that happen unto men upon the earth, that which came to Cassius above all other, is most to be wondered at. For he being overcome in battell at the jorney of Philippes, slue him selfe with the same sworde, with the which he strake Caesar.[2] Againe, of signes in the element, the great comet which seven nightes together was seene very bright after Caesars death, the eight night after was never seene more. Also the brightnes of the sunne was darkened, the which all that yeare through rose very pale, and shined not out, whereby it gave but small heate: therefore the ayer being very clowdy and darke, by the weakenes of the heate that could not come foorth, did cause the earth to bring foorth but raw and unrype frute, which rotted before it could rype. But above all, the ghost that appeared unto Brutus shewed plainly, that the goddes were offended with the murther of Caesar. The vision was thus: Brutus being ready to passe over his army from the citie of Abydos, to the other coast lying directly against it, slept every night (as his manner was) in his tent, and being yet awake, thinking of his affaires: (for by reporte he was as carefull a Captaine, and lived with as little sleepe, as ever man did) he thought he heard a noyse at his tent dore, and looking

1. See 3.2.264–65.
2. See 5.3.41–46.

towards the light of the lampe that waxed very dimme, he saw a horrible vision of a man, of a wonderfull greatnes, and dreadfull looke,
which at the first made him marvelously afraid.[3] But when he sawe
that it did him no hurt, but stoode by his bedde side, and sayd nothing: at length he asked him what he was. The image aunswered him:
I am thy ill angel, Brutus, and thou shalt see me by the citie of Philippes. Then Brutus replied againe, and sayd: Well, I shall see thee
then.[4] Therewithall, the spirit presently vanished from him. After
that time Brutus being in battell neere unto the citie of Philippes,
against Antonius and Octavius Caesar, at the first battell he wan the
victorie, and overthrowing all them that withstoode him, he drave
them into young Caesars campe, which he tooke. The second battell
being at hand, this spirit appeared again unto him, but spake never a
word.[5] Thereuppon Brutus knowing he should dye,[6] did put him selfe
to all hazard in battell, but yet fighting could not be slaine. So seeing
his men put to flight and overthrowen, he ranne unto a little rocke
not farre of, and there setting his swordes point to his brest, fell upon
it, and slue him selfe, but yet as it is reported, with the helpe of his
friend, that dispatched him.[7] [pp. 789–96]

PLUTARCH

From The Life of Marcus Brutus[†]

Marcus Brutus came of that Junius Brutus, for whome the auncient
Romanes made his statue of brasse to be set up in the Capitoll, with
the images of the kings, holding a naked sword in his hand: because
he had valliantly put downe the Tarquines from their kingdom of
Rome. But that Junius Brutus being of a sower stearne nature, not
softned by reason, being like unto sword blades of too hard a temper: was so subject to his choller and malice he bare unto the
tyrannes, that for their sakes he caused his owne sonnes to be executed. But this Marcus Brutus in contrarie maner, whose life we
presently wryte, having framed his manners of life by the rules of
vertue and studie of Philosophie, and having imployed his wit,
which was gentle and constant, in attempting of great things: me

---

3. See 4.3.274–85.
4. See 4.3.281–85.
5. See 5.5.17–19.
6. See 5.5.20.
7. See 5.5.44–51; 65.
† From *Plutarch's Lives of the Noble Grecians and Romanes*, trans. Sir Thomas North
(London, 1579). Markers in the margins of the original text have been removed. Page
numbers to this source appear in square brackets.

thinkes he was rightly made and framed unto vertue. So that his verie enemies which wish him most hurt, bicause of his conspiracy against Julius Caesar: if there were any noble attempt done in all this conspiracie, they referre it whollie unto Brutus, and all the cruell and violent actes unto Cassius, who was Brutus familiar frend, but not so well geven, and condicioned as he. [p. 1055]

* * *

Now there were divers sortes of Praetorshippes at Rome, and it was looked for, that Brutus or Cassius would make sute for the chiefest Praetorshippe, which they called the Praetorshippe of the citie: bicause he that had that office, was as a Judge to minister justice unto the citizens. Therfore they strove one against the other, though some say that there was some little grudge betwext them for other matters before, and that this contencion did sette them further out, though they were allyed together. For Cassius had maried Junia, Brutus sister. Others say, that this contencion betwext them came by Caesar himselfe, who secretly gave either of them both hope of his favour. So their sute for the Praetorshippe was so followed and laboured of either partie, that one of them put an other in sute of lawe. Brutus with his vertue and good name contended against many noble exploytes in armes, which Cassius had done against the Parthians. So Caesar after he had heard both their objections, he told his frendes with whom he consulted about this matter: Cassius cause is the juster, sayd he, but Brutus must be first preferred. Thus Brutus had the first Praetorshippe, and Cassius the second: who thanked not Caesar so much for the Praetorshippe he had, as he was angrie with him for that he had lost. But Brutus in many other thinges tasted of the benefite of Caesars favour in any thing he requested. For if he had listed, he might have bene one of Caesars chiefest frendes, and of greatest authoritie and credit about him. Howebeit Cassius frendes did disswade him from it (for Cassius and he were not yet reconciled together sithence their first contencion and strife for the Praetorship) and prayed him to beware of Caesars sweete intisements, and to flie his tyrannicall favors: the which they sayd Caesar gave him, not to honor his vertue, but to weaken his constant minde, framing it to the bent of his bowe. Now Caesar on the other side did not trust him overmuch, nor was not without tales brought unto him against him: howbeit he feared his great minde, authority, and frends. Yet on the other side also, he trusted his good nature, and fayer condicions. For, intelligence being brought him one day, that Antonius and Dolabella did conspire against him: he aunswered, that these fat long heared men made him not affrayed, but the leane and whitely faced fellowes, meaning that, by Brutus and Cassius. * * * But Cassius being a chollericke man, and hating

Caesar privatlie, more then he did the tyrannie openlie: he incensed
Brutus against him. * * * For Cassius even from his cradell could
not abide any maner of tyrans, as it appeared when he was but a boy,
[p. 1058] * * * Nowe when Cassius felt his frendes, and did stirre
them up against Caesar: they all agreed and promised to take parte
with him, so Brutus were the chiefe of their conspiracie. For they
told him, that so high an enterprise and attempt as that, did not so
muche require men of manhoode, and courage to drawe their swords:
as it stoode them uppon to have a man of suche estimacion as Brutus, to make everie man boldlie thinke, that by his onelie presence
the fact were holie, and just. If he tooke not this course, then that
they shoulde goe to it with fainter hartes, and when they had done
it, they shoulde be more fearefull: bicause everie man woulde thinke
that Brutus woulde not have refused to have made one with them,
if the cause had bene good and honest. Therefore Cassius considering this matter with him selfe, did first of all speake to Brutus, since
they grewe straunge together for the sute they had for the Praetorshippe. So when he was reconciled to him againe, and that they had
imbraced one an other: Cassius asked him if he were determined
to be in the Senate house, the first day of the moneth of Marche,
bicause he heard say that Caesars frendes shoulde move the counsel
that day, that Caesar shoulde be called king by the Senate. Brutus
aunswered him he would not be there. But if we be sent for sayd
Cassius: howe then? For my selfe then sayd Brutus, I meane not to
holde my peace, but to withstande it, and rather dye then lose my
libertie. Cassius being bolde, and taking holde of this worde: Why,
quoth he, what Romane is he alive that will suffer thee to dye for
the libertie? What, knowest thou not that thou art Brutus?[1] Think-
est thou that they be cobblers, tapsters, or such like base mechani-
call people, that wryte these billes and scrowles which are founde
dayly in thy Praetor's chaire, and not the noblest men and best citizens that doe it? No, be thou well assured, that of other Praetors
they looke for giftes, common distribucions amongest the people,
and for common playes, and to see fensers fight at the sharpe, to
shew the people pastime: but at thy handes, they specially require
(as a due det unto them) the taking away of the tyranny, being fully
bent to suffer any extremity for thy sake, so that thou wilt shew thy
selfe to be the man thou art taken for, and that they hope thou art.
Thereuppon he kissed Brutus, and imbraced him: and so each taking
leave of other, they went both to speake with their frendes about it.
[p. 1059] * * * For this cause they durst not acquaint Cicero with
their conspiracie, although he was a man whome they loved dearelie,
and trusted best: for they were affrayed that he being a coward by

1. See 1.2.141–46.

nature, and age also having increased his feare, he woulde quite
turne and alter their purpose, and quenche the heate of their enterprise, the which speciallie required hotte and earnest execucion,
seeking by perswasion to bring all thinges to suche safetie, as there
should be no perill.[2] * * * Furthermore, the onlie name and great
calling of Brutus, did bring on the most of them to geve consent to
this conspiracie. Who having never taken othes together, nor taken
or geven any caution or assuraunce, nor binding them selves one to
an other by any religious othes: they all kept the matter so secret to
them selves, and coulde so cunninglie handle it, that notwithstanding the goddes did reveale it by manifest signes and tokens from
above, and by predictions of sacrifices: yet all this woulde not be
beleved. Nowe Brutus, who knewe verie well that for his sake all
the noblest, valliantest, and most couragious men of Rome did venter their lives, waying with him selfe the greatnesse of the daunger:
when he was out of his house, he did so frame and facion his countenaunce and lookes, that no man could discerne he had any thing
to trouble his minde. But when night came that he was in his owne
house, then he was cleane chaunged. For, either care did wake him
against his will when he woulde have slept, or else oftentimes of him
selfe he fell into suche deepe thoughtes of this enterprise, casting in
his minde all the daungers that might happen: that his wife lying by
him, founde that there was some marvelous great matter that troubled his minde, not beinge wont to be in that taking, and that he
coulde not well determine with him selfe.[3] His wife Porcia (as we
have tolde you before) was the daughter of Cato, whome Brutus
married being his cosin, not a maiden, but a younge widowe after
the death of her first husbande Bibulus, by whome she had also a
younge sonne called Bibulus, who afterwards wrote a booke of the
actes and jeastes[4] of Brutus, extant at this present day. This young
Ladie being excellentlie well seene in Philosophie, loving her husbande well, and being of a noble courage, as she was also wise:
bicause she woulde not aske her husbande what he ayled before she
had made some proofe by her selfe, she tooke a litle rasor suche as
barbers occupie to pare mens nayles, and causing all her maydes
and women to goe out of her chamber, gave her selfe a greate gashe
withall in her thigh, that she was straight all of a gore bloode, and
incontinentlie after, a vehement fever tooke her, by reason of the
payne of her wounde. Then perceiving her husbande was marvelou-
slie out of quiet, and that he coulde take no rest[5]: even in her greatest payne of all, she spake in this sorte unto him: 'I being, O Brutus,

2. Cf. their rationale in 2.1.141–52.
3. See 2.1.61–69.
4. Gestes, i.e., deeds.
5. See 2.1.237–70.

(sayed she) the daughter of Cato, was maried unto thee, not to be thy beddefellowe and companion in bedde and at borde onelie, like a harlot: but to be partaker also with thee, of thy good and evill fortune. Nowe for thy selfe, I can finde no cause of faulte in thee touchinge our matche: but for my parte, howe may I showe my duetie towards thee, and howe muche I woulde doe for thy sake, if I can not constantlie beare a secret mischaunce or griefe with thee, which requireth secrecy and fidelity? I confesse, that a womans wit commonly is too weake to keepe a secret safely: but yet, Brutus, good educacion, and the companie of virtuous men, have some power to reforme the defect of nature. And for my selfe, I have this benefit moreover: that I am the daughter of Cato, and wife of Brutus.[6] This notwithstanding, I did not trust to any of these things before: untill that now I have found by experience, that no paine nor griefe whatsoever can overcome me.' With those wordes she shewed him her wounde on her thigh, and tolde him what she had done to prove her selfe.[7] Brutus was amazed to heare what she sayd unto him, and lifting up his handes to heaven, he besought the goddes to geve him the grace he might bring his enterprise to so good passe, that he might be founde a husband, worthie of so noble a wife as Porcia: so he then did comfort her the best he coulde.[8] Now a day being appointed for the meeting of the Senate, at what time they hoped Caesar woulde not faile to come: the conspirators determined then to put their enterprise in execucion, bicause they might meete safelie at that time without suspicion, and the rather, for that all the noblest and chiefest men of the citie woulde be there. Who when they should see suche a great matter executed, would everie man then set to their handes, for the defence of their libertie. Furthermore, they thought also that the appointment of the place where the counsell shoulde be kept, was chosen of purpose by divine providence, and made all for them. For it was one of the porches about the Theater, in the which there was a certaine place full of seates for men to sit in, where also was set up the image of Pompey, which the citie had made and consecrated in honor of him: when he did beawtifie that parte of the citie with the Theater he built, with divers porches about it. In this place was the assembly of the Senate appointed to be, just on the fifteenth day of the moneth of March, which the Romanes call, Idus Martias: so that it seemed some god of purpose had brought Caesar thither to be slaine, for revenge of Pompeys death. So when the day was come, Brutus went out of his house with a dagger by his side under his long gowne, that no bodie sawe nor

6. See 2.1.292–95.
7. See 2.1.299–302.
8. See 2.1.302–08.

knewe, but his wife onelie. The other conspirators were all assembled at Cassius house, to bring his sonne into the market place, who on that day did put on the mans gowne, called Toga Virilis: and from thence they came all in a troupe together unto Pompeys porche, looking that Caesar woulde straight come thither. But here is to be noted, the wonderfull assured constancie of these conspirators, in so daungerous and waightie an enterprise as they had undertaken. For many of them being Praetors, by reason of their office, whose duetie is to minister justice to everie bodie: they did not onelie with great quietnesse and curtesie heare them that spake unto them, or that pleaded matters before them, and gave them attentive care, as if they had had no other matter in their heades: but moreover, they gave just sentence, and carefullie dispatched the causes before them. So there was one among them, who being condemned in a certaine summe of money, refused to pay it, and cried out that he did appeale unto Caesar. Then Brutus casting his eyes upon the conspirators, sayd, Caesar shall not lette me to see the lawe executed. Notwithstanding this, by chaunce there fell out many misfortunes unto them, which was enough to have marred the enterprise. The first and chiefest was, Caesars long tarying, who came verie late to the Senate: for bicause the signes of the sacrifices appeared unluckie, his wife Calpurnia kept him at home, and the Soothsayers bad him beware he went not abroade.[9] The seconde cause was, when one came unto Casca being a conspirator, and taking him by the hande, sayd unto him: O Casca, thou keptest it close from me, but Brutus hath tolde me all. Casca being amazed at it, the other went on with his tale, and sayd: Why, howe nowe, howe commeth it to passe thou art thus riche, that thou doest sue to be Aedilis? Thus Casca being deceived by the others doubtfull wordes, he tolde them it was a thowsand to one, he blabbed not out all the conspiracie. An other Senator called Popilius Laena, after he had saluted Brutus and Cassius more frendlie then he was wont to doe: he rounded softlie in their eares, and told them, I pray the goddes you may goe through with that you have taken in hande, but withal, dispatche I reade you, for your enterprise is bewrayed. When he had sayd, he presentlie departed from them, and left them both affrayed that their conspiracie woulde out.[1] Nowe in the meane time, there came one of Brutus men post hast unto him, and tolde him his wife was a dying. For Porcia being verie carefull and pensive for that which was to come, and being too weake to away with so great and inward griefe of minde: she coulde hardlie keepe within, but was frighted with everie little noyse and crie she hearde, as those that are taken and possest

9. See 2.1.193–201.
1. See 3.1.13–17.

with the furie of the Bacchantes, asking every man that came from the market place, what Brutus did, and still sent messenger after messenger, to knowe what newes. At length, Caesars comming being prolonged as you have heard, Porciaes weakenesse was not able to holde out any lenger, and thereuppon she sodainlie swounded, that she had no leasure to goe to her chamber, but was taken in the middest of her house, where her speache and sences failed her. Howbeit she soone came to her selfe againe, and so was layed in her bedde, and tended by her women. When Brutus heard these newes, it grieved him, as it is to be presupposed: yet he left not of the care of his contrie and common wealth, neither went home to his house for any newes he heard. Nowe, it was reported that Caesar was comming in his litter: for he determined not to stay in the Senate all that day (bicause he was affrayed of the unluckie signes of the sacrifices) but to adjorne matters of importaunce unto the next session, and counsell holden, faining him selfe not to be well at ease. When Caesar came out of his litter: Popilius Laena, that had talked before with Brutus and Cassius, and had prayed the goddess they might bring this enterprise to passe: went unto Caesar, and kept him a long time with a talke, Caesar gave good eare unto him. Wherefore the conspirators (if so they shoulde be called) not hearing what he sayd to Caesar, but conjecturing by that he had tolde them a little before, that his talke was none other but the verie discoverie of their conspiracie: they were affrayed everie man of them, and one looking in an others face, it was easie to see that they were all of a minde, that it was no tarrying for them till they were apprehended, but rather that they should kill them selves with their owne handes. And when Cassius and certeine other clapped their handes on their swords under their gownes to draw them: Brutus marking the countenaunce and gesture of Laena, and considering that he did use him selfe rather like an humble and earnest suter, then like an accuser: he sayd nothing to his companion (bicause there were many amongst them that were not of the conspiracie) but with a pleasaunt countenaunce encouraged Cassius. And immediatlie after, Laena went from Caesar, and kissed his hande: which shewed plainlie that it was for some matter concerning him selfe, that he had held him so long in talke. Nowe all the Senators being entred first into this place or chapter house where the counsell should be kept: all the other conspirators straight stoode about Caesars chaire, as if they had had some thing to have sayd unto him. And some say, that Cassius casting his eyes upon Pompeys image, made his prayer unto it, as if it had bene alive. Trebonius on thother side, drewe Antonius atoside, as he came into the house where the Senate sate, and helde him with a long talke without. When Caesar was come into the house, all the Senate rose to honor him at his comming in. So when he was

set, the conspirators flocked about him, and amongst them they
presented one Tullius Cimber,[2] who made humble sute for the calling home againe of his brother that was banished. They all made as
though they were intercessors for him, and tooke him by the handes,
and kissed his head and brest. Caesar at the first, simplie refused
their kindnesse and intreaties: but afterwardes, perceiving they still
pressed on him, he violently thrust them from him. Then Cimber
with both his hands plucked Caesars gowne over his shoulders, and
Casca that stoode behinde him, drew his dagger first, and strake
Caesar upon the shoulder, but gave him no great wound.[3] Caesar
feeling him selfe hurt, tooke him straight by the hande he held his
dagger in, and cried out in Latin: O traitor, Casca, what doest thou?
Casca on thother side cried in Graeke,[4] and called his brother to
helpe him. So divers running on a heape together to flie uppon Caesar, he looking about him to have fledde, sawe Brutus with a sworde
drawen in his hande readie to strike at him: then he let Cascaes
hande goe, and casting his gowne over his face, suffered everie man
to strike at him that woulde.[5] Then the conspirators thronging one
upon an other bicause everie man was desirous to have a cut at him,
so many swords and daggers lighting upon one bodie, one of them
hurte an other, and among them Brutus caught a blowe on his
hande, bicause he would make one in murdering of him, and all the
rest also were every man of them bloudied. Caesar being slaine in
this maner, Brutus standing in the middest of the house, would
have spoken, and stayed the other Senators that were not of the
conspiracie, to have tolde them the reason why they had done this
facte.[6] But they as men both affrayd and amazed, fled one upon
anothers necke in haste to get out at the dore, and no man followed
them. For it was set downe, and agreed betwene them, that they
should kill no man but Caesar onely,[7] and should intreate all the
rest to looke to defend their libertie. All the conspirators, but Brutus, determining upon this matter, thought it good also to kill Antonius, bicause he was a wicked man, and that in nature favored
tyranny: besides also, for that he was in great estimation with
souldiers, having bene conversant of long time amongst them: and
specially, having a mind bent to great enterprises, he was also of
great authoritie at that time, being Consul with Caesar. But Brutus
would not agree to it. First, for that he sayd it was not honest: secondly, bicause he told them there was hope of chaunge in him. For

2. Called Metellus Cimber in various places, as in 3.1.27.
3. See 3.1.75.
4. Casca pretended not to know Greek, 1.2.276–78.
5. See 3.1.79.
6. See 3.1.82–84.
7. See 3.1.90–93.

he did not mistrust, but that Antonius being a noble minded and coragious man (when he should knowe that Caesar was dead) would willingly helpe his contry to recover her libertie, having them an example unto him, to follow their corage and vertue. So Brutus by this meanes saved Antonius life, who at that present time disguised him selfe, and stale away.[8] But Brutus and his consorts, having their swords bloudy in their handes, went straight to the Capitoll, perswading the Romanes as they went, to take their libertie againe. Now, at the first time when the murther was newly done, there were sodaine outcryes of people that ranne up and downe the citie, the which in deede did the more increase the feare and tumult. But when they saw they slue no man, neither did spoyle or make havock of any thing: then certaine of the Senators, and many of the people imboldening them selves, went to the Capitoll unto them. There a great number of men being assembled one after another: Brutus made an oration unto them to winne the favor of the people, and to justifie that they had done. All those that were by, sayd they had done well, and cryed unto them that they should boldly come downe from the Capitoll. Whereuppon, Brutus and his companions came boldly downe into the market place. The rest followed in trowpe, but Brutus went formost, very honorably compassed in round about with the noblest men of the citie, which brought him from the Capitoll, thorough the market place, to the pulpit for orations. When the people saw him in the pulpit, although they were a multitude of rakehells of all sortes, and had a good will to make some sturre: yet being ashamed to doe it for the reverence they bare unto Brutus, they kept silence, to heare what he would say. When Brutus began to speake, they gave him quiet audience: howbeit immediatly after, they shewed that they were not all contented with the murther. For when another called Cinna would have spoken, and began to accuse Caesar: they fell into a great uprore among them, and marvelously reviled him. Insomuch that the conspirators returned againe into the Capitol. There Brutus being affrayd to be beseeged, sent back againe the noble men that came thither with him, thinking it no reason, that they which were no partakers of the murther, should be partakers of the daunger. Then the next morning the Senate being assembled, and holden within the temple of the goddesse Tellus, to wete the earth: and Antonius, Plancus, and Cicero, having made a motion to the Senate in that assembly, that they should take an order to pardon and forget all that was past, and to stablishe friendship and peace againe: it was decreed, that they should not onely be pardoned, but also that the Consuls should referre it to the Senate what honors should be appointed unto them. This being agreed

8. See 3.1.96.

upon, the Senate brake up, and Antonius the Consul, to put them in hart that were in the Capitoll, sent them his sonne for a pledge. Upon this assurance, Brutus and his companions came downe from the Capitoll, where every man saluted and imbraced eche other, among the which, Antonius him selfe did bid Cassius to supper to him: and Lepidus also bad Brutus, and so one bad another, as they had friendship and acquaintance together. The next day following, the Senate being called againe to counsell, did first of all commend Antonius, for that he had wisely stayed and quenched the beginning of a civill warre: then they also gave Brutus and his consorts great prayses, and lastly they appoynted them severall governments of provinces. For unto Brutus, they appoynted Creta: Africk, unto Cassius: Asia, unto Trebonius: Bithynia, unto Cimber: and unto the other Decius Brutus Albinus, Gaule on this side the Alpes. When this was done, they came to talke of Caesars will and testament, and of his funeralls and tombe. Then Antonius thinking good his testament should be red openly, and also that his body should be honorably buried, and not in hugger mugger, least the people might thereby take occasion to be worse offended if they did otherwise: Cassius stowtly spake against it. But Brutus went with the motion, and agreed unto it: wherein it seemeth he committed a second fault. For the first fault he did was, when he would not consent to his fellow conspirators, that Antonius should be slayne: and therefore he was justly accused, that thereby he had saved and strengthened a stronge and grievous enemy of their conspiracy. The second fault was, when he agreed that Caesars funeralls should be as Antonius would have them: the which in deede marred all. For first of all, when Caesars testament was openly red amonge them, whereby it appeared that he bequeathed unto every Citizen of Rome, 75 Drachmas a man, and that he left his gardens and arbors unto the people, which he had on this side of the river of Tyber, in the place where now the temple of Fortune is built: the people then loved him, and were marvelous sory for him.[9] Afterwards when Caesars body was brought into the market place, Antonius making his funerall oration in praise of the dead, according to the auncient custom of Rome, and perceiving that his wordes moved the common people to compassion: he framed his eloquence to make their harts yerne the more, and taking Caesars gowne all bloudy in his hand, he layed it open to the sight of them all, shewing what a number of cuts and holes it had upon it. Therewithall the people fell presently into such a rage and mutinie,[1] that there was no more order kept amongst the common people. For some of them cryed out, Kill the murtherers:

9. See 3.2.235–47.
1. See 3.2.165–226.

others plucked up, formes, tables, and stalles about the market place, as they had done before at the funeralls of Clodius, and having layed them all on a heape together, they set them on fire, and thereuppon did put the bodye of Caesar, and burnt it in the middest of the most holy places.[2] And furthermore, when the fire was thoroughly kindled, some here, some there, tooke burning fire brands, and ranne with them to the murtherers houses that had killed him, to set them a fire.[3] Howbeit the conspirators foreseeing the daunger before, had wisely provided for them selves, and fled. But there was a Poet called Cinna, who had bene no partaker of the conspiracy, but was alway one of Caesars chiefest friends: he dreamed the night before, that Caesar bad him to supper with him, and that he refusing to goe, Caesar was very importunate with him, and compelled him, so that at length he led him by the hand into a great darke place, where being marvelously affrayd, he was driven to follow him in spite of his hart. This dreame put him all night into a fever, and yet notwithstanding, the next morning when he heard that they caried Caesars body to buriall, being ashamed not to accompany his funerals: he went out of his house, and thrust him self into the prease of the common people that were in a great uprore. And bicause some one called him by his name, Cinna: the people thinking he had bene that Cinna, who in an oration he made had spoken very evill of Caesar, they falling upon him in their rage, slue him outright in the market place. This made Brutus and his companions more affrayd, then any other thing, next unto the chaunge of Antonius. Wherefore they got them out of Rome, and kept at the first in the citie of Antium, hoping to returne againe to Rome, when the furie of the people were a litle asswaged. The which they hoped would be quickly, considering that they had to deale with a fickle and unconstant multitude, easye to be caried, and that the Senate stoode for them: who notwithstanding made no enquiery of them that had torne poore Cinna the Poet in peeces, but caused them to be sought for and apprehended, that went with fire brands to set fire of the conspirators houses. The people growing weary now of Antonius pride and insolency, who ruled all things in manner with absolute power: they desired that Brutus might returne againe, and it was also looked for, that Brutus would come him selfe in person to playe the playes which were due to the people, by reason of his office of Praetorship. But Brutus understanding that many of Caesars souldiers which served under him in the warres, and that also had lands and houses given them in the cities where they lay, did lye in wayte for him to kill him, and that they dayly by

2. See 3.2.248–51.
3. See 3.2.251ff.

small companies came by one and by one into Rome: he durst no more returne thither, but yet the people had the pleasure and pastyme in his absence, to see the games and sportes he made them, which were sumptuouslie set foorth and furnished with all thinges necessarie, sparing for no cost.

* * * Now the state of Rome standing in these termes, there fell out an other chaunge and alteracion, when the younge man Octavius Caesar came to Rome. He was the sonne of Julius Caesars Nece, whome he had adopted for his sonne, and made his heire, by his last will and testament. But when Julius Caesar his adopted father was slayne, he was in the citie of Apollonia, where he studied tarying for him, because he was determined to make warre with the Parthians: but when he heard the newes of his death, he returned againe to Rome, where to begin to curry favor with the common people, he first of all tooke upon him his adopted fathers name, and made distribution amonge them of the money which his father had bequeathed unto them. By this meanes he troubled Antonius sorely, and by force of money, got a great number of his fathers souldiers together, that had served in the warres with him. And Cicero him selfe, for the great malice he bare Antonius, did favor his proceedings. But Brutus marvelously reproved him for it * * * Now, the citie of Rome being devided in two factions, some taking part with Antonius, other also leaning unto Octavius Caesar, and the souldiers making port-sale[4] of their service to him that would give most: Brutus seeing the state of Rome would be utterly overthrowen, he determined to goe out of Italy, and went a foote through the contry of Luke, unto the citie of Elea, standing by the sea. There Porcia being ready to depart from her husband Brutus, and to returne to Rome, did what she could to dissemble the griefe and sorow she felt at her hart * * * although untill that time she alwayes shewed a constant and pacient mind. [pp. 1060–65]

* * *

Brutus was a carefull man, and slept very litle, both for that his dyet was moderate, as also bicause he was continually occupied. He never slept in the day time, and in the night no lenger, then the tyme he was driven to be alone, and when every bodye els tooke their rest. But nowe whilest he was in warre, and his heade ever busily occupied to thinke of his affayres, and what would happen: after he slumbered a litle after supper, he spent all the rest of the night in dispatching of his waightiest causes, and after he had taken order for them, if he had any leysure left him, he would read some booke till the third watche of the night, at what tyme the Captaines, petty

4. I.e., a sale to the highest bidder.

Captaines and Colonells, did use to come unto him. So, being ready
to goe into Europe, one night very late (when all the campe tooke
quiet rest) as he was in his tent with a litle light, thinking of waighty
matters: he thought he heard one come in to him, and casting his
eye towards the doore of his tent, that he saw a wonderfull straunge
and monstruous shape of a body comming towards him, and sayd
never a word. So Brutus boldly asked what he was, a god, or a man,
and what cause brought him thither. The spirit aunswered him, I
am thy evill spirit, Brutus: and thou shalt see me by the citie of
Philippes. Brutus beeing no otherwise affrayd, replyed againe unto
it: Well, then I shall see thee agayne. The spirit presently vanished
away: and Brutus called his men unto him, who tolde him that they
heard no noyse, nor sawe any thinge at all.[5] Thereuppon Brutus
returned agayne to thinke on his matters as he did before: and when
the daye brake, he went unto Cassius, to tell him what vision had
appeared unto him in the night. Cassius beeing in opinion an Epi-
curian, and reasoning thereon with Brutus, spake to him touching
the vision thus. In our secte, Brutus, we have an opinion, that we
doe not alwayes feele, or see, that which we suppose we doe both see
and feele: but that our senses beeing credulous, and therefore easily
abused (when they are idle and unoccupied in their owne objects)
are induced to imagine they see and conjecture that, which they in
truth doe not. [pp. 1071–72]* * *

* * * [After further narrative Plutarch comments] The selfe same
night, it is reported that the monstrous spirit which had appeared
before unto Brutus in the citie of Sardis, did now appeare againe unto
him in the selfe same shape and forme, and so vanished away, and
sayd never a word. Now Publius Volumnius, a grave and wise Philosopher, that had bene with Brutus from the beginning of this warre, he
doth make mencion of this spirite, but sayth: that the greatest Eagle
and ensigne was covered over with a swarme of bees, and that there
was one of the Captaines, whose arme sodainly fell a sweating, that it
dropped oyle of roses from him, and that they oftentimes went about
to drie him, but all would doe no good. And that before the battell was
fought, there were two Eagles fought betwene both armies, and all
the time they fought, there was a marvelous great silence all the valley
over, both the armies being one before the other, marking this fight
betwene them: and that in the end, the Eagle towardes Brutus gave
over, and flew away. [p. 1078]

* * *

5. See 4.3.284–304.

Brutus thought that there was no great number of men slaine in
battell, and to know the trueth of it, there was one called Statilius,
that promised to goe through his enemies (for otherwise it was
impossible to goe see their campe) and from thence if all were well,
that he woulde lift up a torche light in the ayer, and then returne
againe with speede to him. The torche light was lift up as he had
promised, for Statilius went thither. Nowe Brutus seeing Statilius
tarie long after that, and that he came not againe, he sayd: If Statilius be alive, he will come againe. But his evill fortune was suche,
that as he came backe, he lighted in his enemies hands, and was
slaine. Now, the night being farre spent, Brutus as he sate bowed
towards Clitus one of his men, and told him somewhat in his eare,
the other aunswered him not, but fell a weeping.[6] Thereupon he
proved Dardanus, and sayd somwhat also to him: at length he came
to Volumnius him selfe, and speaking to him in Graeke, prayed him
for the studies sake which brought them acquainted together, that he
woulde helpe him to put his hande to his sword, to thrust it in him to
kill him. Volumnius denied his request, and so did many others: and
amongest the rest, one of them sayd, there was no tarying for them
there, but that they must needes flie. Then Brutus rising up, We
must flie in deede sayd he, but it must be with our hands, not with
our feete. Then taking every man by the hand, he sayd these words
unto them with a cheerefull countenance: It rejoyceth my hart that
not one of my frends hath failed me at my neede, and I do not com-
plaine of my fortune, but only for my contries sake: for, as for me, I
thinke my selfe happier than they that have overcome, considering
that I leave a perpetuall fame of our corage and manhoode, the
which our enemies the conquerors shall never attaine unto by force
nor money, neither can let their posteritie to say, that they being
naughtie and unjust men, have slaine good men, to usurpe tyrannical power not pertaining to them. Having sayd so, he prayed everie
man to shift for them selves, and then he went a litle aside with two
or three only, among the which Strato was one, with whom he came
first acquainted by the studie of Rethoricke. He came as neere to
him as he coulde, and taking his sword by the hilts with both his
hands, and falling downe upon the poynt of it, ran him selfe through.
Others say, that not he, but Strato (at his request) held the sword in
his hand, and turned his head aside, and that Brutus fell downe
upon it: and so ranne him selfe through, and dyed presently. Messala, that had bene Brutus great frend, became afterwards Octavius Caesars frend. * * * Now, Antonius having found Brutus bodie,
he caused it to be wrapped up in one of the richest cote armors he
had. Afterwards also, Antonius understanding that this cote armor

6. See 5.5.4–7 and what follows.

was stollen, he put the theefe to death that had stollen it, and sent the ashes of his bodie unto Servilia his mother. And for Porcia, Brutus wife: Nicolaus the Philosopher, and Valerius Maximus doe wryte, that she determining to kill her selfe (her parents and frendes carefullie looking to her to kepe her from it) tooke hotte burning coles, and cast them into her mouth, and kept her mouth so close, that she choked her selfe. There was a letter of Brutus found wrytten to his frendes, complayning of their negligence, that his wife being sicke, they would not helpe her, but suffred her to kill her selfe, choosing to dye, rather then to languish in paine. Thus it appeareth, that Nicolaus knewe not well that time, sith the letter (at the least if it were Brutus letter) doth plainly declare the disease and love of this Lady, and also the maner of her death. [pp. 1079–80]

PLUTARCH

From The Life of Marcus Tullius Cicero[†]

Cicero was dogge leane, a litle eater, and woulde also eate late, bicause of the greate weakeness of his stomacke: but yet he had a good lowde voyce, though it was somewhat harshe, and lacked grace and comelynesse. Furthermore he was so earnest and vehement in his Oration that he mounted still with his voyce into the highest tunes: insomuche that men were affrayed it woulde one daye put him in hazard of his life. When he came to Athens, he went to heare Antiochus of the citie of Ascalona, and fell in greate likinge with his sweete tongue, and excellent grace, though otherwise he misliked his new [Stoic] opinions in Philosophie . . . Cicero had most affection unto the Academickes, and did studie that sect more then all the rest. . . . [p. 914] [Cicero's Consulship was admired by Cato.] For by decree of the people he was called, father of the contry, as Cato him selfe had called him in his oration: the which name was never given to any man, but onely unto him, and also he bare greater swaye in Rome at that time, than any man beside him. This notwithstanding, he made him selfe envyed and misliked of many men, not for any ill acte he did, or ment to doe: but onely bicause he did too much boast of him selfe. [p. 924] * * *

Nowe touching the conspiracie against Caesar, he was not made privie to it, although he was one of Brutus greatest frendes, and that it grieved him to see thinges in that state they were brought unto,

† From *Plutarch's Lives of the Noble Grecians and Romanes*, trans. Sir Thomas North. (London, 1579). Marginal section headings have been removed. Page numbers to this source appear in square brackets.

and albeit also he wished for the time past, as much as any other
man did. But in deede the conspirators were affrayed of his nature,
that lacked hardinesse: and of his age, the which oftentimes maketh
the stowtest and most hardiest natures, faint harted and cowardly.
Notwithstanding, the conspiracie being executed by Brutus and Cassius, Caesars frendes being gathered together, everie man was
afrayed that the citie woulde againe fall into civill warres. And Antonius also, who was Consul at that time, did assemble the Senate, and
made some speache and mocion then to draw things againe unto
quietnes. But Cicero having used divers perswasions fit for the time,
in the end he moved the Senate to decree (following the example of
the Athenians) a generall oblivion of thinges done against Caesar,
and to assigne unto Brutus and Cassius some governmentes of
provinces. Howbeit nothing was concluded: for the people of them
selves were sorie, when they sawe Caesars bodie brought through
the market place. And when Antonius also did shew them his gowne
all bebloodied, cut, and thrust through with swordes: then they
were like madde men for anger, and sought up and downe the market place if they coulde meete with any of them that had slaine him:
and taking fire brandes in their hands, they ranne to their houses to
set them a fire. But the conspirators having prevented this daunger,
saved them selves: and fearing that if they taried at Rome, they
should have many such alaroms, they forsooke the citie. Then Antonius began to looke aloft, and became fearefull to all men, as though
he ment to make him selfe king: but yet most of all unto Cicero,
above all others. For Antonius perceiving that Cicero began againe
to increase in credit and authoritie, and knowing that he was Brutus
very frend: he did mislike to see him come neere him, and besides,
there was at that time some gealousie betwext them, for the diversi-
tie and difference of their manners and disposicions, Cicero being
affrayed of this, [p. 933] * * * tooke sea alone, to goe into Graece.
But as it chaunceth oftentimes, there was some let that kept him
he could not saile, and newes came to him daily from Rome, as the
manner is, that Antonius was wonderfully chaunged, and that
nowe he did nothing any more without the authoritie and consent
of the Senate, and that there lacked no thing but his person, to
make all things well. Then Cicero condemning his dastardly feare,
returned foorthwith to Rome, not being deceived in his first hope.
For there came suche a number of people out to meete him, that
he coulde doe nothing all day long, but take them by the handes,
and imbrace them: who to honor him, came to meete him at the gate
of the citie, as also by the way to bring him to his house. The next
morning Antonius assembled the Senate, and called for Cicero by
name. Cicero refused to goe, and kept his bedde, fayning that he was

werie with his jorney and paines he had taken the day before: but in deede, the cause why he went not, was, for feare and suspicion of an ambushe that was layed for him by the way, if he had gone, as he was informed by one of his verie good frends. Antonius was marvelously offended that they did wrongfully accuse him, for laying of any ambush for him: and therefore sent souldiers to his house, and commaunded them to bring him by force, or else to sette his house a fire. After that time, Cicero and he were alwayes at jarre, but yet coldly enough, one of them taking heede of an other: untill that the young Caesar returning from the citie of Apollonia, came as lawfull heire unto Julius Caesar Dictator, and had contention with Antonius for the summe of two thowsande five hundred Myriades, the which Antonius kept in his handes of his fathers goodes. Thereuppon, Philip who had maried the mother of this young Caesar, and Marcellus, who had also maried his sister, went with young Caesar unto Cicero, and there agreed together, that Cicero should helpe young Caesar with the favour of his authoritie, and eloquence, as well towardes the Senate, as also to the people: and that Caesar in recompence of his good will should stande by Cicero, with his money and souldiers. For this young Caesar, had many of his fathers old souldiers about him, that had served under him. [p. 934] [For a while Cicero had great influence in Rome. He eventually vanquished Antony and assisted Octavius in acquiring the position of Consul.] But there was Cicero finely colted, as old as he was, by a young man, when he was contented to sue for the Consulship in his behalfe, and to make the Senate agreable to it: wherefore his frendes presently reproved him for it, and shortly after he perceived he had undone him selfe, and together also lost the libertie of his contrie. For this young man Octavius Caesar being growen to be verie great by his meanes and procurement: when he saw that he had the Consulshippe upon him, he forsooke Cicero, and agreed with Antonius and Lepidus. Then joyning his armie with theirs, he devided the Empire of Rome with them, as if it had bene lands left in common betwene them: and besides that, there was a bill made of two hundred men and upwards, whom they had appointed to be slaine. But the greatest difficultie and difference that fell out betwene them, was about the outlawing of Cicero. For Antonius woulde hearken to no peace betwene them, unlesse Cicero were slaine first of all: Lepidus was also in the same mind with Antonius: but Caesar was against them both. Their meeting was by the citie of Bolonia, where they continued three dayes together, they three only secretly consulting in a place environned about with a litle river. Some say that Caesar stuck hard with Cicero [p. 935] the two first dayes, but at the third, that he yeelded and forsooke him. The exchaunge they agreed upon betwene them, was this. Caesar forsooke Cicero: Lepidus, his owne brother Paulus: and Antonius, Lucius Caesar, his uncle by the mothers side.[1] Such place tooke wrath in them, as they regarded no kinred nor blood, and to speake more properly, they shewed that no brute or savage beast is so cruell as man if with his licentiousnes he have liberty to execute his will. [p. 936] * * * Cicero hearing him [Popilius, a colonel] comming, commaunded his men to set downe his litter, and taking his beard in his left hande, as his manner was, he stowtly looked the murderers in the faces, his heade and beard being all white, and his face leane and wrinckled, for the extreame sorowes he had taken: divers of them that were by, helde their handes before their eyes, whilest Herennius did cruelly murder him. So Cicero being three score and foure yeares of age, thrust his necke out of the litter, and had his head cut of by Antonius commaundement, and his hands also, which wrote the Orations (called the Philippians) against him. * * * When these poore dismembred members were brought to Rome, Antonius by chaunce was busily occupied at that time about the election of certaine officers: who when he heard of them and saw them, he cried out alowde that now all his outlawries and proscriptions were executed: and thereuppon commaunded his head and his hands should straight be set up over the pulpit for Orations, in the place called Rostra. This was a fearefull and horrible sight unto the Romanes, who thought they saw not Ciceroes face, but an image of Antonius life and disposicion: who among so many wicked deedes as he committed, yet he did one act only that had some shew of goodnes, which was this. * * * [p. 937]

---

1. See 4.1.1–6.

Possible Sources

APPIAN OF ALEXANDRIA

From The Civil Wars (1578)[†]

[*Antony speaks at Caesar's funeral*]

Piso brought forth *Caesars* body, to the which, infinit numbers in armes ran, to kepe it, and with much noyse and pompe, brought it to the place of speech. There was much lamentation and weeping, ther was rushing of harnesse togither, with repentaunce of the forgetting of revengeance. *Antony* marking how they were affected, did not let it slippe, but toke upon him to make *Caesars* funeral sermon, as Consul, of a Consul, friend, of a friend, and kinsman, of a kinsman (for *Antony* was partly his kinsman) and to use craft againe. And thus he said:

> I do not thinke it meete (O Citizens) that the buriall praise of suche a man, should rather be done by me, than by the whole country. For what you have altogither for the love of hys vertue given him by decree, aswell the Senate as the people, I thinke your voice, and not *Antonies*, oughte to expresse it.

This he uttered with sad and heavy cheare, and wyth a framed voice, declared every thing, chiefly upon the decree, whereby he was made a God, holy and inviolate, father of the country, benefactor and governor, and suche a one, as never in al things they entituled other man to the like. At every of these words *Antonie* directed his countenance and hands to *Caesars* body, and with vehemencie of words opened the fact. At every title he gave an addition, with briefe speach, mixte with pitie and indignation. And when the decree named him father of the Country, then he saide: *This is the testimony of our duety.*

And at these wordes, *holy, inviolate* and *untouched,* and *the refuge of all other,* he said:

---

† From Book 2 of *The Civil Wars* (London, 1578), pp. 156–[59], trans. W. B. Markers in the margins of the original text have been removed.

None other made refuge of hym. But, he, *this holy and untouched*, is kylled, not takyng honoure by violences which he never desired, and then be we verye thrall that bestowe them ono the unworthy, never suing for them. But you doe purge your selves (O Citizens) of this unkindnesse, in that you nowe do use suche honoure towards hym being dead.

Then rehearsing the othe, that all shoulde keepe *Caesar* and *Caesars* body, and if any one wente about to betraye hym, that they were accursed that would not defende him: at this he extolled hys voice, and helde up his handes to the Capitoll, saying:

O *Jupiter* Countries defendour, and you other Gods, I am ready to revenge, as I sware and made execration, and when it seemes good to my companions to allowe the decrees, I desire them to aide me.

At these plaine speeches spoken agaynst the Senate, an uproare being made, *Antony* waxed colde, and recanted hys wordes.

It seemeth (O Citizens) (saide hee) that the things done have not bin the works of men but of Gods, and that we ought to have more consideration of the present, than of the past, bycause the thyngs to come, maye bring us to greater danger, than these we have, if we shall returne to oure olde, and waste the reste of the noble men that be in the Cittie. Therfore let us send thys holy one to the number of the blessed, and sing to him his due hymne and mourning verse.

When he had saide thus, he pulled up his gowne lyke a man beside hymselfe, and gyrded it, that he might the better stirre his handes: he stoode over the Litter, as from a Tabernacle, looking into it, and opening it, and firste sang his Himne, as to a God in heaven. And to confirme he was a God, he held up his hands, and with a swift voice, he rehearsed the warres, the fights, the victories, the nations that he had subdued to his Countrey, and the great booties that he had sent, making every one to be a marvell. Then with a continual crie,

This is the only unconquered of all that ever came to hands with hym. Thou (quoth he) alone diddest revenge thy countrey being injured .300. years, and those fierce nations that onely invaded *Rome*, and only burned it, thou broughtest them on their knees.

And when he had made these and many other invocations, he tourned hys voice from triumphe to mourning matter, and began to lament and mone him as a friend that had bin unjustly used, and did desire that he might give hys soule for *Caesars*. Then falling into moste vehement affections, uncovered *Caesars* body, holding up his vesture with a speare, cut with the woundes, and redde with the bloude of the chiefe Ruler, by the which the people lyke a Quire, did sing lamentation unto him, and by this passion were againe repleate with ire. And after these speeches, other lamentations wyth voice after the Country custome, were sung of the Quires, and they rehearsed again his acts and his hap.

Then made he *Caesar* hymselfe to speake as it were in a lamentable sort, to howe many of his enemies he hadde done good by name, and of the killers themselves to say as in an admiration, *Did I save them that have killed me?* This the people could not abide, calling to remembraunce, that all the kyllers (only *Decimus* except) were of *Pompeys* faction, and subdued by hym, to whom, in stead of punishment, he had given promotion of offices, governments of provinces and armies, and thought *Decimus* worthy to be made his heyre and son by adoption, and yet conspired hys death. While the matter was thus handled, and like to have come to a fray, one shewed out of the Litter the Image of *Caesar*, made of waxe, for hys body it selfe lying flat in the Litter, could not be seene. Hys picture was by a devise turned about, and .xxiii. wounds wer shewed over al his body, and his face horrible to behold. The people seeing this pittifull picture, coulde beare the dolour no longer, but thronged togyther, and beset the Senate house, wherein *Caesar* was kylled, and set it a fyre, and the kyllers that fledde for their lives, they ranne and sought in every place, and that so outragiouslye both in anger and dolour, as they kylled *Cynna* the Tribune being in name lyke to *Cynna* the Pretor that spake evill of *Caesar*, and wold not tarry to heare the declaration of his name, but cruelly tore him a peeces, and lefte not one parte to be put in grave. They caried fire against other mens houses, who manlye defending themselves, and the neighbours entreating them, they refrayned from fyre, but threatned to be in armes the next day. Wherefore the strikers hid themselves, and fled out of the Citie. The people returned to the Litter, and caried it as an holye thing, to be buried in an holy place among the Gods, but bicause the Priests did deny it, they brought hym againe into the common place, where the Pallaice of the old Kings were, and there, with al the bourds and tymber, which they could find in the place, which was muche, beside that every man broughte of himself, with garlandes and other gifts of private persons, makyng a solemne shew, they buryed the body, and abode al night about the fyre, In the whiche place, at the first was made an Altare, but nowe there is a temple of *Caesar*, where he is thought worthy divine honors. For his son by election, *Octavius*, taking the name of *Caesar*, and disposing the state after his example, which then takyng the beginning, and he exceedingly advancing to the degree it is now did thinke his father to deserve honors equall with the Gods, the which at this time having their originall, the

Romaines now use to give the same to hym that ruleth the estate,
unlesse he be a Tyranne, or diffamed at his death, that in olde tyme
could not suffer the name of a Kyng alyve.

SUETONIUS

From The Historie of Twelve Caesars (1606)†

Section 45

Of stature he [Julius Caesar] is reported to have beene tall; of com-
plexion white and cleare; with limbs well trussed and in good plight;
somewhat full faced; his eies black, lively, and quick; also very
healthfull, saving that in his latter daies he was given to faint and
swoune sodainly; yea, and as he dreamed, to start and be affrighted:
twice also in the midst of his martiall affaires, he was surprized
with the falling sicknes. About the trimming of his body, he was
overcurious: so as he would not onely be notted and shaven very
precisely, but also have his haire plucked, in so much as some cast
it in his teeth, and twitted him therewith. Moreover, finding by
experience, that the deformity of his bald head was oftentimes subject to the scoffes and scornes of back-biters and slaunderers, hee
tooke the same exceedingly to the heart: and therefore he both had
usually drawne downe his haire that grew but thin, from the crowne
toward his forehead: and also of all honours decreed unto him from
the Senate and People, he neither received nor used any more willingly, than the priviledge to weare continually the triumphant Law-
rel guirland. Men say also, that in his apparel he was noted for
singularity, as who used to goe in his Senatours purple studded
robe, trimmed with a jagge or frindge at the sleeve hand: and the
same so, as hee never was but girt over it, and that very slack and
loose: whereupon, arose (for certaine) that saying of Sulla, who
admonished the Nobles oftentimes, To beware of the boy that went
girded so dissolutely, [p. 19]

From Section 50

An opinion there is constantly received, that he was given to car-
nall pleasures, and that way spent much: also that he dishonoured
many Dames, and those of noble houses. * * * But above the rest, he
cast affection to Servilia the mother of M. Brutus. * * * [p. 21]

---

† From *The Historie of Twelve Caesars* (London, 1606), trans. Philemon Holland. Markers
in the margins of the original text have been removed. Section numbers are from Holland's translation. Page numbers to this source appear in square brackets:

Section 53

That he was a most sparie drinker of wine, his very enemies would never denie. Whereupon arose this Apophthegm of M. Cato, That of all that ever were, Caesar alone came sober to the overthrow of the State. For, about his foode and diet C. Oppius sheweth hee was so indifferent and without curiosity, that when upon a time his Host set before him upon the bord olde ranke oile in steed of greene, sweet, and fresh, so that other guests refused it, he onely (by his saying) fell to it and eate therof the more liberally; because he would not be thought to blame his Host either for negligence or rusticitie. * * * [p. 22]

Section 59

No religious feare of divine prodigies could ever fray him from any enterprise, or stay him if it were once in hand. As he sacrificed upon a time, the beast made an escape and ran away: yet for all that differred not he his journey against Scipio and Juba. He fortuned also to take a fall then, even as hee went forth of the ship to land: but turning this foretoken to the better presage, 'I take possession,' quoth hee, 'of thee, O Afrike.' Moreover, in verie skorne, and to make but a mockerie of those prophesies, whereby the name of Scipions was fatall to that province, and held luckie and invincible there, he had with him in his Campe the most base and abject fellow of all the Cornelian family, and who in reproch of his life was surnamed Saluito. * * * [p. 25]

Section 76

Howbeit, the rest of his deedes and words overweigh and depresse his good parts downe: so as he might be thought both to have abused his soveraintie, and worthily to have beene murthered. For, he not only tooke upon him excessive honours, to wit, continued Consulship, perpetuall Dictature, and Presidency of Manners; and more than so, the forename of Emperour, the Surname Father of his Countrie; his statue among the Kings, an eminent seate of Estate raised above the rest in the *Orchestra*, among the Senatours: but hee suffered also more stately dignities than beseeming the condition of a mortall wight to bee decreed and ordained for him: namely, a golden Throne in the Curia, and before the Tribunal[1]: a sacred Chariot and therein a frame carrying an Image,[2] at the solemne pomp of his Games *Circenses*: Temples, Altars, his owne Images

---

1. Located in the Forum.
2. An image of Caesar as a deity.

placed neere unto the Gods: a sacred Bedloft for such Images to be bestowed upon: a *flamin*, certaine *Luperci*: and the denomination of one moneth after his owne name. Besides, no honourable offices there were but he tooke and gave at his owne pleasure. His third and fourth Consulship in name onely and title he bare: contenting himselfe with the absolute power of Dictaturship decreed unto him with his Consulares all at one time: and in both yeeres, he substituted two Consuls under him for the three last moneths: so as, in the meane time, he held no Election but of Tribunes and Aediles of the Commons. In steed of Pretours he ordained Provosts, who should administer the affaires of the Citie even whiles he was present. And upon the very last day of the yeare, to wit next before the Kalends of Januarie, the place of a Consulship being vacant by the suddaine death of a Consull he conferred uppon one that made suite to enjoy the same but a few houres. With semblable licentiousnesse despising the custome of his Countrie, he ordained majestrates to continue in office many yeares together. To x. men of Pretours degree he graunted the Consulare Ornaments. Such as were but enfranchized Citizens, and divers mungrell Gaules no better then halfe Barbarians, he admitted Senatours. Furthermore, over the Mint and receipt of the City-revenewes, he set certaine peculiar servants of his owne to be rulers. The charge and commaund of three Legions which he left in Alexandria, he committed wholly to a sonne of Rufinus his freed man, a stale youth and Catanite of his owne. * * * [p. 30]

From Section 77

* * * Nay he proceeded to this point of Arrogancie, that when upon a time in a certaine Sacrifice, the South-sayer brought him word of unlucky Inwards in the beast; and such as had no heart at all, he made answere and said, That those which were to follow afterwards should prove more joy full and fortunate if it pleased him: neither was it to be taken for a prodigious and strange token, if a beast wanted an heart. * * * [pp. 30–31]

From Section 79

To this contumelious and notorious behaviour of his toward the Senate thus despised, he adjoyned a deede much more arrogant: For when as in his returne from the solemne Sacrifice of the Latine Holie dayes, among other immoderate and new acclamations of the people, one out of the multitude had set upon his Statue, a Coronet of Laurell tied about with a white band; and Epidius Marullus, a Tribune of the Commons together with his colleague Caesetius Flavus commanded the said band to be plucked of, and the man to be had away to prison, he taking it to heart, either that this overture to a kingdome sped no better, or, (as he made semblance and pretended himselfe) that he was put by the glorie of refusing it, sharpely rebuked the Tribunes, and deprived them both of their authoritie. Neither for all this, was he wiling afterwards to put away the infamous note of affecting and seeking after the title of a King: albeit he both made answere unto a Commoner saluting him by the name of a King, That he was Caesar and no King: and also at the *Lupercalia*, when Antonius the Consul imposed the Diademe oftentimes upon his head before the *Rostra*, did put it backe againe, and send it into the Capitoll to Jupiter Optimus Maximus. Moreover sundrie rumours ran rife abroad, that he would depart (for ever) to Alexandria or to Ilium, having at once translated and remooved thither the puissance and wealth of the Empire: dispeopeld Italie with mustring of sol-diers; and withall betaken the administration of Rome-Citie unto his friends. * * * [p. 31]

From Section 81

* * * Also, as he offered sacrifice, the Soothsayer Spurina warned him to take heede of danger toward him and which would not be differred after the Ides of March. Now, the verie day before the said Ides, it fortuned that as the birde *Regaliolus* was flying with a little branch of Lawrell, into the Court of Pompeius, a sort of other birdes of diverse kindes from out of the grove hard by, pursued after and there pulled it in peeces. But that night next before the day of his murder, both himselfe dreamed as he lay a sleepe, one while, that he was flying above the clouds: another while, that Jupiter and he shooke hands: and also his wife Calpurnia, imagined, that the Fini-all of his house fell downe, and that her husband was stabbed in her verie bosome: and sodainely withall the chamber doore of it selfe flew open. Hereupon, as also by reason of sickelinesse, he doubted a good while whether he should keepe at home and put off those matters which he had purposed to debate before the Senate, or no? At the last, being counselled and perswaded by Decius Brutus, not to disappoint the Senatours who were now in frequencie assembled and stayed for his comming long since, he went forth when it was well neere eleven of the clocke. And when one met him by the way, and offered him a written pamphlet, which layd open the conspiracie, and who they were that sought his life, he shuffled the same among other skroes and writings which he held in his left hand as if he would have red it anone. After this when he had killed many beasts for sacrifices and could speede of the Gods favour in none, he entred

the *Curia*[3] in contempt of all Religion; and therewith laughed Spurina to scorne: charging him to bee a false Prophet, for that the Ides of March were come: and yet noe harme befell unto him; albeit hee aunswered, That come indeede they were, but not yet past. [p. 33]

Section 82

When they saw once that he had taken his place, and was set, they stood round about him as serviceable attendants readie to do him honor: and then immediatly Cimber Tullus: who had undertaken to begin first, stepped neerer unto him, as though he would have made some request. When Caesar seemed to mislike and put him backe, yea and by his gesture to post him of unto another time, he caught hold of his gowne at both shoulders: whereupon as he cried out, 'This is violence,' Cassius came in too, full afront, and wounded him a little beneth the throat. Then Caesar catching Cassius by the arme thrust it through with his stile or writing punches; and with that being about to leape forward he was met with another wound and stayed. Now when he perceived himselfe beset on everie side and assailed with drawne daggers he wrapped and covered his head with his gowne: but withall he let downe the large lap[4] with his left hand to his legges beneath, hiding thereby the inferiour part also of his bodie, that he might fall more decently: and so, with 3 and 20 wounds he was stabbed: during which time he gave but one grone, without any worde uttered, and that was at the first thrust; although some have written, that as M. Brutus came running upon him he said, . . . 'And thou my sonne.' When all others fled sundrie waies, there lay he a good while dead, untill three of his owne pages bestowed him in a licter: and so with one arme hanging downe, carried him home. Neither in so many wounds, was there, as Antistius his Physitian deemed, any one found mortall, but that which he received second, in his breast. The conspiratours were minded to have dragged his Corps, after hee was thus slaine, into the River Tiberis; confiscated his goods, and repealed all his acts: but for feare of M. Antonius the Consul and Lepidus, Maister of the Horsemen, they held their hands and gave over those courses. * * * [p. 33–34]

Section 85

The common people streight after his funerall obsequies went with burning firebrands and torches to the dwelling houses of Brutus and Cassius: From whence being hardly repelled, they meeting with Helvius Cinna by the way, and mistaking his name, as if he had

---

3. Of Pompey.
4. Which they would wrap over their shoulders.

beene Cornelius Cinna (one who the day before had made a bitter invective as touching Caesar and whom they sought for) him they slew: set his head upon a speare, and so carried it about with them. After this they erected in the Forum a solide Columne almost 20 foote high, of Numidian Marble: with this title graven therupon; PARENTI PATRIAE. 'To the father of his Countrie.' At which piller for a long time they used still to sacrifice, to make vowes and prayers, to determine and end certaine controversies interposing alwaies their oth by the name of Caesar. * * * [p. 35]

Section 89

Of these murderers, there was not one in manner that either survived him above three years, or died of his naturall death. All stood condemned: and by one mishap or other perished: some by shipwracke, others in battaile: and some againe, shortened their own daies, with the verie same dagger, wherewith they had wounded Caesar. [p. 36]

Analogues

SIR THOMAS ELYOT

From The Boke Named the Governour (1531)[†]

[From *Book 2, Chapter 5: On the importance of affability*]

But I had almost forgoten Julius Cesar, who, beinge nat able to
sustaine the burden of fortune, and envienge his owne felicitie, abandoned his naturall disposition, and as it were, beinge dronke with over
moche welth, sought newe wayes howe to be advaunced above the
astate of mortall princes. Wherfore litle and litle he withdrewe
from men his accustomed gentilnesse, becomyng more sturdy in
langage, and straunge in countenance, than ever before had ben his
usage. And to declare more plainely his entent, he made an edict or
decre, that no man shulde prease to come to hym uncalled, and that
they shuld have good awaite, that they spake not in suche familiar
facion to hym as they before had ben accustomed; wherby he so dyd
alienate from hym the hartis of his most wise and assured adherentis, that, from that tyme forwarde, his life was to them tedious, and
abhorring him as a monstre or commune enemie, they beinge knitte
in a confederacy slew hym sitting in the Senate; of which conspiracie was chiefe capitaine, Marcus Brutus, whome of all other he beste
loved, for his great wisedome and prowesse. And it is of some writers
suspected that he was begoten of Cesar, for as moche as Cesar in his
youth loved Servilia, the mother of Brutus, and, as men supposed,
used her more familiarly than honestie required. Thus Cesar, by
omittinge his olde affabilitie, dyd incende his next frendes and companions to sle hym.

But nowe take hede what domage insued to hym by his decre,
wherin he commanded that no man shuld be so hardy to approche
or speke to hym. One whiche knewe of the conspiracie agayne hym,
and by al lykelyhode did participate therin, beinge meved either
with love or pitie, or other wise his conscience remording agayne
the destruction of so noble a prince, consideringe that by Cesars

---

[†] From *The Govenour* by Sir Thomas Elyot (London, 1531).

decre he was prohibited to have to hym any familiar accesse, so that
he might nat plainly detect the conspiraci; he, therto vehemently
meved, wrate in a byll all the forme therof, with the meanes howe it
myght be espied, and sens he mought fynde none other oportunitie,
he delyvered the byll to Cesar the same day that his dethe, and by
al lykelyhode did participate therin, beinge meved either with love
or pitie, or other wise his conscience remording agayne the destruction of so noble a prince, consideringe that by Cesars decre he was
prohibited to have to hym any familiar accesse, so that he might nat
plainly detect the conspiraci; he, therto vehemently meved, wrate
in a byll all the forme therof, with the meanes howe it myght be
espied, and sens he mought fynde none other oportunitie, he delyvered the byll to Cesar the same day that his dethe was prepared, as
he wente towarde the place where the Senate was holden. But he
beinge radicate in pride, and neglecting to loke on that bil, not
esteminge the persone that delivered it, whiche perchance was but of
a mean haviour, continued his way to the Senate, where he inconti-
nently was slaine by the said Brutus, and many mo of the Senate for
that purpose appoynted.

Who beholdinge the cause of the dethe of this moste noble Cesar,
unto whom in eloquence, doctrine, martiall prowesse, and gentilnesse, no prince may be comparid, and the acceleration or haste to
his confusion, causid by his owne edict or decre, will nat commende
affabilite and extolle libertie of speche? Wherby onely love is in the
hartis of people perfectly kendled, all feare excluded, and consequently realmes, dominions and all other autorites consolidate and
perpetuelly stablisshed. The sufferaunce of noble men to be spoken
unto is not onely to them an incomparable suretie, but also a
confounder of repentance, enemie to prudence, wherof is ingendred
this worde, *Had I wist*, whiche hath ben ever of all wise men
reproved.

[From Book 3, Chapter 6: Brutus and Cassius were examples of disloyalty]

This one thinge I wolde were remembred, that by the juste providence of god, disloyalte or treason seldome escapeth great
vengeaunce, all be it that it be pretended for a necessary purpose.
Example we have of Brutus and Cassius, two noble Romaynes, and
men of excellent vertues, whiche, pretendinge an honorable zeale to
the libertie and commune weale of their citie, slewe Julius Cesar
(who trusted them moste of all other) for that he usurped to have the
perpetuall dominion of the empire, supposinge thereby to have
brought the senate and people to their pristinate libertie. But it dyd
nat so succede to their purpose. But by the dethe of so noble a prince

hapned confusion and civil batayles. And bothe Brutus and Cassius, after longe warres vanquisshed by Octavian, nevewe and hiere unto Cesar, at the last falling in to extreme desperation, slewe them selfes. A worthy and convenient vengeaunce for the murder of so noble and valyaunt a prince.

[From *Book 3, Chapter 16: Caesar, Pompey, and Ambition*]

Also Pompei, and Julius Cesar, the one suffrynge no piere, the other no superior, by their ambycion caused to be slaine betwene them people innumerable, and subverted the best and mooste noble publyke weale of the worlde, and fynally havynge lyttel tyme of rejoysinge theyr unlefull desire, Pompeie, shamefully fleinge, had his heed striken of, by the commaundement of Ptolomee, king of Egipt, unto whome as unto his frende he fledde for succour. Cesar, the vainquyssher, was murdred in the Senate with daggers, by them, whome he mooste specially favoured.

I could occupie a great volume with histories of them whiche, coveytynge to mount into excellent dignities, dyd therby bringe in to extreme perylles bothe them selves and their countreys. For as Tacitus saith, wonderfull elegantly, with them whyche desire soveraygnetie, there is no meane place betwene the toppe and the stepe downe. To the which wordes Tulli agreinge, sayeth that hygh autorities shulde nat moche be desired, or rather nat to be taken at some tyme, and often tymes to be left and forsaken.

JOHN HIGGINS

From The Mirror for Magistrates (1587)[†]

[*Fols. 77a–78b: Caesar's Biographical Background*]

* * *

If ever erst the fame of auncient *Romayne* facts
Have come to pearce thine eares before this present time,
I thinke amongst the rest, likewise my noble actes
Have shewde them selves in sight, as *Phoebus* fayre in prime.
When first the *Romayne* state began aloft to clime,   5
And wanne the wealth of all the worlde beside,
When first their force in warlike feates were tryde,
My selfe was victour hee that did the *Romaynes* guyde.

† From *The Mirror for Magistrates* (London, 1587).

     I *Caius Julius Caesar Consull* had to name,
That worthie *Romayne* borne, renownde with noble deeds: 10
What neede I here recyte the linage whence I came,
Or else my great exploytes? perdy 'tis more then needes:
But onely this to tell, of purpose now proceedes:
Why I a *Romayne* Prince, no *Britayne*, here
Amongst these *Britayne* Princes now appeere,   15
As if amongst the rest a *Britayne* Prince I were.

     And yet because thou maist perceyve the story all
Of all my life, and so deeme better of the end:
I will againe the same to mind yet briefly call,
To tell thee how thou maist me prayse or discommend.   20
Which when thou hast, perdy, as I recyte it, pend,
Thou shalt confesse that I deserved well,
Amongst them here my tragedie to tell,
By conquest sith I wanne this Ile before I fell.

     Of stature high and tall, of colour fayre and white,   25
Of body spare and leane, yet comely made to see:
What neede I more of these impertinent recyte,
Sith *Plutarch* hath at large describde it all to thee.
And eke thy selfe that thinkst thou seest and hearest me,
Maist well suppose the rest, or take the viewe   30
Thou maist by talke of those which erst me knewe,
And by my statures tell of my proportion true.

     In journey swift I was, and prompte and quicke of witte,
My eloquence was likte of all that hearde me pleade,
I had the grace to use my tearmes, and place them fitte,   35
My roling Rhetoricke stoode my Clients oft in steade:
No fine conveyance past the compasse of my heade.
I wan the spurres, I had the laud and prayse,
I past them all that pleaded in those dayes,
I had of warlike knowledge, Keasar, all the keyes.   40

     At seventeene yeeres of age, a *Flamin* was I chose,
An office great in *Rome* of priesthoode Princely hie,
I married eke *Cossutia* whereof much mischiefe rose,
Because I was divorc'st from her so speedily.
Divorcement breeds despite, defame is got thereby.   45
For such as fancies fond by chaunge fulfil,
Although they thinke it cannot come to ill,
The wrong they shew doth cry to God for vengeance still.

Of these the stories tell, what neede I more recyte,
Or of the warres I waged *Consul* with the *Galles*?   50
The worthiest writers had desire of me to write,
They plac'st my life amongst the worthies and their falles.
So Fame me thinks likewise amids the *Britaynes* calles
For *Caesar* with his sword, that bare with them the sway,
And for the cause that brought him into such decay,   55
Which by his noble acts did beare their freedome first away.

When I in *Fraunce* had brought the *Galles* to bende,
And made them subject all obaysant unto mee:
Mee thought I had unto the worlde his ende
By west subdued the Nations whilome free.   60
There of my warres I wrot an historye
By nights, at leisure times so from my Countrey far:
I did describe the places and the sequelles of my war
The Commentaryes calde of *Caesars* acts that ar.

At length I did perceave there was an Island yet   65
By west of *Fraunce*, which in the *Ocean* sea did lye:
And that there was likewise no cause or time to let,
But that I might with them the chance of Fortune trye.
I sent to them for hostage of assuraunce, I,
And wild them tribute pay unto the *Romayne* stoute,   70
Or else I woulde both put theyr lives & goods in doubte,
And also reave away the best of all theyr route.

But they a people fearce and recklesse of my powres,
Abused those which brought th'ambassage that I sent:
Now sith (quod they) the land and region here is oures,   75
Wee will not *Caesar* to thy rightlesse hestes assent.
By dome of frendly Goddes first this Ile wee hent,
Of *Priames* bloud wee are, from *Greece* we *Trojanes* came.
As *Brutus* brought us thence, & gave this land his name,
So for our fredome we will freely fight to keepe the same.   80

* * *

[Fols. 82a–83a: Caesar invades Britain and returns to Rome to war
against Pompey and his sons]

But glory won, the way to holde and keepe the same,
To holde good Fortune fast, a worke of skill:
Who so with prudent arte can stay that stately dame
Which sets us up so high upon her hauty hill,
And constant aye can keepe her love and favour still,   85

Hee winnes immortall fame and high renowne:
But thrise unhappy hee that weres the stately crowne,
Yf once misfortune kicke and cast his scepter downe.

    For when in *Rome* I was *Dictator* chose,
And Emperour or Captayne sole for aye: 90
My glory did procure mee secret foes,
Because above the rest I bare the sway.
By sundry meanes they sought my deepe decaye.
For why, there coulde no *Consuls* chosen bee,
No *Pretor* take the place, no sentence have decree,   95
Unlesse it likte mee first, and were approvde by mee.

    This they envide that sude aloft to clime,
As *Cassius*, which the *Pretorship* did crave,
And *Brutus* eke his friende which bare the crime
Of my dispatch, for they did first deprave   100
My life, mine actes,[1] and sought my bloud to have,
Full secretly amongst them selves conspirde, decreede
To bee attemptors of that cruell bloudy deede,
When *Caesar* in the *Senate* house from noble hart should bleede.

    But I forewarned was by *Capis* tombe,   105
His *Epitaph* my death did long before forshowe:
Cornelius Balbus sawe mine horses headlesse ronne
Without a guide, forsakeing foode for woe.
Spurina warned mee that sooth of thinges did knowe,
A wrenne in beake with Laurell greene that flewe   110
From woods to *Pompeys* Court, whom birdes there slew,
Forshowde my dolefull death, as after all men knew.

    The night before my slaughter, I did dreame
I caried was, and flewe the clouds above:
And sometime hand in hand with *Jove* supreame   115
I walkte mee thought, which might suspitions move.
My wife *Calphurnia, Caesars* only love,
Did dreame shee sawe her crest of house to fall,
Her husband thrust through breast a sword withall,
Eke that same night her chamber dores themselves flewe
    open all.   120

    These thinges did make mee doubte that morning much,
And I accrazed was and thought at home to stay:

---

1. Cassius and Casca do this in Act I.

But who is hee can voyde of destnyes such,
Where so great number seekes hym to betray.
The traytour *Brutus* bad mee not delay,   125
Nor yet to frustrate there so great assembly sate:
On which to heare the publique pleas I gate,
Mistrusting naught mine end and fatall fate.

    There met mee by the way a *Romayne* good,
Presenting mee a scrole of every name: 130
And all their whole devise that sought my bloud,
That presently would execute the same.
But I supposde that for some suit hee came,
I heedelesse bare this scrole in my left hand,
And others more, till leasure, left unscand,   135
Which in my pocket afterwards they fand.

    Spurina as I came at sacrifizes was,
Nere to the place where I was after slayne:
Of whose divinings I did litle passe,
Though hee to warne mee oft before was fayne.   140
My hauty hart these warnings all disdayne.
(Quod I) the Ides of Marche bee come, yet harme is none.
(Quod hee) the Ides of Marche be come, yet th'are not gone.
And reckelesse so to Court I went, and tooke my throne.

    Assoone as I was set, the traytors all arose,   145
And one approached nere, as to demaund some thing:
To whom as I layd eare, at once my foes
Mee compast round, their weapons hid they bring.
Then I to late perceiv'd the fatall sting.
O this (quoth I) is violence: then *Cassius* pearst my breast: 150
And *Brutus* thou my sonne (quoth I) whom erst I loved best?
Hee stabde mee in, and so with daggers did the rest.

    You Princes all, and noble men beware of pride,
And carefull will to warre for Kingdomes sake:
By mee, that set my selfe aloft the world to guide,   155
Beware what bloudsheds you doe undertake.
Ere three & twenty wounds had made my hart to quake,
What thousands fell for *Pompeys* pride and mine?
Of *Pompeys* life that cut the vitall line,
My selfe have told what fate I found in fine.   160

    Full many noble men, to rule alone, I slewe,
And some themselves for griefe of hart did slay:

For they ne would mine Empyre stay to vewe.
Some I did force to yeelde, some fled away
As loth to see theyr Countryes quite decay.   165
The world in *Aphrike, Asia*, distant far,
And *Europe* knew my bloudsheds great in war,
Recounted yet through all the world that ar.

     But sith my whole pretence was glory vayne,
To have renowne and rule above the rest,   170
Without remorce of many thousands slayne,
Which, for their owne defence, their warres addrest:
I deeme therefore my stony harte and brest
Receiv'd so many wounds for just revenge, they stood
By justice right of *Jove*, the sacred sentence good.   175
That who so slayes, hee payes the price, is bloud for bloud.

Shakespeare and Roman History

T. J. B. SPENCER

From Shakespeare and the Elizabethan Romans[†]

Shakespeare has, at various times, received some very handsome compliments for his ancient Romans; for his picture of the Roman world, its institutions, and the causation of events; for his representation of the Roman people at three critical stages of their development: the turbulent republic with its conflict of the classes; the transition from an oligarchic to a monarchic government which was vainly delayed by the assassination of Julius Caesar; and the final stages by which the rule of the civilized world came to lie in the hands of Octavius Caesar. These are quite often praised as veracious or penetrating or plausible. Moreover, the compliments begin early, and they begin at a time when no high opinion was held of Shakespeare's learning. The name of Nahum Tate, for example, is not a revered one in the history of Shakespeare studies; yet in 1680 he wrote:

> I confess I cou'd never yet get a true account of his Learning, and am apt to think it more than Common Report allows him. I am sure he never touches on a Roman Story, but the Persons, the Passages, the Manners, the Circumstances, the Ceremonies, all are Roman.[1]

And Dryden, too, in conversation said "that there was something in this very tragedy of *Coriolanus*, as it was writ by Shakespeare, that is truly great and truly Roman".[2] And Pope (for all his comparison of Shakespeare to "an ancient majestick piece of *Gothick* Architecture") declared in his Preface that he found him

---

† From *Shakespeare Survey* 10 (1957): 27–38. Excerpts: pp. 27–31, 33–34, 37–38. A lecture delivered to the Shakespeare Conference at Stratford-upon-Avon, 6 September 1955. Reprinted with the permission of Cambridge University Press.

1. Letter before *The Loyal General, A Tragedy* (1680); *The Shakspere Allusion Book . . . 1591 to 1700* (Oxford, 1932), II, 266.

2. Reported by Dennis; see D. Nichol Smith, *Eighteenth Century Essays on Shakespeare* (Glasgow, 1903), p. 309.

very knowing in the customs, rites, and manners of Antiquity.
In *Coriolanus* and *Julius Caesar*, not only the Spirit, but Manners, of the *Romans* are exactly drawn; and still a nicer distinction is shewn, between the manners of the *Romans* in the time
of the former and of the latter.[3]

The odd thing is that this veracity or authenticity was approved at a
time when Shakespeare's educational background was suspect; when
the word "learning" practically meant a knowledge of the Greek and
Roman writers; when the usual description of Shakespeare was
"wild"; when he was regarded as a member of what Thomas Rymer
called "the gang of the strolling fraternity".

There were, of course, one or two exceptions; Rymer wrote,
towards the end of the seventeenth century, in his most cutting way
about *Julius Caesar*:

> *Caesar and Brutus* were above his conversation. To put them
> in Fools Coats, and make them Jack-puddens in the *Shakespear*
> dress, is a *Sacriledge*. . . . The Truth is, this authors head was
> full of villainous, unnatural images, and history has only
> furnish'd him with great names, thereby to recommend them to
> the World.[4]

There was, too, the problem of Shakespeare's undignified Roman
mobs. It was obvious that Cleopatra's vision of a Rome where

> mechanic slaves
> With greasy aprons, rules, and hammers, shall
> Uplift us to the view

was derived from Shakespeare's own London. And Casca's description: "The rabblement hooted and clapped their chopped hands and
threw up their sweaty night-caps . . ."—this was the English populace and not the Roman *plebs*. Dennis thought that the introduction
of the mob by Shakespeare "offends not only against the Dignity of
Tragedy, but against the Truth of History likewise, and the Customs
of Ancient *Rome*, and the majesty of the *Roman* People".[5] But the
opinions of Rymer and Dennis were eccentric; the worst they could
say against Shakespeare's Romans was that they were not sufficiently dignified; and this counted for very little beside the usual
opinion of better minds that Shakespeare got his Romans right.

More surprising, therefore, was Shakespeare's frequent neglect
of details; and it was just at *this* time that the scholars and critics (if
not the theatrical and reading publics) were becoming sensitive to

3. D. Nichol Smith, *op. cit.* pp. 53, 62.
4. *A Short View of Tragedy* (1693), p. 148.
5. D. Nichol Smith, *op. cit.* p. 26.

Shakespeare's anachronisms, his aberrations from good sense and common knowledge about the ancients, and were carefully scrutinizing his text for mistakes. It was apparent that, when it came to details, Shakespeare's Romans often belonged to the time of Queen Elizabeth and King James. And the industrious commentators of the eighteenth century collected a formidable array of nonsense from his plays on classical antiquity: how clocks strike in ancient Rome; how Cleopatra has lace in her stays and plays at billiards; how Titus Lartius compares Coriolanus's *hm* to the sound of a battery; and so on. Above all, it could be observed that Shakespeare was occasionally careless or forgetful about ancient costume. Coriolanus stood in the Forum waving his hat. The very idea of a Roman candidate for the consulship standing waving his hat was enough to make a whole form of schoolboys break into irrepressible mirth. Pope softened the horror by emending *hat* to *cap*; and Coriolanus was permitted to wave his cap, not his hat, in the texts of Theobald, Hanmer, Warburton, and Dr Johnson, and perhaps even later. What seemed remarkable and what made the eighteenth-century editors so fussy about these anachronisms was Shakespeare's inconsistency in his historical reconstructions: his care and scrupulosity over preserving Roman manners, alongside occasional carelessness or indifference. The very reason they noticed the blunders was that they jarred against the pervading sense of authenticity everywhere else in the Roman plays.

I take it that Dryden and Pope were right; that Shakespeare knew what he was doing in writing Roman plays; that part of his intention was a serious effort at representing the Roman scene as genuinely as he could. He was not telling a fairy tale with Duke Theseus on St Valentine's Day, nor dramatizing a novelette about Kings of Sicilia and Bohemia, but producing a *mimesis* of the veritable history of the most important people (humanly speaking) who ever lived, the concern of every educated man in Europe and not merely something of local, national, patriotic interest; and he was conscious of all this while he was building up his dramatic situations and expositions of characters for the players to fulfil. It can, therefore, hardly fail to be relevant to our interpretations of the plays to explore the views of Roman history in Shakespeare's time. It is at least important to make sure that we do not unthinkingly take it for granted that they were the same as our own in the twentieth century to which we belong or the nineteenth century from which we derive. It is worth while tracing to what extent Shakespeare was in step with ideas about ancient Rome among his contemporaries and to what extent (and why) he diverged from them.

"Histories make men wise." Ancient, and in particular Roman, history was explored as the material of political lessons, because it was one of the few bodies of consistent and continuous historical material available. Modern national history (in spite of patriotism) could not be regarded as so central, nor were the writers so good; and the narratives in the scriptures were already overworked by the parson. Roman history was written and interpreted tendentiously in Europe in the sixteenth century, as has happened at other times. In writing his Roman plays Shakespeare was touching upon the gravest and most exciting as well as the most pedantic of Renaissance studies, of European scholarship. Although Shakespeare himself turned to Roman history after he had been occupied with English history for some years, nevertheless it was Roman history which usually had the primacy for the study of political morality. Yet in spite of the widespread interest in ancient culture among educated persons, the actual writing of the history of the Greeks and Romans was not very successful in England in the sixteenth century. There was no history of the Romans in Shakespeare's lifetime comparable (for example) to the *History of Great Britain* by John Speed or the *Generall Historie of the Turkes* by Richard Knolles. Sir Walter Raleigh did not get very far in his *History of the World* and dealt only with the earlier and duller centuries of Rome. Probably the reason for the scarcity of books of Roman history and their undistinguished nature was that the sense of the supremacy of the ancients and of the impudence of endeavouring to provide a substitute for Livy and Tacitus was too strong.[6] So explained William Fulbecke, who published a book called *An Historicall Collection of the Continuall Factions, Tumults, and Massacres of the Romans* in 1601 and dedicated it to Sackville, Lord Buckhurst (the primary author of *A Mirror for Magistrates*). "I do not despaire" (wrote Fulbecke) "to follow these Romanes, though I do not aspire to their exquisite and industrious perfection: for that were to climbe above the climates: but to imitate any man, is every mans talent." His book is a poor thing. And so is Richard Reynoldes' *Chronicle of all the Noble Emperours of the Romaines* (1571). And the translations of the Roman historians, apart from North's Plutarch, before the seventeenth century are not particularly distinguished. But for this very reason the books on Roman history are useful evidence for the normal attitude to the Romans and their story in Shakespeare's lifetime. For it is not so much what we can find in Plutarch, but what Shakespeare noticed in Plutarch that we need to know; not merely

---

6. Cf. A. Momigliano, *Contributo alla storia degli studi classici* (Rome, 1955), pp. 75–6: "To the best of my knowledge, the idea that one could write a history of Rome which should replace Livy and Tacitus was not yet born in the early seventeenth century. The first Camden Praelector of history in the University of Oxford had the statutory duty of commenting on Floras and other ancient historians (1622) . . . Both in Oxford and Cambridge Ancient History was taught in the form of a commentary on ancient historians."

Plutarch's narrative, but the preconceptions with which his biographies could be read by a lively modern mind about the turn of the seventeenth century; for

> men may construe things after their fashion
> Clean from the purpose of the things themselves.

It is by no means certain that we, by the unaided light of reason and mid-twentieth-century assumptions, will always be able to notice the things to which Shakespeare was sensitive.

First then, the title of William Fulbecke's book is worth attention: *An Historicall Collection of the Continuall Factions, Tumults, and Massacres of the Romans and Italians during the space of one hundred and twentie yeares next before the peaceable Empire of Augustus Caesar.* There is not much of the majesty of the Roman People (which Dennis desiderated) in these continual factions, tumults and massacres. In his preface Fulbecke writes:

> The use of this historic is threefold; first the revealing of the mischiefes of discord and civill discention. . . . Secondly the opening of the cause hereof, which is nothing else but ambition, for out of this seed groweth a whole harvest of evils. Thirdly the declaring of the remedie, which is by humble estimation of our selves, by living well, not by lurking well: by conversing in the light of the common weale with equals, not by complotting in darke conventicles against superiors.[7]

Equally tendentious is what we read on the title-page of the translation of Appian as *An Auncient Historic and exquisite Chronicle of the Romanes Warres, both Civile and Foren* in 1578;

> In the which is declared:
> Their greedy desire to conquere others.
> Their mortall malice to destroy themselves.
> Their seeking of matters to make warre abroad.
> Their picking of quarels to fall out at home.
> All the degrees of Sedition, and all the effects of Ambition.
> A firme determination of Fate, thorowe all the changes of Fortune.
> And finally, an evident demonstration, That peoples rule must give
>   place, and Princes power prevayle.

This kind of material (the ordinary stuff of Roman history in the sixteenth century) does not lend itself to chatter about the majesty of the Roman people. In fact, the kind of classical dignity which we associate perhaps with Addison's *Cato* or Kemble's impersonation of Coriolanus is not to be taken for granted in Shakespeare's time. The

7. Sig. A2.

beginning of Virgil's *Aeneid*, with its simple yet sonorous *arma virumque cano*, might by us be taken as expressive of true Roman dignity. Richard Stanyhurst, however, in his translation of Virgil in 1582 rendered it:

> Now manhood and garboyles I chaunt. . . .

"Garboyles", it will be remembered, was Antony's favourite word to describe the military and political exploits of Fulvia.

So much for Roman history as "garboyles". Secondly, besides the "garboyles" and encouraging them, there was a limitation in viewpoint due to the fact that the moral purpose of history in general, and of Roman history in particular, was directed towards *monarchs*. When Richard Reynoldes published his *Chronicle of all the noble Emperours of the Romaines, from Julius Caesar orderly . . . Setting forth the great power, and devine providence of almighty God, in preserving the godly Princes and common wealthes* in 1571, he gave the usual panegyric: "An historic is the glasse of Princes, the image most lively bothe of vertue and vice, the learned theatre or spectacle of all the worlde, the councell house of Princes, the trier of all truthes, a witnes of all tymes and ages . . ." and so forth. The really important and interesting and relevant political lessons were those connected with *princes*. It was this that turned the attention away from republican Rome to monarchical Rome: the Rome of the Twelve Caesars and their successors. Republican Rome was not nearly so useful for models of political morality, because in sixteenth-century Europe republics happened to be rather rare. (Venice, the important one, was peculiar, not to say unique, anyway.) Republics were scarce. But there were aspiring Roman Emperors all over the place.

Sometimes the political lesson was a very simple one. In dedicating his *Auncient Historie and exquisite Chronicle of the Romanes Warres* in 1578, the translator states:

> How God plagueth them that conspire againste theyr Prince, this Historie declareth at the full. For all of them, that coniured against *Caius Caesar*, not one did escape violent death. The which this Author hathe a pleasure to declare, bycause he would affray all men from disloyaltie toward their Soveraigne.

We need not, perhaps, put too much emphasis upon this argument, because the book was being dedicated to the Captain of the Queen's Majesty's Guard. But more sophisticated writers showed the same interest. Sir Walter Raleigh in his *History of the World* on occasions pointed the suitable political moral. But the problems that interested him and set him off on one of his discussions were those relevant to the political situation in the sixteenth and early seventeenth centuries. The story of Coriolanus, for example, does not interest him at all; he compresses Livy's fine narrative into nothingness, though he spares a few words for Coriolanus's mother and wife who prevailed upon him "with a pitiful tune of deprecation".[8] But the problem of the growth of tyranny fascinates him. He never got as far as Julius Caesar. He had to wind up his *History* at the beginning of the second century B.C. But he gets Caesar into his discussion. The problem of the difference between a benevolent monarchy and an odious tyranny, and the gradations by which the one may merge into the other—that was the real interest; and Imperial Rome was the true material for that.

So that, in spite of literary admiration for Cicero, the Romans in the imagination of the sixteenth century were Suetonian and Tacitan rather than Plutarchan. An occasional eccentric enthusiasm for one or both of the two Brutuses does not weigh against the fact that it was the busts of the Twelve Caesars that decorated almost every palace in Europe. And it required a considerable intellectual feat to substitute the Plutarchan vision of Rome (mostly republican) for the customary line of the Imperial Caesars. Montaigne and Shakespeare were capable of that feat. Not many others were. The Roman stuff that got into *A Mirror for Magistrates* naturally came from Suetonius and historians of the later Caesars. One of the educators of Europe in the sixteenth century was the Spaniard Antonio de Guevara. His *Dial of Princes* (which was a substitute for the still unprinted *Meditations* of the Emperor Marcus Aurelius) was translated by North with as much enthusiasm as Plutarch was. Guevara, whose platitudinous remarks on politics and morals—he was a worthy master for Polonius—gave him a European reputation, naturally turned to Imperial Rome to illustrate his maxims and observations on life. The Emperor Marcus Aurelius was his model of virtue (though he included love-letters from the Emperor to a variety of young women in Rome—which seems rather an incongruous thing to do for the over-virtuous author of the *Meditations*); and when Guevara wanted examples of vices as well as virtue, to give more varied moral and political lessons, he again naturally turned to the Roman monarchs.

* * *

In Shakespeare's three principal Roman plays we see a steadily advancing independence of thought in the reconsideration of the Roman world. In *Julius Caesar*, it seems to me, he is almost precisely in step with sound Renaissance opinion on the subject. There has been a good deal of discussion of this play because of a supposed ambiguity in the author's attitude to the two principal characters. It

8. *The History of the World*, IV, vii, §i; *Works* (Oxford, 1832), V, 531–2.

has been suggested, on the one hand, that Brutus is intended to be a short-sighted political blunderer who foolishly or even wickedly struck down the foremost man in all the world; Dante and survivals of medieval opinion in the sixteenth century can be quoted here. We have, on the contrary, been told, on very high authority in Shakespeare studies, that Shakespeare followed the Renaissance admiration for Brutus and detestation for Caesar. It has also been suggested that Shakespeare left the exact degrees of guilt and merit in Caesar and Brutus deliberately ambiguous in the play, to give a sense of depth, to keep the audience guessing and so make the whole dramatic situation more telling. But all this, it seems to me, obscures the fact that the reassessment and reconsideration of such famous historical figures was a common literary activity in the Renaissance, not merely in poetry and drama (where licence is acceptable), but in plain prose, the writing of history. It seems hardly legitimate to talk about "tradition", to refer to "traditional" opinions about Caesar and Brutus, when in fact the characters of each of them had been the subject of constant discussion. In the nineteenth century you could weigh up the varying views of Caesar held by Mommsen or Froude or Anthony Trollope or Napoleon III of France, and read their entertaining books on the subject. It was not so very different in the sixteenth century. I am not suggesting that Shakespeare read the great works on the life and character of Julius Caesar by Hubert Goltz (1563) or by Stefano Schiappalaria (1578) where everything about him was collected and collated and assessed and criticized. But other people did. And Shakespeare, writing a play of the subject, could hardly live in such intellectual isolation as to be unaware of the discussion. It would, I think, be quite wrong to suggest by quotation from any one writer such as Montaigne that Caesar was generally agreed to be a detestable character. On the contrary, the problem was acknowledged to be a complicated and fascinating one; and the discussion began early, and in ancient times. Men have often disputed (wrote Seneca in his *De Beneficiis*, a work translated both by Arthur Golding and by Thomas Lodge), whether Brutus did right or wrong. "For mine owne part, although I esteemed *Brutus* in all other thinges a wise and vertuous man, yet meseemeth that in this he committed a great errour"; and Seneca goes on to explain the error: Brutus

> imagined that such a Citie as this might repossesse her ancient honour, and former lustre, when vertue and the primitive Lawes were either abolished, or wholly extinguished; Or that Iustice, Right, and Law, should be inviolably observed in such a place, where he had seene so many thousand men at shocke and battell, not to the intent to discerne whether they were to obay and

serve, but to resolve under whom they ought to serve and obay. Oh how great oblivion possessed this man! how much forgot he both the nature of affaires, and the state of his Citie! to suppose that by the death of one man there should not some other start up after him, that would usurpe over the common-weale.[9]

Likewise William Fulbecke (writing in 1586, though his book was not published until 1601), while seeing the calamities Caesar was bringing upon the Roman state, could not praise Brutus for permitting himself to participate in political assassinations:

> M. Brutus, the chiefe actor in Caesars tragedie, was in counsel deepe, in wit profound, in plot politicke, and one that hated the principality whereof he devested Caesar. But did Brutus looke for peace by bloudshed? did he thinke to avoyd tyrannie by tumult? was there no way to wound Caesar, but by stabbing his own conscience? & no way to make Caesar odious, but by incurring the same obloquie?[1]

Fulbecke summarized his position in the controversy: "Questionlesse the Romanes should not have nourished this lyon in their Citie, or being nourished, they should not have disgraced him."

* * *

There may very well be, in Shakespeare's writings, a good many vestiges of the medieval world-picture. His mind may have been encumbered, or steadied, by several objects, orts, and relics of an earlier kind of intellectual culture. But it is scarcely perceptible in his Roman plays, which can be brought to the judgment bar of the Renaissance revivification of the ancient world, and will stand the comparison with the major achievements of Renaissance Humanism (as Ben Jonson's will not). We find there a writer who seems in the intellectual current of his times. Shakespeare had what might be described as the scholarship of the educated creative writer—the ability to go and find out the best that is known and thought in his day; to get it quickly (as a busy writer must, for Shakespeare wrote more than a million words in twenty years); to get it without much trouble and without constant access to good collections of books (as a busy man of the theatre must, one often on tour and keeping up two homes); and to deal with his sources of information with intelligence and discrimination. The favourite notions of learning get around in ways past tracing. Anyone who is writing a play or a book on any subject has by that very fact a peculiar alertness and sensitivity

---

9. Lodge's translation in *The Workes of Lucius Annaeus Seneca, Both Morall and Naturall* (1614), pp. 30–1; *Of Benefits*, ii, xx.
1. *Op. cit.* sig. Zı^v.

to information and attitudes about his subject. Shakespeare did not write in isolation. He had friends. It would be an improbable hypothesis that he worked cut off from the intellectual life of his times. Indeed, all investigations of the content of his plays prove the obvious: that he was peculiarly sensitive to the intellectual tendencies of his age, in all spheres of thought. His scholarship was of a better quality than Jonson's, because (one might guess) he was a better listener, not so self-assertive in the company of his betters, and was therefore more able, with that incomparable celerity of mind of his, to profit from any well-informed acquaintance.

Finally, in understanding the picture of the ancient world in these plays, the part played by Shakespeare himself in creating our notions of the ancient Romans should not be forgotten. It has become difficult to see the plays straight, to see the thing in itself as it really is, because we are all in the power of Shakespeare's imagination, a power which has been exercised for several generations and from which it is scarcely possible to extricate ourselves. * * *

Shaping a Narrative

ERNEST SCHANZER

[Caesar in Literary Tradition]†

* * *

In considering medieval and Renaissance attitudes to Caesar, one must distinguish between the popular tradition, in which he figures as an image rather than a person, the first of the Emperors, the Mirror of Knighthood, one of the Nine Worthies, the World Conqueror;[1] and the response of educated men who had access to some of the ancient historians, biographers, and poets. Where in the popular tradition Caesar was extolled and his assassins execrated, educated men, both in the Middle Ages and the Renaissance, derived from their reading of the ancients a predominantly divided response. This is already notable in John of Salisbury's Mirror for Magistrates, the *Polycraticus* (1160), where a knowledge of Cicero, Lucan, and Suetonius, coupled with that of early Christian and medieval writers, has resulted in a wavering and mixed response, not dissimilar to Cicero's. In the *De Regimine Principum* (1270) of Thomas Aquinas we find, side by side, much as in Suetonius and Dio, the two opposed views of Caesar as the virtuous, just, and merciful Emperor and as the tyrannical usurper who richly deserved his death. As I have argued elsewhere,[2] even in Dante, who is commonly taken as a typical exponent of the medieval apotheosis of Caesar, we get glimpses of an essentially divided attitude, in spite of the fate allotted in the *Inferno* to Brutus and Cassius. Dante's divided attitude towards Caesar, as far as it can be inferred from the scant references to him in his works, seems to have been the reverse of Cicero's, stemming from an apparent lack of esteem for his personal qualities and an

---

† From *The Problem Plays of Shakespeare: A Study of "Julius Caesar," "Measure for Measure," and "Antony and Cleopatra"* (New York: Schocken Books, 1965), pp. 16–22. Reprinted by permission of Taylor & Francis Books UK.
1. See [Friedrich] Gundolf, [*Caesar: Geschichte seines Ruhms* (Berlin: G. Bondi, 1924)], ch.2.
2. 'Dante and Julius Caesar', *Medium Aevum*, vol. 24 (1955), pp. 20–22.

approval of his historic role in founding the Empire. His attitude
seems closest to that of Plutarch, for with both writers what appears
to be scant liking for Caesar as a man is coupled with a belief in him
as the agent of Destiny, and with an enthusiastic admiration for the
virtues of Cato of Utica.

The young Petrarch's divided response to Caesar is very similar
to Cicero's and partly derived from it, resulting from admiration for
Caesar's personal qualities and achievements and hatred of him as
the destroyer of the Republic. But in addition to this we find a radical change of attitude in the course of the poet's life. As Dr. Hans
Baron puts it, 'In the years when he had first conceived his *Africa*,
and had been associated with Rienzo, he had given enthusiastic
praise to the *Respublica Romana*, at the expense of the Emperors.
In his old age, profound admiration for Caesar reigned once more
supreme. . . . His growing interest in Caesar—whom in his youth he
had considered the destroyer of Roman liberty—sprang largely from
his conviction that Caesar was the prototype of those enlightened
tyrants at whose courts Petrarch spent the second half of his life.'[3]
In this opposition of attitudes towards Caesar between the young
republican and the old courtier, Petrarch provides in his own person
an epitome of the Caesar controversy that divided the humanists of
the early Italian Renaissance. Dr. Baron has well brought out how
closely this division between Caesar's detractors and admirers
reflected that between civic humanists, mostly Florentine, and
those attached to the courts of Princes. Thus, much as in Caesar's
own day, the polemics concerned with him and his assassins formed
part of the political struggle between republican and anti-republican
forces. These polemics reached a climax in the prolonged controversy, beginning in 1435, between the Florentine Poggio Bracciolini
and the Veronese humanist at the court at Ferrara, Guarino. But
while this partisan controversy banished for a time any mixed
response to the Caesar story among its most vocal participants, it
inevitably reasserted itself among readers of Plutarch and Suetonius, of Cicero, Appian, and Petrarch—in other words, among all
educated men. It makes its most surprising appearance in Orlando
Pescetti's *Cesare* (1594), for this play was dedicated to Alfonso d'Este,
whom, in his dedication, Pescetti compares to Caesar and claims as
one of his descendants. Yet it is Brutus who is treated, throughout
the play, with the greatest sympathy, while of Caesar we are given a
divided, though predominantly unsympathetic, picture, based in the
main on Lucan, Plutarch, Appian, and Muret.[4]

3. *The Crisis of the Early Italian Renaissance* (1955), vol. 1, pp. 95–6.
4. A strong case for Pescetti's *Cesare* as a source of Shakespeare's play has been made by
   Alexander Boecker, *A Probable Source of Shakespeare's 'Julius Caesar'* (1913). Some of the
   verbal echoes seem too close for coincidence. For instance, the notion, put forward in

In France the tradition of a divided response is continued in the Caesar plays of Muret (first publ. 1553) and Grévin (1558), where, as H. M. Ayres has shown,[5] Plutarchian narrative and Lucanic sentiments are presented in a Senecan mould, with Caesar transformed into a Hercules-like braggart, but with his Plutarchian stoicism and other noble qualities unimpaired. MacCallum thus can speak of Muret's 'divided admiration for Brutus and Caesar'.[6] And the same holds true of Garnier's *Cornélie* (1574), which Shakespeare may have known in Thomas Kyd's translation (1594).[7] Garnier, much as Plutarch, Suetonius, and Dio, presents two antithetical images of Caesar. Cassius (iv.1) depicts him as a usurping tyrant, who 'hath vnpeopled most part of the earth' by his 'bloody jarres'. This is followed by the Chorus of Caesar's friends, who see him as the great conqueror who brings peace to Rome, the merciful victor who '(abhorring blood) at last / Pardon'd all offences past.'[8] When Caesar appears on the stage (iv.2), he begins his speech as the vainglorious, boastful victor, but in conversation with Antony reveals his clemency, his trust in his friends, his Stoic contempt of death.

Montaigne's divided attitude is very similar to Cicero's, stemming from the keenest admiration for Caesar's personal qualities and the strongest abhorrence of his political pursuits. One sentence brings this out most pointedly: 'When I consider the incomparable greatnesse and unvaluable worth of his minde, I excuse Victorie, in that shee could not well give him over, in this most unjust and unnatural cause.' He speaks enthusiastically of Caesar's mildness and extraordinary clemency towards his enemies, and continues: 'Never was man, that shewed more moderation in his victorie, or more resolution in his adverse fortune. But all these noble inclinations, rich gifts, worthy qualities, were altered, smothered and eclipsed by this

---

both plays by Brutus, that Antony should not be killed, for, once the head is off, the limbs are powerless

> (Col troncar della testa all'altre membra
> Troncasi ogni valore, ogni possanza . . .

> For he can do no more than Caesar's arm
> When Caesar's head is off . . .)

is too unusual to be accepted as a plausible coincidence. Therefore, unless one assumes an English intermediary play that closely echoed Pescetti's, I think we have to accept the notion that Shakespeare had looked at *Il Cesare* in the Italian original. As Boecker points out, *Il Cesare* also provides an interesting parallel to Shakespeare's play in that it is named after Caesar, who, though constantly discussed, plays a subordinate part in the action and only appears in two of the five acts, while Brutus is the central, as well as the most sympathetic, character throughout.

5. 'Shakespeare's *Julius Caesar* in the Light of some other Versions', *P.M.L.A.*, vol. 25 (1910), pp. 203 ff.
6. M. W. MacCallum, *Shakespeare's Roman Plays and their Background* (1910), p. 27.
7. See Joan Rees, '*Julius Caesar*—an Earlier Play, and an Interpretation', *M.L.R.*, vol. 50 (1955), pp. 135 ff.
8. I quote from Kyd's translation, *Works*, ed. Boas (1901).

furious passion of ambition; by which he suffered himselfe to be so farre mis-led, that it may be well affirmed, she onely ruled the Sterne of all his actions. . . . To conclude, this only vice (in mine opinion) lost, and overthrew in him the fairest naturall and richest ingenuitie that ever was; and hath made his memorie abhominable to all honest mindes, insomuch as by the ruine of his countrey, and subversion of the mightiest state and most flourishing Common-wealth, that ever the world shall see, he went about to procure his glorie.'[9]

All the evidence suggests that in England, too, such a divided response was the prevailing one among educated men. It is found already in Sir Thomas Elyot's *Governour* (1531), a work which, as Mr. J. C. Maxwell has shown,[1] Shakespeare seems to have drawn on for at least one passage in *Julius Caesar*. Elyot speaks of 'this moste noble Cesar, unto whom in eloquence, doctrine, martiall prowesse, and gentilnesse, no prince may be comparid', 'the perfecte paterne of Industrie', 'nat so much honoured for his lernynge as he is for his diligence'. But 'beinge radicate in pride', he 'abandoned his naturall disposition, and as it were, being dronke with ouer moche welth, sought newe wayes howe to be aduaunced aboue the astate of mortall princes. Wherfore litle and litle he withdrewe from men his accustomed gentilnesse, becomyng more sturdy in langage, and straunge in countenance, than euer before had ben his usage . . . wherby he so dyd alienate from hym the hartis of his most wise and assured adherentis, that, from that tyme forwarde, his life was to them tedious, and abhorring him as a monstre or commune enemie, they beinge knitte in a confederacy slewe hym sitting in the Senate'.[2]

In the account of his death by Caesar's ghost in the 1587 additions to *The Mirror for Magistrates* he sees himself successively as overthrown by cruel Fortune (ll. 319–20), as the victim of the envious conspirators 'that sude aloft to clime' (l. 329), and as killed in just revenge for his savage slaughter of his enemies.

> But sith my whole pretence was glory vayne,
> To haue renowne and rule aboue the rest,
> Without remorce of many thousands slayne,
> Which, for their owne defence, their warres addrest:
> I deeme therefore my stony harte and brest
> Receiu'd so many wounds for iust reuenge, they stood
> By iustice right of *Ioue*, the sacred sentence good,
> That who so slayes, hee payes the price, i[n] bloud for bloud.
>
> (ll. 401–8)

---

9. *Essays*, transl. Florio (1603), Bk. II, ch. 33.
1. 'Julius Caesar and Elyot's Governour', *N. & Q.*, vol. 201 (1956), p. 147.
2. *The Governour*, Everyman edition, pp. 101, 105, 133, 134.

He alternates between praise and condemnation of his deeds. No wonder D. S. Brewer is moved to speak of 'the equivocal, not to say contradictory attitude to Caesar expressed by the writer in the *Mirror for Magistrates*'.[3]

Finally, the divided response at its most blatant is found in the anonymous play commonly called *Caesar's Revenge* (published in 1606 but, on stylistic evidence, placed by general consent in the nineties).[4] It seems based mainly on Appian, but, in its depiction of Caesar in its second half, clearly draws also a good deal on Lucan and on the Muret-Grévin tradition. In the early scenes Caesar is portrayed in a wholly sympathetic manner. On his first entry after Pharsalia he does not boast of his victory but weeps for the destruction caused by the civil broils, blaming his own ambition, which led him to inflict wounds on his mother, Rome. We next see him enamoured of Cleopatra, and weeping for Pompey's death. Brutus points to the dram of evil that douts Caesar's noble substance:

> To what a pitch would this mans vertues sore,
> Did not ambition clog his mounting fame.
>
> (ll. 210–11)[5]

And Cicero, who in this play is one of Caesar's sturdiest admirers and later one of his chief mourners, exclaims (much like the historical Cicero):

> *Caesar* although of high aspiring thoughtes,
> And vncontrould ambitious Maiesty,
> Yet is of nature faire and courteous.
>
> (ll. 1028–30)

Having given us in the first part of the play the fair, courteous Caesar, in its remainder we are shown Caesar's uncontrolled, ambitious Majesty, the Caesar of Muret and Grévin. He now declares that he will 'leaue Heauen blind, my greatnes to admire' (l. 1216), that

---

3. 'Brutus' Crime: A Footnote to *Julius Caesar*', R.E.S., N.S., vol. 3 (1952), pp. 52–3.
4. In a note in N. & Q., vol. 199 (1954), pp. 196–7, I have argued that this play was one of the sources of *Julius Caesar*. I feel no longer so confident of Shakespeare's knowledge of it. The fact that in both plays Brutus's evil spirit is turned into Caesar's ghost, which is sometimes mentioned as if it were the chief point of identity between the two plays, does not suggest indebtedness. For in North's translation of the *Caesar* we read of 'the ghost that appeared unto Brutus' and declared himself to be his 'ill angel' (*op. cit.*, pp. 106–7). A ghost and Brutus's ill angel? Most Elizabethans would have identified it as Caesar's ghost, come to seek revenge for his murder. But the appearance on the battle-field of Caesar's ghost in the company of Discord, who has come from the Underworld, so strikingly parallels Antony's prophecy about 'Caesar's spirit, ranging for revenge, / With Atè by his side come hot from hell' that, joined with the other points of resemblance, it makes Shakespeare's knowledge of the play still seem probable to me. And the style of *Caesar's Revenge* to my mind rules out the possibility that it was the later play.
5. Line references are to the Malone Society reprint of the play.

Alexander 'Must to my glory vayle his conquering crest' (l. 1267), and caps it all with the announcement,

> Of *Ioue* In Heauen, shall ruled bee the skie,
> The Earth of *Caesar*, with like Maiesty.
>
> (ll. 1510–11)

In the eyes of his friends Caesar is 'faire vertues flowre / Crowned with eternall honor and renowne' (ll. 1841–2), while to the conspirators, who are shown to be inspired by genuine devotion to the commonwealth, he is a tyrant and the great enemy of Rome.

After the assassination we find Brutus stricken with guilt at having murdered his friend and benefactor. To put an end to his mental torments he implores Caesar's ghost to kill him (ll. 2316 ff.). And, oddly reversing the parental relationship, he compares himself to Althea, who murdered her son:

> *Althea* raueth for her murthered Sonne,
> And weepes the deed that she her-selfe hath done:
> And *Meleager* would thou liuedst againe,
> But death must expiate *Altheas* come [?staine].
> I, death the guerdon that my deeds deserue . . .
>
> (ll. 2321–5)

And he slays himself, anticipating, much in the manner of Othello, an eternity of tortures in Hell (ll. 2516–25). Caesar's ghost, on the other hand, now glutted with the blood of his enemies, looks forward to his blissful abode in the Elysian fields.

> There with the mighty champions of old time,
> And great *Heroes* of the Goulden age,
> My dateless houres Ile spend in lasting ioy.

With these words the play ends. Dante's divine punishment has been combined with a divided attitude to Caesar and his assassins which is much like that of Appian and Dio.

* * *

CRITICISM

Early Commentary

SAMUEL JOHNSON

From The Works of William Shakespeare (1765)[†]

Of this tragedy many particular passages deserve regard, and the contention and reconcilement of Brutus and Cassius is universally celebrated; but I have never been strongly agitated in perusing it, and think it somewhat cold and unaffecting, compared with some other of Shakespeare's plays; his adherence to the real story, and to Roman manners, seems to have impeded the natural vigour of his genius.

VII.102

GEORGE STEEVENS

From Shakespeare in the Theatre (1772–73)[‡]

* * *

[g] [2–4 June 1772]

An opinion is universally prevalent with respect to the writings of Shakespeare, that he was no friend to the fair sex, but that on the contrary he embraced every opportunity of treating the ladies with the utmost severity, and represented them as often as possible in a disagreeable light to the public. How a charge so unjust should be so generally credited would appear to me a matter of much surprize, if I was not perfectly sensible that nine-tenths of our modern Critics take their opinions entirely upon trust, and never once prudently examine whether their theatrical belief is really orthodox.

[†] From Samuel Johnson, *The Works of William Shakespeare* (London, 1765), 8 vols., 5.5.33.

[‡] From *Shakespeare: The Critical Heritage*, ed. Brian Vickers (London: Routledge & Kegan Paul, 1979), 5 vols., 5: 498–500. Reprinted by permission. Attributed to George Steevens, who is known to have written under various pseudonyms for the *General Evening Post* in the period 1771–73.

The gentlemen who are thus pleased to censure our immortal poet for his cruelty to the ladies tell us triumphantly of Goneril and Regan in *Lear*, of Lady Anne in *Richard the Third*, of the Queen in *Cymbeline*, of the Queen in *Hamlet*, and ascend the climax of critical exultation with a mention of the Queen in *Macbeth*. In the several characters here enumerated I readily grant that Shakespeare has by no means drawn a flattering picture of the softer sex, and even acknowledge that a Devil more incarnate than the latter could not possibly be coloured by the pencil of human imagination.[1] Yet while I make this acknowledgement I shall enter also with confidence into Shakespeare's defence, and beg to ask what the reader thinks of Juliet, Imogen, Ophelia, Portia in the *Merchant of Venice*, Portia in *Julius Cæsar*, Veturia and Volumnia in *Coriolanus*, Isabella in *Measure for Measure*, of Rosalind and Cælia in *As You Like It*, of Hero and Beatrice in *Much Ado*, of Helena, Diana, and the Countess of Roussillion in *All's Well that Ends Well*, of Constance in *King* John, Desdemona in *Othello*, of Cordelia in *Lear*, and several other women of less importance in these and the different pieces, which I have not particularly pointed out. I fancy a great majority, even from this trifling retrospect of parts, will be found in favour of the fair; and our bard of course will not only be rescued from the imputation of injustice to the sex but be allowed the title of strenuous advocate for the dignity of female reputation.

The charge, however, of making his women generally depraved is not the only one which the Critics have brought against Shakespeare; they insist that as vehicles for dramatic action his feminine characters are most insignificant, and even Colley Cibber admits the justice of this accusation so far that he enters into a laboured justification of the poet from his total want of actresses. But instead of granting the conclusion drawn I deny the premises absolutely, and declare that Shakespeare has no need of an excuse. His women are always as important as the nature of his fable requires them, and if in some places his men engross the principal business of a play there are other places where his women have equally the advantage. If Falstaff for instance not only banishes all brothers from the throne of humour in the *Merry Wives*, Rosalind is no less distinguished in the comedy of *As You Like It*. If Othello renders Desdemona comparatively insignificant, Imogen throws all the male characters at a considerable distance behind her in *Cymbeline*; in *Much Ado*, there is no knowing where to place the superiority—and in *Romeo*, capital as the lover is made, Juliet is entrusted with the most interesting part of the business. Possibly indeed, upon a minute comparison of

1. Cf. Steevens in the 1773 edition.

character and character the scale will preponderate in favour of the men, and that too essentially; but won't it do the same in real life? Are not men the grand agents in the fall of empires, as well as in the management of domestic duties; and don't they settle the marriage of a child, no less than direct the revolutions of Government? Shakespeare consequently gave them only that natural pre-eminence which they possess in the unavoidable course of things, and the Critics expose themselves constantly to contempt in asserting that his women are palpably contemptible.

From the foregoing observations a reader of common sense will see the indispensible necessity of judging for himself in every thing relative to the stage. No error is more general than what I have here endeavoured to expose, yet none is more obvious to the meanest capacity; and I dare say that many, on the perusal of these indigested hints, who think that Shakespeare's women are not only depraved in the majority but dramatically insignificant also, will be astonished at the grossness of a mistake into which they never could have fallen, if they had merely exercised a moderate portion of reflection.

* * *

Had the critics, however, turned to *Macbeth* or *Julius Cæsar* they might have seen that a very excellent play could have been written without the assistance even of a love episode. Lady Macbeth has no conjugal struggles of tenderness on her husband's account. She is his accomplice in guilt, and is therefore anxious for her own sake that his villainy is successful. But none of the finer feelings are alarmed for his safety; they are all rooted up in her soul, and no one incident in the piece arises from the source of female affection.[2]

Julius Cæsar, in the circumstance of Portia's anxiety about Brutus, is to be sure an instance of conjugal tenderness which seems at a first view to refute the assertion with which we set out. But when the reader recollects that the scene between Portia and Brutus is rather a *preparation* for a situation than a real situation, and when he moreover recollects that no circumstance of consequence is produced by the heroism of Portia to advance the piece, he will probably think with us that *Julius Cæsar* is no more to be set down as a play of tenderness than the bloody usurper of the Scottish diadem.

* * *

2. Cf. Steevens in the 1773 edition.

From Unsigned Essay on *Julius Caesar* (1789)[†]

There are no characters of our immortal Shakespeare in which dramatic excellence and historical truth are more powerfully combined than in those which constitute his play of *Julius Cæsar*. This drama is remarkable for containing a greater variety of beautiful sentiments than any composition that ever came from the pen of man; and that frigid critic will deservedly meet our indignation who, upon hearing it read or seeing it exhibited, shall be so little transported with its excellence as to remind us that it is deficient in the unities of time and place.

This play has been censured, but certainly without justice, for the conversation which takes place at its opening between Flavius, Marullus, and certain holiday-making Plebeians. This, say some delicate critics, is low humour, ill suited to the grandeur of the business which follows, and unlikely to have passed between the Commons and their Tribunes. They who make such observations must be told that the lower class of an hardy and free people (and the Romans were not then quite reduced to slavery) are distinguished by a certain degree of saucy wit and a fondness for joking with their superiors, particularly when a festival (as this was of the Lupercal) gives a kind of licence to such indulgences. The Englishman's observation must have been strangely limited who has not noticed such a tendency in the commonalty of his own country. Upon the whole, I cannot but consider this as happy an introduction of a good play as can be met with in the works of the most artful dramatist. (67–8)

So much for the introduction of this play. I shall now examine the character of Mark Antony, who, if not the hero of the piece, is certainly one of the leading persons in it. The minute exactness with which our poet has followed Plutarch in most instances leaves us little room to doubt that he had earnestly consulted that excellent biographer in order to give his characters as much of historical truth as was consistent with the plan of his drama. Mark Antony appears to me the only character in which truth is sacrificed to poetry. But Shakespeare perhaps knew that had he represented him in his true colours he must have given up his most perfect dramatic character, and have disgusted his audience by the exhibition of a mean, drunken, brutal, and I believe an ignorant soldier. Perhaps from Plutarch it would not be possible for our poet, or any other person, to have extracted a satisfactory and decisive history of that Roman

† From *Shakespeare: The Critical Heritage*, ed. Brian Vickers (London: Routledge and Kegan Paul, 1981), 6 vols., 6:500–505. Reprinted by permission. The piece originally appeared in the *Lounger's Miscellany*, nos. 12 (10 January 1789) and 13 (17 January 1789).

who created such confusion, and so disgraced the annals of his country. Between the mildness and moderation of his biographer Plutarch, and the vehemence and rancour of his great political enemy Cicero, it is probable that an account might be furnished more thoroughly illustrating his true character than that which should be taken from the single record of either of those writers. Plutarch tells us that he addicted himself to the study of oratory at Athens; but he does not add that he made any proficiency in that science. Cicero ridicules him for his general ignorance and his particular inability to speak. Shakespeare, on the contrary, has made him a most eloquent and persuasive orator. Plutarch mentions that he spoke over the dead body of Cæsar. Cicero has alluded to his speech in terms perhaps ironical, calling it, '*præclara oratio.*'[1] And Shakespeare has given the substance of that speech, which, though most excellent in itself, is certainly not such a one as Antony was likely to have delivered. The art of this speech consists in the appearance of blunt and honest simplicity in the speaker, which Antony would not probably have assumed because he could not have carried it through. The particular style of oratory to which he had devoted his studies, we are told, was the Asiatic, or diffuse and flowery. Here, however, every thing is plain; no rhetorical flourish, no circumlocution, no unnecessary or ornamental Epithet: '*He only speaks right on.*' And while he is declaring to his hearers that '*he comes not to steal away their hearts;*'—that '*he is no orator, as Brutus is; but, as they knew him all, a plain, blunt man, that loves his friend;*' [3.2.216ff.] he has in fact so stolen away their hearts as to have reduced the mob entirely to his own management, and so established his own oratory superior to that of Brutus as to have reversed every inclination of the people to support the enemies of Cæsar. Had he attained to this degree of eloquence it is not probable that Plutarch would have left so shining a qualification unmentioned; or that Cicero would have stigmatized him for his stupidity, which he does frequently in his *Philippics*, particularly the second. (68–70)

The impression left upon our minds, respecting Shakespeare's representation of this character, is that he was not indeed free from vices, but endued with a sufficient number of good qualities to conciliate our favour; that he was brave and generous, '*one that loved his friend;*' polite, debauched, and eloquent. I believe it would be difficult to fix any of these qualities upon him from true history, except his debauchery, which was of the most ignominious kind. (70–1)

That Antony was polite, or as Enobarbus calls him in Shakespeare, '*our courteous Antony,*' no one will readily agree to who is acquainted with the *Philippics* of Cicero, in which, after every allowance is made for the bitterness of an enemy and the capacity of that

1. *Philippics*, 1.2: 'The speech Marcus Antonius made that day was a noble one'.

orator to vilify or extol his subject, sufficient proof is established
that he is a sordid and sottish debauchee; content with gratifying
his lusts in the lowest and most ignominious manner. His dishon-
esty is sufficiently apparent in his forgeries of Cæsar's Will. Thus
much for the excellent dramatic character Mark Antony; in the exhibition of which, perhaps, it may be said, *the farther the poet has
departed from the truth of history, the nearer he has approached to the
excellence of the drama.* (72)

Having devoted the foregoing Paper to an examination of the real
and dramatic character of Mark Antony, I shall now endeavour to
shew that the other *dramatis personæ* represent to us an history of
those great commotions as complete, faithful, and accurate as can
be extracted from the annals of any history. Shakespeare seems to
have obtained from Plutarch, and that only through the medium of
translation, a thorough knowledge of the minds and manners of
those great persons whom he has brought forward; such were the
vast powers of his mind. And with judgement no less discerning, he
has conveyed his knowledge in such a manner as to have given every
common spectator as accurate an idea of each character as if the
biography of each were submitted to his particular attention. In this
play is contained all that great and interesting series of events which
took place from the beginning of the conspiracy against Julius
Cæsar to the issue of the battle at Philippi—perhaps the most
important period that the political history of the world can furnish;
and our Bard has scarcely omitted any one circumstance that could
give life and spirit to his piece; nor has he admitted any one of consequence in which he is not warranted by the records of antiquity. It
might, indeed, afford some satisfaction in passing through this play,
to point out those particular instances of the author's minute attention to history, for which it is so remarkable, as well as to note some
trivial deviations from that standard of truth which, however, is
never suffered to be out of sight. Such a discussion cannot tend to
diminish the value of a performance which can be increased by no
commendations, nor lessened by any censures. (73–4)

* * * Concerning the character of Cassius, the Poet has left us in
a state of uncertainty as to the motives by which he was instigated
to form a conspiracy agains Julius Cæsar. Nor is this, I believe, any
where exactly ascertained in history. Plutarch seems to be in doubt
whether his conduct arose from private pique or private enmity, or a
general abhorrence of tyrants and a zeal for the public good. His artful mode of rousing the spirit of Brutus is well preserved and faithfully delineated. Nor has he omitted the circumstance of letters
being thrown into the windows of Brutus. Cicero is frequently mentioned by Plutarch upon this occasion, only to inform us that he had
no concern in the conspiracy. Accordingly, we find Shakespeare has

kept him in the background, when he must have undoubtedly had great temptation to bring him forward as the constant opponent of Antony, and the great source of Roman eloquence. Herein he has sacrificed at least something which might have been ornamental to truth. This great character is presented indeed to us; but with such scrupulous reserve that we cannot help lamenting that he is not more engaged in the business of the drama. The sickness of Ligarius is mentioned, and forms another proof of the strictness with which the Poet observes the truth of history. Perhaps it might have given his audience a clearer and more just idea of this character, if he could have contrived to inform them that this Caius Ligarius is the same who owed his life to the oratory of Cicero and the clemency of Cæsar. Our Poet has not forgotten to inform us that the time which intervened between the forming and executing the plan of the conspiracy was spent by Brutus in unquiet nights, '*musing and sighing with his arms across*' [2.1.240]; that the conspirators disdained to bind each other by an oath; that prodigies and apparitions distinguished the night before their deed was perpetrated; that Brutus's wife Portia made trial of her own constancy by voluntarily inflicting a wound upon herself; and that she then remonstrated with her husband upon his withholding from her those secrets to which, as his wife, she was entitled to be privy. And all this information is conveyed to us in a manner so fully, faithfully, and beautifully that we know not which most to admire, the accuracy of the historian or the sublimity of the Poet. The circumstances of the conspiracy, and the order and arrangement in which the several persons concerned in it act their different parts in that great tragedy, are equally to be noticed for their truth and beauty. [Quotes 2.2.4ff.]

The dialogue which follows between Cæsar and Decius is natural and necessary to further the business of the play; but I doubt whether it can be met with in any authentic record. The truth is that Cæsar did go to the Capitol; and, according to Plutarch, really pretended he was sick in order to shorten his attendance there. Shakespeare's variation is so trifling as to be scarcely worthy of notice. Plutarch's account is not more exact than our Bard's of what follows. (75–6)

The sequel of this story is not less exact than the part which has gone before. That mildness of character which is generally found the companion of real spirit and firmness is highly manifest in Brutus, and indeed eventually becomes the source of his unfortunate end. In the consultation of the conspirators he had before objected to the motion of the wary Cassius, who proposed that Antony should fall together with Cæsar; in which instance the generosity of his temper got the better of his prudence. Another instance of this generous disposition occurs in his granting permission to Antony to

speak in the order of Cæsar's funeral; which request of Antony's
Cassius, with his usual caution and penetration, objected to. But,
finding his objection too weak to overturn Brutus's notions of justice,
he concludes his ineffectual remonstrance: '*I know not what may fall;
I like it not.*' [3.1.243] The varying commotions of the people, and the
effect wrought upon them by the speeches of the different orators,
are such as every one acknowledges to be justly represented; but at
the same time such as no man could paint who was not most inti-
mately acquainted with the interests, actions, and passions of every
order of mankind. (76–7)

To all this is added a circumstantial and interesting history of the
war against Brutus and Cassius, which Antony seems to have undertaken for the sole purpose of smothering that spark of liberty which
had just appeared to the Roman people; and also that he might erect
to himself a throne of absolute power upon the downfall of those
enemies to tyranny. When we consider that the only materials from
which our Poet composed this excellent piece were the Lives of Plutarch, it is matter of great wonder that every incident should have
been so exactly introduced in its proper place; and that the shades
of character, which mark the different persons of the drama, should
have been more strongly and more distinctly preserved than even
by Plutarch himself. (77–8)

WILLIAM HAZLITT

[*Julius Caesar* (1817)]†

* * * Otherwise, Shakespear's JULIUS CAESAR is not equal as a
whole, to either of his other plays taken from the Roman history. It
is inferior in interest to *Coriolanus*, and both in interest and power
to *Antony and Cleopatra*. It however abounds in admirable and
affecting passages, and is remarkable for the profound knowledge of
character, in which Shakespear could scarcely fail. If there is any
exception to this remark, it is in the hero of the piece himself. We do
not much admire the representation here given of Julius Caesar, nor
do we think it answers to the portrait given of him in his Commentaries. He makes several vapouring and rather pedantic speeches,
and does nothing. Indeed, he has nothing to do. So far, the fault of
the character is the fault of the plot.

* * *

† From William Hazlitt, *Characters of Shakespear's Plays* (London: C. H. Reynell, 1817),
33–41. Excerpts: pp. 33–34, 38–41.

Shakespear has in this play and elsewhere shown the same penetration into political character and the springs of public events as
into those of every-day life. For instance, the whole design of the
conspirators to liberate their country fails from the generous temper
and overweening confidence of Brutus in the goodness of their cause
and the assistance of others. Thus it has always been. Those who
mean well themselves think well of others, and fall a prey to their
security. That humanity and sincerity which dispose men to resist
injustice and tyranny render them unfit to cope with the cunning
and power of those who are opposed to them. The friends of liberty
trust to the professions of others, because they are themselves sincere, and endeavour to reconcile the public good with the least possible hurt to its enemies, who have no regard to any thing but their
own unprincipled ends, and stick at nothing to accomplish them.
Cassius was better cut out for a conspirator. His heart prompted his
head. His habitual jealousy made him fear the worst that might happen, and his irritability of temper added to his inveteracy of purpose,
and sharpened his patriotism. The mixed nature of his motives made
him fitter to contend with bad men. The vices are never so well
employed as in combating one another. Tyranny and servility are to
be dealt with after their own fashion: otherwise, they will triumph
over those who spare them, and finally pronounce their funeral panegyric, as Antony did that of Brutus.

> "All the conspirators, save only he,
> Did that they did in envy of great Caesar:
> He only in a general honest thought
> And common good to all, made one of them."

The quarrel between Brutus and Cassius is managed in a masterly
way. The dramatic fluctuation of passion, the calmness of Brutus,
the heat of Cassius, are admirably described; and the exclamation of
Cassius on hearing of the death of Portia, which he does not learn
till after their reconciliation, 'How 'scaped I killing when I crost you
so?' gives double force to all that has gone before. The scene between
Brutus and Portia, where she endeavours to extort the secret of the
conspiracy from him, is conceived in the most heroical spirit, and
the burst of tenderness in Brutus—

> "You are my true and honourable wife;
> As dear to me as are the ruddy drops
> That visit my sad heart"—

is justified by her whole behaviour. Portia's breathless impatience to
learn the event of the conspiracy, in the dialogue with Lucius, is full
of passion. The interest which Portia takes in Brutus and that which
Calphurnia takes in the fate of Caesar are discriminated with the

nicest precision. Mark Antony's speech over the dead body of Caesar has been justly admired for the mixture of pathos and artifice in it: that of Brutus certainly is not so good.

The entrance of the conspirators to the house of Brutus at midnight is rendered very impressive. In the midst of this scene, we meet with one of those careless and natural digressions which occur so frequently and beautifully in Shakespear. After Cassius has introduced his friends one by one, Brutus says—

> "They are all welcome.
> What watchful cares do interpose themselves
> Betwixt your eyes and night?
> *Cassius.* Shall I entreat a word?   (*They whisper.*)
> *Decius.* Here lies the east: doth not the day break here?
> *Casca.* No.
> *Cinna.* O pardon, Sir, it doth; and yon grey lines,
> That fret the clouds, are messengers of day.
> *Casca.* You shall confess, that you are both deceiv'd:
> Here, as I point my sword, the sun arises,
> Which is a great way growing on the south,
> Weighing the youthful season of the year.
> Some two months hence, up higher toward the north
> He first presents his fire, and the high east
> Stands as the Capitol, directly here."

We cannot help thinking this graceful familiarity better than all the formality in the world.—The truth of history in JULIUS CAESAR is very ably worked up with dramatic effect. The councils of generals, the doubtful turns of battles, are represented to the life. The death of Brutus is worthy of him—it has the dignity of the Roman senator with the firmness of the Stoic philosopher. But what is perhaps better than either, is the little incident of his boy, Lucius, falling asleep over his instrument, as he is playing to his master in his tent, the night before the battle. Nature had played him the same forgetful trick once before on the night of the conspiracy. The humanity of Brutus is the same on both occasions.

> ———"It is no matter:
> Enjoy the honey-heavy dew of slumber.
> Thou hast no figures nor no fantasies,
> Which busy care draws in the brains of men.
> Therefore thou sleep'st so sound."

HARLEY GRANVILLE-BARKER

[Characters] (1946)†

* * *

From the beginning Shakespeare's dramatic development has lain in the discovering and proving of the strange truth that in the theatre, where external show seems everything, the most effective show is the heart of a man.

* * *

A hero, let us be clear, is the character of which a dramatist, not morally, but artistically, most approves.* * * Shakespeare's sympathy with Brutus does not imply approval of the murder of Cæsar; it only means that he ultimately finds the spiritual problem of the virtuous murderer the most interesting thing in the story. Brutus best interprets the play's theme: Do evil that good may come, and see what does come!

* * *

Brutus

That the development of Brutus should be slow is proper enough; such characters do not too readily reveal themselves. Shakespeare builds the man up for us trait by trait; economically, each stroke of value, seldom an effect made merely for its own sake. With his usual care that the first things we learn shall be essential things, that very first sentence—measured, dispassionate, tinged with disdain—by which Brutus transmits to Cæsar the cry in the crowd:

A soothsayer bids you beware the Ides of March,

gives us so much of the man to perfection; and its ominous weight is doubled in his mouth, its effect trebled by the innocent irony. Brutus draws aside from the procession to the games, withdrawn into himself.

> I am not gamesome: I do lack some part
> Of that quick spirit that is in Antony.
> Let me not hinder, Cassius, your desires;
> I'll leave you.

† From Harley Granville-Barker, *Prefaces to Shakespeare* (London: Sidgwick & Jackson, Ltd., 1946), 52–88. Reprinted by permission of The Society of Authors as the Literary Representative of the Estate of Harley Granville-Barker. Excerpts: pp. 52, 53, 54–55, 63–66, 77–79, 85–88.

The strain of self-consciousness, that flaw in moral strength! A suspicion of pose! But self-consciousness can be self-knowledge.

*   *   *

The plain fact is, one fears, that Shakespeare, even if he can say he understands Brutus, can in this last analysis make nothing of him; and no phrase better fits a playwright's particular sort of failure. He has let him go his own reasoning way, has faithfully abetted him in it, has hoped that from beneath this crust of thought the fires will finally blaze. He can conjure up a flare or two, and the love and grief for Portia might promise a fusing of the man's whole nature in a tragic passion outpassing anything yet. But the essential tragedy centred in Brutus' own soul, the tragedy of the man who, not from hate, envy nor weakness, but

> . . . only, in a general honest thought
> And common good to all . . .

made one with the conspirators and murdered his friend; this, which Shakespeare rightly saw as the supremely interesting issue, comes to no more revelation than is in the weary

> . . . Cæsar, now be still:
> I killed not thee with half so good a will.

Shakespeare's own artistic disposition is not sufficiently attuned to this tragedy of intellectual integrity, of principles too firmly held. He can apprehend the nature of the man, but not, in the end, assimilate it imaginatively to his own. He is searching for the hero in whom thought and emotion will combine and contend on more equal terms; and when the end of Brutus baffles him, here is Hamlet, as we have seen, all waiting to begin. For the rest, he at least reaps the reward, a better than Brutus did, of integrity and consistency. He never falsifies the character, and, in its limited achievement, it endures and sustains the play to the end. He had preserved, we may say, for use at need, his actor's gift of making effective things he did not fully understand; and the Brutus of the play will make call enough on the actor even should he know a little more about Brutus the Stoic than Shakespeare did.

Cassius

Cassius is blest—and cursed—with a temperament. He is compounded, that is to say, of qualities contradictory enough to keep him in a ferment. He is passionate, but self-conscious; he is an egoist and yet clear-sighted, and yet unwise. Does he really admire Brutus? He plays on his weaknesses and follows his lead. He is self-willed, but he feeds on sympathy. He is brave and as nervous as a cat. He sways between more obvious inconsistencies besides. For all his cleverness he is simple; and rash simplicity is his doom at last. He kills Cæsar remorselessly; but he swears—and it is no boast—that he would take his own life as soon rather than suffer shame. He would take Antony's too, from pure policy; yet in the flush and confusion of a bloody triumph he can pause to think of the danger innocent old Publius may run. He tricks Brutus, his friend, by the letters laid in the Præ- tor's chair and thrown in at the window; but when the rest go smiling to lure Cæsar to death, though he sees to it they go, he holds back.[1] Truly it might rather be from caution than conscience, for he is not apt at hiding his feelings; and he knows he has not hidden them from Cæsar, whose sharp eye caught his acrid looks as he passed him coming from the games; while Cassius, as sharp, guessed that the low talk with Antony was of him. But though he knows that Cæsar "bears him hard" he talks the most reckless treason to Casca. It is well-calculated recklessness, however. He has gauged that seeming tardiness aright; he strikes fire from the flint. In all he is alert and vibrant; he can do anything but do nothing.

What better sort of character, then, for getting such a play as this under way?

* * *

Octavius Cæsar

He tags to the three another figure; and perhaps nothing in the play is better done within its limits, than is the outline of Octavius Cæsar, the man who in patience will reap when all this bitter seed has been sown. He appears three times, speaks some thirty lines, and not one of them is wasted. We see him first with Antony and Lepidus. He watches them trade away the lives of their friends and kinsmen. And when Antony, left alone with him, proposes to 'double-cross' Lepidus, he only answers,

> You may do your will;
> But he's a tried and valiant soldier.

It is the opening of a window into this young man's well-ordered mind. Lepidus is a good soldier, he approves of Lepidus. But Antony is powerful for the moment, it won't do to oppose Antony. Lepidus must suffer then. Still, should things turn out differently, let Antony

---

1. His absence, of course, is in question. It may be that the stage direction of the Folio is faulty. But, if he is there, it is unlikely that Cæsar, naming the others, would ignore, him, or that he, being ignored, would stay silent.

remember that this was his own proposal, and that Octavius never approved of it.[2]

By the next scene, however, this quiet youth has grown surer—not of himself, that could hardly be, but of his place amid the shifting of events.

> *Antony.* Octavius, lead your battle softly on,
>   Upon the left hand of the even field.
> *Octavius.* Upon the right hand, I; keep thou the left.
> *Antony.* Why do you cross me in this exigent?
> *Octavius.* I do not cross you; but I will do so.

He is quite civil about it; but he means to have his way, his chosen place in the battle and chief credit for the victory. And Antony does not argue the point. When the opponents in the coming battle are face to face, Cassius and Antony, and even Brutus may outscold each the other for past offences. The practical Octavius, with a mind to the present and to his own future, is impatient of such childishness.

> Come, come, the cause: if arguing make us sweat,
> The proof of it will turn to redder drops.
> Look, I draw sword against conspirators:
> When think you that the sword goes up again?
> Never, till Cæsar's three-and-thirty wounds
> Be well aveng'd; or till another Cæsar
> Have added slaughter to the sword of traitors.

This is the first time he has spoken out, and he speaks to some purpose. Nor does he give place to Antony again. When we see them together for the last time in victorious procession, Octavius has the lead.

> All that serv'd Brutus, I will entertain them.

'I,' not 'we.' And Shakespeare gives him the play's last word.

* * *

Calpurnia and Portia

The boy Lucius has sometimes been played by a woman. This is an abomination. Let us not forget, on the other hand, that Calpurnia was written to be played by a boy. Producers are inclined to make a fine figure of her, to give her (there being but two women in the play) weight and importance, to fix on some well-proportioned lady,

---

2. *Julius Cæsar* begins the cycle of Shakespeare's greater plays, and *Antony and Cleopatra* ends it. The later relations of Octavius and Antony are implicit in this little scene. The realist, losing grip, will find himself 'out-realised' by his pupil.

who will wear the purple with an air. But Shakespeare's intention is as plain as daylight; and in a part of twenty-six lines there can be no compromise, it must be hit or miss. Calpurnia is a nervous, fear-haunted creature. Nor does she, like Portia, make any attempt to conceal her fears. She is desperate and helpless. Portia, with her watchful constancy, can win Brutus' secret from him. Cæsar treats Calpurnia like a child. Her pleading with him is a frightened child's pleading; her silence when Decius and the rest come to fetch him to the Senate-house—silence broken, for better emphasis, by just one cry—is as pathetic in its helplessness. What happens to her during the remainder of the scene? We have but one cue, Cæsar's

> Give me my robe, for I will go.

This is the last line of a speech to Calpurnia, but perhaps it is spoken to the servant who, a minute or so before, brought the news from the augurers. I would rather take it, though, as a hint for dividing her from the group of eager men who are now surrounding her husband. She stands tremulous, watching him go in to taste some wine with these good friends; then she goes herself to do his bidding for the last time. Failing the right sort of Calpurnia, quite half the dramatic value of her scene will be lost.

A quiet beauty is the note of Portia, and Shakespeare sounds it at once. Her appearance is admirably contrived. The conspirators have gone, Brutus is alone again, and the night's deep stillness is recalled.

> Boy! Lucius! Fast asleep? It is no matter;
> Enjoy the honey-heavy dew of slumber:
> Thou hast no figures nor no fantasies
> Which busy care draws in the brains of men;
> Therefore thou sleep'st so sound.

But so softly she comes, that for all the stillness he is unaware of her, until the soft voice, barely breaking it, says,

> Brutus, my lord!

Portia is a portrait in miniature. But how suited the character itself is to such treatment, and how Shakespeare subdues his power to its delicacy! The whole play is remarkable for simplicity and directness of speech; nothing could exemplify her better. For she is seen not as a clever woman, nor is she witty, and she speaks without coquetry of her "once-commended beauty." She is home-keeping and content; she is yielding, but from good sense, which she does not fear will seem weakness. Her friends perhaps call her a dull woman. But she has a dignity of soul and an innate courage that might well leave the cleverest of them humble.

Note how everything in the scene—not the words and their meaning only—contributes to build up this Portia. The quiet entrance, the
collected thought and sustained rhythm of her unchecked speech,
the homely talk of supper-time and of the impatient Brutus scratch-
ing his head and stamping, and of his present risk of catching cold;
nothing more wonderful than this is the foundation for the appeal to

> . . . that great vow
> Which did incorporate and make us one . . .

Nor does the appeal at its very height disturb the even music of the
verse. For with her such feelings do not ebb and flow; they lie deep
down, they are a faith. She is, as we should say, all of a piece; and her
very gentleness, her very reasonableness is her strength. Even her
pride has its modesty.

> I grant I am a woman, but, withal,
> A woman that Lord Brutus took to wife;
> I grant I am a woman; but, withal,
> A woman well-reputed, Cato's daughter;
> Think you I am no stronger than my sex,
> Being so father'd and so husbanded?

The repeated phrase and the stressed consonants give the verse a
sudden vigour; they contrast with the drop back to simplicity of

> Tell me your counsels, I will not disclose 'em.
> I have made strong proof of my constancy,
> Giving myself a voluntary wound
> Here, in the thigh: can I bear that with patience
> And not my husband's secrets?

To this, with imperceptibly accumulating force, with that one flash
of pride for warning, the whole scene has led. A single stroke, powerful in its reticence, as fine in itself as it is true to Portia.

Then, lest she should seem too good to be true, Shakespeare adds
a scene of anti-climax; of a Portia confessing to weakness, all nerves,
miserably conscious that her page's sharp young eyes are fixed on
her; outfacing, though, the old soothsayer, and, with a final effort,
spiritedly herself again. While, for one more touch of truth, he gives
us,

> O Brutus!
> The heavens speed thee in thine enterprise.

Murder is the enterprise, and Cato's daughter knows it. But he is her
Brutus, so may the heavens speed him even in this.

❊   ❊   ❊

Modern Commentary

IRVING RIBNER

From Historical Tragedy†

* * *

There is a tradition slow in dying among Shakespearian critics which would separate the history plays from the mainstream of Shakespearian tragedy, as though a concern with history precluded involvement in the ethical questions which are the province of tragedy. Such a separation, as I have elsewhere argued,[1] is meaningless and unnecessary. Shakespeare's contemporaries made no distinction between history and tragedy; it was, in fact, a commonplace of Renaissance neo-classicism that history was the most suitable subject matter for tragedy, a doctrine which Ben Jonson very notably expressed when in the preface to the 1605 edition of *Sejanus* he pointed to his 'truth of argument' as evidence that he had 'discharged the other offices of a tragic writer'.

In *Richard III* Shakespeare framed a play to complete an historical tetralogy whose subject was the fate of England, and at the same time he created a tragedy in which the degradation of England and her salvation through purgation of evil within herself were mirrored in the life-journey of the tragic hero who was her king. Just as the story of Richard III had already been shaped by Shakespeare's predecessors into a vehicle for tragedy, that of King John had been given tragic potentialities in the two-part *Troublesome Reign of* John which was Shakespeare's source. In *Richard II* and *Julius Caesar*, we find Shakespeare approaching the matter of history with a surer hand, and out of it creating tragedy of singular power. In these plays he is learning lessons which are to have fruition in the great tragedies of the succeeding decade. After *Julius Caesar* we are ready for *Hamlet*.

† From Irving Ribner, *Patterns in Shakespearean Tragedy* (New York: Barnes and Noble, 1960), 36–64. Reproduced by permission of Taylor & Francis Books UK. Excerpts: pp. 36–37, 53–61, 62–63, 64.
1. *The English History Play in the Age of Shakespeare* [Princeton, 1957], particularly pp. 28–30.

But the very fact that these plays do accomplish the ends of the Tudor historian, that they use the past in order to teach political wisdom to the present, conditions their scope as tragedy. Like the other tragedies, these embody intellectual statements which character and action support, and which are particularly implicit in the pathways to destruction taken by the central figures. But the salvation of the body politic receives greater emphasis than that of the individual man. That the plays are histories conditions the symbolic function of character. The hero-king stands always for England, and the principle implicit in his life-journey is one of national destiny, although this may be related closely to his own damnation or salvation. The fate of Brutus or Caesar is secondary to that of Rome, and as tragic heroes they also reflect in specific human terms principles of general political conduct.

*   *   *

In *Julius Caesar* Shakespeare experiments with a unique manipulation of two tragic situations within a single play.[2] The tragedies of Caesar and of Brutus are each both ethical and political, and each hero's career reflects a similar pattern of action. Both tragedies are combined by and subordinated to the larger theme which governs the play: the tragedy of Rome to which Caesar and Brutus each in his own way contributes.

In *Julius Caesar* Shakespeare further extended the pattern he had developed from *Titus Andronicus* through *Richard II*, to develop for the first time a full-scale tragedy of moral choice, drawing upon the tradition of the English morality play.[3] In such a tragedy the hero is faced with a choice between good and evil; through his own imperfections he makes a wrong choice, comes to see the error of his choice in his consequent suffering, and before his death renounces it. This progression is fully displayed in Brutus and partially in Caesar. Shakespeare dwells on the scope and terms of each moral choice itself, the forces militating for and against it, and the exact process by which the hero is led to commit his error. In *Julius Caesar* and the plays which follow it characters come more and more to represent particular moral positions.

Before we can understand *Julius Caesar* as tragedy, we must see clearly its political issues, and about these there has been wide dis-

---

2. *Julius Caesar* was written almost certainly in 1599. See Chambers, *William Shakespeare*, 1, 397; T. S. Dorsch, ed., *Julius Caesar* (London, 1955), pp. vii-viii. M. W. MacCallum, *Shakespeare's Roman Plays and Their Background* (London, 1910), p. 174, would date it in 1600 or 1601, but the evidence, well summarized by Dorsch, is all to the contrary.

3. This has been well argued by Virgil K. Whitaker, *Shakespeare's Use of Learning* (San Marino, 1953), pp. 224–50, although we cannot accept the terms of Brutus' moral choice as Whitaker explains them, and he fails to perceive that Caesar undergoes a similar tragic progression.

agreement.[4] We must recognize, to begin with, that Caesar is not a king and that at no place in the play does Shakespeare call him a king. The very opposite is made clear in the second scene when Cassius says:

> I had as lief not be as live to be
> In awe of such a thing as I myself.
> I was born free as Caesar; so were you.
>
> (I.ii.95–97)

A king was not like other men. He derived his power, according to Tudor theory, because he was God's agent on earth, designated by God through the legitimacy of his lineal descent. Caesar has no such claim. He is an adventurer who, by force, has replaced another adventurer, Pompey, and he is now reaping the civil acclaim which had been Pompey's, as the first scene makes clear. If Caesar is to be crowned it will be by the mob. The people cheer in approval when Caesar refuses the crown at the Lupercal, as Casca explains, but Casca makes it equally clear that this refusal is only a temporary gesture and that the people are fickle and may be brought easily by Caesar to accede to his will (I.ii.235–78). The Senate in conferring the crown would be acceding merely to Caesar's power seconded by the mob. It is wrong to regard *Julius Caesar* as a play about a king who is murdered by rebellious citizens. It is a play about a great general who aspires to be a king and who is murdered on the eve of his success.

Plutarch had seen the desire for kingship as the cause of Caesar's tragedy:

> But the chiefest cause that made him mortally hated was the covetous desire he had to be called king; which first gave the people just cause and next his secret enemies honest colour, to bear him ill will.[5]

Plutarch's view of Caesar is one of several which came down to the Renaissance. One view, to be found in many Elizabethan tracts in defence of monarchy, saw him as a great hero designated by God to

---

4. Many critics have argued that the play is without political implications at all, most recently Vernon Hall, Jr., in *Studies in The English Renaissance Drama*, pp. 106–24. Ernest Schanzer, 'The Problem of *Julius Caesar'*, *SQ*, vi (1955), 297–308, has argued that Shakespeare was deliberately ambiguous in his political attitudes, creating a 'problem play'. Perhaps the most common view today is that first given wide currency by McCallum (pp. 212–27) and more recently repeated by Whitaker and J. E. Phillips, *The State in Shakespeare's Greek and Roman Plays* (New York, 1940), pp. 172–88. These writers see the play as a vindication of absolute monarchy, represented by Caesar, with Brutus as the tragic hero who falls into the tragic error of opposing the political system ordained by God. This view tends to slight the role of Caesar in the play and to ignore the fact that he is not a king and that in no place does Shakespeare call him one. I have treated the play's political issues at greater length in *JEGP*, lvi (1957), 10–22.
5. *Shakespeare's Plutarch*, ed. C. F. Tucker Brooke (New York, 1909), 1, 90.

establish monarchy in a corrupt society, only to be struck down by rebels who brought ruin to their country and damnation to their souls. On the other hand, stemming from Plutarch and repeated by a long line of Renaissance writers, is the view of Caesar as a great hero who became so puffed up with pride and ambition that he destroyed the most noble edifice ever created by man, the Roman republic.[6] This view of Caesar, the would-be tyrant, is in every Renaissance Caesar play which has come down to us. Such a view lent itself readily to treatment in the popular manner of Renaissance Senecanism, and I would suggest that it is this view which Shakespeare explored in his own *Julius Caesar*.[7]

The charge of illogic so often levelled against Brutus stems from his Orchard soliloquy (II.i.9–34), in which he justifies his action against Caesar. There is illogic in the action of Brutus, but it is not in his decision that Caesar is a danger to Rome. The Orchard speech is not only logical; it focuses upon the basic question of the play, the usurpation of power. Caesar must be destroyed, as Brutus sees it, not because he has been a tyrant, but because he aspires to unlawful power, and such power must inevitably corrupt the most virtuous man and make a tyrant of him:

> But 'tis a common proof,
> That lowliness is young ambition's ladder,
> Whereto the climber-upward turns his face;
> But when he once attains the upmost round,
> He then unto the ladder turns his back,
> Looks in the clouds, scorning the base degrees
> By which he did ascend. So Caesar may.
> Then, lest he may, prevent.
>
> (II.i.21–28)

In terms of Tudor political doctrine these lines are not without logic.[8] Tudor theorists justified the absolutism of a lawful king on the grounds that, as an agent of God, he executed God's purposes. But an absolute ruler without God's sanction and thus without the check of responsibility to God—as Caesar would be if he were crowned— would be a tyrant. An ordinary man, no matter how great, could not

---

6. T. J. B. Spencer, 'Shakespeare and the Elizabethan Romans', *Shakespeare Survey 10* (Cambridge, 1957), pp. 37–38, has shown that Caesar was a subject for wide discussion in Shakespeare's England, and that there were many conflicting views. There is no one view which we can call the typically Elizabethan one.

7. That Shakespeare in earlier plays may have referred to Caesar in a more favourable light cannot influence our view of *Julius Caesar*, for as Schanzer has shown by an examination of all the Caesar references in the plays, Shakespeare's attitude towards Caesar apparently changed after his reading of Plutarch and his consideration of the matter in preparation for *Julius Caesar*. See *SQ*, VI (1955), 299–300.

8. J. Dover Wilson, ed., *Julius Caesar* (Cambridge, 1949), p. xxxi, has been virtually alone among modern commentators in denying the illogic of these lines.

aspire to kingship; he could only aspire to tyranny, and this is precisely what Brutus fears. He estimates properly the political threat of Caesar. His sin is the manner in which he opposes that threat. To attain a public good he commits a private evil; his tragedy, like that of King John, affirms that public morality can be built only upon private virtue.

Brutus' fears, we must conclude, far from being foolish, are, in Tudor terms, well grounded, and they were probably Shakespeare's fears as well. The succession issue was perhaps the most vital political problem in England when *Julius Caesar* was written in 1599, and the possibility that a powerful general with no legitimate claim, but with the support of the rabble, might make a bid for the throne was a fear not lightly to be discounted. The abortive attempt of Essex some two years later attests to the ever-present possibility in 1599. If the history play used events of the past to mirror contemporary political problems, *Julius Caesar* is no exception.

There are, as I have suggested, two tragic heroes in *Julius Caesar*, Brutus and Caesar, although the one is treated more fully than the other. Each brings about his own destruction, and together they bring chaos to Rome. Each is among the greatest men the world has ever known, but each makes a wrong moral choice. The source of Caesar's tragedy Shakespeare found not primarily in Plutarch, but chiefly as part of the long tradition of Senecan Caesar plays which preceded his.[9] It was a tragic pride and ambition which became apparent upon his return to Rome after the defeat of Pompey's sons in Spain. It is touched upon only lightly by Plutarch, who concludes that Caesar 'reaped no fruit of all his reign and dominion, which he had so vehemently desired all his life, pursued with such extreme danger, but a vain name only, and a superficial glory that procured him the envy and hatred of his country' (I.105–6), but it is amplified in Renaissance accounts of which Montaigne's may furnish a convenient example:

> But all these noble inclinations were stifled and corrupted by that furious passion of ambition by which he was so forcibly carried away, that we may safely declare that it held the rudder and steered all his actions. . . .
>
> To sum up, this single vice, in my opinion, destroyed in him the richest and most beautiful nature that ever was, and made his memory abominable to all good men, since it led him to seek his glory in the ruin of his country and the subversion of the most powerful and flourishing Republic the world will ever see.[1]

---

9. See H. M. Ayres, 'Shakespeare's *Julius Caesar* in the Light of Some Other Versions', *PMLA*, xxv (1910), 183–227.

1. *The Essays*, trans. by E. J. Trechmann (New York, Modern Library, 1946), pp. 636–7.

The greatest man in the world had risen so high that he was ripe for the inevitable fall. Above all else, Caesar wanted to be king, and to attain a power to which he was not entitled, he would accept the support of the mob. This inordinate desire for kingship is the height of Caesar's tragic folly, the *hubris* which will destroy him. On the day of his assassination he remains firm in his decision to remain at home until Decius Brutus offers him the prospect of a crown:

> the Senate have concluded
> To give this day a crown to mighty Caesar.
> If you shall send them word you will not come,
> Their minds may change.
>
> (II.ii.93–96)

This is the temptation which he cannot resist, and it is the immediate cause of his destruction. Shakespeare has carefully prepared his audience for the wrong moral choice which now follows.

That Caesar can never be a fitting king for Rome has been indicated in the second scene of the play. Caesar here turns to Antony preparing to run in the Lupercal:

> Forget not, in your speed, Antonius,
> To touch Calpurnia; for our elders say,
> The barren, touched in this holy chase,
> Shake off their sterile curse.
>
> (I.ii.6–9)

Shakespeare introduces Calpurnia's sterility to make clear to the audience that Caesar has no heirs, and that should he die as king, Rome would be left in that very state of civil chaos, without a lawful claimant to the throne, which Tudor Englishmen so feared would follow the death of their own Elizabeth.

Caesar's pride is shown in the pomposity of his boastful speeches:

> danger knows full well
> That Caesar is more dangerous than he:
> We are two lions litter'd in one day,
> And I the elder and more terrible.
>
> (II.ii.44–47)

An audience could not receive such lines as other than almost ludicrous posturing; Caesar is denying the limitations of his nature as a man. His pride is shown also in his refusal to heed the words of the soothsayer: 'He is a dreamer; let us leave him; pass' (I.ii.24). Elizabethans generally believed that prophecies were to be taken seriously, and certainly that no prudent statesman could run the risk of ignoring them. This is again stressed in Caesar's reaction to Calpurnia's

dream (II.ii); here his folly is underscored dramatically by the audience's knowledge of how right Calpurnia actually is. Throughout
the first three acts Shakespeare shows us a strutting, vainglorious
Caesar, denying his kinship to humanity and claiming the qualities
of a god. The pathetic irony of this tragic delusion Shakespeare indicates by ingenious little touches. When Caesar has proclaimed that
he is impervious to the fears which might visit lesser men, this is followed immediately by a reminder that this god suffers, in fact, from
one of the most human of afflictions: 'Come on my right hand, for
this ear is deaf' (I.ii.213).

This technique is used again in the boastful vaunt which Caesar
delivers just before his death:

> I could be well moved, if I were as you;
> If I could pray to move, prayers would move me:
> But I am constant as the northern star,
> Of whose true-fix'd and resting quality
> There is no fellow in the firmament.
> The skies are painted with unnumber'd sparks,
> They are all fire and every one doth shine,
> But there's but one in all doth hold his place:
> So in the world; 'tis furnish'd well with men,
> And men are flesh and blood, and apprehensive;
> Yet in the number I do know but one
> That unassailable holds on his rank,
> Unshaked of motion: and that I am he.
>
> (III.i.58–70)

In the flashing daggers of the conspirators we are shown the pathetic
delusion in these lines, that no man is constant as the Northern Star.
Caesar cannot escape the limitations of his own flesh and blood; he
is just a man after all, weak and subject to the fate of any man who
would make himself a god. His death is an ironic commentary upon
his own pretensions.

Caesar's wrong moral choice is his decision to go to the Senate to
accept a crown to which he has no lawful claim. The traditional
debate which in the earlier drama accompanied the choice of the
morality play hero occupies the scene in which this choice is made,
with Calpurnia filling the role of good angel and Decius Brutus that
of bad. The temptation of Decius causes Caesar to deny the pleas of
his wife. In the pattern of the total play, however, it is Marc Antony
rather than Decius who performs the traditional role of the tempter,
for Antony thrice offers Caesar the throne at the feast of the Lupercal. Antony after Caesar's death is used as a symbol of those very
elements for which Caesar stood, and which Brutus because of his
own sinful moral choice cannot destroy.

Antony must triumph, but that the triumph is one of evil rather than good is made implicit by Antony's own immorality, his ruthless manipulation of the mob for personal revenge at the expense of Rome, and particularly in the cold brutality of the proscription scene:

> ANTONY: These many, then, shall die; their names are prick'd.
> OCTAVIUS: Your brother too must die; consent you, Lepidus?
> LEPIDUS: I do consent,—
> OCTAVIUS: Prick him down, Antony.
> LEPIDUS: Upon condition Publius shall not live,
>   Who is your sister's, son, Mark Antony.
> ANTONY: He shall not live; look, with a spot I damn him.
>   (IV.i.1–6)

Caesar's spirit is victorious in spite of Brutus, and a cold-blooded exchange of kinsmen is the fruit of such victory.[2] From Antony's triumph emerge the very evils Brutus had vainly sought to stem. If there is any hope for Rome it is not in Antony, but in the young Octavius who, before the end of the play, we see emerging as the force which will put Antony down (V.i. 19–20).

We have no evidence that Caesar ever becomes aware of the sin which has led to his downfall. This form of recognition and regeneration Shakespeare reserves for his treatment of Brutus, in whom he seems to have been more deeply interested. There are two facets to the tragedy of Brutus, the one directly related to the other. His failure to lead the conspiracy to success stems directly from his other failure: to live up to his own ideals of conduct. Brutus has been called an idealist philosopher, lacking in those public virtues which the successful leader must have, unable to cope with the crude realities of politics.[3] This inability springs from the root of his tragedy, his own separation of public from private morality. All of his tactical errors—his rejection of the oath, his refusal to murder Antony, his insistence that Antony be allowed to speak at Caesar's funeral—all spring from his unwillingness to accept the logical consequences of his own immoral act. He argues from the standpoint of a morality which has already been corrupted.

Cassius knows the logical consequences of Caesar's murder, that once the immoral course has been taken, a reassertion of morality can only spring from self-deception and lead to disaster. Of all the conspirators, Cassius alone sees that Brutus has forfeited the moral

---

2. It is difficult to reconcile this scene with G. Wilson Knight's view that 'the murder of Caesar is a gash in the body of Rome, and this gash is healed by love', with Antony as the spirit of love bringing peace and order to a troubled world. See *The Imperial Theme* (London, 1951), p. 63.

3. See John Palmer's analysis in *The Political Characters of Shakespeare*, pp. 1–64.

stature which made him at first the obvious choice for leader, and he sees the folly of his attempt to reassert it. In this Cassius too plays a tragic role, for in spite of his clear insight he allows Brutus to prevail to the destruction of all. While Cassius is fully developed as a complex personality, he is used to fill a thematic function in the total play. Shakespeare needs a contrast to Brutus who will logically accept the immorality of Caesar's death and who will show the audience the self-deception of Brutus.

Under the leadership of Cassius, the conspirators might have achieved an immediate success, but it could not have been a lasting one, for the conspiracy itself was evil, and even had it been properly managed, it could have brought only disaster to Rome. Great as Caesar's threat to Rome might have been, to oppose it by conspiracy and murder was wrong. The death of Caesar may have been as essential to the preservation of Rome as was the death of Prince Arthur to the stability of England, but Shakespeare can no more condone Brutus' action than he can King John's order for the death of Arthur. In order to attain a goal of public good, Brutus commits a private crime: he murders his friend. This is his wrong moral choice and the source of his tragedy. The crime of Brutus, the virtuous murderer, is a violation of the closest bonds which tie man to man, bonds with which the audience instinctively identifies. We have a sharp dramatic antithesis between an abstract political ideal and the ordinary human goodness which it violates. Brutus is aware of this violation, and he is willing to face it.

* * *

Brutus, more than Caesar, carries on the dramatic tradition of the morality play hero who must choose between good and evil forces which vie for his soul, and in this scheme Cassius plays the symbolic role of the seducer who makes clear for the audience those very qualities which lead Brutus to make his fatal error. But what Shakespeare castigates as Brutus' evil choice is not his decision that Caesar is a threat to Rome, but rather his decision to join Cassius in conspiracy and murder, and this is an important distinction. As disasters begin to mount after Antony's funeral oration, Brutus, like a morality hero, slowly becomes aware of the error of his choice. This growing awareness Shakespeare makes clear in the quarrel scene in the fourth act.

Cassius, as we have seen, has been committed all along to the immoral consequences of the first sinful act, and he has argued that they be accepted. He has always, however, given in to Brutus' counter-arguments. This has been true in the matters of the oath (II.i. 114–40) and of Antony's death. Now Cassius argues the necessity for a relatively slight immorality, that his bribe-taking officer,

Lucius Pella, should not have been condemned. The pathetic irony
of Brutus' self-deception breaks forth in all its vehemence:

> Remember March, the ides of March remember:
> Did not great Julius bleed for justice' sake?
> What villain touch'd his body, that did stab,
> And not for justice? What, shall one of us,
> That struck the foremost man of all this world
> But for supporting robbers, shall we now
> Contaminate our fingers with base bribes,
> And sell the mighty space of our large honours
> For so much trash as may be grasped thus?
> I had rather be a dog, and bay the moon,
> Than such a Roman.
>
> (IV.iii.18–28)

Through these lines comes the vain effort of a man trying to convince
himself of the truth of what he already is beginning to know is false.
The audience knows that every man but Brutus himself stabbed, 'and
not for justice', and as Cassius persists in his demands, this truth
must be brought home to Brutus with an overwhelming certainty. He
accepts the renewed friendship of Cassius, but it is a despairing gesture, and his awareness of his error emerges finally in the simple line,
'You have done what you should be sorry for' (IV.iii.65).

* * *

Shakespeare in *Julius Caesar* was interested in two great figures from
Roman history, and he treated both in accordance with the historical
and literary tradition which he inherited: Caesar as the noble hero
overthrown by his pride and ambition, and Brutus as the virtuous
would-be saviour of his country who, through his own insufficiency,
brings only greater tragedy to Rome. Of the two tragedies, that of
Brutus more completely attracted his interest. As an historical dramatist, Shakespeare was fully aware of the political implications of his
theme. He saw, on the one hand, a lesson in the civil chaos which
results when a great and noble leader tries to overthrow long-
established institutions and seeks with the support of the mob to
attain a kingship to which he has no lawful claim. On the other hand,
he saw the chaos which results when men of noble instincts violate
their own natures and enter into evil so that political good may result.

I have dwelt upon the political issues in *Julius Caesar* because in
this play these issues are at the root of the tragic conflict. The
heroes of Roman history were viewed by Shakespeare's audience at
a distance which blurred their human imperfections and made of
them supermen such as the world had never again beheld. There is
always a grandeur and magnificence about them, and it is thus easy

for Shakespeare to envisage them as embodiments of moral principles. In *Julius Caesar* we find such characters, each embodying a
specific moral attitude, subjected to imaginative exploration. There
is a higher degree of intellectual symbolism in this play than in *King
John* or *Richard II*, and Shakespeare can approach his subject with a
higher and more impersonal degree of objectivity. He is not bound
here by the peculiarly Tudor views of history, as he had been in the
English historical tragedies. In *Julius Caesar* Shakespeare learned
techniques which he was to apply in later plays. He could now, better than ever before, embody intellectual statement in dramatic
character, and in character conflict expose the implications of clash-
ing ideologies.

* * *

G. WILSON KNIGHT

[Love and Honor]†

The human element in *Julius Caesar* is charged highly with a general
eroticism. All the people are 'lovers'. This love is emotional, fiery, but
not exactly sexual, not physically passionate: even Portia and Brutus
love with a gentle companionship rather than any passion. Though
the stage be set for an action 'most bloody, fiery, and most terrible',
though the action be fine, spirited, and adventurous, and noble blood
be magnificently spilt in the third act, yet the human element is
often one of gentle sentiment, melting hearts, tears, and the soft fire
of love. There are many major and minor love-themes. There is love
expressed or suggested between Brutus and Cassius, Brutus and Caesar, and Antony and Caesar; Brutus and Portia, Brutus and Volumnius, Brutus and Lucius; Caesar and Decius, Cassius and Lucius
Pella, Cassius and Titinius; Ligarius and Brutus, Artemidorus and
Caesar. Probably there are other instances. The word 'lover' is amaz-
ingly frequent, sometimes meaning little more than 'friend', but
always helping to build a general atmosphere of comradeship and
affection. Love is here the regal, the conquering reality: the murder of
Caesar is a gash in the body of Rome, and this gash is healed by love,
so that the play's action emphasizes first the disjointing of 'spirit' from
'matter' which is evil, fear, anarchy; and then the remating of these
two elements into the close fusion which is love, order, peace.

† From G. Wilson Knight, *The Imperial Theme* (London: Methuen & Co., 1951). Reprinted
by permission. Excerpts: pp. 63, 66–69, 70–71, 80–81, 83, 87–89, 94.

*   *   *

[W]hatever we may think of Caesar as a man, we must see him also as a symbol of something of vast import, resplendent majesty, and starry purpose.

Antony recognizes this fully. He loves Caesar. That is, he sees him as man and as hero and does not, like Brutus, distinguish between the two. Cassius despises him as a man, and therefore will not believe in him at all as a hero; Brutus loves him as a man but believes in him only too powerfully as a hero, and thinks him therefore dangerous. To Antony the two aspects are indistinguishable. This is equivalent to saying that Antony ardently, almost passionately, loves Caesar: for in such love—and only then—the spiritual and personal elements are blended. That is ever the function of love: in creation or recognition, it mates the spiritual with the material. Antony, the lover, can thus unify our difficulties: in his words—and in his only, not in Caesar's—do we feel the dualism of Caesar's 'spirit' and physical being perfectly unified. In his words only we see the Caesar of history:

> O mighty Caesar! dost thou lie so low?
> Are all thy conquests, glories, triumphs, spoils,
> Shrunk to this little measure?   (iii.i.148)

We are suddenly at home here strangely: this is how we want to see Caesar, how we expect to see him, how we are never allowed to see him till he is dead. The conspirators' swords are 'rich with the most noble blood of all this world' (iii.i. 155). Again,

> Thou art the ruins of the noblest man
> That ever lived in the tide of times.
> Woe to the hand that shed this costly blood!
>
>   (iii.i.256)

He sees him as a man he loved; also as a supremely noble man; and, still further, as a symbol of government and peace. Now that he is rashly slain, forces of disorder will rage unchecked:

> Domestic fury and fierce civil strife
> Shall cumber all the parts of Italy.   (iii.i.263)

Caesar's 'spirit' will have its revenge. In his oration he again stresses both Caesar's lovable personality and his importance as victor and national hero. His personal and national goodness are here entwined: to Antony Caesar is Rome's lover. Caesar hath 'wept' (iii. ii. 96) for the poor of Rome, his captives' ransoms filled Rome's 'general coffers' (iii.ii.94). He is thus a national friend or lover over and beyond his love for Antony:

> He was my friend, faithful and just to me: (III.ii.90)

or his love for Brutus:

> For Brutus, as you know, was Caesar's angel:
> Judge, O you gods, how dearly Caesar loved him.
>   (III.ii.185)

So the people of Rome should 'mourn for him' (III. ii. 108) as for a dear friend. Caesar is now shown as a general lover. The common people, if they heard his will, would

> go and kiss dead Caesar's wounds,
> And dip their napkins in his sacred blood,
> Yea, beg a hair of him for memory,
> And, dying, mention it within their wills,
> Bequeathing it as a rich legacy
> Unto their issue.   (III.ii.137)

Notice the strongly erotic emotion here. Throughout Antony's speech, love—whether of Caesar for Brutus, Antony or Rome, or of Antony or Rome for Caesar—is stressed in contrast to the ever more sarcastically pronounced suggestion of 'honour': 'honourable men whose daggers have stabbed Caesar' (III. ii. 156). 'Love' is pitted against 'honour'. Even Caesar's mantle is suffused with emotion, almost sentimentality:

> If you have tears, prepare to shed them now.
> You all do know this mantle: I remember
> The first time ever Caesar put it on;
> 'Twas on a summer's evening, in his tent,
> That day he overcame the Nervii.   (III.ii.173)

So personal can be Antony's appeal. At the other extreme he sees Caesar's murder as a treason which plunges Rome in disaster. When 'great Caesar fell', Rome fell too:

> O! what a fall was there, my countrymen;
> Then I, and you, and all of us fell down,
> Whilst bloody treason flourish'd over us.
>   (III.ii.194)

Then Antony shows them Caesar's body itself:

> Kind souls, what! weep you when you but behold
> Our Caesar's vesture wounded? Look you here,
> Here is himself, marr'd, as you see, with traitors.
>   (III.ii.199)

Antony emphasizes the personal element throughout. But he is also aware of the political aspect. The idea of Caesar as an abstract principle of order is not, in his mind, divided from Caesar his friend, the lover of Rome, now a stricken lifeless body. He thinks of the wounds, the torn mantle that was Caesar's. Elsewhere he refers to Caesar's 'spirit': here, and usually, he sees Caesar as a lovable, noble, and great man whose murder is a senseless and wicked act. So close are the personal and public elements twined in his thoughts that he readily suggests that personal reasons must have urged the conspirators to their deed:

> What private griefs they have, alas, I know not,
> That made them do it . . .   (III.ii.217)

Although Antony is, of course, ready to stress all that may suit his purpose, yet his attitude throughout his oration is exactly in line with his other thoughts and acts. He only has to be sincere to win over the citizens to his side:

> I am no orator, as Brutus is;
> But, as you know me all, a plain blunt man,
> That love my friend.
>   (III.ii.221)

It is true: he does not need to act. He reads the will, Caesar's bequests to the Roman people. The citizens recognize Caesar now as 'royal'. He is 'most noble Caesar', and 'royal Caesar' (III. ii. 248, 249). The final effect is clinched in Antony's

> Here was a Caesar! When comes such another?
>   (III.ii.257)

Though making a division between Caesar the man and Caesar the national hero and dictator, Brutus, Cassius, and indeed Caesar himself, have all plunged Rome and themselves in disaster. * * * [T]he central act, Caesar's assassination, is shown as a rough breaking of 'spirit' from 'body', whether of Caesar or Rome. Antony's love alone heals the dualism. Throughout he avoids this distinction. He unifies the dualism created by the poet in presenting Caesar as almost a dualized personality. It is the way of love. It unifies both the mind or soul of the subject, and the thing, person, or world that is loved, blending 'spirit' in 'body', seeing the physical afire with spirit-essence. So Antony alone knows the one Caesar better than Brutus and Cassius, better than Caesar himself, better than we who faithfully react to the impressions of the early scenes. Because he loves and is moved by love he sees things simplified, unified. His acts tend likewise to heal the gaping dualism of 'spirit' and 'matter' that has resulted from the gashing of Rome's civic body. Portents have blazed their terrors over Rome, the spirit of Rome being torn from its body;

and supernatural portents, omens, ghosts continue after Caesar's death. Fierce civil chaos is threatened now, as Antony prophesies: the body of Rome disorganized, disjointed by lack of any controlling spirit. Antony speaks, acts, fights to heal Rome. The wounds of Rome, the separation of 'spirit' from 'body', are thus healed by a lover and his love. Caesar's 'spirit' is then at peace.

Caesar we must therefore be ready to regard as Antony sees him; and yet, as I have elsewhere shown, we are forced by the play's symbolic effects to see the action largely through the eyes of Brutus. That we may do this Caesar is also shown to us as he appears to Brutus: he is both man and demi-god curiously interwoven. But it will be clear that Brutus' failure to unify his knowledge of Caesar is a failure properly to love him, love being the unifying principle in all things, regularly opposed in Shakespeare to disorder, treachery, evils of all kinds: this is the continual 'music'-'tempest' contrast throughout the plays. Now Brutus' failure to love his friend, Caesar, is one with his worship of abstract 'honour'. Therein we have the key to his acts: he serves 'honour' always in preference to love. Both his 'love' for Caesar and his 'honour' are given exact expression. Cassius asks Brutus if he would not have Caesar made king:

> I would not, Cassius; yet I love him well.
> But wherefore do you hold me here so long?
> What is it that you would impart to me?
> If it be aught toward the general good,
> Set honour in one eye and death i' the other,
> And I will look on both indifferently:
> For let the gods so speed me as I love
> The name of honour more than I fear death.
>
> (i.ii.82)

This love Brutus sacrifices to his 'honour'.

*   *   *

Brutus' honour pains and slays Portia, drives Cassius in their quarrel almost to madness, while Brutus remains ice-cold, armed appallingly in 'honesty'. He shows little emotion at his dear ones' death. You can do nothing with him. He is so impossibly noble: and when we forget his nobility he becomes just 'impossible'. Thus when he would for once solace himself for a while with Lucius—his truest love—and Lucius' music, his 'evil spirit' denies his right to such relief. * * * Brutus has put love from him. He rides roughshod over domestic happiness * * *. His acts disturb Portia, dislocate meals and sleep. So, too, Caesar and Calpurnia are roused from bed, and Caesar's hospitality desecrated. Cassius, on the contrary, invites people to dinner. The contrast is important. Such pursuit of an ethical ideal in and for itself, unrelated to the time and people around, is seen at the last to be perilous. It is a selfishness. His ethic is no ethic, rather a projection of himself. * * * [H]e projects his mental pain on his country. He alone bears the responsibility of Caesar's death, since he alone among the conspirators sees—and so creates —its wrongfulness; he alone bears the burden of the conspiracy's failure. He only has a guilty conscience—anguished by an 'evil spirit'. But Cassius, at the last, is 'fresh of spirit' (v.i.91). And yet, Brutus has glory by his losing day. He suffers, not because he is less than those around him but because he is, in a sense, far greater. He is the noblest Roman of them all. He suffers, and makes others suffer, for his virtue: but such virtue is not enough. Virtue, to Brutus, is a quality to be rigidly distinguished from love. Love, in fact, ever conflicts with it. He denies the greatest force in life and the only hope in death. He thus fails in life and dies sadly, pathetically searching at the end for some one 'honourable' enough to slay him.

* * *

Love is powerful in Cassius, but does not come easily. He is too sincere to be happy. * * * He is always, as it were, safe, invulnerable to chance, his own soul is a fortress:

> I know where I will wear this dagger then;
> Cassius from bondage will deliver Cassius:
> Therein, ye gods, you make the weak most strong;
> Therein, ye gods, you tyrants do defeat:
> Nor stony tower, nor walls of beaten brass,
> Nor airless dungeon, nor strong links of iron,
> Can be retentive to the strength of spirit.
>
> (i.iii.89)

This assurance is born of a unity of soul. He is not divided, like Brutus.

* * *

Throughout the play Cassius' love of Brutus is emphasized. We find many emotions in him: envy, ardour, love. He possesses a certain spiritual loneliness and a sense of ultimate security, he is the captain of his soul. But he is not happy: rather given to gloom and foreboding. He is romantic, compact of poetry. Intellect is subsidiary with him, and he is more at home with realities than abstractions. He does not understand Brutus' ethical finesse. Yet respect for his friend causes him to give way to Brutus time after time, thereby ruining his own conspiracy. * * * After Caesar's death he is maddened by Brutus' obsession with 'honour'. His complaint is typical.

He interceded for a friend, Lucius Pella, whom Brutus subsequently punished for accepting bribes. Cassius ever champions personal emotions, personal fears and forebodings, antipathies and envies, personal love. Brutus ever upholds an intellectual ideal of 'honour'. They meet, one passionate and ardent, the other aloof, scornful, self-righteous:

> CASSIUS.   Most noble brother, you have done me wrong.
> BRUTUS.   Judge me, you gods! wrong I mine enemies?
>   And, if not so, how should I wrong a brother?
> CASSIUS.   Brutus, this sober form of yours hides wrongs;
>   And when you do them—
>
> (IV.ii.37)

Throughout the quarrel Cassius is passionate in anger, grief, or love. Brutus is cold, aureoled in self-righteousness, unreachable, remote: but beneath emotion surges, too, in him. Cassius is the first to give way, to admit fault. Typically, he fights throughout, not, like Brutus, with reason, but with emotion. He is in this the more feminine of the two. * * * Brutus loves him not: a 'friendly eye' would not see such faults. Brutus' ethical scorn still lacerates him unmercifully. At last, he exposes the riches of his thwarted longing, passion-soul:

> Come, Antony, and young Octavius, come,
> Revenge yourselves alone on Cassius,
> For Cassius is aweary of the world;
> Hated by one he loves; braved by his brother;
> Check'd like a bondman; all his faults observed,
> Set in a note-book, learn'd and conn'd by rote,
> To cast into my teeth. O, I could weep
> My spirit from mine eyes! There is my dagger,
> And here my naked breast; within, a heart
> Dearer than Plutus' mine, richer than gold:
> If that thou be'st a Roman, take it forth;
> I, that denied thee gold, will give my heart:
> Strike, as thou didst at Caesar; for, I know,
> When thou didst hate him worst, thou lovedst him better
> Than ever thou lovedst Cassius.
>
> (IV.iii.93)

Here Cassius challenges the rich worth of his emotional nature against the other integrity of Brutus. But what is there in Brutus that dare so boast its spiritual 'gold'? And Cassius wins, by power of love. They celebrate their new strength with a bowl of wine. His 'heart' is thirsty, he 'cannot drink too much of Brutus' love' (IV.iii.162). Cassius is wrung with sorrow at Portia's death, and shows more grief than Brutus. And he gives way to Brutus on points of strategy. He is, indeed, the more experienced soldier:

> I am a soldier, I,
> Older in practice, abler than yourself
> To make conditions.   (iv.iii.30)

Yet, as always, he gives way to Brutus. At this point he is, indeed, far more concerned with his and Brutus' love than any military expedients:

> O my dear brother!
> This was an ill beginning of the night:
> Never come such division 'tween our souls!
> Let it not, Brutus.
>   (iv.iii.233)

Cassius' love thus saves the conspiracy from the final disgrace of 'division', enables it to meet its end intact.

* * *

The Caesar of history swims into our ken in Antony's first words after the assassination. Love heals the severance of 'body' from 'spirit'. Perhaps Cassius was wrong. He was blind to Caesar's greatness. To see ahead and fear is evil and unreal: reality is now, and love. Cassius who ever looks ahead, foreboding ill, yet treasures also a spiritual fortress which has no fear, and finally falls back only on this soul-treasure in his breast. Caesar's spirit has proved his course of action wrong (v.iii.45); but not his heart 'richer than gold'. As failure nears, his love is brighter, he steps free. Antony's victory is the conquest of love, love which saw only in Caesar a true friend and a great man, that made no 'god' comparisons nor foolishly stressed his physique, and, seeing the real Caesar, was content to trust him with Rome's fate. And Cassius' death, too, is a conquest of love. Time and again he sacrifices his conspiracy for Brutus. Brutus ruins an otherwise seaworthy plot. But Cassius drinks his fill of Brutus' love at the last, and dies 'fresh of spirit' in the cause of friendship. Brutus refuses love for honour. In incident after incident he brushes love aside. He alone is throughout wholly responsible for the dualism which wrenches 'spirit' from 'body', in Rome or in his own mind.

* * *

JOHN W. VELZ

[Role-Playing]†

* * *

Numerous characters in *Julius Caesar* adopt, or consider adopting, roles which other characters have played. The title of this article is drawn from one of the hypothetical transfers; Cassius contemplates in soliloquy his preliminary success in luring Brutus toward the conspiracy and muses that

> If I were Brutus now, and he were Cassius,
> He should not humour me.

> (I.ii.311–312)

As he works on the crowd in Act III, Antony, in mock self-deprecation, also imagines himself a Brutus:

> I am no orator, as Brutus is,
> . . . . .
>   But were I Brutus,
> And Brutus Antony, there were an Antony
> Would ruffle up your spirits.

> (III.ii.219–230)

Portia supposes herself an alter-Brutus. Protesting to her husband by "that great vow / Which did incorporate and make us one" (II.i.272–273), she demands to be made a party to the conspiracy. Because she is fused in marriage with Brutus, she believes that she shares his nature and can adopt his role.[1] That she cannot play the part adequately is underlined by her pathetic nervous crisis in II.iv just before the assassination. At Philippi in V.iv, Lucilius actually does adopt the name and role of Brutus, enabling the real Brutus to escape encirclement:

> And I am Brutus, Marcus Brutus, I!
> Brutus, my country's friend; know me for Brutus![2]

---

† From John W. Velz, "'If I were Brutus Now . . . ': Role-playing in *Julius Caesar*." *Shakespeare Studies* 4 (1968): 149–59. Reprinted by permission. Excerpts: pp. 150–56.

1. Maurice Charney considers that "it is significant how often Portia uses Brutus' words—it strengthens the bond between them and attests to Portia's dependence on her husband." (*Shakespeare's Roman Plays: The Function of Imagery in the Drama*, [Cambridge, Mass., 1961], p. 61.).

2. V.iv.7–8. This speech is unassigned in the Folio, and some scholars have believed that it is Brutus who insists on his identity here (most recently Mildred E. Hartsock in "The Complexity of *Julius Caesar*," PMLA, LXXXI [1966], 60). But Plutarch makes it virtually certain that Lucilius is the speaker here. In "Marcus Brutus" he recounts the exploits of Brutus' lieutenants in the second battle, "who valliantlie ranne into any daunger, to save Brutus life. Amongest them there was one of Brutus frendes called Lucilius, who seeing

But in a sense this instance of "becoming" Brutus is as hypothetical as the musings of Cassius and Antony, because moments later Lucilius makes it plain that Brutus is *sui generis*. When common soldiers take him a captive to Antony, he contrasts his lot with Brutus':

> I dare assure thee that no enemy
> Shall ever take alive the noble Brutus.
> . . . . .
> When you do find him, or alive or dead,
> He will be found like Brutus, like himself.
>   (V.iv.21–25)

It is not only Brutus whose abilities, ideals, or lot are echoed in the imitation of others. Three Roman heroes who do not appear on the stage are nevertheless present in the behavior or attitudes of characters conscious of following heroic precedent. As he prepares to take the field at Philippi, Cassius remembers Pharsalus, calling Messala to witness

>   that against my will
> (As Pompey was) am I compell'd to set
> Upon one battle all our liberties.   (V.i.74–76)

He recalls that Pompey was pushed into a disastrous battle by the bad advice of his own allies—an analogy to the strategy conference in which he himself has yielded to Brutus (IV.iii.195–224), and a sinister portent for the action yet to come. Portia identifies herself proudly not only as the wife of Brutus, but also as the daughter of Marcus Porcius Cato; a woman "so father'd, and so husbanded" (II.i.297) can keep secrets and play a Stoic's role, she insists. As she reveals that to play this role she has wounded herself, Portia becomes a miniature of her Stoic father, whose famous self-immolation at Utica Brutus alludes to at V.i.102–103. Like Portia, Young Cato sees himself in their father's heroic role:

> I am the son of Marcus Cato, ho!
> A foe to tyrants, and my country's friend.
> I am the son of Marcus Cato, ho!   (V.iv.4–6)

Dying, as his father died, in the struggle against tyranny, he may "be honour'd, being Cato's son" (V.iv.11). The third hero who is vicariously present in the play is Lucius Junius Brutus. Aware of the rever-

---

a troupe of barbarous men making no reckoning of all men else they met in their way, but going all together right against Brutus, he determined to stay them with the hazard of his life, and being left behinde, told them that he was Brutus . . ." (Geoffrey Bullough, ed., *Narrative and Dramatic Sources of Shakespeare* [New York, 1964], V, 128–129.) The marginalium on this passage reads "The fidelitie of Lucilius unto Brutus."

ence in which Marcus Brutus holds his idealistic ancestor, Cassius shrewdly reminds him that

> There was a Brutus once that would have brook'd
> Th' eternal devil to keep his state in Rome
> As easily as a king.
>
> (I.ii.157–159)

Cassius' technique is masterful. He has built toward this climactic appeal with vague contrasts between the decadent present and the noble past (148–156), and he follows it with the device of fastening an exhortation to Marcus Brutus on the very statue of his ancestor (I.iii.145–46). The implied analogy serves its purpose; Brutus later thinks of the ancient republicanism of his family as he fills the gap in the allusive instigation Cinna has thrown in at his window:

> Thus must I piece it out:
> Shall Rome stand under one man's awe? What, Rome?
> My ancestors did from the streets of Rome
> The Tarquin drive, when he was call'd a king.
>
> (II.i.51–54)

And it is at this point that Brutus makes his moral commitment:

> Am I entreated
> To speak, and strike? O Rome, I make thee promise,
> If the redress will follow, thou receivest
> Thy full petition at the hand of Brutus.[3]
>
> (II.i.55–58)

Pompey, Marcus Cato, and Lucius Junius Brutus are, then, a triumvirate of republicans whose struggle against tyranny in the noble past is consciously re-enacted by Cassius, Portia, Young Cato, and Brutus. Balanced against these idealists who model themselves on a bygone heroism are those characters in the play who are firmly committed to the decadent present which Cassius complained of and who successively assume the role of the tyrant, Caesar. The name and the spirit of Caesar dominate the last half of the play from the moment when Antony foresees "Caesar's spirit, ranging for revenge" (III.i.270). Antony himself is that imperious spirit for the moment, as he orders Octavius' servant to keep his master out of Rome and then proceeds to defeat the conspirators with his oration.[4] It is

---

3. The Second Plebeian also sees Brutus in a traditional family role; after Brutus justifies tyrannicide in his oration, this man shouts enthusiastically, "Give him a statue with his ancestors" (III.ii.51) Caius Ligarius, too, thinks of Brutus as "deriv'd from honourable loins" (II.i.322).
4. Norman Sanders disagrees; he argues that "Antony in his oration . . . [like Brutus in his] never attempts to attract the power of Rome to himself. Rather, what he does achieve by verbal means is what the conspirators did physically in the case of Caesar: that is, to

Octavius, however, who will emerge as Caesar, both in spirit and in name. At the beginning of Act V he points out that Antony's prediction of the conspirators' military strategy was erroneous and he insists on rearranging Antony's own battle plan:

> ANT.   Octavius, lead your battle softly on
>   Upon the left hand of the even field.
> OCT.   Upon the right hand I. Keep thou the left.
> ANT.   Why do you cross me in this exigent?
> OCT.   I do not cross you; but I will do so.[5]

Antony gives another order, restraining Octavius from an immediate charge on the enemy, but as he gives it he calls Octavius "Caesar."[6] Octavius himself asserts his inheritance of Caesar's name and is avenging power when he interrupts the flyting which preoccupies Antony, Brutus, and Cassius:

> Look,
> I draw a sword against conspirators.
> When think you that the sword goes up again?
> Never, till Caesar's three and thirty wounds
> Be well aveng'd; or till another Caesar
> Have added slaughter to the sword of traitors.
>
> (V.i.50–55)

Addressed to "Caesar," Brutus' reply (56) tacitly validates Octavius' assertion that he is "another Caesar," and neither Brutus' patronizing "Young man" (60) nor Cassius' taunting "A peevish school-boy" (61) can seriously diminish this claim. At the end of the play Antony looks back to the conspiracy, but practical Octavius looks ahead to the spoils of victory; the future and the role of Caesar will be his.[7]

The assumption of Caesar's role first by Antony and then by Octavius points to one reason why Shakespeare included so much role-playing in Julius Caesar; it is the means of underscoring a major

---

deprive someone else of power" ("The Shift of Power in 'Julius Caesar'," *REL*, V [1964], 32). But in IV.i Antony is firmly in command: he orders Lepidus about and labels him "a slight unmeritable man" (12); it is he who provides Octavius with intelligence of the movements of Brutus and Cassius and who calls for a council of war.

5. V.i.16–20. It has often been observed that Shakespeare modified his source in this episode; in Plutarch it is Brutus who insists on having the right wing and Cassius who yields to him. Maurice Charney suggests that "Shakespeare seems to be deliberately developing Octavius" (op. cit., p. 76n) and he points out that Octavius' "I will do so" echoes Caesar's imperious insistence on his will at II.ii.71: "The cause is in my will: I will not come" (p. 76).

6. V.i.24. The first reference to Octavius in the play prefigures this climactic admission that Octavius is a reincarnation of Caesar; Antony asks the servant at III.i.276 "You serve Octavius Caesar, do you not?" reminding us of Octavius' family relationship to Julius Caesar. But three times in Acts III and IV he is "young Octavius" and six more he is simply "Octavius."

7. Sanders (op. cit., p. 34n) suggests that the roles of Julius Caesar and Octavius might effectively be doubled to underline the shift of power to this new Caesar.

concern of the action, the process by which a new Caesar emerges
from the wreckage of the conspiracy. That Caesarism is a foregone
conclusion is clear in III.ii. The First Plebeian, swayed by Brutus'
oration, spontaneously demands a Caesarean triumph for his new
idol: "Bring him with triumph home unto his house."[8] Immediately
the thought of Brutus as a new Caesar grips the crowd:

> 3. Pleb.   Let him be Caesar.
> 4. Pleb.   Caesar's better parts
> Shall be crown'd in Brutus.
>
> (III.ii.52–53)

It is bitter irony that Brutus, the character in the cast who least
desires to be a Caesar, should be the first to be offered the role.
When Antony's appeal to their emotions begins to reverse the impact
of Brutus' sober speech, the Plebeians again assume that there will
be a successor to Caesar:

> 2. Pleb.   If thou consider rightly of the matter,
> Caesar has had great wrong.
> 3. Pleb.   Has he, masters?
> I fear there will a worse come in his place.
>
> (III.ii.111–113)

And the oration sweeps to a climax in which the idea of Caesarism
is inherent: "Here was a Caesar! when comes such another?" (III.
ii.254). The crowd shouts "Never, never!" but Antony has caught
their earlier mood, and he knows that the role of Caesar will be
transferred to the man who can play it best.

Role-playing is, then, crucial to the plot of Julius Caesar; it is common in both of the two opposed sets of characters, and the roles each
faction elects to play convey thematic or philosophical values. The
republicans see themselves in roles from the heroic past, while the
monarchists look to a prototype who appears onstage and who
belongs fully to the Rome of the present. The outcome of the action
is implicit in this subtle difference.

The dominance of Caesarism is also suggested by the fact that
numerous other characters, especially republicans, adopt Caesar's
characteristic trick of speech. Seventeen times in the three scenes in
which he appears, Caesar refers to himself as "Caesar." Some critics
have been harsh with him for this idiosyncrasy, regarding it as an
indication of his fatuousness. But Shakespeare could have found the
impersonal style in Caesar's Commentaries,[9] and he may have

---

8. III.ii.50. This citizen obviously is fond of processions; a moment later he repeats the
   suggestion: "We'll bring him to his house with shouts and clamours" (54).
9. Norman N. Holland believes he did (*The Shakespearean Imagination*, [New York,
   1964], p. 138). Without discussing the question of style, T. W. Baldwin finds the evi-

thought it a mark of the Roman (perhaps of the noble Roman) to see oneself from the outside, to talk of oneself as of an object. Certainly the last of Caesar's impersonal references to himself comes at the moment of his death, when the time for pretense is past: "Then fall Caesar!" Whether Caesar's mode of speech is pompous or noble, it echoes throughout the play as others unconsciously imitate it, giving us the sense that they are playing Caesar's role. Cassius calls himself by his name twelve times; Brutus speaks of "Brutus" eleven times. Antony (4), Casca, Portia, Metellus, Octavius ("Caesar"), Pindarus, Titinius, and Lucilius all echo the Caesarean mode of speech.[1] When instances occur in the last half of the play, it is as though we were hearing the voice of Caesar, even from his enemies, after he himself is gone.

In a different sense, Caesar's voice echoes in III.iii, as Cinna the Poet unconsciously reenacts the events of II.ii and III.i. His death is a pathetic microcosm of the assassination. Like Caesar, Cinna goes to his death despite a portentous dream. Like Caesar, he speaks of his unwillingness to leave his home:

> Caes.   The cause is in my will: I will not come.
>
> (II.ii.71)

> Cin.   I have no will to wander forth of doors.
>
> (III.iii.3)

Yet each man is drawn "forth" despite premonitions of disaster.[2] Cinna, on his way to Caesar's funeral "as a friend" (III.iii.22), surely expects no attack from the Plebeians who love Caesar; his violent death, like Caesar's, comes at the hands of men he considers friends.[3] And as the Plebeians repeat "Tear him to pieces! . . . Tear him . . . tear him . . . Tear him . . . tear him!" (III.iii. 28–35) we are reminded of the imagery of dismemberment Brutus has applied to Caesar's assassination:

---

dence for Shakespeare's having studied the *Commentaries* in school inconclusive. See *William Shakespeare's Small Latine & Lesse Greeke* (Urbana, Ill., 1944), II. 569–572.

1. It is perhaps significant that characters often use third person for first at moments of profound seriousness or emotional intensity, when pose is unlikely: Portia pleading to be more than a harlot to Brutus, Titinius killing himself out of friendship for Cassius, Pindarus sadly leaving Cassius' dead body, Casca committing himself to the conspiracy. This third-person pattern is supported by more than twenty passages where characters use the name of the person addressed where we would expect a second-person pronoun: e.g., "it sufficeth / That Brutus leads me on"; "I should not then ask Casca what had chanc'd." From a different perspective, R. A. Foakes has discussed the prevalence and the importance of personal names in *JC*; see "An Approach to *Julius Caesar*," *SQ*, V (1954), 259–270.

2. The word "forth" echoes and re-echoes somberly: see II.ii.8, 10, 28, 38, 48, 50, and III. iii.3, 4.

3. Compare Caesar at II.ii.126–127:

> Good friends, go in, and taste some wine with me;
> And we, like friends, will straightway go together.

O, that we then could come by Caesar's spirit,
And not dismember Caesar! But, alas,
Caesar must bleed for it.[4]

(II.i.169–171)

Unconscious adoption of the role of Caesar, whether ironic (as in the reflection of his style by others) or pathetic (as in the echoes of his words and attitudes by Cinna), does more than suggest the continuing presence of Caesar after his death. As echoes of his words or style reverberate through the play, they provide a continuity to the unconscious ear which tends toward unity. Roles which are played not once but again and again by successive "actors" have an effect as much structural as thematic. A crucial repetition of this sort underscores the assassination as the moral center of the play and draws events in the first, third, fourth, and fifth acts toward that moral center and toward one another.

Four characters in Julius Caesar offer their deaths to others.[5] Caesar begins the sequence at the Lupercal. As Casca cynically tells it,

he pluck'd me ope his doublet, and offer'd them his
throat to cut. And I had been a man of any occupation,
if I would not have taken him at a word, I would I
might go to hell among the rogues.

(I.ii.261–265)

Though Casca's reaction to this flamboyant gesture is facetious, it has a more profound meaning as an ironic adumbration of the assassination—it is Casca who first rears his hand against Caesar in III.i. As Caesar offers his throat to the populace he also foreshadows his own readiness to die at the last moment of his life: "*Et tu, Brute?*— Then fall Caesar!" (III.i.77). Antony recreates the assassination for the Plebeians in his oration, giving special emphasis to Caesar's willingness to die:

. . . when the noble Caesar saw him [Brutus] stab,
Ingratitude, more strong than traitors' arms,
Quite vanquish'd him: then burst his mighty heart;
And in his mantle muffling up his face,
          . . . great Caesar fell.

(III.ii.186–191)

---

4. Most of these echoes of Caesar's death in Cinna's are discussed by Norman H. Holland, who draws conclusions different from mine. See "The 'Cinna' and 'Cynicke' Episodes in *Julius Caesar*," *SQ*, XI (1960), 439–444.
5. The fact is noted briefly by Adrien Bonjour in *The Structure of Julius Caesar* (Liverpool, 1958), p. 30, n. 33.

When he offers to let the conspirators kill him over Caesar's body in III.i, Antony plays the same role that Caesar has played at the Lupercal. Though the stakes are higher and the emotion more intense, Antony does not expect to be taken at his word any more than Caesar did; he can afford this melodramatic offer, since before his entrance he has been told of Brutus' solemn promise:

> . . . so please him come unto this place,
> He shall be satisfied; and, by my honour,
> Depart untouch'd.
>
> (III.i.140–142)

As he elaborates his paradoxical appeal, Antony proposes his death as an analogue to Caesar's. He is to die at "Caesar's death's hour" (154) beside his corpse (162), at the same bloody hands (158) which wield "those your swords, made rich / With the most noble blood of all this world" (155–156). Antony's speech becomes an exaggeration of Caesar's loss of will to live; Shakespeare here makes Antony repeatedly "beg" (164) his death of the conspirators: "there is no hour so fit" (153), he is "apt to die" (160), he beseeches the assassins to fulfill their pleasure (157–159), he can imagine no more pleasing death (161). Yet, no matter how sincerely he feels his loss, how closely he identifies himself with his dead friend, Antony shows the ability to take advantage of this emotional moment, a trait which will enable him to assume the role of a pragmatic tyrant, at least temporarily.

The third offer of death is Brutus'; he tells the Plebeians that

> as I slew my best lover for the good of Rome, I have the
> same dagger for myself, when it shall please my country
> to need my death.
>
> (III.ii.46–48)

Adrien Bonjour suggests that Brutus' offer is as shallow as Caesar's in I.ii, manifesting his realistic awareness of how to mold a crowd with theatrics.[6] Remembering Brutus' desire to make Caesar's death a sacrifice (II.i.166–174), we may take him more literally here. He offers himself as he has offered Caesar—an immolation "for the good of Rome." Like Antony before him, Brutus offers to die by the same weapon that killed Caesar.

Cassius continues the pattern in IV.iii, when he offers Brutus his dagger and urges him to stab him to the heart.[7] The offer is as hyper-

---

6. Ibid., p. 20.
7. Twice before Cassius has impulsively volunteered his own death. When Casca tells him that Caesar is to be crowned on the Ides of March, Cassius replies:

> I know where I will wear this dagger then;
> Cassius from bondage will deliver Cassius.   (I.iii.89–90)

bolic as the theatrical gestures of Caesar and Antony which it echoes, but Cassius is not insincere here, any more than Brutus was in III.ii. The bitterness of broken friendship is in his words as he remembers that Brutus has stabbed a friend before:

> Strike, as thou didst at Caesar; for I know,
> When thou didst hate him worst, thou lov'dst him better
> Than ever thou lov'dst Cassius.
>
> (IV.iii.104–106)

As Cassius offers himself to the blow,

>   there is my dagger,
> And here my naked breast,   (IV.iii.99–100)

Shakespeare provides an emphatic piece of stage business which must remind the audience of earlier occasions at which bared breasts are mentioned or seen. Caesar, of course, has opened his doublet to the crown in I.ii; Cassius himself has appeared onstage in I.iii with his bosom audaciously exposed to the thunderstorm.[8] Most emphatic of all, at an intense moment in his oration, Antony has pulled the mantle off Caesar's body to reveal him "marr'd, as you see, with traitors" (III.ii.199).

When, one after another, they offer to die on the swords or knives of others, Antony, Brutus, and Cassius do more than unconsciously recreate the role which Caesar originated at the Lupercal. Each of them at the moment of his offer is fully conscious of his own relationship to the assassination: each of them speaks of Caesar's death when he offers his own. And the behavior of these three imitators of Caesar looks forward to Philippi as well as back to the central event of the play, for Brutus and Cassius both will die in a sense offering their deaths to Caesar. When Cassius dies on the words:

When he wrongly believes that the conspiracy has been discovered, he threatens to kill himself:

>   If this be known,
> Cassius or Caesar never shall turn back,
> For I will slay myself.   (III.i.20–22)

Brutus keeps him from the rash act; the scene is an ironic prefiguration of Cassius' impulsive and mistaken suicide at Philippi.

8. Shakespeare concentrates the image in I.iii; Cassius emphasizes that he is "unbraced" (48), bare-bosomed (49), and that he presents himself directly to the lightning (51–52) which itself "seem'd to open / The breast of heaven" (50–51). Cassius, who offers to have his heart taken out of his bosom (IV.iii.102–103), may recall to us Cinna the Poet, whose name has been plucked out of his heart (III.iii.33–34); and Cassius' request of Brutus during the quarrel foreshadows his request of Pindarus at the end of his life:

>   with this good sword,
> That ran through Caesar's bowels, search this bosom.   (V.iii.41–42)

> Caesar, thou art reveng'd,
> Even with the sword that kill'd thee,
>
> (V.iii.45–46)

he echoes the proposals of Brutus and Antony that they should be victims of the same weapons that killed Caesar. And Brutus' attitude at his death mirrors both the willingness of Caesar to die and the four willing offers of death which have punctuated the play:

> Caesar, now be still;
> I kill'd not thee with half so good a will.
>
> (V.v.50–51)

The effect of the repeated pattern of offers is, therefore, dual: to lead us radially to the central assassination, and to heighten the poetic justice with which Brutus and Cassius die by the sword in the fifth act.[9]

Role-playing is recurrent and striking behavior among the characters in Julius Caesar. The roles men deliberately choose to play delineate the opposed forces in the action and sketch the theme of Caesarism triumphant over political idealism. At the same time, there are other roles which men play without awareness that these are parts which others have played before them. This unconscious role-playing is one means by which Shakespeare draws *Julius* Caesar into structural coherence.[1]

---

9. The fact that Caesar, Brutus, and Cassius all are killed with swords is doubtless responsible for a number of references to stabbing scattered through the play. Casca facetiously puts the case that "if Caesar had stabb'd their mothers" the Plebeians would have forgiven him (I.ii.271–272). In two passages already quoted (I.iii.89–90; IV.iii.99–100) Cassius speaks of daggers turned against himself. Portia reveals that she has wounded herself with a knife; Titinius kills himself onstage with Cassius' sword; and Messala, carrying the news of Cassius' death to Brutus, chooses an apt metaphor:

> . . . I go to meet
> The noble Brutus, thrusting this report
> Into his ears. I may say thrusting it;
> For piercing steel and darts envenomed
> Shall be as welcome to the ears of Brutus
> As tidings of this sight.   (V.iii.73–78)

1. I wish to express my gratitude to the Folger Shakespeare Library for the Fellowship under which this article was written in the spring of 1968.

JAN H. BLITS

From Caesar's Ambiguous End[†]

Despite its apparent simplicity, *Caesar* is very ambiguous, particularly in its presentation of Caesar.[1] Although dominating the world around him, the play's titular hero appears in only three scenes, speaks fewer than 150 lines, and is killed before the play is half over. Moreover, while his greatness is indisputably reflected in the men around him, in his influence over them and especially in the way they act in relation to him,[2] Caesar himself seems almost idle and much of what we see of him hardly measures up to what he says about himself. For example, he declares he is "as constant as the northern star" and as immovable as Mount Olympus soon after appearing indecisive about whether to attend the Senate; he asserts his superiority to every sort of adulation and blandishment when he appears to have been duped by Decius' flattery shortly before; and he claims to be absolutely fearless and even more dangerous than Danger itself only to seem to yield first to Calphurnia's fear for his safety and then to his own fear of what the senators might whisper about his courage were he to give way to her fear.[3] Shakespeare, it seems, has deliberately fashioned a Caesar who is at once great and small, victor and vanquished, triumphant hero and vainglorious fool. On the one hand, he is made to seem indecisive, insolent, self-deceiving, and petty; on the other, he is shown to be so much the master of the world that even the heavens reflect his image and herald his fall.

* * *

† From Jan H. Blits, *The End of the Ancient Republic: Shakespeare's "Julius Caesar"* (London: Rowman and Littlefield, 1993), 63–91. Reprinted by permission. Excerpts: pp. 63–64, 65, 77–79, 80–87, 87–91.

1. See Mungo MacCallum, *Shakespeare's Roman Plays and Their Background* (London: Macmillan and Co., 1967), esp. 218ff.; Ernest Schanzer, *The Problem Plays of Shakespeare* (New York: Schocken Books, 1965), 10ff.; Allan Bloom, *Shakespeare's Politics* (New York: Basic Books, 1964) 75f., 88–91.

2. Caesar is essentially right when he boasts, "The things that threaten'd me / Ne'er look'd but on my back; when they shall see / The face of Caesar, they are vanished." (II.ii.10–12) When Caesar first appears (I.ii.1–24) we see that Casca, who will stab him from behind, is the first to attend to his words; and although he jeers at Caesar behind his back (I.ii.231ff.), he is as obsequious as Antony to his face. Brutus, too, does his bidding, as does Cassius, his most resentful detractor, even though he complains bitterly in private that he ". . . must bend his body/If Caesar carelessly but nod on him." (I.ii.116f.) With the possible exception of Cicero, all of Caesar's republican enemies act one way in public and another in private. Caesar arrogates the prerogatives of at least a king, and all of Rome's nobles hold him in awe and pay him the deference he claims. See also V.i. 39–44.

3. II.ii.4–107, III.i.31–77.

Yet, while Caesar's actions are ambiguous, his ambition to become a god is not.[4] And if his actions are examined with a view to that ambition rather than to the commonly supposed ambition to become king, they appear not only consistent but brilliantly conceived and perfectly executed. They demonstrate characteristic political traits that enabled Caesar to "get the start of the majestic world, / And bear the palm alone" (I.ii.129f.)—his extraordinary ability to beguile his enemies while flattering his supporters.

* * *

The ambiguity of Caesar's end stems largely from the fact that his death is at once the epitome and the antithesis of an heroic death and that Caesar intends it to be understood by opposite groups in these opposite ways. To the Senate and the old regime in general, he intends it to be seen as the culmination of Olympian greatness and strength; to the people and the new regime, as the martyrdom of a new sort of god.[5] Thus, on the one hand, Caesar strives to embody perfectly all the traits of manliness. When confronted by the "very dangerous" Cassius, he insists he is not liable to fear, "for always I am Caesar" (I.ii.189–209). Similarly, when Calphurnia urges him not to go to the Senate, he first claims absolute fearlessness and equanimity concerning death:

> Cowards die many times before their deaths;
> The valiant never taste of death but once.
> Of all the wonders that I yet have heard,
> It seems to me most strange that men should fear,
> Seeing that death, a necessary end,
> Will come when it will come.

and then goes so far as to claim superiority to Danger itself:

> Danger knows full well
> That Caesar is more dangerous than he.
> We are two lions litter'd in one day,
> And I the elder and more terrible.
>
> (II.ii.32–37; 44–47)

And, finally, in front of the Senate he goes still further, declaring his absolute constancy and superiority to everything around him:

4. See esp. II.ii.44–48 and III.i.58–74. Although his essay begins, "*Julius Caesar* is the story of a man who became a god" (*Shakespeare's Politics*, 75), Bloom does not develop this theme. While pointing out that "Caesar conceives of himself as a god" (*ib.*, 90) and was in fact "worshipped as a divinity, as were many of those who inherited his name" (*ib.*, 75), he nonetheless judges his actions finally in terms of ambition for the crown.

For the fact that Caesar was ranked among the gods, not only by formal decree, but in the belief of the people, see Suetonius, *Divus Julius*, 88.

5. Caesar "collaborates, as it were, in his own deification." [John] Palmer, *Political Characters* [1961], 37.

I could be well mov'd, if I were as you;
If I could pray to move, prayers would move me;
But I am constant as the northern star,
Of whose true-fix'd and resting quality
There is no fellow in the firmament.
The skies are painted with unnumber'd sparks,
They are all fire, and every one doth shine;
But there's but one in all doth hold his place.
So in the world: 'tis furnish'd well with men,
And men are flesh and blood, and apprehensive;
Yet in the number I do know but one
That unassailable holds on his rank,
Unshak'd of motion; and that I am he,
Let me a little show it, even in this,
That I was constant Cimber should be banish'd
And constant do remain to keep him so.

(III.i.58–73)

In front of the people, on the other hand, Caesar suppresses all such heroic claims to divinity and affects not just equality but even inferiority. To the one group his death is meant to show him as immovable as Mount Olympus and as constant as the northern star; to the other, as weak as the weakest mortal and as poor as the poorest man:

But yesterday the word of Caesar might
Have stood against the world; now lies he there,
And none so poor to do him reverence.

(III.ii.120–122)

Caesar's double-faced death is the direct result of Rome's new political situation. Caesar claims to be "in the world" what the northern star is in the sky. He claims to be a universal god. Rome's universal empire brings forth a "new heaven" as it establishes a "new earth" (A&C I.i.17). The gods of republican Rome were gods of the city. Essentially civic or public, they defended Rome's public good from the twin dangers of private corruption at home and military defeat abroad. They were emphatically worldly or political. Like the city they defended, which defined itself chiefly by opposition to enemies or outsiders, their worship was necessarily confined within a narrow or particular horizon. Their existence was inseparable from the primacy of the public realm. Universal empire, however, necessarily destroys that realm by obliterating the distinctness or particularity of Rome and, with it, the public realm which the old gods defended and upon which their existence and worship depended. Universal empire requires an universal god, but, as the success of Antony's funeral oration shows, an universal god is worshipped by private individuals, not by citizens. Its worship is personal because its horizon is universal. As universal empire destroys the separateness of a political community, it establishes the separateness of its individual members. Men are no longer primarily citizens. They are now first and foremost individuals, whose deepest concerns are essentially private and whose relation to their gods is therefore immediate and direct.

    * * * Rome conquered the world by destroying the cities around her and readily accepting as citizens those she conquered so she could use them to conquer still more. To conquer everyone, Rome had to embrace everyone, so that her very conquests eventually transformed her basic principle of universal force into universal love.[6] It is therefore appropriate that Decius' interpretation of Calphurnia's dream alludes to Christian saints (II.ii.85–90), Antony's oration compares Caesar's "sacred blood" to that of Christian martyrs (III.ii.132–39), and Octavius alludes to the crucifixion of Jesus when speaking of Caesar's wounds (V.i.53). Cassius indignantly insists that Caesar, although worshipped as a god, is no more than a pitiful mortal. Yet it is because of Rome's conquest of the world and Caesar's conquest of Rome that such a "man / Is now become a god" (I.ii.114f.). While Rome's universal empire, reducing all men to private individuals, diminishes the glory of this world,[7] Caesar's death, at once an act of heroism and martyrdom, both connects and separates pagan and Christian, republican and imperial Rome. It begins the new as it completes the old.[8]

Shakespeare's ambiguous presentation reflects the problematical relation between the old and the new Rome, and hence the dual character of Caesar's death and divinity. But it also demonstrates the political skills which enabled Caesar to reach the top in Rome. It reflects the means he used as well as the ends he pursued. We saw this in his manipulation of the people at the Lupercal. We see it again in his handling of Decius on the morning of the ides.

    The scene with Decius (II.ii) is generally thought to show Caesar at his worst—superstitious, irresolute, arrogant and easily flattered. The keynote is struck at the end of the conspirators' meeting in the previous scene when Cassius warns,

6. Machiavelli, *Discourses*, II.3; [Harvey C.] Mansfield, *Machiavelli's New Modes and Orders* [1979], 198.

7. "It is a diminished world into which Shakespeare takes us after the death of Caesar." Palmer, *Political Characters*, 46. Rome has become Caesar's patrimony; cp. III.ii.249 with I.ii.152f.

8. That there may ultimately be something otherwordly about Coriolanus' isolating pride and uncompromising integrity is suggested by his last words to the Roman people: "Despising / For you the city, thus I turn my back. / There is a world elsewhere." (III. iii.133–135) The rest of his life shows that that other "world" is nowhere on earth.

> But it is doubtful yet
> Whether Caesar will come forth to-day or no;
> For he is superstitious grown of late,
> Quite from the main opinion he held once
> Of fantasy, of dreams, and ceremonies.
> It may be these apparent prodigies,
> The unaccustom'd terror of this night,
> And the persuasion of his augurers,
> May hold him from the Capitol to-day.

And Decius confidently assures him,

> Never fear that: if he be so resolv'd,
> I can o'ersay him; for he loves to hear
> That unicorns may be betray'd with trees,
> And bears with glasses, elephants with holes,
> Lions with toils, and men with flatterers;
> But when I tell him he hates flatterers,
> He says he does, being then most flattered.
> Let me work;
> For I can give his humour the true bent,
> And I will bring him to the Capitol.

(II.i.193–211)

Dreams and flattery indeed lie at the heart of the scene. As Caesar tells Decius that Calphurnia's dream keeps him from going to the Senate that day, so Decius' flattering reinterpretation of the dream apparently causes him to change his mind and go. Yet it is Caesar who, in telling the dream, gives Decius' ingratiating humor "the true bent," flattering him by letting him believe he can flatter Caesar, and, in so doing, induces him to betray his own purpose without his ever becoming aware that he has done so. The counterpart of the Lupercal scene, Caesar's exchange with Decius directly presents his political indirection. It shows him secretly defeating by openly gratifying his secret enemies.

As the scene begins, Caesar is awake despite the early hour. We know why the conspirators are up, but it is less clear why he should be. The violence and noise of the storm in the night and Calphurnia's cries in her sleep may have awakened him:

> Nor heaven nor earth have been at peace to-night:
> Thrice hath Calphurnia in her sleep cried out,
> "Help, ho! they murther Caesar!"

(1–3)

But he may be awake for another reason as well. From what Casca tells Cicero, we learn that Caesar was with him, Antony and perhaps others during the night and that he intends to go to the Senate in the

morning (I.iii.36–38). And, if only by rumor, Casca knows certain
senators plan that day to make him king everywhere but in Italy:

> Indeed, they say the senators to-morrow
> Mean to establish Caesar as a king;
> And he shall wear his crown by sea and land,
> In every place, save here in Italy.
>
> (I.iii.85–88)

Since Casca has heard this report, at best, secondhand, it would be
unreasonable to believe it could not have reached Caesar as well,
either through Casca, Antony, other senators, partisans, or spies.[9]
But if Caesar has heard the rumor, he must assume his very dangerous enemies such as Cassius have, too. Caesar nevertheless does not
send for a bodyguard or take any other precaution against attack.
Instead, he prepares to go to the Senate, as planned. When Calphurnia enters and expresses fear for his safety, he first dismisses
her concern out of hand, but yields when she suggests a pretext and
begs on her knee. He yields to her fears just as Decius arrives. While
surely strengthening Caesar's suspicions, Decius' unexpected arrival
is not enough to confirm them or to indicate where, when or how his
assailants might attack. Caesar has no reason to assume the republicans will make the mistakes they do. For all he knows, they might
strike him in the obscurity of his home, use a furtive means such as
poison, or even employ hired agents. Caesar's yielding to Calphurnia
thus gives him an opportunity to test Decius' intentions. "And you
are come in a very happy time," he tells him,

> To bear my greeting to the senators,
> And tell them that I will not come to-day:
> Cannot, is false; and that I dare not, falser;
> I will not come to-day. Tell them so, Decius.
>
> (60–64)

Caesar refuses to go or to explain why he will not go. But when
Decius asks for some cause, lest he be laughed at by the senators,
Caesar first reiterates his refusal—

> The cause is in my will: I will not come;
> That is enough to satisfy the Senate.

—but then, expressly to gratify Decius, relates Calphurnia's dream
and explains that she keeps him home because of it:

---

9. Caesar seems almost the only man in Rome ignorant of the plot against him. Popilius,
though not one of the conspirators, wishes them well (III.i.12ff.), and Artemidorus, a
foreign-born partisan of Caesar's, knows even of the last-minute inclusion of Ligarius
among the conspirators (II.iii.4).

But for your private satisfaction,
Because I love you, I will let you know:
Calphurnia here, my wife, stays me at home.
She dreamt to-night she saw my statue;
Which like a fountain with an hundred spouts
Did run pure blood; and many lusty Romans
Came smiling, and did bathe their hands in it.
And these does she apply for warnings and portents
And evils imminent; and on her knee
Hath begg'd that I will stay at home to-day.

And Decius replies,

This dream is all amiss interpreted;
It is a vision fair and fortunate:
Your statue spouting blood in many pipes,
In which so many smiling Romans bath'd
Signifies that from you great Rome shall suck
Reviving blood, and that great men shall press
For tinctures, stains, relics, and cognizance.
This by Calphurnia's dream is signified.

(71–90)

Caesar, though guarded, seems impressed by Decius' interpretation: "And this way have you well expounded it." (91) Decius, encouraged by this response, continues in his bid to make good on his boast to Cassius. He asserts that the interpretation refers to the Senate's (previously undisclosed) decision "To give this day a crown to mighty Caesar" (94),[1] and then, professing his "dear, dear love" (102), warns of what the senators might whisper about Caesar's courage were he to stay home because of his wife's bad dreams. Caesar, apparently swallowing it all, declares how foolish Calphurnia's fears now seem, expresses shame for having yielded to them, asks for his robe, and announces he will go.

While Caesar never looks more foolish than at this moment, he has learned everything he needs to know. As well as he knows how to interpret auspicies to suit his own purpose (37–48), he also knows how to present Decius with materials which he will interpret in such a way as unwittingly to divulge his own intentions. Contrary to first impressions, Caesar does not learn the details of her dream from Calphurnia. At the beginning of the scene, he says only that she thrice cried out in her sleep, "Help, ho! they murther Caesar!" and nothing in their conversation when she appears suggests they have spoken since she awoke. Calphurnia reminds Caesar of "the

---

1. Note that Decius omits the important limitation on the kingship that Casca mentions (I.iii.85–88).

things that we have heard and seen" and reports in vivid detail the "most horrid sights seen by the watch," which she says frighten her (13–26), but does not mention her dream, and in fact never does. Calphurnia's dream is Caesar's fabrication. He attaches to the dream the interpretation she gave to the horrid sights, and thus replaces her explanation of her fears, and hence his reason for staying home, with one of his own.[2] The ruse works perfectly. In challenging the interpretation Caesar offers, Decius confirms the central facts. What was true of Caesar's statue in the dream will be true of Caesar himself in Rome—he will indeed spout blood like a fountain. Decius thus acknowledges that Calphurnia was correct in her "vision" and wrong only in judging whether Caesar's assassination will be good or bad. Only whether her "vision" was "fair and fortunate" was "amiss interpreted." No wonder Caesar tells him, "And this way have you well expounded it." Caesar has learned he will be slain that day and his murder will be what he wants—a bloody public spectacle in the Capitol.

The victory Decius imagines he has secretly won over Caesar is Caesar's real, secret victory over him. Once he hears Decius's words, Caesar never again wavers.[3] He greets the rest of the assassins with urbane provocations, reminding them of their debts to him as well as their dependence, and when in public shows no concern whatever for what anyone could possibly give or take from him. Just as on the way to the Senate he displays indifference to what affects himself and concern for what affects others, so when he arrives in the Capitol he appropriates all giving (and even the Senate) to himself:

> What is now amiss
> That Caesar and his Senate must redress?
>
> (III.i.31f.)

From the moment he learns that he will be assassinated in a manner that will epitomize his life, Caesar acts like the god he claims to be.[4]

Caesar does not aspire to be king but rather to force future kings to aspire to the rank of "Caesar." Unwilling to follow in the path of any established tradition, however illustrious, he seeks to found a new tradition in which his name is superior to any other honor and confers all legitimate title to rule. He intends to establish a Caesarian

---

2. Contrary to what Caesar implies, Calphurnia was frightened because the sights were so dreamlike and yet not a dream (13–26).
3. Michael Platt, *Rome and Romans According to Shakespeare* (Salzburg Studies in English Literature: *Institut für Englishe Sprache und Literatur*, 1976), 201.
4. In Plutarch (*Caesar*, 66.4–5), Suetonius (*Divus Julius*, 82.1–2) and Appian (*The Civil Wars*, II.108), Caesar struggles with his killers. In Shakespeare, he does not.

monarchy, but a monarchy in his name, not in his person.[5] Thus the cry of "Caesar" is fully audible to the partly deaf Caesar. Caesar, whose deafness is Shakespeare's invention, is in a sense deaf to everything but his name, and especially to the warning of danger (I.ii.12–24). His name, he claims, makes him more than a man by rendering him independent of fear:

> Would he were fatter! But I fear him not:
> Yet if my name were liable to fear,
> I do not know the man I should avoid
> So soon as that spare Cassius.
> I rather tell thee what is to be fear'd
> Than what I fear; for always I am Caesar.
>
> (I.ii.195–198,208f.)

Caesar's goal is to establish the divinity of "Caesar," to show that his name is the greatest power and to possess that name is to possess such power. "Would you praise Caesar, say 'Caesar,' go no further." (A&C III.ii.13) To be great, greatness will have to bear his name.

Caesar is ambitious for his name. He lives and dies for it. In this respect he is characteristically, if perversely, Roman. * * * It is often pointed out how frequently and grandiloquently Caesar refers to himself by name.[6] Nineteen times he calls himself "Caesar." Fittingly enough, his last word is his name: "Then fall Caesar!" (III.i.71) But Caesar is by no means alone in referring to himself in this manner. Brutus and Cassius do so more than a dozen times each, and even Casca does once, as does Portia. Moreover, all of these self-references occur in the context of either the characters' proudest Roman declarations or their most shameful defeats. They are all associated with manliness.[7] Cassius can therefore draw Brutus into the conspiracy by invoking "the great opinion / That Rome holds of his name" (I.ii.315f.), and initially arouse him against Caesar by comparing the fates (and inherent qualities) of their names:

> Brutus and Caesar: what should be in that "Caesar"?
> Why should that name be sounded more than yours?

5. *Non Rex sum sed Caesar* ("I am not king but Caesar."): Plutarch, *Caesar*, 60.2, Suetonius, *Divus Julius*, 79.2, Appian, *Civil Wars*, II.108. As Bloom (*Shakespeare's Politics*, 91) points out, Caesar's name did, of course, soon become synonymous with the grandest sort of monarchy. Beginning with Octavius (see III.i.276; V.i.24, 54, 57) and extending down to our own day, emperors have continued to rule as Caesars, Kaisers, Czars, and Shahs.

6. E.g., by MacCallum, *Shakespeare's Roman Plays*, 230f., Palmer, *Political Characters*, 36ff., and Platt, *Rome and Romans*, 203ff.

7. Brutus' most republican speech (II.i.46–58) is the only speech in the play beginning and ending with the speaker's own name; note in context I.iii.90, the only line of its sort in the play. It would be difficult to exaggerate the importance of names in *Caesar*. Despite the play's relative brevity, the names of leading characters are mentioned much more often in *Caesar* than in any other Shakespearean play. Whereas Hamlet's name occurs 85 times, Macbeth's 42, Othello's 34 and Lear's 15, Caesar's appears 229 times, Brutus' 144, Cassius' 75 and Antony's 70. Only *Antony and Cleopatra* comes close to *Caesar*.

Write them together, yours is as fair a name;
Sound them, it doth become the mouth as well;
Weigh them, it is as heavy; conjure with 'em,
"Brutus" will start a spirit as soon as "Caesar".
Now in the names of all the gods at once,
Upon what meat doth this our Caesar feed,
That he is grown so great? Age, thou art sham'd!
Rome, thou hast lost the breed of noble bloods!
When went there by an age, since the great flood,
But it was fam'd with more than with one man?
When could they say, till now, that talk'd of Rome,
That her wide walks encompass'd but one man?
Now is it Rome indeed, and room enough,
When there is in it but one only man.
O, you and I have heard our fathers say,
There was a Brutus once that would have brook'd
Th' eternal devil to keep his state in Rome
As easily as a king.

                                        (I.ii. 140–159)[8]

To Brutus, who vows he loves "The name of honour" more than he
fears death (I.ii.88), as to other honor-loving Romans, names are
most real. The name is the thing itself.

Caesar is hardly dead before his name is used as he intended. At
his funeral the crowd urges that Brutus be the next Caesar, and
Antony exclaims to them, "Here was a Caesar! when comes such
another?" As Bloom remarks, Caesar's "own person would not have
sufficed to this role; but the edifice carefully constructed by him *plus*
the memory of his martyrdom formed an almost eternal imperium."[9]
Caesar constructs the memory of his martyrdom, however, as carefully as the edifice of his Olympian grandeur. His death turns him
into a god not only by saving him from the errors of humanity and its
weaknesses, as Bloom argues, but also, or especially, by publicly
demonstrating his human weakness and private suffering, as Antony
shows. Caesar is not merely spared infamy by his murder; he is raised
to the status of a god.

Shakespeare indicates both by what he omits from his historical
sources and by what he adds to them that Caesar's actions are to be
understood as having been undertaken with a view to his ambitious
death. Unlike Plutarch and Suetonius, who discuss the numerous
projects Caesar was planning at the time of his murder,[1] Shake-

---

8. The ironic implication, we should note, is that Rome does indeed belong to "one man."
   Owing to Brutus' namesake, Rome belongs especially to him.
9. *Shakespeare's Politics*, 91.
1. Plutarch, *Caesar*, 58.2–5; Suetonius, *Divus Julius*, 44f.

speare suppresses all his future plans for Rome[2] and avoids the impression that any were cut short by his death, but at the same time he invents his careful preparations for his assassination. According to the sources, Octavius was in Greece when he heard of Caesar's murder and only then decided to return to Rome.[3] In Shakespeare, "Caesar did write for him to come to Rome," and Octavius is "within seven leagues of Rome" at the time of the assassination and "is already come to Rome" before the end of the funeral (III.i.278ff.; III. ii.264ff.). It is important to note that neither Caesar's letters nor Octavius's arrival, both of which are wholly Shakespeare's inventions, serve any merely dramatic purpose. Octavius does not appear on stage until Act IV, scene i, which is to say, not for another year and a half. Only Caesar's preparations for the aftermath of his slaying require his heir's early return. And that the letters anticipate his killing is corroborated by three additional facts: the letters cause Octavius to act stealthily before the assassination; although written by Caesar, they direct Octavius not to Caesar but to Antony (and hence are not summonses for help); and Octavius' servant shows no surprise at hearing his master called "Octavius Caesar" (III.i.276ff.).[4]

While heightening the ambiguity and general sense of spiritual emptiness around him, Shakespeare's alterations also suggest that Caesar, having assured his preeminence among his rivals, has little to live for but much to die for. He is indeed "at the end of his career." Owing to his vast political accomplishments, there is no place left in the world for a man like him. If anyone in the Roman plays is interested in the sort of enterprises Plutarch says he planned, it is not Caesar but his successors (A&C II.vii. 17ff.). As Bloom notes, "One can hardly imagine that such a man could settle down to the career of a peaceful public administrator."[5] Nor would Caesar be content, like some later Caesars, to use his political position to indulge his private lusts. Caesar's achievements may have destroyed the ancient political world, but he remains a completely political man to the end, seeking immortal fame and glory, not bodily pleasure. His passions and aims are personal only in the sense that he seeks a political victory that is entirely his own, one in which what is personally his replaces what belongs to the city as such. There is nothing hedonistic or private about this Caesar. Even in private with his wife, he lacks privacy. Caesar could, of course, seek to become a living god. Indeed, Cassius says he is already on his way to becoming one

---

2. One possible exception is I.iii.85–88, which some editors understand as a remote allusion to Caesar's planned expedition against the Parthians.
3. Plutarch, *Brutus*, 22.2, *Antony*, 16.1; Suetonius, *Divus Augustus*, 8.2; Appian, *Civil Wars*, III.9–11.
4. In addition, Antony knows exactly where to find Caesar's will.
5. *Shakespeare's Politics*, 90.

(I.ii.114ff.). But, as Caesar's last appearance in the Capitol vividly demonstrates and as Shakespeare's apparently unfavorable presentation of him generally suggests, there is no way to distinguish genuine praise and love from the mere flattery and fear of a man who dominates the world and in whom all obedience and giving are concentrated.

But Caesar looks forward to death not so much because life holds no more conquests for him as because death alone promises him his true crowning conquest. Fulfilling his ambition to recreate Rome in his own image, it allows him to set a single goal for ambitious men beyond their reach—to be Caesar—while at the same time establishing himself as a new sort of god—one that is universal, above political rule, possessing and inspiring a sort of strength that is thought to be superior to manliness and inseparable from pity, and directly and immediately related to its worshippers. Combining reverence based on pity or love with reverence based on awe, Caesar's double-faced death, epitomizing both his political and military lives, brings together the sublime remoteness of "the northern star" and the personal closeness of "sweet Caesar's wounds" (III.ii.227) and "sacred blood." Caesar therefore goes to his death not only knowingly but willingly. Indeed, he goes to it in some sense like a traditional Roman—"pleas'd to . . . seek danger where he was like to find fame."

Yet, as Shakespeare presents it, Caesar's lasting achievement, like his death on the one hand and Brutus' problematical virtue on the other, seems ultimately more melancholic than glorious. It diminishes men's hearts as it expands their horizons and, by depriving them of opportunities for noble actions and triumphs in this world, forces them finally to seek glory and salvation in the next. In Titinius' words, "The sun of Rome is set. Our day is gone; / . . . our deeds are done." (V.iii.63f.) There are no worldly causes left worthy enough to fight for. Caesar's own victory, however, shares this unhappy fate. The fulfillment of Roman ambition necessarily comes too late, for it can come only at the end of the Republic's decline and not at the peak of its strength. Caesar's triumph—the end of the Republic which reveals its true beginnings—presupposes the corruption, as it implies the destruction, of republican Rome. Caesar's glory is therefore in some sense hollow or vain, though in another sense immortal. It is inseparable from a diminution of the hearts of men and an accompanying disillusionment or disenchantment with the beauty of this world. The world can no longer seem "majestic" to men who must live in Caesar's shadow (see esp. I.ii.91–136). Caesar claims to be in the world what the northern star is in the sky. But the northern star, as Caesar seems to forget, is visible only at night. It may indeed display an unrivaled "true-fix'd and resting quality," but its quality and glory stand out only against a darkened sky.

PAUL A. CANTOR

[Rhetoric, Poetry, Republic]†

* * *

It has frequently been noted that by comparison with Shakespeare's other tragedies, * * * *Julius Caesar* [is] basically rhetorical in mode, rather than lyrical.[1] * * * [T]he verse seems strictly governed by the dramatic context, with the result that neither contains the kind of lyric poetry that stands out in much of Shakespeare's work. * * * If one were to quote some memorable lines from either of the Republican Roman plays, they would almost certainly be from a public speech, say Antony's "Friends, Romans, countrymen," that is, lines more appropriate to a handbook of oratory than of lyric poetry. There are no songs in * * * *Julius Caesar.* * * * The stage directions of *Julius Caesar* do call for a song (IV.iii.266), but Shakespeare apparently did not bother to write one for the play, and in any case Brutus' boy has barely begun singing when he falls asleep. * * * Like any other private activity, poetry is judged in Rome by a political standard. What matters to the city is not the beauty of a poem, but the effect it will have on its citizens.

The Rome of *Julius Caesar* is actively hostile to poets.[2] Of the two who appear in the play, the first is torn to pieces by a mob that confuses him with a conspirator because it takes names for reality. In an almost surrealistic scene, the dreamer poet, who did not want to go out into the marketplace but was led forth by something he cannot explain (III.iii.1–4), is given a mock trial by the citizens of Rome. Faced with the impossible rhetorical task of answering his accusers "directly," "briefly," "wisely," and "truly" (III.iii.9–12), the poet Cinna finds that even his resources of irony are not enough to save him from execution. As the plebeians carefully check, Cinna does give one answer "directly" (l.23), one answer "briefly" (ll.24–25), and one answer "truly" (ll.26–27), but he never gives an answer "wisely," for in his situation to answer directly, briefly, and truly is not to answer "wisely," in the sense of "prudently."[3] His one attempt to give a wise

† From Paul A. Cantor, *Shakespeare's Rome: Republic and Empire* (Ithaca, NY: Cornell University Press, 1976), 110–14. Copyright © 1976 by Cornell University Press. Used by permission.
1. See Harry Levin, "Introduction to *Coriolanus*," *The Complete Pelican Shakespeare* (Baltimore: Penguin Books, 1969), p. 1213, and Brower, pp. 217–18.
2. See [Maurice] Charney [1961], pp. 65–66, and [Lawrence] Danson [1974], pp. 62–63.
3. A comparison of Brutus' speech with Antony's in the preceding scene will confirm the point that in addressing the people, to speak directly, briefly, and truly is not to speak wisely.

answer is interpreted by the plebeians as a wisecrack and turns his
audience of judges against him:

> *Cinna.*   Wisely I say, I am a bachelor.
> 2. *Plebeian.*   That's as much as to say, they are fools that marry.
>   You'll bear me a bang for that.

> [III.iii.16–18]

The questions the plebeians originally fired at Cinna (ll.5–8) added
up to one: Are you with us or against us, are you part of our city?
With his single answer, he apparently declares himself in the eyes of
the plebeians as their enemy, for they think his claim that it is wise to
be a bachelor calls into question the wisdom of all who marry. Cinna's independence is a challenge to the communal way of life of the
city. Later in the play, Brutus apparently feels a similar challenge to
his authority when a "vilely" rhyming poet breaks in upon a Roman
political conference, claiming the right to advise the generals on how
to make peace (IV.iii.132). Displaying a degree of irascibility unusual
for him, Brutus virtually throws the poet out with the words: "What
should the wars do with these jigging fools?" (IV.iii.137). If poetry
has no relevance to war, if it does not serve the public interest, Brutus does not want to hear it, and he resents being told what to do by
a merely private man. In general, Rome's hostility to poetry reflects
a deeper hostility to any private interest that claims to be independent of the city, especially independence of mind or freedom from
the city's opinions. Significantly, the poet Brutus wants expelled is a
"cynic" (IV.iii.133), one of those men who openly despises political
life and the honors of the city.[4]

The absence of any sustained lyrical passages in * * * *Julius Caesar* is in keeping with the focus on political concerns in Republican
Rome. With their minds fixed on public life, the Republican Romans
tend to sound as if they were always speaking at a rostrum, making
grandiloquent oratorical gestures at each other even when they are
talking two at a time (see, for example, * * * I.iii.89–100). In *Julius
Caesar* * * * the measure of a man's power is his skill as an orator,
and most of the turning points * * * involve the success or failure of
rhetorical attempts at persuading fellow Romans to one course of
action or another.[5] To take only a few examples, *Julius Caesar* opens
with Flavius and Marullus trying to persuade the plebeians to
remember Pompey and abandon Caesar's cause, we then see Cassius trying to persuade Brutus to join a conspiracy against Caesar,

---

4. In North's Plutarch, the character who breaks in upon Brutus and Cassius "cared
   for never a Senator of them all." See *Shakespeare's Plutarch*, p. 146, and [Allan]
   Bloom [1964] p. 101, p. 110.
5. See [Harry] Levin ["Introduction to Coriolanus (1969)"], p. 1213.

later Brutus must persuade his fellow conspirators to do things his way in murdering Caesar, in Act II, scene ii, Calphurnia tries to persuade Caesar to stay at home, while Decius Brutus must persuade him to go to the Senate as planned, and of course the whole play builds up to the great rhetorical combat between Brutus and Antony for the allegiance of the citizens of Rome. * * *

* * * [A]lthough we are continually witness to characters trying to bring fellow Romans around to their opinions, we rarely get to see how they arrived at those opinions for themselves. The use of rhetoric presupposes that one thinks one knows the truth: rhetoric is fundamentally an art of convincing people of truths one thinks one has already found, not of seeking truth in the first place. The rhetorical texture of the Republican Roman plays is thus one more indication of the fixity of opinions in Shakespeare's Rome. Everyone in the city thinks that he knows what is right and that the only problem is winning others over to his own views. This point is confirmed by looking at the few soliloquies in *Julius Caesar* * * * where one might expect to find characters in the process of doubt, self-examination, and the open search for truth. We will see, however, that the Republican Romans use rhetoric even when talking to themselves, so dominated are they in their thinking by the city.

In *Julius Caesar* the soliloquy serves mostly as a stage device, a convenient way, for example, for a character to reveal his plans to the audience (I.ii.308–22). Antony's one soliloquy (III.i.252–75) is really a dialogue, an address to the dead Caesar, which has the character of a solemnly pledged oath. The soliloquy is not used to lay bare an actual process of thought, to show a character groping for a decision. Brutus' main soliloquy begins with a conclusion, "It must be by his death" (II.i.10), and then proceeds to justify it, as if Brutus were addressing a crowd. Having already arrived at a decision, he is searching for reasons that would convince the world that what he has decided to do is just; he appeals to "common proof" (l.21), considers how his argument can best be manipulated for rhetorical effect (ll.28–30), and ends with a kind of proverb in the form of a beast fable (ll.32–34). This soliloquy can be viewed as a trial-run for Brutus' oration in Act III, scene ii, which it resembles closely.[6] * * * Since Brutus always sets his sights by what is viewed as noble in Rome, he thinks he has a straightforward principle for resolving the question of his divided loyalties and does not experience the kind of perplexing moral dilemma that grips either Macbeth or Hamlet. Like Volumnia, Brutus automatically places the public interest before his

6. See Brower, pp. 224–26.

private interest (II.i.10–12), an attitude reflected in the public character of even his most private speech.[7]

* * *

R. A. FOAKES

[Assassination and Mob Violence][†]

Julius Caesar, *Assassination, and Mob Violence*

Julius Caesar has struck many commentators as having a simplicity and clarity that differentiates it from the earlier histories, but at the same time, it is a play that offers a fresh perspective on violence and war. Caesar is the first dramatic character to be assassinated on the public stage for political reasons. The assassin as a killer hired privately for payment was already an established figure in the drama,[1] but political assassination as a public course of action chosen deliberately for a cause is different in kind. Shakespeare has Macbeth refer to the killing of Duncan as 'assassination' in his only use of the word, the first recorded in the *OED* as meaning the taking of life by treacherous violence, and the term 'assassin' soon gained currency in the seventeenth century, but commonly with reference to the murder of a public figure for reward.

The name Caesar had long been available to signify an absolute monarch or emperor, as can be seen in Shakespeare's use of it in, for example, *Henry VI*, Part 3 where the King, wandering in disguise, laments his loss of power: 'No bending knee will call thee Caesar now' (3.1.18). If an English monarch could be equated with Caesar, then a play about Julius Caesar might have some topical connection with concerns in the late years of Elizabeth's reign about the legitimacy of rebellion.[2] Shakespeare, however, was innovative in his play in rejecting the common view of Rome as an empire under the sway of the Caesars, a view derived from Suetonius, in favour of a republican idea of Rome derived from Plutarch.[3] By Shakespeare's time there was a vast European literature offering

---

7. See Bloom, p. 95.
† From R. A. Foakes, *Shakespeare and Violence* (Cambridge, UK, and New York: Cambridge University Press, 2003), 160–66. Reprinted with the permission of Cambridge University Press.
1. See Martin Wiggins, *Journeymen in Murder: the Assassin in English Renaissance Drama* (Oxford: Clarendon Press, 1991), and above, p. 31.
2. David Daniell, Introduction to his edition of *Julius Caesar*, Arden Shakespeare, Series 3 (Walton-on-Thames: Thomas Nelson and Sons, 1998), 28–9.
3. As argued by T. J. B. Spencer, 'Shakespeare and the Elizabethan Romans', *Shakespeare Survey*, 10 (1957), 27–38, cited in Daniell, 47.

opinions for or against Julius Caesar, appointed 'dictator' in Rome, who might be perceived as a tyrant, but also as the pattern for a benevolent monarch. Equally Brutus might be viewed as a lover of freedom, or alternatively as an example of a traitor, placed in the lowest circle of Hell in Dante's *Inferno*, whose death provided 'an evident demonstration, that peoples rule must give place, and Princes power prevail'.[4] Shakespeare achieves an extraordinary nuanced balancing act in his representation of both Brutus and Caesar.

Caesar's hesitations, his changes of mind, his falling sickness and deafness, his treatment of the senators as 'Good friends' (2.2.126), and his refusal to listen to Artemidorus ('What touches ourself shall be last served', 3.1.8), all help to moderate our sense of his personality, so that it seems in character that he refuses the crown offered him before the people by Antony. At the same time, Caesar is waited on as the man in power, admired by Antony, who is all obedience: 'When Caesar says "Do this", it is performed' (1.2.10). Caesar was above all famous as a warrior, and North's translation of Plutarch's life of him is devoted largely to his achievements in battle, including his invasion of England and his well-known message to Rome after his victory over King Pharnaces in Asia Minor, 'Veni, vidi, vici' [I came, I saw, I conquered].[5] Cassius tries to downplay this aspect of Caesar by boasting to Brutus that he rescued Caesar from drowning, carrying him on his back just as Aeneas carried his father Anchises from burning Troy. Later, in his funeral oration, Antony reminds the plebeians that the mantle on Caesar's body is the one he wore when he 'overcame the Nervii' (3.2.174). The idea of Caesar as warrior, as related to epic heroes, underlies the action of the play, but Shakespeare is concerned to emphasize the gap between the public image of authority earned by past achievements, and the present weaknesses and limitations of Caesar as a man. The senators look to him to conduct state affairs in the Capitol, and his authority and potential brutality are glimpsed in the violent punishment of the tribunes of the people, Marullus and Flavius, who are 'put to silence', according to Casca, suggesting they were executed for 'pulling scarves off Caesar's images' (1.2.281–2).[6]

Caesar also projects an image of himself as embodied in his name, an image of constancy and courage in authority: 'always I am Caesar' (1.2.209), a name that cannot be 'liable to fear'. So it is also

4. Geoffrey Bullough, *Narrative and Dramatic Sources of Shakespeare* (London: Routledge; New York: Columbia University Press), v, 24 (citing Appian, 1578).
5. The Latin phrase was added by the French translator Jaques Amyot, and taken over by Sir Thomas North in his English version.
6. According to Plutarch, they were imprisoned by Caesar's followers, and Caesar deprived them of their offices.

understandable that Brutus should be anxious when the people
appear to 'Choose Caesar for their king' (1.2.79). By the same token,
Brutus could be seen as representing freedom: he is conscious of his
descent from Lucius Junius Brutus who by tradition drove the tyrant
Tarquin from Rome (1.2.157–9; 2.1.53–4), and he conspires to kill
Caesar in the name of honour and freedom. With selective emphasis Caesar can be perceived as a dictator and Brutus as a republican
idealist. The play was staged and read in the United States for
decades after independence as embodying, in the words of the
advertisement of the 1770 production in Philadelphia, 'The noble
struggles for liberty by that renowned patriot, Marcus Brutus'.[7] The
rise of fascism suggested a different take on the play. Rather than
celebrating the heroism of Brutus, the remarkable production by
Orson Welles in New York in 1937 presented Caesar as Mussolini,
with black-shirted followers giving him Nazi salutes.[8] The play was
subtitled 'Death of a Dictator', and its emphasis was on the ineffec-
tiveness of Brutus and the libertarian ideal as they are overwhelmed
by the forces of fascism.

   Shakespeare's play may be adjusted to support such interpretations, but they diminish its complexity. Caesar is an ambiguous figure, not a tyrant, however much those around him seem to push him
towards adopting that role; and Brutus is nudged by Cassius towards
inventing for himself reasons for Caesar's overthrow, even as he
acknowledges that 'the quarrel / Will bear no colour for the thing he
is' (2.1.28–9). It is Cassius who reconstructs Caesar as a tyrant
(1.3.92, 103), harping on the notion that Brutus and the conspirators are 'underlings' (1.2.139) or in bondage to Caesar (1.2.60, 96;
1.3.90, 113). Brutus worries that Caesar might be ambitious and
might like to be crowned as emperor (2.1.12–16), but it is only when
he has to show leadership and encourage the gathered conspirators
that he adopts the language of Cassius and speaks of 'high-sighted
tyranny' (2.1.118). Even then he urges on his companions as if they
were going against an abstraction not a man. Brutus and the other
conspirators think that by killing Caesar they have destroyed not a
tyrant but tyranny itself, and can substitute for tyranny an alterna-
tive abstraction: 'Liberty! Freedom! Tyranny is dead!', cries Cinna,
echoed by Cassius and then Brutus (3.1.78, 81, 110). Cassius, the
instigator of what for him has been a plot against an enemy, is caught
up in the general fervour as the assassination is successful, and
imagines the conspirators will be known as 'The men who gave their
country liberty' (3.1.118).

7. Cited by Daniell, Introduction to *Julius Caesar*, 105.
8. See *ibid.*, 110.

In all the build-up to the assassination of Caesar there is no mention of what is to happen after his death. By his insinuations that the conspirators are underlings, and that the name of Brutus will start a spirit as soon as Caesar's, Cassius works on his friend by implying that he would make as good a ruler as Caesar, but always the main emphasis is on achieving freedom from bondage. The question who is to exercise power, and by what means, is never directly addressed. Brutus remains blind to the conseqences of his actions, never more so than when he calls on his comrades to bathe their hands in Caesar's blood, and wave their red weapons while crying 'Peace, Freedom and Liberty'. The bleeding body of Caesar is onstage through much of Act 3, and his ripped and blood-stained mantle is displayed by Antony, a vivid emblem of the violence that mocks the conspirators' cry of 'Peace'. The question who is to ensure peace and freedom, who is to govern after Caesar, is not discussed by them, and it lies at the heart of the play. Its absence allows an interpretation of Brutus as acting for the 'common good to all', in Antony's words (5.5.72), though he is concerned only with the general idea or name of liberty in conspiring against the idea of tyranny, and has no concern for the common good. So he could be played as embodying a republican ideal in America, provided that the struggle for liberty excluded the mob, and the scene of the lynching of Cinna the poet (3.3) was omitted. In the reduced and much altered blackshirt version with which Orson Welles launched the Mercury Theater in New York in 1937, he restored this scene, which had long been omitted in productions designed to enhance the stature of Brutus. It is a brief scene of great power that shows a remarkable anticipation of modern interpretations of the psychology of crowds. In thirty-eight lines Shakespeare dramatizes the critical moment when a bunch of citizens becomes a mob: 'The most important occurrence within the crowd is the *discharge*. Before this the crowd does not exist; it is the discharge which creates it.' The 'discharge' here occurs not when Cinna begins to answer the questions put to him by the plebeians, but is triggered when he reveals his name. At that point they cease to hear him, and join together in the cry 'tear him', as he becomes for them the embodiment of a hated name. As a mob, then, they finally rush off to set fire to the houses of the conspirators, to 'burn all': 'A crowd setting fire to something feels irresistible; so long as the fire spreads everyone will join it and everything hostile will be destroyed.'[9]

The violence of the killing of Caesar, displayed so vividly onstage by Brutus and the other conspirators when they coat their arms and

9. Elias Canetti, *Crowds and Power*, transl. Carol Stewart (London: Gollancz; New York: Viking Press, 1962), 17, 20.

swords in his blood, and when the funeral orations take place in the presence of his bloody corpse and his clothes covered in blood, indirectly produces the violence of the mob. The Mercury production began in darkness, and the lights came up to reveal Caesar, uniformed to suggest Mussolini, silencing everyone by speaking Casca's line (1.2.14), 'Bid every noise be still.'[1] Caesar's death brought an end to his ability to control noise, to keep crowds in awe, and the consequences of the assassination were brought home in the carefully orchestrated scene in which the poet Cinna wandered onstage to encounter a group of men who ignored his offer of poems; he tried to withdraw, only to find his way blocked, as other groups surrounded him in an ever-tightening circle. They began to tear his poems, and finally united as a mob, daggers drawn, and Cinna disappeared, screaming as he was murdered.[2] Welles saw Brutus as a man of principle, but also as an ineffectual liberal, desiring reform, but having no idea how to bring it about. He reduced the play to ninety minutes of continuous action, cut out Octavius, and the scene where Caesar's ghost appears, and curtailed the part of Antony. The play, for him, effectively ended once Antony set mischief afoot by stirring up the plebeians at the end of 3.2. The following scene, in which the innocent poet Cinna is lynched, thus took on tremendous importance. Brutus deluded himself into thinking he could destroy Caesar's name or spirit by stabbing his body, and the mob's destruction of Cinna for the sake of his name enacts a horrifying parallel. Brutus bathed in Caesar's blood with no thought for his victim, but anticipating the re-enactment of the murder on the stage:

> How many times shall Caesar bleed in sport
> That now on Pompey's basis lies along,
> No worthier than the dust?

> (3.1.114–16)

His cold-blooded triumph in the murder of Caesar is put in perspective by the violent death of Cinna.

Shakespeare's play completes the narrative of the rebellion, which is launched before dawn as the conspirators debate where the east lies (2.1.101–11), and is rounded off symbolically at the end of another bloodstained day with the death of Cassius:

> O setting sun,
> As in thy red rays thou dost sink tonight,
> So in his red blood Cassius' day is set.

> (5.3.60–2)

---

1. Frank Brady, *Citizen Welles* (New York: Charles Scribner's Sons, 1989), 123.
2. [Frank] Brady, *Citizen Welles* [1989], 125.

The violence of the assassination breeds other forms of violence. The mob's lynching of Cinna is the most terrible. The first concern of the triumvirate is to name and agree to execute all the supporters of the conspirators (4.1). Immediately after this scene the play jumps in time to the civil war that ensues. Shakespeare diverts us with the quarrel between Brutus and Cassius, the report of the suicide of Portia, and the appearance of the ghost of Caesar to Brutus. It is a fine sequence that eloquently establishes a sense that, however much they try to cheer themselves up, Cassius and Brutus are troubled by an unspoken awareness that all has been in vain, and the mood is one of resignation. When Brutus promises his boy Lucius, 'If I do live, / I will be good to thee' (4.3.264–5), he knows as we know that he will not live.

The scene prepares for the final encounter with the forces of Octavius and Antony at Philippi. Once again the stage is stained with blood, as young Cato is killed fighting, while Cassius dies on the sword with which he stabbed Caesar, and Brutus runs on his own sword. It is only in death that Cassius and Brutus find the freedom they thought to achieve with the assassination of Caesar (5.5.54). The bodies of Cassius and Brutus lie onstage marking the end of the 'day' of rebellion. In a final irony, Titinius puts a crown on the dead Cassius (5.3.97), who had so objected to the idea that Caesar might accept a crown. Shakespeare's main interest, however, is not in the completion of the cycle of violence, which happens relatively swiftly, but in the originating act and its immediate consequences. He shows at length how Brutus can only condition himself to participate in the murder of Caesar by turning him into an abstraction, an embodiment of tyranny. Brutus has no substantial motive, but this 'noblest Roman of them all' can be seduced by a foggy idealism into killing one who loves him (1.2.309). This is the mystery Shakespeare explores, and the death of Cinna the poet is the central scene of the play, in showing how all the lofty talk of freedom from bondage by the conspirators leads after the murder at once not to liberty, but to chaos and an explosion of spontaneous random violence.

* * *

PERFORMANCE HISTORY

SIDNEY HOMAN

From Shakespeare's Theater of Presence[†]

Late in the play Brutus sees a hybrid ghost containing both Caesar's spirit and the specter of Brutus's own troubled conscience. This "optical bifurcation" disturbs a play that, on the surface, seems given to the secular, masculine world of realpolitik. Actually, the supernatural has been present much earlier in the portents seen near Caesar's assassination, but the men—though not the women in the play—have either not witnessed such portents or, if they have, have used them as confirmation for their own practical political ends. *Julius Caesar* itself is rooted in historical fact, *has happened*, but the presence here of the supernatural, of what challenges mortal vision, suggests a sphere of influence beyond the rationale of history. Commentators on *Julius Caesar* have also been divided not only as to the ghost's significance[1] but to that of the larger play.[2] These bifurcations—the hybrid ghost who in Plutarch is sim-

---

† From Sidney Homan, *Shakespeare's Theater of Presence: Language, Spectacle, and the Audience* (Lewisburg, PA: Bucknell University Press, 1986), 87–104. Reprinted by permission of Associated University Presses. Excerpts: pp. 87–88, 98–104.

1. For example. Bernard Breyer, dismayed by the "few meager lines" given to the ghost's appearance, observes that it is "mighty unimpressive for a stellar role." "A New Look at *Julius Caesar*," *Essays in Honor of Walter Clyde Curry*, ed. Richmond C. Beatty et al. (Nashville, Tenn.: Vanderbilt University Press, 1954), p. 162. It has been called "a dramatic condensation of the immortality" achieved by Caesar during his life (Brigid Brophy, *Black Ship to Hell* [New York: Harcourt, Brace, and World, 1962], p. 77), a manifestation of "the Caesar-principle" (Kenneth Burke, *The Philosophy of Literary Form* [New York: Vintage, 1957], p. 281), and thereby a "visible symbol" of his power and significance (Edward Dowden, *Shakespeare: A Critical Study of His Mind and Art* [New York: Harper and Brothers Publishers, 1881], p. 256). A reminder that "Caesar is never for a moment absent" (John Palmer, *Political and Comic Characters in Shakespeare* [London: Macmillan, 1962], p. 58), the ghost is the "reaffirmation of the monarchic principle" (J. E. Phillips, *The State in Shakespeare's Greek and Roman Plays*, Columbia University Studies in English and Comparative Literature 149 [New York: Columbia University Press, 1940], p. 187), the personification of a great man (Virgil Whitaker, *Shakespeare's Use of Learning* [San Marino, Calif.: Huntington Library, 1964], p. 230), the Northern Star (Roy Walker, "Unto Caesar: A Review of Recent Productions," *Shakespeare Survey* 11 [1958]: 132–35). Conversely, the ghost has been seen as a premonition of the ill that the conspirators have failed to eradicate (Derek Traversi, *Shakespeare: The Roman Plays* [Stanford, Calif.: Stanford University Press, 1963], p. 70), or the unwanted, repudiated parts of Brutus's personality that break through despite his attempts to deny them (Lynn de Gerenday, "Play, Ritualism, and Ambivalence in *Julius Caesar*," *Literature and Psychology* 24 [1974]: 30). It has been called Brutus's evil spirit and thus an ironic counterpart to his earlier reputation as Caesar's "angel" (David C. Green, *"Julius Caesar" and Its Sources*, Salzburg Studies in English Literature [Salzburg, Austria: University of Salzburg Press, 1979], pp. 269–70) * * * However, E. E. Stoll would take the ghost "not intellectually or philosophically, but as a matter of art." *Shakespeare Studies Historical and Comparative in Method* (New York: The Macmillan Co., 1927), p. 209.

2. Perhaps Coleridge initiates the debate with his question, "What character does Shakespeare mean Brutus to be?" See *Coleridge's Shakespearean Criticism*, ed. T. M. Raysor (Cambridge, Mass.: Harvard University Press, 1930), 1:16. For William R. Bowden, Brutus is well-intentioned but lacking any real vision ("The Mind of Brutus," *Shakespeare Quarterly* 17 [1966]: 57–67); Moody E. Prior doubts "whether the most fruitful

ply Brutus's evil spirit, as well as the co-presence of the secular and the supernatural, and of male and female vision—when added to *Julius Caesar*'s current status as a "problem play"[3] are at one, I think, with the issue of how we—both characters and audience—interpret what we see onstage, or what in modern criticism would be called the relation between the sign and the signifier.

I believe that in *Julius Caesar* we are confronted with two incompatible plays. One is exclusive, grounded in the facts, depicting a political world in which males confidently, for a time, "read" events in terms of their own prescriptive standards, a world in which what we see is what we *can* see. The other play, one that will prove dominant, includes but goes beyond this secular drama, enacting a mystical, timeless world to which the women, Portia and Calphurnia, prove especially sensitive, one mocking the conspirators' progressive, cause-and-effect mentality with its own cyclical, and therefore cynical "history." This second world demands a sense of visual play for which the playless conspirators prove inadequate, and is a world rendering invalid the Romans' attempt to read Caesar accurately in life, not to mention that Caesar existing in death who visits Brutus on the eve of battle. For the rationalistic conspirators, interpretation is both the issue and their curse.

* * *

Against this cyclical inevitability, whose dominant metaphor is found in the repetition of roles and scenes, there stands the image of the playwright himself. Through language and spectacle, and in full comprehension of his subject, Shakespeare has fashioned a historical event, recreated it through the theater, to the degree that, as T. J. B. Spencer observes, twentieth-century man tends to see ancient Rome much as Shakespeare himself enacts it.[4] The playwright's view even dominates here over that of Plutarch, who lived closer to the period and served as the playwright's primary source. Nor could the admittedly greater erudition of Ben Jonson give his two Roman tragedies a comparable status.

---

way to approach *Julius Caesar* is as the tragedy of Brutus ("The Search for a Hero in *Julius Caesar,*" *Renaissance Drama*, N.S. 2 [1969]: 81–101). For Phyllis Rackin, Brutus dies "unconvinced," still believing that all men were true to him, never fully understanding the realities of political life ("The Pride of Shakespeare's Brutus," *Library Chronicle* 32 [1966]: 18–30), while Gordon Ross Smith sees him as an inflexible character, self-righteous, alternating between an imperious will and childish impulsiveness ("Brutus, Virtue, and Will," *Shakespeare Quarterly* 10 [1959]: 367–79). * * * A very excellent review of the conflicting readings of the play, at least up to 1966, is provided by Mildred E. Hartsock, "The Complexity of *Julius Caesar,*" *PMLA* 81 (1966): 56–62.

3. Ernest Schanzer, *The Problem Plays of Shakespeare: A Study of "Julius Caesar," "Measure for Measure," "Antony and Cleopatra"* (New York: Schocken Books, 1963), p. 34.

4. T. J. B. Spencer, "Shakespeare and the Elizabethan Romans," *Shakespeare Studies* 10 (1957): 27–38.

Yet, with no less equal energy and intention, the characters, Brutus in particular, try to "fashion" (2.1.220) the present, to "play" with it for a desired end. In this sense Brutus is a failed playwright, or, as Sigurd Burckhardt argues, he, like Shakespeare, is the playwright responsible for committing an act.[5] A common complaint about Brutus's playwriting skills, however, is that he is too cold, too abstract, not sufficiently attuned to the ears and eyes of his audience.[6] He sees not so much the bodies of men but the abstraction "conspiracy" (2.1.77). Unlike his own playwright, Brutus, in fact, would divorce language from spectacle, preferring the "word" of men (2.1.125), indeed "good words" before physical action itself (5.1.29). His funeral oration is a case in point. The language is abstract, nontactile, and while there are superficial appeals to the audience for its response, Brutus's questions are actually *rhetorical* in the most limited sense of that word. He plays *to* an audience, but not in concert *with* it, and it is a telling fact that when he pauses for their "reply," the audience affirms "None, Brutus, none" (3.2.34–35). His own play, the assassination of Caesar, reverses Shakespeare's since it is based not so much on the past (Brutus has no clear present complaint about Caesar's policies) as on the future (he would murder Caesar for what he might become). Like a playwright or poet, he must also use the physical as the root for language and symbolic vision: "For Antony is but a limb of Caesar" and "O that we then could come by Caesar's spirit, / And not dismember Caesar!" (2.1.165, 169–70). Yet, in attempting to separate what cannot be separated if the theater is to work, Brutus fails to produce the very play he would fashion. Disdaining "savage spectacle" (3.1.223), he would convert the physical act of assassination, as Brents Stirling rightly observes, to a theater of "sacrificers" (2.1.166), in which, contradicting the normal balance in such rituals between the body and the service over that body, the physical source of the sacrifice would cease to be a factor.[7] Brutus's concept of both sacrifice and theater is thus limited, his play at length seen by his audience, under Antony's tutelage, as a "piteous spectacle" (3.2.198), and ultimately as only a "gallant show" (5.1.13). In point of fact, he will not "come by" ("eliminate") Caesar's spirit; nor will he avoid dismembering the body. This theatrical cleavage is the equivalent to the "gaping dualism" that G. Wilson Knight finds in Brutus as he con-

5. Sigurd Burckhardt, "How Not to Murder Caesar," *Centennial Review* 11 (1967): 141–56. Schanzer suggests that Brutus is tortured not so much by what he has lost as by what he has "gained," by "the kind of world which he has helped bring into existence" (*Problem Plays*, p. 63).
6. See particularly the fine article by John S. Anson, "*Julius Caesar*: The Politics of the Hardened Heart," *Shakespeare Studies* 2 (1966): 11–33.
7. Brents Stirling, "Or Else This Were a Savage Spectacle," *PMLA* 66 (1951): 765–74; and reprinted in his *Unity in Shakespearian Tragedy* (New York: Columbia University Press, 1956), pp. 40–54.

trasts his cold abstractions of "honor" with the physical and communal nature of "love."[8]

In this regard Cassius is Brutus's counterpart; he would sacrifice
a diminished language to spectacle. He is physical, tactile. In his
opening line he asks if Brutus will "see" the "order of the course"
(1.2.25) and then "observe[s]" something other than a "show of love"
in Brutus's eyes (32–34). Uneasy with the symbolic, with anything
other than what is here and now, and as perceived by himself, Cassius is not given to art in any exalted sense, loving neither plays nor
music (1.2.203–4). Like the unplayful Tribunes in the first scene, he
would "disrobe the images" (1.1.64). His language is used instead
for the practical purpose of inciting others to action: "my weak
words / Have struck but thus much show of fire" (1.2.176–77). Nor
is he above the stratagem of having "writings" thrown in Brutus's
window (1.2.316–18).[9]

Though we might want to qualify the word, Antony is a *compromise* between the extremes of Brutus and Cassius. Of "quick spirit"
(1.2.29) and given to "sports" (2.1.189), with that word embracing
everything from athletic contests to theatrical spectacles, he stages
the offstage coronation reported by Casca, with the audience clapping and hissing the performers "as they use to do the players in the
theatre" (1.2.258–61). Antony's own staged sincerity in the presence
of the conspirators and his self-conscious address to Caesar's dead
body ("O, pardon me" [3.1.254–75]) culminate, of course, in the
funeral oration, where he combines the conceptual (the challenge
to Brutus as an honorable man) and the visual. Making himself
and then Caesar the object of the address, rather than attempting to
justify a past event, *playing* to his audience, his speech itself is
replete with highly theatrical details. When he comes down from the
pulpit, lifts Caesar's mantle, and asks the mob to form a circle
around the body (the otherwise formal "theater" of the oration now
becoming theater-in-the-round), Antony demonstrates a sense of
staging unmatched in the play. Significantly, Brutus is absent, by his
own wish, during this performance. Still, even this "shrewd contriver" (2.1.158) cannot practice his theatrics so effectively as to rise
above history, and at the end it will be the efficient but playless Octavius whose star is in the ascendancy.

All three "playwrights" pale, of course, beside their ultimate cre-
ator. Nor does any character have a sense of play equal to the complexities of its world. Curiously, *Julius Caesar* opens with tribunes

8. G. Wilson Knight, "The Eroticism of *Julius Caesar,*" in *The Imperial Theme* (London:
Methuen and Company, 1954), pp. 63–95.
9. On this issue of characters being like playwrights shaping or attempting to shape reality,
see William B. Toole, "The Metaphor of Alchemy in *Julius Caesar,*" *Costerus* 5 (1972):
135–51.

chastising workmen for playing, for celebrating in a holiday spirit Caesar's return. The occasion for play, the feast of the Lupercal, will itself be quickly converted to the arena of serious political work. Mildred Hartsock notes that the only characters not caught up in the complexities of the world, and hence able to see the tragic connection between man's attempt to fashion events and history's inflexible hand, are the two poets and the soothsayer.[1] More often, the theater is dismissed as something irrelevant to the seeming "realities" of the world: the Soothsayer is only a "dreamer" (1.2.24), the staged coronation "mere foolery" (1.2.236), and that imagination by which we escape the confines of the present is on a par with a belief in "unicorns" (2.1.204). As with the trust in portents, or the belief in a world beyond the immediate reaches of the senses, particularly the visual senses, the theater is here associated with what is womanish and, in the almost exclusively male world of *Julius Caesar*, unflatteringly so. Cassius dismisses those who read the portents for supernatural commentary as being governed by their "mothers' spirits" (1.3.83). In similar fashion Decius associates a belief in dreams with women (2.2.99). Misinterpretation of the object of the immediate senses is an "error soon conceiv'd, / That never com'st unto a happy birth, / But kill'st the mother that engend'red" it (5.3.69–71).

Nevertheless, when the play metaphor surfaces most graphically, it is a male speaker who imagines a production that will never exist, a *Julius Caesar* having little in common with the complex play world that the speaker himself presently inhabits. Cassius's "How many ages hence / Shall this our lofty scene be acted over / In states unborn and accents yet unknown" generates in turn Brutus's "How many times shall Caesar bleed in sport, / That now on Pompey's basis lies along / No worthier than the dust!" (3.1.111–16). Here are Romans "speaking centuries before the Renaissance" and anticipating "a Globe audience in 1599 watching a stage representation of their deed."[2] To be more accurate, the laudatory play they envision never comes from Shakespeare's pen.

Only at the end of the play, near death, do these characters who mistake themselves for flesh-and-blood people see the world of *Julius Caesar* with any real perspective. Brutus's "I know my hour is come" ends a speech that opens with the revelation to Volumnius that the ghost of Caesar has twice appeared to him (5.5.20), and later when he says that his "tongue / Hath almost ended his life's history" and that he has "but labor'd to attain this hour" (5.5.39–42), the theatrical metaphor, so long missing in Brutus's conscious

1. Hartsock, "The Complexity of *Julius Caesar*," p. 62.
2. Sidney Homan, *When the Theater Turns to Itself: The Aesthetic Metaphor in Shakespeare* (Lewisburg, Pa.: Bucknell University Press, 1981), pp. 11–12.

mind, subtly reasserts itself: the actor playing Brutus is about to end
his speaking role, and he has worked for the stage's two-hours' traffic to bring himself to this final scene. Now for Brutus history itself
becomes cyclical and cynical rather than progressive and positive:
"O Julius Caesar, thou art mighty yet! / Thy spirit walks abroad, and
turns our swords / In our own proper entrails" (5.3.94–96). Earlier
he parallels this observation with one a bit more general: "but this
same day / Must end that work the Ides of March begun" (5.1.112–
13.). In his own words Brutus is late developing a sense of "his life's
history" (5.5.40). Just as Caesar near death was given to superstition's
imaginative world—the theater in essence—both Brutus and Cassius, in now qualifying the otherwise secular, rational tenets of their
Stoicism and Epicureanism, respectively, "change" their minds and
"partly credit things that do presage" (5.1.77–78).

The ghost scene (4.3.239–308) stands as a vortex for the enlarged
vision called for and yet so rarely found in the play. It is a moment
when Brutus can see through, albeit briefly, to the mystical or supernatural that coexists with the natural, external world, as well as to
the cyclical history encompassing his own present actions.

The scene itself does not come upon the play suddenly but rather
has been anticipated, though, like Brutus in his serene moment
before death, we as audience can realize this only in retrospect. Brutus himself had earlier defined the night as that time "when evils are
most free" (2.1.79), as a time when he envies the peaceful sleep of his
servant Lucius since he has "no figures nor no fantasies, / Which
busy care draws in the brains of men" (231–32). Prophetically, he
had found the sleepless period "since Cassius first did whet [him]
against Caesar" or the space between "the acting of a dreadful thing
/ and the first motion" as being "like a phantasma or a hideous
dream" (2.1.61–65).

As noted, Shakespeare couples Plutarch's spirit embodying Brutus's ill conscience with the ghost of Caesar. That ill conscience
may find its origin in the Cobbler's pun on "bad soles" (1.1.13), and
surfaces at length in Antony's prophetic remark at the funeral oration that "the evil that men do lives after them" (3.2.75). Several
commentators have seen the ghost as Brutus's other half, as the Caesar element in himself,[3] as the embodiment of "his subjective fears
and misgivings,"[4] the "proof" that Caesar and Brutus are ultimately
the same being,[5] as the spirit that "Brutus cannot stop . . . because
he is infused with it himself in all of its paradoxical glory."[6] Perhaps

3. Albert Kearney, "The Nature of an Insurrection: Shakespeare's *Julius Caesar,*" *Studies*
(Dublin) 63 (1974): 141–52.
4. MacCallum, *Roman Plays,* p. 269.
5. Rackin, "Pride of Brutus," p. 28.
6. Simmons, *Pagan World,* p. 107.

this notion of the ghost as part of Brutus, or as a manifestation of a half that has hitherto been suppressed in the play, is anticipated in Portia's description of herself as her husband's half: "am I yourself / But, as it were, in sort or limitation?" (2.1.282–83). She observes this, we will recall, after the conspirators have left, and her most pressing subject is the "sick offense within [Brutus's] mind" that keeps him from bed and restful sleep (2.1.268).

The ghost scene itself is set outside the confines of the daylight, political world, and forms part of what John Crawford has charted as the play's larger movement from the external to the internal.[7] Appropriately, Brutus observes that "the deep of night is crept upon . . . talk," and to his question "There is no more to say?" Cassius replies with a simple "No more" (226, 229). The failed playwright, as I have called him, given to language rather than spectacle, the man who attempted earlier to divorce the conceptual from the physical, is here bereft of words themselves, indeed has grown "much forgetful" (255).[8] The sure, inflexible Brutus of the Quarrel Scene is now twice given to the qualifying "I think" (274, 276). The intellectual of the conspiracy, the classic orator at the funeral, now speaks with an almost awkward simplicity: "*Bru.* Well; then I shall see thee again? / *Ghost.* Ay, at Philippi. / *Bru.* Why, I will see thee at Philippi then" (284–86).

In representing not one but two entities, the ghost itself defies normality or probability. Like Hamlet's father's ghost, both dead and living, it comes from a world not fully encompassed by orthodox notions of reality. And it must be invoked; Hamlet's "Speak, I am bound to hear" (1.5.6) is here Brutus's "Speak to me what thou art" (281).[9] Potentially a god, an angel of conscience, and a demonic spirit, the ghost demands that sense of play implicit in an enlarged vision, the ability to entertain a double, an inclusive rather than an exclusive notion of reality.[1] Nor can anyone onstage, upon waking, share Brutus's vision or, more properly, what he has both seen and heard. Like Bottom waking from his forest adventure with "when my cue comes, call me, and I will answer" (4.1.200–201), Lucius wakes with the line "the strings, my lord, are false" (291) and thus reveals that for him the time covered during the ghost's appearance does not

---

7. John W. Crawford, "The Religious Question in *Julius Caesar*," *Southern Quarterly* 15 (1977): 297–302.
8. See T. Walter Herbert, "Shakespeare Announces a Ghost," *Shakespeare Quarterly* 1 (1950): 247–54.
9. In *The Structure of "Julius Caesar"* (Liverpool: Liverpool University Press, 1958), p. 48, Adrien Bonjour observes that "for the first time in the play Brutus is clearly led to contemplate acting himself in flagrant opposition to his own philosophical ideal. . . ."
1. On this issue of the necessity of entertaining doubles see René Girard, "Lévi-Strauss, Frye, Derrida, and Shakespearean Criticism," *Diacritics* 3 (1973): 34–38.

exist, since to his own mind he has continued speaking, without interruption, from Brutus's earlier observation about slumber rewarding him with sleep as he plays the instrument (269). Nor can Brutus find anyone else to verify the appearance. As most of those who have directed the play would do, I take his questions to Lucius, Varrus, and Claudio as a tactful way of detecting whether those onstage have shared his vision, without at the same time raising suspicions that he alone has seen the ghost. After first claiming that Lucius cried in his dream, thereby making his question "Didst thou see any thing?" (297) seem reasonable, he repeats the stratagem with Varrus and Claudio. As the offstage audience, we confirm what they cannot, though Brutus, caught in the historical confines of the stage, cannot take any comfort in this "fact."

Maurice Charney's observation that throughout the play the name of Caesar becomes a kind of "talisman"[2] takes on a very special meaning in this scene that another commentator sees as bordering on "the occult," with Brutus functioning as a "tragic conjurer," working in a setting complete with bell, book, candle (and an ill-burning one at that),[3] and music.[4] Until this moment Brutus has been convinced of his own clear vision. Here his otherwise unreliable eyes help shape the "subjective apparition of Caesar himself."[5] The very play that introduces Brutus to Cassius with the subject of eyes is now flooded with reference to vision: "heavy eyes" (256), "Let me see, let me see" (273), the "weakness of mine eyes" (276), the opening questions to the ghost as Brutus struggles with the evidence of his eyes (275, 278).

By his own admission Brutus sees the ghost once more (5.5.17–18), and for us the question must be, in this play that enacts the limitations of man's vision of himself, his role in history, and of his place in a world that embraces the natural and the mystical: just how much does Brutus see? Like Othello in his final speech, does Brutus, so late in the play, achieve something approaching tragic vision? There is no sure critical consensus here. It has been argued that once Brutus's optimistic prophecy about Rome after Caesar is rejected, another "voice" in the form of Caesar's cryptic ghost must fill the void, and so here Brutus's "evil spirit" shows the prophet

2. Maurice Charney, *Shakespeare's Roman Play: The Function of Imagery in the Drama* (Cambridge, Mass.: Harvard University Press, 1961), p. 70.
3. See Vincent F. Petronella, "Dramatic Conjuring in Shakespeare's *Julius Caesar*," *Dalhousie Review* 57 (1977): 130–40.
4. See John Hollander, *The Untuning of the Sky* (Princeton, N.J.: Princeton University Press, 1961), p. 150, where he suggests that the reference to false strings shows "the discordant conspirators, now jangling and out of tune even among themselves." And F. W. Sternfeld, *Music in Shakespearean Tragedy* (London: Routledge and Kegan Paul, 1963), pp. 80–81.
5. A. W. Bellringer, "*Julius Caesar*: Room Enough," *Critical Quarterly* 12 (1970): 46.

offering up his last sign by giving up the ghost.[6] Conversely, Brutus's subsequent behavior, unlike that of Macbeth after he has seen the ghost, is not that of a guilty man since the spirit is "another pointer to the unavoidable outcome; it signifies power rather than judgment."[7] Or the scene allows Brutus's inner self to surface briefly in a play where otherwise it is never "fully confronted or reflected upon."[8]

Though he predates him by little more than a year on the Globe stage and was, indeed, performed by the same lead actor, Brutus is surely no Hamlet. His vision of the ghost comes late rather than early, and unlike Hamlet, Brutus does not wax desperate with imagination almost from the start. If Hamlet is too circumspect, to the degree that he renders himself incapable of the decisive action distinguishing the elder Hamlet, Brutus, although an intellectual and an idealist, focuses more on the events of the world than on human motivation or questions about reality as it is intersected by the unreality of dreams and the theater. John Russell Brown speaks of the ghost as an actor's subtext—the motivation and rationale of a character existing just below the conscious, written text—which has momentarily come to the surface.[9] More often in *Julius Caesar* that subtext, as it includes the forces at once psychological, historical, mystical, and cyclical that shape human behavior, must be inferred by the audience. Brutus prefers another type of play, one where "our looks [do not] put on our purposes, / But bear it as our Roman actors do, / With untir'd spirits and formal constancy" (2.1.225–27). For him, to his Conscious mind, the theater is only secular, a tool at best, only a metaphor for reality (as when we spoke during World War II of "the European Theater"), a way of picturing the abstractions of political and ethical thought and thus only their handmaiden, inauthentic in itself, let alone being a superior way of understanding reality. This concept of the theater is, I think, at once Brutus's strength and glaring limitation. His kinsmen are to be found in those public figures like Theseus and Claudius who, with varying degrees of both success and integrity, try to manage in the immediate world. Unlike Hamlet, a man given to theater, they do try to prove "most royal," having "been put on" (5.2.397–98).

Yet a serenity comes to Brutus following the ghost's appearance. We have already observed those moments near his death when he sees his life in some perspective, as a kind of theatrical "history," which, of course, is what it is. Such late-come vision is brief, to be sure, but we are no less grateful. One critic cites the paradox: "the

6. Anderson, "Language of Sacrifice," p. 20.
7. Bellringer, "Room Enough," p. 46.
8. Ruth Nevo, *Tragic Form in Shakespeare* (Princeton, N.J.: Princeton University Press, 1972), p. 46.
9. John Russell Brown, "Shakespeare's Subtext: I," *Tulane Drama Review* 8 (1963): 90.

flood [of history] cannot be gauged by the reasoning mind," and the only wisdom we can have is at the end, when the end is known.[1] Harriet Hawkins comments that here Shakespeare's audience has "the retrospective foreknowledge of a historian, a playwright, or a god," and if we misconstrue the world the fault "lies in human nature itself," when we are compelled to be actors ourselves rather than spectators.[2] No less than for us, Brutus's knowledge comes late, yet it comes nevertheless. Moments before the entrance of Antony and Octavius, Brutus can at last avert his look with impunity from the visible world, for now, and only now, obscured vision is a blessing rather than a curse: "Night hangs upon my eyes, my bones would rest, / That have but labor'd to attain this hour."

JOHN NETTLES

From Brutus in *Julius Caesar*[†]

＊　＊　＊

In the orchard, talking to the conspirators, Brutus is seen most clearly in all his paradoxical glory. He is mistaken in his assessment of the wrongs visited upon the Roman people by Caesar, mistaken in the belief that Caesar can be carved as a dish fit for the gods, not butchered as a carcass fit for hounds, mistaken in the belief that the populace will understand what the conspirators are doing and applaud them as purgers of the body politic, and, lastly and fatally, mistaken in assuming that Mark Antony poses no threat and need not be killed along with Caesar. The stage is set for tragedy, a tragedy born of Brutus's inability to understand anything of the world in which he finds himself. Far from creating a wonderful commonwealth by sacrificing Caesar he lets loose the dogs of war and in the conflict Brutus loses everything he ever owned or loved. That is the price he pays for his mistakes.

The killing of Caesar is a bloody mess. Desperately seeking to give the murder some resonant ritual quality, he has to resort, above all things, to the hunters' practice of daubing their hands with the blood of the butchered quarry. Then Brutus commands his fellow conspir-

1. Norman Rabkin, "Structure, Convention, and Meaning in *Julius Caesar*," *Journal of English and Germanic Philology* 63 (1964): 253.
2. Harriet Hawkins, *Likeness of Truth in Elizabethan and Restoration Drama* (Oxford: Clarendon Press, 1972), pp. 146, 151.
† From *Players of Shakespeare 4*. Ed. Robert Smallwood (Cambridge, UK and New York: Cambridge University Press, 1998), 177–92. Reprinted with the permission of Cambridge University Press. Excerpts: pp. 183–89, 191–92.

ators to walk 'to the market place' and 'waving our red weapons o'er our heads / Let's all cry, "Peace, freedom, and liberty"' (III.i.108–10). The sight must have been astonishing in its presumption.

Brutus is surprised at the adverse reaction of the people and senators who, instead of rejoicing at Caesar's death, fly away and barricade themselves in their houses as if Doomsday were come. But Brutus thinks he has only to address them and apprise them of the true nature of his actions for them to applaud him as the sav-iour of Rome. It is a peculiar speech in many ways, not least in that there is no reasoned justification for the killing of Caesar, just the bald statement that Caesar was ambitious and that if he had been allowed to live the Roman citizens would all have become slaves. Brutus, because he loved Rome more than Caesar, therefore took upon himself the job of rescuing Romans from such a fate. No public reasons, nor any other kind of reasons, are rendered for Caesar's death. The people are asked to believe Brutus for his hon-our and have respect to his honour that they may believe. That is as far as the reasoning goes. The assumption he is asking them to make must be that Brutus is an honourable man and as such would be incapable of dishonourable actions carried out for dis-honourable reasons. What reasons he actually did have for killing Caesar, honourable or otherwise, are not clearly stated. Caesar is killed for his ambition, says Brutus. How, or if, that ambition, if it existed, would lead to tyranny which would justify assassination is never explained.

In the playing of it the speech seems too short, even perfunctory, really to fulfil its purpose, and, particularly when contrasted with Mark Antony's much longer oration, it appears not a little arrogant in its brevity and lack of substance. Brutus has laid himself wide open to the piercing oratory of Mark Antony who deals very specifi-cally and clearly with facts about the real world, not politically expe-dient suppositions. The very weakness in Brutus's position (which Brutus himself has seen in the orchard monologues) is taken up and mercilessly exposed to the public gaze. Mark Antony is a consider-able orator but he is helped enormously in his attack on the con-spirators by the grotesque shortcomings of Brutus's thinking. As a target they do not come any bigger than Marcus Brutus.

Brutus's characteristic inability to think straight is evident throughout the course of the drama. He shouts at Cassius for not passing on some of that money to pay his legions, seemingly unaware of the paradox involved in accepting tainted money at two removes which he would refuse on principle to collect himself directly:

> . . . What, shall one of us,
> That struck the foremost man of all this world

But for supporting robbers, shall we now
Contaminate our fingers with base bribes?

(IV.iii. 21–4)

In so far as he is willing to accept the money so vilely raised, the answer has to be 'yes'. (Incidentally, I think that the phrase 'But for supporting robbers' is descriptive, not of Caesar, but of Cassius and Brutus, the sense of the lines being 'shall we who heroically killed great Caesar soil our heroic hands with criminally obtained money for no better reason than to support robbers?')

So far, so inexplicable; but perhaps there is another reason for Brutus's passion and contradictory behaviour in the tent scene which does seem on the face of it to be a mighty storm in a very small tea-cup. I think the scene has more to do with Brutus's grief for the death of his wife than with base bribes. Brutus may be a blunderer in the world of public affairs, but all the indications are that his private life with Portia is very rich indeed. The loveliest words Brutus speaks describe his feelings for her:

You are my true and honourable wife,
As dear to me as are the ruddy drops
That visit my sad heart

(II.i.288–90)

The words sing in the air; they are unforced and flow with a beautiful necessity indicative of great feeling. When she dies, Brutus cannot howl with grief; a Roman does not do that. But he can shout at Cassius, the other love in his life, and shout he does. Cassius has never seen him so angry, but the anger is not quite what it appears to be. It is, I think, Brutus expressing his sorrow for Portia's death. Once he has done that, he can then play the charade with Titinius and Messala of pretending that he has not heard of Portia's death before their arrival. Now he can play for their benefit, and for his own, the noble Roman who can bear great loss with patience and equanimity:

Why, farewell, Portia. We must die, Messala.
With meditating that she must die once,
I have the patience to endure it now.

(IV.iii.188–90)

And he can play this role so well because he has spent the previous half hour letting his feelings out with rare passion.

The endgame for Brutus begins with his characteristically mistaking what is going on. He is no better a military strategist than he is a political philosopher, and against the advice of Cassius, he marches to Philippi to face Mark Antony and Octavius Caesar

there. Before the battle Cassius asks him what he will do if they
are defeated; Brutus answers that he will place his trust in a
benign providence which will see him safely through the worst
ordeals. His belief in this 'providence' is so absolute that he despises
those men, like Cato, who commit suicide for fear of what might be.
Cassius then asks Brutus if he will not contemplate suicide in the
event of defeat: will he be prepared to be led in triumph through the
streets of Rome? No, says Brutus, because he bears 'too great a mind'
(v.i.112). Hasn't he contradicted himself? In any event, at the end of
the play he commits suicide.

What character, then, have we discovered Brutus to be? He is a
man who thinks much, but none too well; a man whose assumptions
about the world he lives in are almost all mistaken; a man who, acting on these assumptions, achieves the exact opposite of what he
intended. He is a political disaster—and yet he is not without a certain nobility. There is sense in Mark Antony's praise of him as the
noblest Roman of them all. Brutus believes what he believes with
passionate intensity. He honestly believes that he is acting altruisti-
cally for the good of Rome. He honestly believes the reasons are
sufficient for the purpose of justifying his actions. That those reasons are palpably not sufficient is a judgement we make of them—
Brutus himself sincerely thinks otherwise. The confidence he has in
his powers of thought borders on arrogance. 'Brutus thinks it, therefore it must be right', he seems to be saying. He is a dangerous man;
a man who acts on the directions of a defective judgement. He
believes passionately in what he does. He acts according to high principles, sincerely, for the good of Rome. If he has nobility, then it
consists of that; but it is an odd kind of nobility. One may sincerely
believe almost anything but it is not believing sincerely that, of itself,
makes a man noble. Whether or not a man is noble must have something to do with the quality of reasoning that leads to that belief.
After all, Hitler sincerely believed that Jews should be killed. We
would not call him noble because of his sincerity: we would call him
the reverse because of the nature of his belief.

Here is the main problem with playing the character Brutus. The
reputation, and the expectations we have of the man, are destroyed
in the course of the play. Whatever he was before the play begins,
during the play he is shown over and over again to be a man over-
impressed with his own judgement, a man totally unsuited to political action, a man of endless opinion and no knowledge, a man who
destroys the very things he wants to preserve. And at the end of the
two hours traffic of the stage it seems he still has no knowledge of
the enormity of his mistakes or the extent of his responsibility
for them:

My heart doth joy that yet in all my life
I found no man but he was true to me.
I shall have glory by this losing day
More than Octavius and Mark Antony
By this vile conquest shall attain unto.

(v.v.34–8)

It sounds noble, but it seems dreamlike in its distance from reality; he is again, it seems, inventing a world in which he can play the hero rather than recognizing a real world in which he is, arguably, the greatest villain. But we, the audience, can see what he is doing—and I the actor can see it.

Brutus began the play mistaking the world he was in and he ends the drama, and his life, in the same fashion. The contradictions in his character remain unresolved; there is no getting of wisdom for Brutus. Hamlet goes on an extraordinary voyage of discovery, he is hurt to the quick by his experiences, he is changed by them, he learns from them, his wisdom grows because of them: and this being so, the Hamlet at the end of the play is a very, very different character from that at the beginning. Brutus, it appears, goes through no such transformation. His suffering is not rewarded with spiritual catharsis. Brutus remains the same at the end as he was at the beginning, only increasingly bewildered by his situation, unable to understand or change it.

The problem remains of how to play him. This is a big problem. Actors always want, and rightly so, to make their creations understandable, sympathetic, accessible and attractive. The problem with Brutus, I suspect, is that if you play what is written Brutus is not understandable, becomes unsympathetic, is certainly inaccessible, and for all this remains strangely unattractive behind the noble appearance. The solution, at least the solution we have gone for in this, Sir Peter Hall's production of 1995–6, is to play the contradictions and shortcomings of Brutus for all that they are worth and not to gloss over them, hide them, or in some way lessen them. The point of Brutus is precisely the contradiction he embodies, the contradiction between appearance and reality. Brutus appears a noble Roman stuffed with high principles and lofty thought, an ideal man to lead his fellows. The reality is that Brutus is that most dangerous of men, a misconstruer of events and men, who is given power to demonstrate how mortal that can be.

From the practical point of view of putting Brutus on the stage decisions have of course to be made as how precisely to present the man properly and fairly as a rounded human being. True, the intellectual weakness of his thinking must be shown clearly; true his heroic affectation must not be underplayed. But equally the gentler, more ordinarily emotional aspect of his character must be portrayed for the no better, but still very good, reason that it will bring Brutus closer to the audience, make him appear less removed and Olympian, and more accessible. Brutus may sometimes appear beyond the reach of normal understanding, but still we must try to make him a human being and not a one-dimensional caricature of bad political thinking.

We are on fertile ground. There are a number of exchanges which happily demonstrate this finer behaviour. True, some of them might appear of little account, but they all show Brutus in a kinder light than when he is inveighing against Caesar or plunging unknowingly into the chaos of civil war. This first conversation with Cassius illustrates perfectly what I wish to say and to play. Cassius chides Brutus for not being as loving and gentle towards him as he has been before. Brutus's apology is immediate, admirably sincere and comprehensive: it is not haughty or distant but direct and deeply felt. It has simplicity and honesty. Great advantages accrue from playing the attractiveness of Brutus's honesty here for many reasons, but chiefly because it gives an inkling of what Brutus was before the opening of the play, and more because it can provide Brutus with an extraordinary journey as he walks, half unknowingly, from the moral uplands of honour, love, and gentleness into the dark pit of murder, terror, and civil war. Brutus must appear downcast at first sight, yes, but nonetheless noble, honest, loving and decent. In pursuit of this effect we have chosen what I believe to be the better option of making Brutus's remark about Antony

> . . . I do lack some part
> Of that quick spirit that is in Antony   (I.ii.28–9)

less bitter and contemptuous than some commentators would have it. This serves an important double purpose. Firstly, it presents Brutus initially in a gentle, perhaps even a wittily wistful, fashion and secondly points up dramatically how much Brutus misunderstands and underestimates Mark Antony, a man who at this stage does not figure large in Brutus's thoughts at all, certainly not to the point of exciting any deep emotion of envy, fear, or contempt. No, Brutus must appear at first as he would like to think himself: upright, grave, honest, noble, and above all, honourable. The playing, I think, should be straightforward and unadorned—time for histrionics later.

The orchard scene has been analyzed at length for its political content. There is difficult verse from an increasingly complex man, but there is also a small, simple, but effective counterpoint to all the anguish running through the scene which resurfaces in Act Four, Scene Three, and I think that Brutus takes great delight in it.

Perhaps an audience should too. That counterpoint is Lucius, the
young and innocent boy-servant who is having a very hard time chez
Brutus. If it is not his master demanding attention deep in the night,
it is his mistress hearing strange voices and sending him off on
pointless errands. Lucius can provide a lovely, near-comic relief in
the orchard scene and certainly we play for this to happen. The
comedy lies in the fact that Lucius is not very good at being the servant boy, willing though he may be. At the beginning of the scene
Brutus calls, not once but several times, for Lucius. Lucius is asleep.
Brutus asks Lucius if tomorrow is the ides of March; Lucius does
not know. Someone knocks at the gate; Lucius has to be told to go
and answer it (at least in our production he has, for he has fallen
asleep again). The conspirators finally leave and Brutus calls for
Lucius once more—and once more, predictably, Lucius is asleep. It
is a sweet and human moment and Brutus responds, perhaps more
wisely than he knows, when he contrasts his state to that of Lucius:

> Thou hast no figures nor no fantasies,
> Which busy care draws in the brains of men;
> Therefore thou sleep'st so sound.

(II.i.231–3)

Later in the play, towards the end of the tent scene, Lucius is once
more called upon by Brutus, this time to sing and play. Again the
gentle youth falls asleep, innocently asleep. Brutus was not kind and
loving to Caesar, but he is touchingly kind and loving to Lucius:

> If thou dost nod, thou break'st thy instrument;
> I'll take it from thee; and, good boy, good night

(IV.iii.269–70)

says he, remembering perhaps his own long-lost innocence which
allowed him, too, such peaceful slumber. In any event it is a moment
of blessed calm and sensitivity in a play of such noise and cruelty
and as such we have sought to play it as feelingly as possible in order
to show, among other things, how Brutus achieves a certain nobility
in his domestic life which he signally fails to do in his public life.

This is achingly clear in his confrontation with his wife Portia.
Cassius and the conspirators have left. There follows a beautiful
scene about two people who love each other very much. Brutus loved
Caesar too, but he loves Portia better. They both die because of him,
but one death Brutus willed the other he did not, and how very much
he did not is evidenced by this scene. The language is the language
of deep devotion and affection, not of a new love, hot and untried,
but of a deep, mature, considered and abiding love—and all the more
touching for that. If nothing else, the scene will show how much
Brutus has changed, for we may see through Portia's eyes the lovely

man Brutus must once have been. Again, as in the opening scene, I try to make the playing as deeply felt and unaffected as possible; no place here for Brutus to go into rhetorical overdrive as he has done with the conspirators a few minutes earlier. All that is needed is honest playing and the point will have been made.

There is, of course, a problem. There always is with Brutus. He promises faithfully to tell his wife everything he is thinking and doing. Caius Ligarius appears, Brutus seemingly instantaneously forgets Portia and rushes off to kill Caesar. That is the way he is. Sir Peter Hall thinks this to be yet another example, albeit a poignant one, of Brutus's feverish state of mind: he is in a phantasma, or a hideous dream, and sometimes knows not what he does. Yes he is, and I believe that the language he uses, standing with dripping knife over the body of Caesar, reinforces that view. He says that he is very regretfully going to kill Caesar. He is not going to like doing it much, for the man is his friend, but he has to do it for the good of Rome; but when he actually does the deed his language is the language of delight, of exultation, of blood lust. I think and I play that Brutus liked it very much, this killing of Caesar. Ambition's debt may be paid, but my goodness how Brutus enjoyed collecting! No use in underplaying this or trying to gloss over it. From the gallows humour of:

> So are we Caesar's friends, that have abridged
> His time of fearing death
>
> (iii.i.104–5)

to the exuberant exultation of:

>   Stoop, Romans, stoop,
> And let us bathe our hands in Caesar's blood
> Up to the elbows, and besmear our swords;
> Then walk we forth, even to the market-place,
> And waving our red weapons o'er our heads,
> Let's all cry, 'Peace, freedom, and liberty!'
>
> (iii.i.105–10)

Brutus's repressed motives seem to be evident, and I believe the actor must play the scene so that the audience is aware of this, that is to say with an overweening joy. There is nothing noble about this killing. Brutus, with bloodied hands, stands shoulder to shoulder with those other conspirators who killed out of personal hatred, malice and envy. He is no better than they.

It is an unattractive prospect to play Brutus at this point in the drama as a vicious killer, but that is what he has become and this is what must be played despite his speech to the people in which he reiterates yet again that he killed Caesar not because he loved him less but because he loved Rome more. Typically, there is no glimmer of a hint in Brutus's oration that he is being insincere. True, he uses many a rhetorical trick; true, he is good with form but short of substance, but he believes what he is saying while he is saying it. We may say, as an audience, that he is self-deceived, but the actor must, I think, play him as if he were what he thinks he is, with all the oratorical ability at his command. There is no good point in the actor nudging the audience into an understanding that Brutus cannot truly believe in what he is saying, because Brutus does believe it; the self-deception is absolute, it seems, and because of this his own bloody end is guaranteed.

As I have said before, the curious feature of Brutus's journey towards that end is that there is no development of insight or understanding in him. He fails to acquire wisdom. He continues to make awful mistakes; he continues to change his mind from moment to moment; he continues to contradict himself despite his 'great mind'! A man who understands so little of himself and the world will soon be destroyed by that world. So it is with Brutus, but even in this extremity the speech just before his death that I quoted earlier ('My heart doth joy' (v.v.34ff.)) betrays no awareness of his own personal failure unless one can so colour the line 'my bones would rest, / That have but laboured to attain this hour' that it means 'All the great things I strove for are turned to dust and ashes'. I have tried in performance to gloss this line to show, however late in the day, some degree of self-awareness in Brutus, some knowledge of the enormity of what he has brought about, but I do not think it works because it flies in the face of everything we have learned of Brutus. I believe the better option is to present him at the end as in the orchard, a man who does not know himself, a man who deceives himself and cannot develop or grow because of these flaws in his nature. This is not to say that the man is essentially evil. By all accounts, before the events of the play,

> His life was gentle, and the elements
> So mixed in him, that Nature might stand up
> And say to all the world, 'This was a man!'

> (v.v.73–5)

But during the drama he casts himself in the role of noble hero and the saviour of Rome and thereby is o'erparted to a tragic degree.

ROBERT F. WILLSON JR.

From Shakespeare in Hollywood, 1929–1956[†]

* * *

Despite the budgetary problems, casting challenges, and debates over interpretation, Mankiewicz delivers a film that far outstrips the other major Hollywood Shakespeare productions discussed in this book. His use of the camera to create a particular mood or emotional climate is often inspired. The opening, for example, features the emblem of a Roman eagle over which the credits are scrolled; following this is a prologue quotation from Plutarch featuring a telling line: "Caesar had grown odious to moderate men through the extravagance of the titles and honors heaped upon him." The Roman marketplace then appears, with the title "Rome 44 B.C." imposed upon the shot, as the camera focuses on a bust of Caesar adorned with garlands. Here are the "titles" remarked upon by Plutarch, accompanied by the boisterous crowd of citizens in a holiday mood. Rebuked by Marullus—"You blocks, you stones, you worse than senseless things!"—the plebes guiltily disperse as Flavius disdainfully pulls a garland from Caesar's bust. The camera pulls back to a long shot in which we see both Marullus and Flavius "detained" by Roman police troops. The prominence of Caesar's power, signified in the eagle, his bust, and the presence of Gestapo-like police, is thus immediately asserted.

Throughout the film, Mankiewicz relies heavily on busts and statues to establish a compelling mise-en-scène and underscore thematic elements. When Cassius tries to persuade Brutus to join the conspiracy, the scene is shot on the ramps of the Coliseum-like structure that Caesar and his entourage have entered and where the general will be offered the crown (1.2). As Cassius observes that "There was a Brutus once . . ." (159), he stands next to a bust of Lucius Junius Brutus, who expelled the corrupt Tarquin and founded the Roman republic. That Caesar is in no way as vicious as the tyrant Tarquin greatly qualifies Cassius's suggestion that his friend follow the example of his famous namesake and ancestor. As is sometimes the case in other scenes featuring a bust or statue of some famous Roman, we are invited to consider the great difference in stature between the memorialized statesman and the flawed or

† From Robert F. Willson Jr., *Shakespeare in Hollywood, 1929–1956* (Madison: Fairleigh Dickinson University Press, 2000), 148–52. Reprinted by permission of Associated University Presses.

naive politicians who plot assassination before our eyes. Still, to have Cassius woo Brutus by recalling the figure of a legendary Brutus, famous for a decisive and popular act that saved Rome from slavery, is an effective touch. Later, in Brutus' garden, just before the arrival of the conspirators, Brutus reads over the letter urging him to "Speak, strike, redress!" as he stands next to another bust of his noble ancestor. In this private space, marked by the chiaroscuro effect of shadows of tree branches cast on pale garden walls, the bust seems to confirm in the hero's mind that he is destined to act in a manner that will destroy a "king" and bring further honor to his name. Mankiewicz makes us believe that the busts and statues are omens just as significant as lions or "men in fire" walking the Roman streets.

Caesar too is not immune to the messages of statues, as we learn in 2.2, when he recounts to Decius Brutus Calpurnia's dream in which his statue "Did run pure blood, and many lusty Romans / Came smiling and did bathe their hands in it." His ubiquitous image can be seen in the bust located prominently in his main room, where this scene takes place. Unlike that of Brutus' ancestor, this bust has come to stand for absolute power; Caesar's careful study of it represents the kind of vanity that goes before the great man's fall. Decius' counterinterpretation of the dream—that the blood running from the statue represents Caesar's special favor, which all men seek—plays to that vanity, changing Caesar's mind about coming to the Senate. In a play that tests men's judgment and their ability to decipher and use omens and signs to their best advantage, marble statues deliver critical "speeches" to those who will listen. Caesar proves deaf to this warning—and he pays a dear price.

The statue that speaks most profoundly in the play and film is of course that of Pompey, the great soldier and triumvir whom Caesar defeated in the Battle of Pharsalus in 48 B.C. It becomes the central monument in the Senate as Calhern's Caesar (himself a rigid, monolithlike figure as he declares "I am constant as the northern star") falls at its base; Mankiewicz shoots the assassination scene (3.1) by using Pompey's statue as the focal point. As Casca and the other conspirators set upon Caesar, Brutus retreats toward the base of the monument, and it is toward Brutus and the statue that the mortally wounded general staggers, ending his last walk with the famous words "Et tu, Brute? Then fall, Caesar!" as Brutus stabs him. This segment recalls and realizes Calpurnia's dream, as all the murderers bathe their hands in Caesar's blood, at the same time making Brutus into the instrument of Pompey's revenge. Just as suddenly Antony appears at the end of a long corridor, and we glimpse him from the vantage point of Pompey's statue as he moves cautiously toward the murder scene. After shaking hands with all the conspirators and being allowed by Brutus to prepare the body and speak the eulogy (over Cassius' sound objections), Antony is left alone to denounce the "butchers" and plan his revenge. Brando as Antony kneels next to Caesar's body, but the base of Pompey's statue, smeared with blood, is prominently part of the frame as he speaks. The visual message is clear: Antony has now taken over from Brutus the position of de facto ruler of Rome. That message is confirmed by his despotic manipulation of the crowd in the Forum scene (3.2) and by his actions in 4.1, where he, Octavius, and Lepidus compile the list of those who must be murdered under their regime. The scene takes place in Caesar's apartment, and Antony can be seen turning the bust of his predecessor toward him as he speaks to Octavius of the need to "make head" against the forces of Cassius and Brutus. Antony, not the Roman populace, has inherited the place and power of Caesar, yet we know that he too will be subject to the turning of fortune's wheel, as Octavius' presence signifies. The spirit of Caesar, after all, will find its home in him, not Antony.

The motif of prophetic statues or busts is completed in two climactic scenes, both emphasizing Brutus' fall. In the first of these, Caesar's ghost shows itself to Brutus on the eve of the Philippi battle, reminding the noblest Roman that they will meet again there (4.3). Mankiewicz creates the ghost as a shadowy, diaphanous figure glimpsed against the inside of Brutus' tent. The effect is not particularly imposing or frightening, in part because the director lacked the budget necessary to invent a truly terrifying spectre. Yet the figure looks like a statue, one that moves only to speak, and then only by moving his lips. Even in death, the image seems to say, Caesar continues to impose his will on the living; the leader has not fallen but in fact stands upright in a clean toga, apparently healed of the wounds made by the conspirators' blades, ready to exact his revenge.

In the second of these scenes, Brutus asks Strato to hold his sword so that he may run upon it, thereby ending his life and depriving Antony and Octavius of the prize of his imprisonment (5.5). Brutus is desperate to die because Cassius is gone (he finds his helmet on the ground) and his hopes for victory have been dashed. Strato fulfills his master's wishes—"I found no man but he was true to me," Brutus declares—though reluctantly; the shot recalls the one in the Senate, where Brutus occupied Strato's place as he stabbed Caesar. Indeed, Brutus' final words remind us of that moment: "Caesar, now be still. I killed not thee with half so good a will" (51). As the tragic hero falls at his servant's feet, Mankiewicz holds the shot, creating the image of a monument depicting a slave standing over his fallen master. This shot conforms with the general style of the film, which

Jack Jorgens describes: "The characters, filmed from eye-level mostly in medium and long shot, have a statuesque feel."[1] It also conveys the message that Brutus has been, like Caesar, sacrificed to history, victim of a slave he yearned to set free.

*   *   *

1. Jack J. Jorgens, *Shakespeare on Film* (Bloomington: Indiana University Press, 1977), 101.

Film and Audiorecording Bibliography†

1907	*Le Mort de Jules César*, directed by George Méliès. France.
1908	*Julius Caesar*, directed by William V. Ranous (?). United States.
1909	*Giulio Cesare*, directed by Giovanni Pastrone. Italy.
1910	*Brutus* (adaptation), directed by Enrico Guazzoni. Italy.
1911	*Julius Caesar*, directed by Sir Frank R. Benson. With Benson, Guy Rathbone, Murray Carrington. UK.
1913	*Julius Caesar* (one scene, Brutus and Cassius), nd. United States.
1913	*Giulio Cesare*, nd. Gloria Films. Italy.
1914	*Giulio Cesare*, directed by Enrico Guazzoni. With Amleto Novelli, Gianna Terribili Gonzalez. Italy.
1950	*Julius Caesar*, directed by David Bradley. With Charlton Heston. Avon Productions. United States.
1953	*Julius Caesar*, directed by Joseph Mankiewicz. With Sir John Gielgud, Marlon Brando, James Mason. M.G.M. United States.
1970	*Julius Caesar*, directed by Stuart Burge. With Charlton Heston, Sir John Gielgud, Jason Robards. Commonwealth United Entertainment, Inc. (Republic Entertainment). UK.
1987	*Julius Caesar*, directed by Herbert Wise. With Charles Gray, Richard Pasco, Keith Michell, David Collings. BBC (originally broadcast on the BBC series "The Shakespeare Plays," 1978). UK.

† More details relating to the early film versions of *Julius Caesar* can be found in Charles W. Eckert, ed., *Focus on Shakespearean Films* (Englewood Cliffs, NJ: Prentice-Hall, Inc., 1972). I have relied on Eckert, p. 169, in the compilation of information concerning the pre-1950 films.

Related Films

2002   *Julius Caesar*, directed by Uli Edel. With Jeremy Sisto, Richard Harris, Christopher Walken, Chris Noth. Victory 11. United States.

2005   *Julius Caesar's Rome*, nd. A&E Television Network/History Channel. United States.

Audio Recordings

n.d.   *Julius Caesar*. Cambridge, UK.: The Marlowe Society of Cambridge University. Directed by George Rylands.

1954   *Julius Caesar*. New York: Columbia Entré. With Orson Welles and other members of the Mercury Theater. (A reissue of Columbia Masterworks set MC 10, 1939.)

ca. 1964   *Julius Caesar*. New York: Shakespeare Recording Society. With Sir Ralph Richardson and Anthony Quayle.

ca. 1985   *Julius Caesar*. New York: Caedmon Audio. With Sir Ralph Richardson, Anthony Quayle, John Mills, Alan Bates, and Michael Gwynn.

1996   *Julius Caesar*. New York: Caedmon Audio. With Sir Ralph Richardson and Anthony Quayle.

1998   *Julius Caesar*. London: Distributed by the Penguin Group. Arkangel Productions. With Michael Feast, Adrian Lester, John Bowe.

2003   *Julius Caesar*. Auburn, California: Audio Partners. (In "The Complete Arkangel Shakespeare, Vol. 15.")

Selected Bibliography

As with many other Shakespearean tragedies, the materials that bear on *Julius Caesar* are voluminous. This bibliography represents only some of what is available to readers.

•Indicates works included or excerpted in this Norton Critical Edition.

Bibliographies

Velz, John W. *Shakespeare and the Classical Tradition: A Critical Guide to Commentary, 1660–1960.* Minneapolis: University of Minnesota Press, 1968.
Walker, Lewis, comp. *Shakespeare and the Classical Tradition: An Annotated Bibliography, 1961–1991.* New York and London: Routledge, 2002.

Background and Sources

The most comprehensive collection of source materials on *Julius Caesar* can be found in Volume 5 (*The Roman Plays*, pp. 3–211) of Geoffrey Bullough's eight-volume set *Narrative and Dramatic Sources of Shakespeare* (London: Routledge and Kegan Paul; New York: Columbia University Press, 1957–1975). Bullough's volume includes large portions of Thomas North's translation of Plutarch's *Lives*, first published in London in 1579. The excerpts from the *Lives* in this volume are taken from North's first edition. (The excerpts from Appian (trans. 1578), Suetonius (trans. 1606), Elyot (1531), and Higgins (1587) are likewise taken from the first editions.)

In addition, Bullough presents some analogs in his volume, including sections of *Caesar's Revenge*, an anonymous play printed in 1607 that, according to the title page, was performed by the students of Trinity College, Oxford.

Although source study constituted a significant portion of the early scholarly conversation, no edition can represent all of the relevant material. For further discussion on Shakespeare's sources and historical background, see the entries listed here.

Barroll, J. Leeds. "Shakespeare and Roman History." *Modern Language Review* 53 (1958): 327–43.
Honigmann, E. A. J. "Shakespeare's Plutarch." *Shakespeare Quarterly* 10.1 (1959): 25–33.
Martindale, Charles, and Michelle Martindale. *Shakespeare and the Uses of Antiquity.* London and New York: Routledge, 1990.
Miles, Gary B. "How Roman are Shakespeare's 'Romans'?" *Shakespeare Quarterly* 40.3 (1989): 257–83.
Miola, Robert A. *Shakespeare's Reading.* Oxford and New York: Oxford University Press, 2000.
Miola, Robert A. "*Julius Caesar* and the Tyrannicide Debate." *Renaissance Quarterly* 38.2 (1985): 271–89.

Miola, Robert A. "Shakespeare and His Sources: Observations on the Critical History of *Julius Caesar.*" *Shakespeare Survey* 40 (1987): 77–90.

Muir, Kenneth. *The Sources of Shakespeare's Plays.* New Haven: Yale University Press, 1978.

Ornstein, Robert. "Seneca and the Political Drama of *Julius Caesar.*" *Journal of English and Germanic Philology* 57 (1958): 51–56.

Parker, Barbara L. "'A Thing Unfirm': Plato's Republic and Shakespeare's *Julius Caesar.*" *Shakespeare Quarterly* 44.1 (1993): 30–43.

Platt, Michael. *Rome and Romans According to Shakespeare.* Institut für Englische Sprache und Literatur. Salzburg: Universität Salzburg, 1976.

Roe, John. *Shakespeare and Machiavelli.* Cambridge, UK: Boydell & Brewer, 2002.

Ronan, Clifford. *"Antike Roman": Power Symbology and the Roman Play in Early Modern England, 1585–1635.* Athens and London: The University of Georgia Press, 1997.

Sacharoff, Mark. "Suicide and Brutus' Philosophy in *Julius Caesar.*" *Journal of the History of Ideas* 33 (1972): 115–22.

• Schanzer, Ernest. *The Problem Plays of Shakespeare: A Study of "Julius Caesar," "Measure for Measure," and "Antony and Cleopatra."* New York: Schocken Books, 1965.

Spencer, T. J. B., ed. *Shakespeare's Plutarch.* Harmondsworth, UK : Penguin Books, 1964. Rpt. 1968.

• Spencer, T. J. B. "Shakespeare and the Elizabethan Romans." *Shakespeare Survey* 10 (1957): 27–38.

Velz, John W. "The Ancient World in Shakespeare: Authenticity or Anachronism? A Retrospect." *Shakespeare Survey* 31 (1978): 1–12.

Velz, John W. "*Orator* and *Imperator* in *Julius Caesar.* Style and the Process of Roman History." *Shakespeare Studies* 15 (1982): 55–75.

Criticism

Much of the critical commentary regarding *Julius Caesar* as a tragedy considers the play in light of Shakespeare's other Roman plays, particularly *Antony and Cleopatra.* I have included very few of those studies here, instead concentrating on commentaries that highlight the play on its own. Even so, the list following is not exhaustive; it is selective.

EARLY CRITICISM

• Granville-Barker, Harley. *Prefaces to Shakespeare.* London: Sidgwick & Jackson, 1946. [*Prefaces* was first published in a series, 1927–47.]

• Hazlitt, William. *Characters of Shakespear's Plays.* London: 1817.

• Johnson, Samuel. *The Works of William Shakespeare.* London: 1765.

• Steevens, George. *"Julius Caesar (1772–73)."* In *Shakespeare" The Critical Heritage.* Ed. Brian Vickers (5: 498–500). London, Henley, and Boston: Routledge & Kegan Paul, 1979.

• Unsigned essay. "An Essay on *Julius Caesar.*" In *Shakespeare: the Critical Heritage.* Ed. Brian Vickers (6: 500–505). London, Boston, and Henley: Routledge & Kegan Paul, 1981.

MODERN CRITICISM

Anderson, Peter S. "Shakespeare's Caesar: the language of sacrifice." *Comparative Drama* 3 (1969): 3–26.

Anson, John S. "Julius Caesar: The Politics of a Hardened Heart." *Shakespeare Studies* 2 (1966): 11–33.

Baines, Barbara J. "Political and Poetic Revisionism in *Julius Caesar*." *The Upstart Crow* 10 (1990): 42–54.

Barroll, J. Leeds. "The Characterization of Octavius." *Shakespeare Studies* 6 (1970): 231–88.

Barton, Anne J. "*Julius Caesar* and *Coriolanus*: Shakespeare's Roman World of Words." In *Shakespeare's Craft*. Ed. Philip J. Highfill (24–47). Carbondale: Southern Illinois University Press, 1982.

Batson, Beatrice, ed. *Shakespeare's Christianity: The Protestant and Catholic Poetics Of Julius Caesar, Macbeth, and Hamlet*. Waco: Baylor University Press, 2006.

• Blits, Jan H. *The End of the Ancient Republic: Shakespeare's "Julius Caesar."* London: Rowman and Littlefield, 1993.

Bonjour, A. *The Structure of "Julius Caesar."* Liverpool: University of Liverpool Press, 1958.

Bono, Barbara J. "The Birth of Tragedy: Tragic Action in *Julius Caesar*." *English Literary Renaissance* 24.2 (1994): 449–70.

Brower, Reuben A. *Hero and Saint: Shakespeare and the Greco-Roman Heroic Tradition*. Oxford: Oxford University Press, 1971.

Brown, John Russell. *Shakespeare: The Tragedies*. Basingstoke, UK, and New York: Palgrave, 2001.

Bulman, James C. *The Heroic Idiom of Shakespearian Tragedy*. Newark: University of Delaware Press, 1985.

Bushnell, Rebecca. "*Julius Caesar*." In *A Companion to Shakespeare's Works*. Vol. 1: *The Tragedies*. Ed. Richard Dutton and Jean E. Howard (339–56). Oxford: Blackwell, 2003.

• Cantor, Paul A. *Shakespeare's Rome: Republic and Empire*. Ithaca, NY: Cornell University Press, 1976.

Charney, Maurice. *Shakespeare's Roman Plays*. Cambridge, MA: Harvard University Press, 1961.

Clemen, Wolfgang. *Shakespeare's Dramatic Art*. London: Methuen, 1972.

Daiches, David. *Shakespeare: "Julius Caesar."* Studies in English Literature 65. London: Edward Arnold, 1976.

Davis, Lloyd. "Embodied Masculinity in Shakespeare's *Julius Caesar*." *EnterText* 1 (2003): 161–82.

Dean, Leonard. "*Julius Caesar* and Modern Criticism." *English Journal* 50 (1961): 451–56.

Drakakis, John. "'Fashion it thus': *Julius Caesar* and the Politics of Theatrical Representation." In *Shakespeare and Politics*. Ed. Catherine M. S. Alexander (206–28). Cambridge, UK, and New York: Cambridge University Press, 2004.

Felheim, Marvin. "The Problem of Time in *Julius Caesar*." *Huntington Library Quarterly* 13 (1950): 399–405.

Foakes, R. A. "An Approach to *Julius Caesar*." *Shakespeare Quarterly* 5.3 (1954): 259–70.

• Foakes, R. A. *Shakespeare and Violence*. Cambridge, UK, and New York: Cambridge University Press, 2003.

Girard, René. "Collective Violence and Sacrifice in *Julius Caesar*." *Salmagundi* 88 (1991): 399–419.

Greene, Gayle. "'The power of speech to stir men's blood': The Language of Tragedy in Shakespeare's *Julius Caesar*." *Renaissance Drama* 11 (n.s.) (1980): 67–93.

Hadfield, Andrew. *Shakespeare and Republicanism*. Cambridge, UK, and New York: Cambridge University Press, 2005.

Hapgood, Robert. "'Speak hands for me': Gesture as Language in *Julius Caesar*." *Drama Survey* 5 (1966): 162–170. Rpt. in *Essays in Shakespearean Criticism*. Ed. James L. Calderwood and Harold E. Tolliver (405–14). Englewood Cliffs, N.J.: Prentice Hall, 1970.

Hardin, Richard F. *Civil Idolatry: Desacralizing the Monarchy in Spenser, Shakespeare, and Milton.* Newark: University of Delaware Press, 1992.

Hopkins, D. J. *City/Stage/Globe: Performance and Space in Shakespeare's London.* London and New York: Routledge, 2008.

Kahn, Coppélia. *Roman Shakespeare: Warriors, Wounds and Women.* London and New York: Routledge, 1997.

Kezar, Dennis. "*Julius Caesar* and the Properties of Shakespeare's Globe," *English Literary Renaissance* 28.1 (1998): 18–46.

Kirschbaum. Leo. "Shakespeare's Stage-Blood and Its Critical Significance." *Publications of the Modern Language Association* 64 (1949): 517–29.

• Knight, G. Wilson. *The Imperial Theme.* London: Methuen, 1951.

Knight, W. Nicholas. "Brutus' Motivation and Melancholy." *The Upstart Crow* 5 (1984): 108–24.

Leggatt, Alexander. *Shakespeare's Political Drama: The History Plays and the Roman Plays.* London and New York: Routledge, 1988.

Lever, J. W. *The Tragedy of State.* London: Methuen, 1971.

Liebler, Naomi Conn. *Shakespeare's Festive Tragedy.* London and New York: Routledge, 1995.

McAlindon, T. *Shakespeare's Tragic Cosmos.* Cambridge, UK, and New York: Cambridge University Press, 1991.

MacCallum, M. W. *Shakespeare's Roman Plays and their Background.* London: Macmillan, 1910. New edition with introduction by T. J. B. Spencer, 1967.

McGowan, Margaret M. "Caesar's Cloak: diversion as an art of persuasion in sixteenth century writing." *Renaissance Studies* 18 (2004): 437–48.

Marshall, Cynthia. "Portia's Wound, Calphurnia's Dream: Reading Character in *Julius Caesar.*" *English Literary Renaissance* 24.2 (1994): 471–98.

Mehl, Dieter. *Shakespeare's Tragedies: An Introduction.* Cambridge, UK, and New York: Cambridge University Press, 1986.

Miles, Geoffrey. *Shakespeare and the Constant Romans.* Oxford: Clarendon Press, 1996.

Miola, Robert. "*Julius Caesar* and the Tyrannicide Debate." *Renaissance Quarterly* 38.2 (1985): 271–89.

Miola, Robert. *Shakespeare's Rome.* Cambridge, UK, and New York: Cambridge University Press, 1983.

Muir, Kenneth. *Shakespeare's Tragic Sequence.* London: Hutchinson University, 1972.

Paster, Gail Kern. "'In the spirit of men there is no blood': Blood as a Trope of Gender in *Julius Caesar.*" *Shakespeare Quarterly* 40.3 (1989): 284–98.

Pinciss, G. M. "Rhetoric as Character: The Forum Speech in *Julius Caesar.*" *The Upstart Crow* 4 (1982): 113–21.

Prior, Moody E. "The Search for a Hero in *Julius Caesar.*" *Renaissance Drama* 2 (n.s.) (1969): 81–101.

Rackin, Phyllis. *Shakespeare's Tragedies.* New York: Frederick Ungar, 1978.

Rebhorn, Wayne. "The Crisis of the Aristocracy in *Julius Caesar.*" *Renaissance Quarterly* 43.1 (1990): 75–111.

• Ribner, Irving. *Patterns in Shakespearian Tragedy.* New York: Barnes & Noble, 1960.

Richmond, Hugh M. *Shakespeare's Political Plays.* New York: Random House, 1967.

Sanders, Norman. "The Shift of Power in *Julius Caesar.*" *Review of English Literature* 5 (1964): 24–35.

Simmons, J. L. *Shakespeare's Pagan World: The Roman Tragedies.* Charlottesville: University Press of Virginia, 1973.

Sohmer, Steve. *Shakespeare's Mystery Play: The Opening of the Globe Theatre, 1599.* (Manchester: Manchester University Press, 1999).

Stirling, Brents. "Brutus and the Death of Portia." *Shakespeare Quarterly* 10.2 (1959): 211–17.

Stirling, Brents. *Unity in Shakespearean Tragedy.* New York: Columbia University Press, 1956.

Thomas, Vivian. *Shakespeare's Roman Worlds.* London and New York: Routledge, 1989.

Tice, Terrence N. "Calphurnia's Dream and Communication with the Audience in Shakespeare's *Julius Caesar.*" *Shakespeare Yearbook* 1 (1990): 37–49.

Toole, William B. "The Cobbler, the Disrobed Image and the Motif of Movement in *Julius Caesar.*" *The Upstart Crow* 4 (1982): 41–55.

Traversi, D. A. *Shakespeare: The Roman Plays.* Palo Alto: Stanford University Press, 1963.

Velz, John W. "Cassius as a 'Great Observer.'" *Modern Language Review* 68 (1973): 256–59.

Velz, John W. "Clemency, Will and Just Cause in *Julius Caesar.*" *Shakespeare Survey* 22 (1969): 109–18.

• Velz, John W. "'If I were Brutus now . . .': Role-Playing in *Julius Caesar.*" *Shakespeare Studies* 4 (1968): 149–59.

Velz, John W. "Two Emblems in Brutus' Orchard." *Renaissance Quarterly* 25.3 (1972): 307–15.

Visser, Nicholas. "Plebeian Politics in *Julius Caesar.*" *Shakespeare in Southern Africa* 7 (1994): 22–31.

Well, Charles. *The Wide Arc: Roman Values in Shakespeare.* New York: St. Martin's Press, 1992.

Wilders, John. *The Lost Garden: A View of Shakespeare's English and Roman History Plays.* London and Basingstoke: Macmillan, 1978.

Willson, Robert F. Jr. "*Julius Caesar.* The Forum Scene as Historic Play-Within." *Shakespeare Yearbook* 1 (1990): 14–27.

Wilson, Richard. *Will Power: Essays on Shakespearean Authority.* Hemel Hempstead, UK: Harvester Wheatsheaf, 1993.

Yoder, R. A. "History and the Histories in *Julius Caesar.*" *Shakespeare Quarterly* 24.3 (1973): 309–27.

Zander, Horst, ed. *Julius Caesar: New Critical Essays.* London and New York: Routledge, 2005.

Performance and Film Studies

The best survey of stage history is John Ripley, *Julius Caesar on Stage in England and America, 1599–1973* (Cambridge, UK, and New York: Cambridge University Press, 1980). However, it is best supplemented with particular essays and studies, some of which are listed here.

Brode, Douglas. *Shakespeare in the Movies.* Oxford and New York: Oxford University Press, 2000.

Brown, John Russell. *Shakespeare's Dramatic Style.* London: Heinemann, 1970.

Crowl, Samuel. "'Our Lofty Scene': Teaching Modern Film Versions of *Julius Caesar.*" In *Teaching Shakespeare into the Twenty-First Century.* Ed. Ronald E. Salomone and James E. Davis (222–31). Athens: Ohio University Press, 1997.

Coursen, H. R. *Reading Shakespeare on Stage.* Newark: University of Delaware Press, 1995.

Field, B. S. *Shakespeare's "Julius Caesar": A Production Collection.* Chicago: Nelson- Hall, 1980.

France, Richard. "Orson Welles's Anti-Fascist Production of *Julius Caesar.*" *Forum Modernes Theater* 15 (2000): 145–61.

Homan, Sidney. *Directing Shakespeare: A Scholar Onstage.* Athens: Ohio University Press, 2004.

• Homan, Sidney. *Shakespeare's Theater of Presence: Language, Spectacle, and the Audience* (Lewisburg, PA: Bucknell University Press, 1986).

Houseman, John. *Entertainers and the Entertained*. New York: Simon and Schuster, 1986.

Keyishian, Harry. "Storm, Fire, and Blood: Patterns of Imagery in Stuart Burge's *Julius Caesar*." In *Shakespeare in Performance: A Collection of Essays*. Ed. Frank Occhiogrosso (93–104). Newark: University of Delaware Press, 2003.

• Nettles, John. "Brutus in *Julius Caesar*." In *Players of Shakespeare 4*. Ed. Robert Smallwood (177–92). Cambridge, UK, and New York: Cambridge University Press, 1998.

Rutter, Carol Chillington. "Facing History, Facing Now: Deborah Warner's *Julius Caesar* at the Barbican." *Shakespeare Quarterly* 57.1 (2006): 71–85.

Walker, Roy. "Unto Caesar: A Review of Recent Productions." *Shakespeare Survey* 11 (1958): 128–35.

• Willson, Robert F. Jr. *Shakespeare in Hollywood, 1929–1956*. Madison, NJ: Fairleigh Dickinson University Press, 2000.